A Catalogue of Nineteenth Century
Printing Presses

A Catalogue of Nineteenth Century Printing Presses

Harold E. Sterne

Oak Knoll Press &
The British Library

2001

Second revised and expanded edition

Published in 2001 by **Oak Knoll Press**
310 Delaware Street, New Castle, Delaware, 19720 USA
and
The British Library
96 Euston Road, London NW1 2DB, England

British Library Cataloguing-in-Publication Data
A CIP Record is available from The British Library

ISBN: 1-58456-047-9 (USA)
ISBN: 0-7123-0663-3 (UK)

Original printing: 1978 by Ye Olde Printery, Cincinnati, Ohio

Author: Harold E. Sterne
Typographers: Harold E. Sterne and MidAtlantic Books & Journals, Inc.
Publishing Director: J. Lewis von Hoelle

Library of Congress Cataloging-in-Publication Data

Sterne, Harold E., 1929-
A catalogue of nineteenth century printing presses / Harold E. Sterne. - 2nd rev. and expanded ed.
p. cm.
Rev. ed. of: Catalogue of nineteenth century printing presses. c1978.
Includes bibliographical references and index.
ISBN 1-58456-047-9 (acid-free paper)
1. Printing-press—History—19th century—Catalogs. 2. Printing-press—History—19th century—Pictorial works. I. Sterne, Harold E., 1929-Catalogue of nineteenth century printing presses. II. Title.

Z249.S827 2001
681'.62'09034—dc21

00-053037

Printed in the United States of America on 60# archival, acid-free paper meeting the requirements of the American Standard for Permanence of Paper for Printed Library Materials.

contents

Preface – vii

Acknowledgements – ix

Introduction – xi

Hand Presses – 1

Cylinder Presses – 17

Platen Presses – 119

Lever Presses – 185

Lithographic Presses – 211

Rotary Presses – 223

Miscellaneous Equipment – 241

Addendum, Chandler & Price Serial Numbers – 255

Bibliography – 256

Index -- 257

This book is dedicated to
all those who want to preserve
the art of letterpress printing
for future generations.

preface

In 1978 Hal Sterne realized that there was a need for a book of images of old printing presses. Although he was the manager of a large modern commercial printing company, he was also an amateur printer. Like many trades that become obsolete – calligraphy, hand bookbinding and steam railroading, among many others – letterpress printing became an occupation done for pleasure. Hobby printers use old – sometimes-antique -- letterpress equipment, usually platen jobber presses. These presses are generally small enough to go into a home basement or garage, and were the workhorses of the job printing industry from about 1850 until about 1950.

During that hundred years a wide range of these "jobber" presses were manufactured. The same was true of all the other varieties of letterpress and lithographic printing presses: cylinder presses, iron hand presses, and rotary presses. When they were manufactured, they were state-of-the-art commercial presses, but by 1950 most of them were long obsolete. As letterpress gave way to much faster offset printing, these old letterpress machines were often sold for scrap – but some were saved from the scrap heap by hobby printers, collectors, and printing museums.

Anyone attempting to identify, save, repair, or use one of these old presses was confronted with a lack of information. The first step was of course identification, and Hal effectively solved that problem with the 1978 first edition of his *Catalogue of Nineteenth Century Printing Presses.* Simply by leafing through the *Catalogue* one could usually find and identify a press.

Another great service that Hal performed, in 1981, was to reprint two of Ralph Green's fact-filled books, *The Iron Hand Press in America* and *A History of the Platen Jobber.* With these books available it become much easier to identify and then find some basic information about many old presses, most of them manufactured before the twentieth century.

I have used the *Catalogue of Nineteenth Century Printing Presses* countless times in the last 22 years. Although for many years I have collected old printing machinery catalogues, I could never hope to cover the range of presses that Hal included in his book. Whenever I was confronted by a press with no manufacturer's name on it, the *Catalogue* was always the first reference to check. Or, if I got a letter or a phone call referring to a Cincinnati Type Foundry "Nonpareil Press," I would find several detailed wood engravings reprinted in the book.

Before the halftone process of printing photographs came into general use in the late 1890s, most illustrations in newspapers, magazines, books, (and, of course, trade catalogues) were done by wood engraving. Photographs or drawings were transferred to the end grain of blocks of type-high Turkish boxwood. Skilled engravers then cut away the surface areas that were not to print, leaving type-high lines and areas that were inked and then printed along with the type. It was a cumbersome and slow process, requiring much skilled hand work, yet it had a close affinity with letterpress printing.

Catalogue illustrations were ideal for wood engraving because the process made the precision rendering of small details possible. In fact the process survived for catalogue illustration until well into the middle of the twentieth century because of this clarity, which was not usually possible in a halftones made from photographs. Because boxwood blocks were limited in size, to provide larger areas for engraving often two or more blocks were lined up and clamped tightly together. Occasionally a straight white line can be seen in a wood engraved illustration, where the two blocks have slightly separated over time.

If we look at any of the illustrations in this book, we can see a remarkable affinity: these wood engravings were originally printed by the very printing presses that they were used to illustrate. The fact that they are reproduced in the present book by offset-lithography dilutes the effect only slightly.

Five varieties of presses are shown in this catalogue, each preceded by a short introduction. Of these, only three are small enough to be used by amateurs. Lithographic presses capable of printing from the stone are the province of artists; small ones are still being made today. Iron hand presses are very much in demand, and bring high prices, although mainly for display; very few are used for printing. Platen presses, both bench models and treadle styles, are in use all over the world by enthusiastic amateur printers.

The illustrations in this book were gathered by Hal Sterne mainly from printing trade catalogues and ads in publications like *The Inland Printer.* There is an inherent paradox in looking at these catalogues now, intended as they were to be seen for a brief moment in time, when we realize that that brief moment passed more than a hundred years ago. When we see these old catalogue pages, we are peering through a dusty window-pane into the past, evoking in many of us pleasant feelings of curiosity and nostalgia

Now, in the year 2000, Hal Sterne has performed another service. He has revised and expanded his 1978 book. He has added additional 150 images of presses, so that (if there was ever any doubt of it) this book is now certainly the most comprehensive collection of press images ever put together. Another very useful improvement in this edition is the dating, whenever possible, of the presses. When there was no date available from the original source of the image, wherever possible a range of dates during which the press was manufactured has been given. The range of dates information for platen presses and iron hand presses comes from Ralph Green's *A History of the Platen Jobber* and his *The Iron Hand Press in America.* In my experience Ralph Green is the only reliable source for these dates, and he is nearly always accurate. Putting dates next to the presses adds extra usefulness to the book.

Here, then, is the new, bigger, and better edition of *Catalogue of Nineteenth Century Printing Presses.* We are in Hal Sterne's debt for having assembled this book – the family album of the printing industry of the nineteenth century.

--Stephen O. Saxe

acknowledgements

It is not possible to compile this kind of book without the assistance of many people. It would have been impossible even to begin had it not been for my long-time friend, Ted Ringman, now deceased, who had an uncanny knack for finding old printing catalogues wherever he went. He gave me an original salesman's catalog of used printing equipment from the 1800's which is the source of the majority of the illustrations found in this book.

The many people who helped me with the first edition of my book in 1978 are mentioned in that book. Dave Peat and Steve Saxe generously allowed me to use their vast libraries of old catalogues and magazines making possible the many new illustrations found in this second edition. Of special interest, from Dave Peat, is the original wood engraving on page 210 that shows the great detail in which all of these wonderful engravings were made. I would be remiss if I did not mention the great care that Rich Hopkins took in producing the negatives for the additional illustrations which captured all the details from old, faded, and sometimes torn and yellowed pages.

In order to include the old ads in their entirety, some presses still need to be shown vertically and others horizontally. Since the page size of the second edition is twice that of the first edition, the inconvenience of turning the book has been minimized. The chapters in this book are in chronological order of press development. An attempt was made to place the presses in alphabetical order by manufacturer wherever possible.

It is a privilege to have the preface of my book written by Steve Saxe, well known author of several books on printing history. I thank Eunice Lebowitz Cohen, former Brandeis slide curator, for her editorial assistance and Steve Saxe for the final accuracy check. This work could not have been accomplished had it not been for my able research assistant, editorial assistant, copy reader, proof reader, typist, and loving wife, Judilee.

I hope The Catalog of Nineteenth Century Printing Presses will continue to whet the reader's appetite for research and jog memories to find a press that is a little different from the ones pictured here.

Harold E. Sterne
January 2001

introduction

Looking at the wood engravings of old nineteenth century printing presses is fascinating, for by close observation, one can see the subtle changes that each manufacturer made in his own machine. Identifying these uniquely different presses which at first glance seem to look alike, has meant studying texts of many excellent printing histories and poring over countless old catalogues in historical societies and private libraries. This work is a collection of old engravings of presses representing a multitude of manufacturers, some of whom are almost unknown today. The printer and historian will find perusing these pages much easier than searching the catalogues and turning the fragile leaves from which these engravings were selected.

This book should be of interest to everyone in our printing industry. Some "old timers" may remember working on an old press, or at least junking an old clunker to make room for a more modern piece of equipment. Some may remember these presses from Dad's shop, or from the back room of the town's weekly newspaper. Printers who have never seen anything quite as old as a press made in the eighteen hundreds may wonder how a beautifully printed sheet could have been produced from that "hunk of iron."

Indeed, it is a marvel to look at a specimen of beautiful four-color work that came off the delivery of one of these ornate monsters, and to admire the skill and devotion to craftsmanship that produced such superb work from that equipment.

Were those the "good old days"? They certainly were not! Struggling all day on a Washington hand press that yielded a daily production of 2,000 sheets, or feeding a cylinder press at 2,000 sheets an hour cannot be remembered as the "good old days." Those were the days when every printer clamored for changes in his press that would solve production problems and improve the quality of the work.

We can see how each kind of press helped advance the art of printing. Each innovation incorporated into a printing press meant that the printed word and the printed picture could be disseminated faster and in greater quantity.

We admire the engineering feats that allowed these machines to operate as well as they did with the technology available. As we look at these illustrations, we must also marvel at how much we have progressed since the turn of that century.

My first interest in letterpress came 57 years ago when at the age of fourteen I started working after school as a clean-up boy in a letterpress shop. I was fascinated, watching hand type being set and platen presses being hand fed as well as watching the more automatic Kluge. Unfortunately after the boss found out that I was under 16 and couldn't get a work permit to be around equipment, I was fired. I then took a printing course in high school and with my great interest and "previous experience" it was the only course in which I made an A. As soon as I saved enough money from my non printing jobs I bought a used 10 x 15 Chandler & Price job press with a Miller feeder along with a new type cabinet and 24 fonts of new type. As I remember I could not find used type and cabinet and had to buy new. I sold job work to the neighborhood merchants. By the time I was ready to think about college I was hooked on printing and started looking for a college that offered a degree in Printing Management. Hearing that Carnegie Tech was the best, I applied there. This was right after World War II and as they gave preference to veterans, I applied to the next closest school, West Virginia Institute of Technology, where I received a degree in Printing Plant Management in 1951. They had a lot of letterpress equipment and only one sheet-fed offset press.

I had mastered the linotype so had no problem finding summer employment as a jobber pressman and linotype operator. One summer I worked at a weekly newspaper running a linotype full time, plus, on Wednesday nights I fed the Babcock "Optimus" that printed the paper. I vividly remember operating that obsolete piece of nineteenth century equipment featured in this book. I graduated from college during the Korean War and decided to join the Air Force since they promised me a job as a printer. Even though my Air Force jobs involved offset equipment, I kept my hand in letterpress, moonlighting in local letterpress plants as a Heidelberg pressman and a linotype operator until I went to Officer Candidate School and became commander of the same printing squadron. Once back in civilian life, I left letterpress and for the next 35 years had several management jobs in large offset plants but never lost my love for letterpress.

In the 1970's my wife and I started an antique letterpress shop in an artist colony in Indiana. There we printed "Wanted" posters and newspaper headlines on an old Reliance hand press and sold wood type and type cases. This enterprise rekindled my interest in letterpress and I started accumulating type and presses for my second basement hobby shop.

I retired in 1990 and again became involved in letterpress full time as founder and co-owner of a mail order letterpress supply house. We eventually purchased old, well known letterpress equipment manufacturers: Cowen Pressroom Products, Vandercook, and Kelsey, and the entire type inventory from American Type Founders. Writing this book brought back memories from my early days in printing and reinforced my desire to continue to enjoy letterpress in retirement.

hand presses

Wooden hand presses were the only printing presses in existence before the nineteenth century. They had been in use for almost 300 years. From the time of Gutenberg (Ca.1398-1468) and his invention of movable type, the hand press had been wooden, varying in style according to the printer. The first wooden printing presses were probably converted from presses used in other trades, such as wine making, coin making, and metal working. The foremost problem in working hand presses was getting enough pressure between the bed and the platen. Wooden presses needed 2 pulls to print an entire sheet.

Builders experimented to improve the primitive designs with the limited pressure mechanism available. Between the sixteenth century and the nineteenth century clamps, screws, bars and other devices, which may have been made from metal rather than wood, facilitated changes in the manner that the platen was pressed against the bed. Unfortunately none of these technical improvements resulted in a good sheet reproduced with one pull of the lever to turn a screw.

The original common wood press used a screw for pressure, as did the Stanhope, the first iron hand press, built in 1800. Then George Clymer used a crossbeam, which pivoted on one end and pulled down at the other end, with a lever and a toggle mechanism, on his Columbian. The Wells and Smith presses used equal length toggle joints. The Stansbury Press used a torsion toggle. Finally all the Washington style presses used a "figure 4" toggle mechanism that put pressure on the top beam. More than 30 companies sold iron hand presses in the United States.

The following is a chronological list of presses and dates they first appeared:

1813 Columbian, *George Clymer, Philadelphia*
1818 Ruthven, *Adam Ramage, Philadelphia*
1819 Wells, *John J. Wells, Hartford, Connecticut*
1821 Washington, *Rust & Turney, New York*
1822 Stansbury, *Cincinnati Type Foundry, Cincinnati*
1822 Smith, *R. Hoe & Co., New York*
1827 Couillard, *Phineas Dow, Boston*
1829 Washington, *Samuel Rust, New York*
1831 Tufts, *Otis Tufts, Boston*
1832 Adams, *Seth Adams, Boston*
1834 Smith, *Cincinnati Type Foundry, Cincinnati*
1834 Philadelphia, *Adam Ramage, Philadelphia*
1835 Smith, *R. Hoe & Co., New York*
1835 Washington, *R. Hoe & Co., New York*
1836 Eagle, *James Maxwell, New York*
1836 Austin, *Fred J. Austin, New York*
1845 Cosfeldt, *F. J. Cosfeldt, Philadelphia*
1845 *Worrall & Co., New York*
1845 Franklin, *Dickinson & Williamson, Cincinnati*
1845 American, *Adam Ramage, Philadelphia*
1850 Bronstrup, *Fred Bronstrup, Philadelphia*
1850 Sheridan, *B. Sheridan, New York*
1851 Washington, *Cincinnati Type Foundry, Cin'nati*
1851 Jones, *Guilford & Jones, Cincinnati*
1852 Foster, *Charles Foster, Philadelphia*
1854 Taylor, *A.B. Taylor Mfg. Co., New York*
1856 Stansbury, *Cincinnati Type Foundry, Cincinnati*
1857 Improved Washington, *R. Hoe & Co., N. Y.*
1867 Taylor, *A.B. Taylor Son & Co., Chicago*
1867 Stansbury, *R. Hoe & Co., New York*
1874 Washington, *Franklin Type Foundry, Cincinnati*
1880 Washington, *J.T. Carroll, New York*
1881 Madison, *W.G. Walker, Madison, Wisconsin*
1881 Washington, *Palmer & Rey, San Francisco*
1887 Washington, *Marder Luse & Co., Chicago*
1888 Washington, *Shniedewend & Lee, Chicago*
1893 Washington, *Challenge Machinery Co., Chicago*
1895 Reliance, *Paul Shniedewend & Co., Chicago*

The iron hand press, developed in the nineteenth century, resulted in a very strong impression, and had enough strength to print up to four newspaper pages with one pull of the handle. The R. Hoe & Co. made a 30 x 46" press that was capable of printing that many pages. Although faster and more powerful presses were needed to get out the daily newspapers, production did not increase significantly when these presses were made from iron rather than wood. It still required two men to print only 200 to 250 sheets per hour. In order to get a good print it was necessary to wet the paper, a time consuming task. But the quality was greatly improved with the iron hand press and the work was not nearly as strenuous as with the wooden press.

In 1800 the earliest iron hand press was the Stanhope, built in England, still using a screw with compounded levers. The Stanhope had appeared in newspaper plants in the United States by 1811. The biggest advantage was that the iron platen could be twice as large as the wooden platen. In 1813 George Clymer, a skilled mechanic from Philadelphia, invented the very ornate Columbian, the first press to eliminate the screw. This press used an eagle as an adjustable counterweight. The cost of this elaborate iron press resulted in disappointing sales in the U.S. Clymer moved to London in 1817, at the age of 63. The Columbian was well received there, as it was more powerful than its competitor, the Stanhope. As the first iron hand presses began to achieve great success, R.W. Cope designed and built the Albion in England.

John Wells, a Connecticut ink maker, developed a press to make linseed oil for his inks. Seeing the need for an improved hand press, he adapted the toggle joint he used in his oil press to build the Wells hand press, which was patented in 1819.

Redesigning went on with ideas crossing from the States to England for the first two decades of the nineteenth century. In 1829 Samuel Rust of New York received his patent for the lighter weight Washington iron hand press. Rust's design eliminated the cast iron frame. His patent was based on two cast iron beams held together with rods, threaded on each end inside a column and held together with a nut at the top and bottom. This allowed the press to be taken apart for easy moving. The Washington designed by Rust was very popular due to the use of the toggle action and springs to bring down the platen for a powerful impression, and also because it weighed less and cost less.

At the Hoe Company, Robert Hoe's brothers-in-law, Peter and Mathew Smith, designed an iron hand press with a frame shaped like the outline of an acorn. This Hoe press was naturally often referred to as the Acorn press.

There were still dozens of manufacturers of the iron hand press in the United States in the mid 1800's but there were only four or five styles of presses being made. Each manufacturer waited for the original patent to expire so that he could add his own improvements and still sell the machine under the name of the popular press, such as a Washington style press. The iron Washington hand press with the "figure 4" toggle designed by Rust was later taken over by the Hoe Co.

The durability of the iron hand press was indisputable, and many of the presses manufactured in the 1800's were in service as proof presses well into the twentieth century. Today these are much sought after antiques not only by printing houses for their lobbies, but also by collectors, museums and by amateur printers who want to duplicate the work of our forefathers by using hand set type and wetted paper. Even today scaled plans are available for making wooden hand presses. There are a few people in the United States who have used these plans to make their own wooden hand press and there are those craftsmen who are creating new iron hand press reproductions for today's limited market.

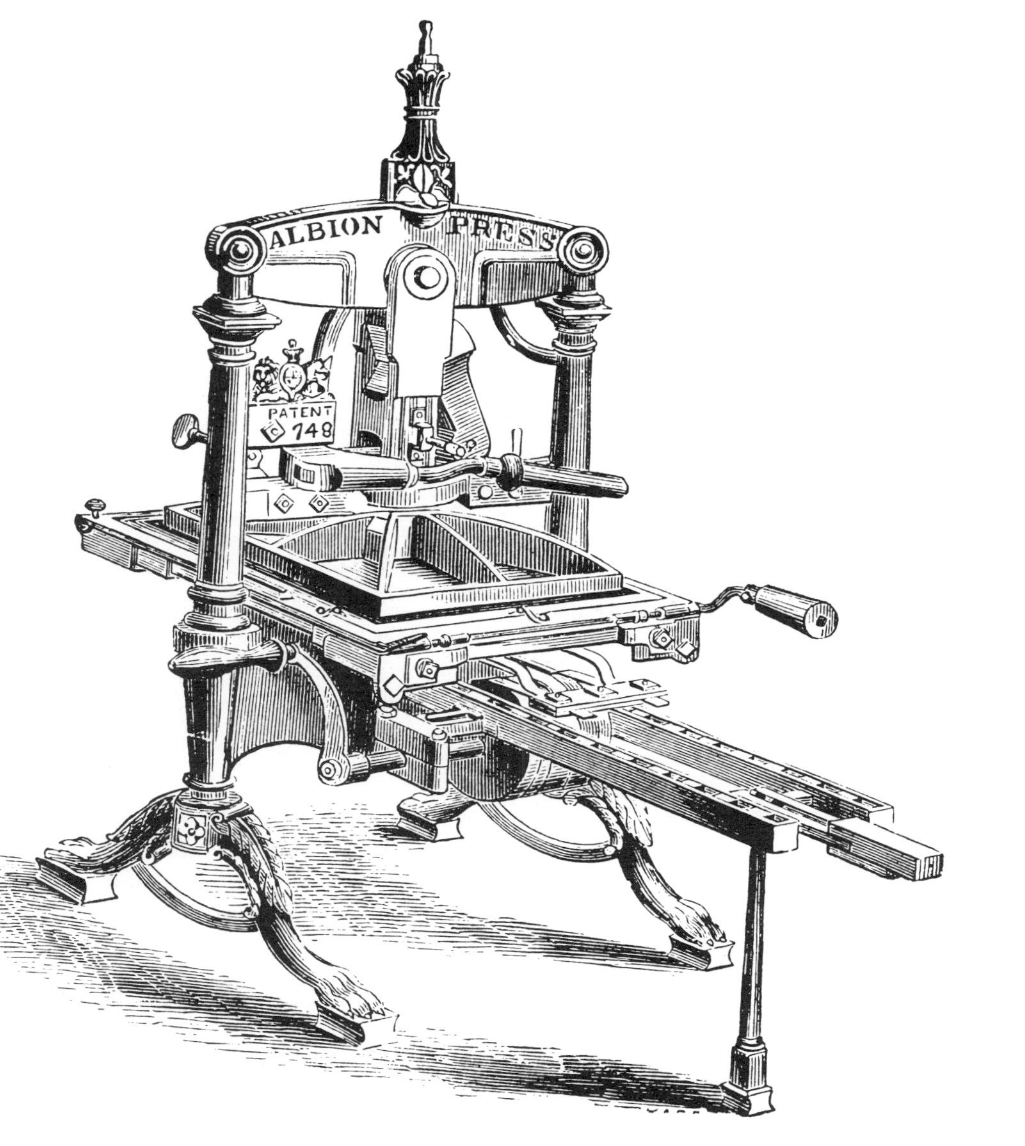

The Albion Press invented by R. W. Cope in London. Circa 1823

Alexandra Press. One of many styled after the Albion. Circa 1863

The Bronstrup Press successor to Adam Ramage. Circa 1850

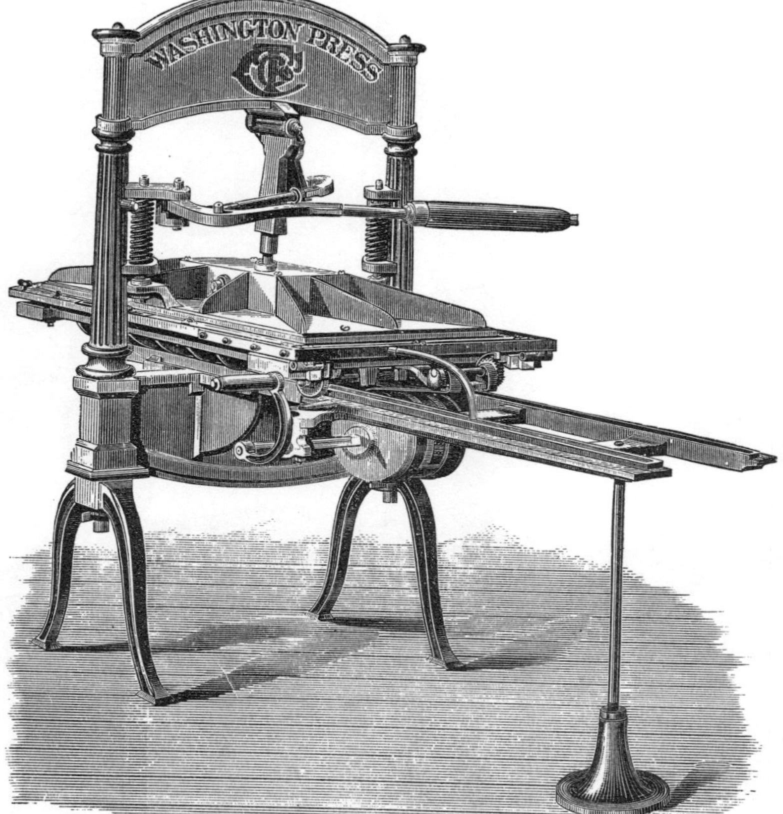

Washington Hand Press.

No. 2—23x31½, without wheels,	$225	No. 7—27x43, Rolling Bed,	$325
" 3—23x34, Rolling Bed,	275	" 8—29x43, " "	350
" 5—25x39, " "	300	Boxing,	7

Two pairs of points, one wrench, one sheeps-foot, pair of bearers, and one extra frisket go with each press
*By regular column is meant 13 ems pica.

THE LATEST PATENTED IMPROVEMENT in Washington Hand Presses consists in placing wheel tracks by side the ordinary ways; and instead of sliding the bed out with great friction in the usua. way, it is rolled easily out and in on wheels, so arranged that they are free and do not support the bed when it is in position to receive the impression. It is a great saver of muscle, and is now put upon most of the presses we make. The cost is only $25.00 extra on any size.

Cincinnati Type Foundry Co.,

MANUFACTURERS AND DEALERS IN ALL KINDS OF

TYPE AND PRINTING MACHINERY, HAND, JOB AND POWER PRESSES.

Send for Circulars and Estimates to

CHAS. WELLS, Treasurer, No. 201 Vine Street, Cincinnati, O.

Circa 1870

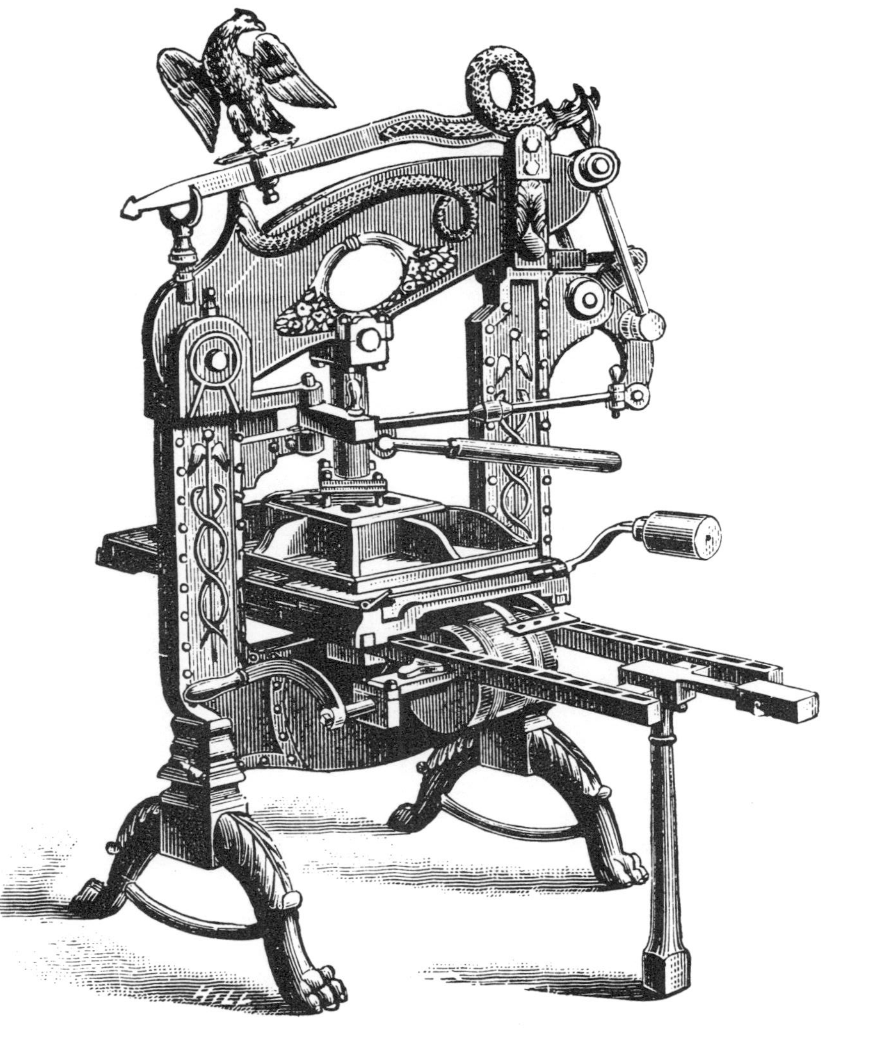

The Columbian Press invented by George Clymer in Philadelphia.
Circa 1813.

The Foster Press made in Cincinnati. Purchased by R. Hoe & Co. in 1857.

WASHINGTON HAND PRINTING PRESSES.

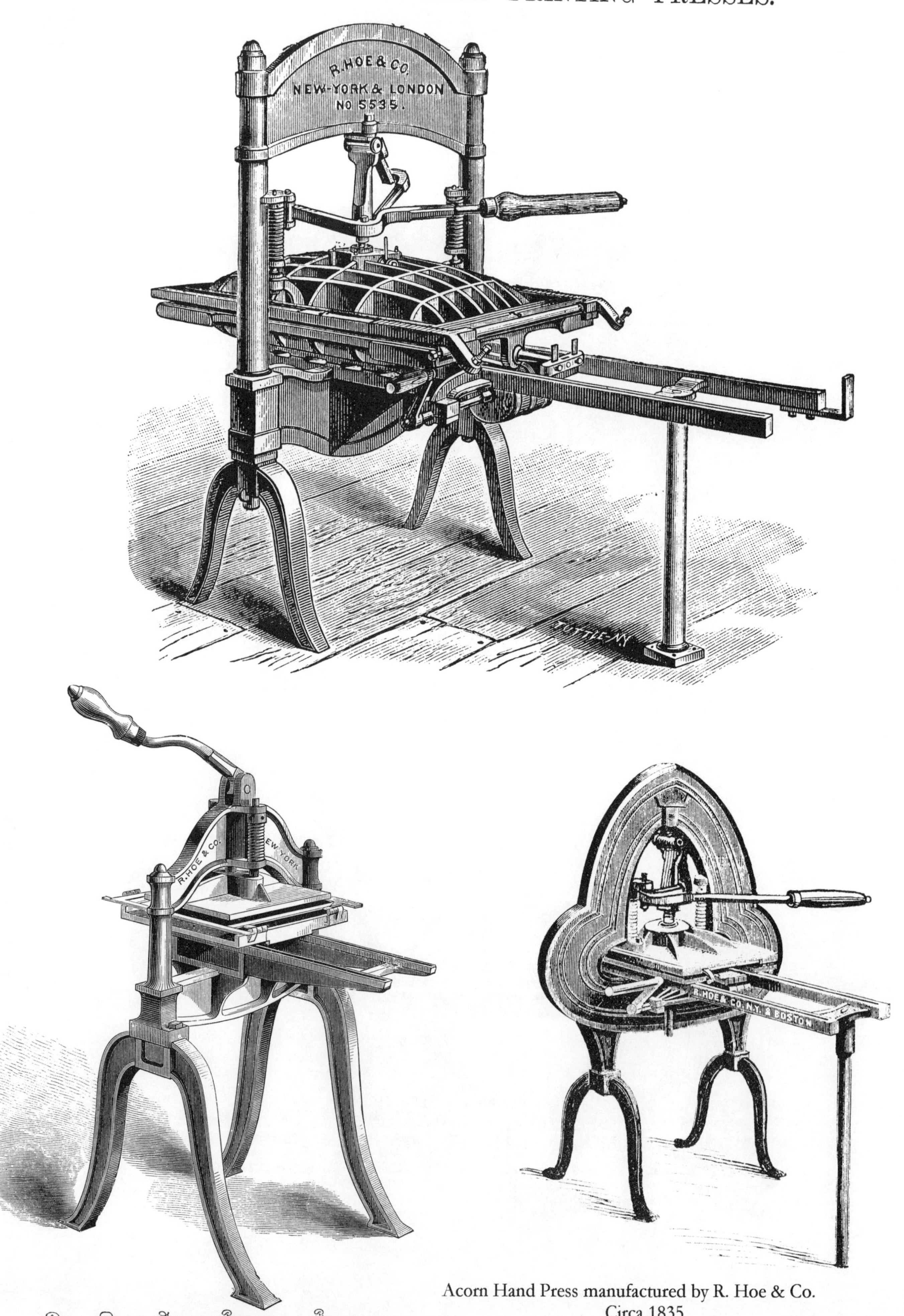

New Hand-Lever Printing Press.

Acorn Hand Press manufactured by R. Hoe & Co.
Circa 1835

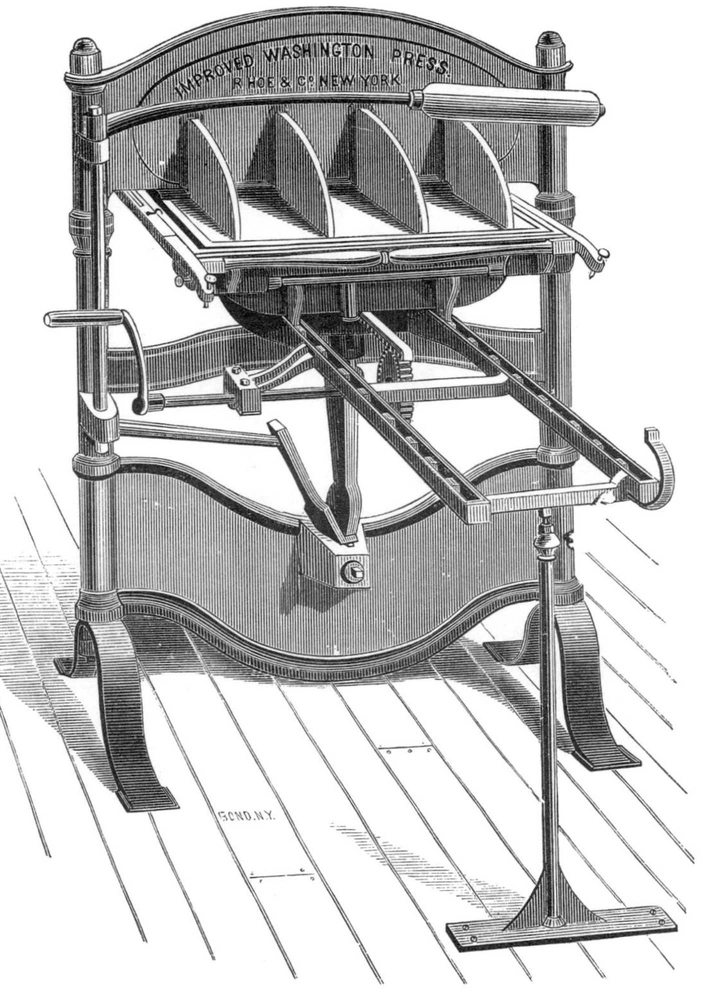

Improved Washington Press.

This is a modification of the Washington Press as represented on preceding page. It takes up much less room in height, and is equally simple, quick and powerful in its operation. The sizes and prices are the same.

Circa 1866.

R. Hoe & Co., 29 and 31 Gold Street, New-York.

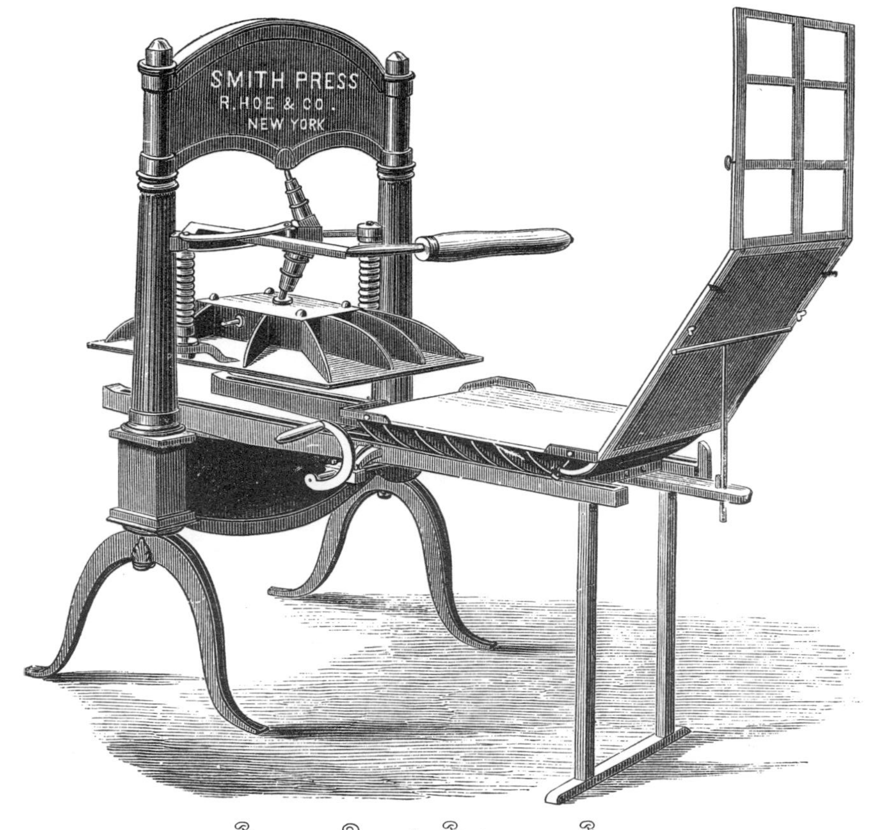

Patent Smith Printing Press.

Sizes and Prices same as those of Washington Presses.

Directions for Putting-up Washington and Smith Hand Presses.

Observe that all the connecting parts are marked or indented by points.

After setting the frame upon its legs and putting on the ribs and bed, lay the platen on the bed, placing under it two bearers about type high. Then put the springs in their places and the nuts over them, and pass the suspending rods through them, observing to place the rods so that the indentations on them correspond with those on the platen. Give the nuts two or three turns, then run in the bed so as to bring the platen under the rods, and screw them fast to the platen, after which put in the bar-handle, standard and lever, (or wedge and knees if a Smith Press.)

Circa 1860.

Patent Washington Printing Press.

The celebrity which our Patent Washington and Smith Hand Presses have obtained, and their exclusive and constant use in almost every Printing Office in the United States and other countries, during the last twenty years, renders any remarks upon their superiority unnecessary. They are elegant in appearance, simple, quick and powerful in operation, and combine every facility for the production of superior printing. Each press is tried at the manufactory, and warranted for one year.

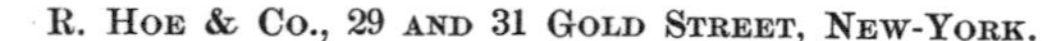

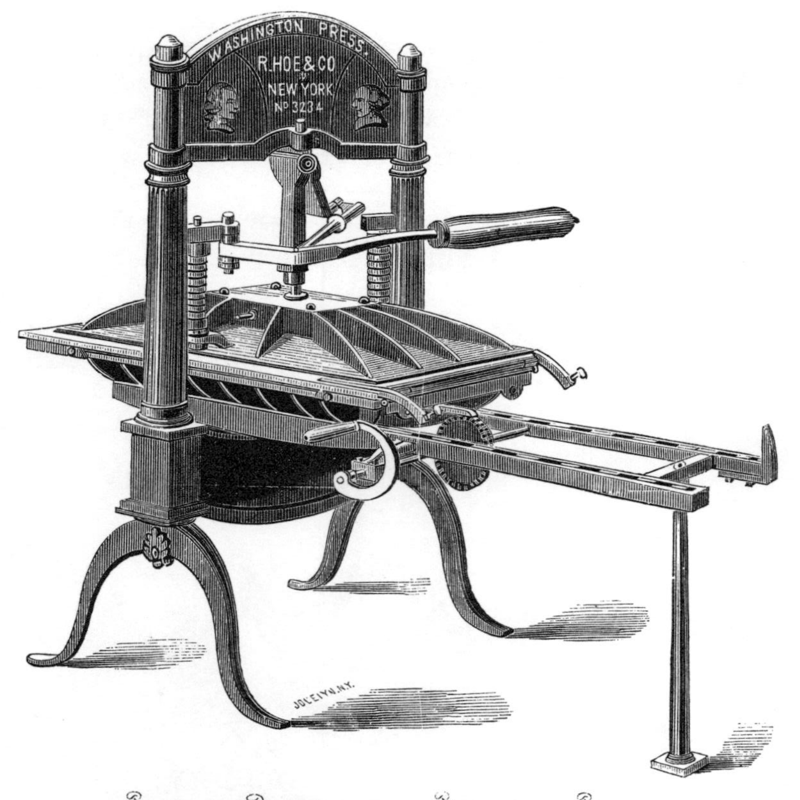

Patent Washington Printing Press.

The celebrity which our Patent Washington and Smith Hand Presses have obtained during the last forty years, renders any remarks upon their superiority unnecessary. They are elegant in appearance, simple, quick and powerful in operation, and combine every facility for the production of superior printing. Each press is tried at the manufactory, and warranted for one year.

Improved Inking Apparatus for the Hand Press.

The large distributing cylinder, which is turned by a crank, vibrates. There are two rollers to ink the form, unless the order be for one roller only, moving in a carriage with four wheels, those on one end being plain, those on the other having a projecting flange. Two wrought iron rails lie on the bed, outside of the chase; one of them grooved to receive the projecting flanges on one pair of the wheels, the other level on the surface. Projecting from the frame are two short rails, on which the wheel rests while the rollers are receiving ink from the cylinder. The machine must be set up behind the press so that the short rails on it agree exactly. both in height and width, with the rails on the bed of the press when it is run out. The journal boxes of the inking rollers have adjusting screws, so that they may bear more or less on the type, as circumstances require.

Sizes and Prices.

With Vibrating Cylinder, Railway and Carriage to work one ink roller.

Foolscap	$50.00.
Medium	55.00.
Super Royal	60 00.
Nos. 1 & 2	65.00.
" 3 & 4	70.00.
" 5 & 6	75.00.

R. Hoe & Co., 29 and 31 Gold Street, New-York.

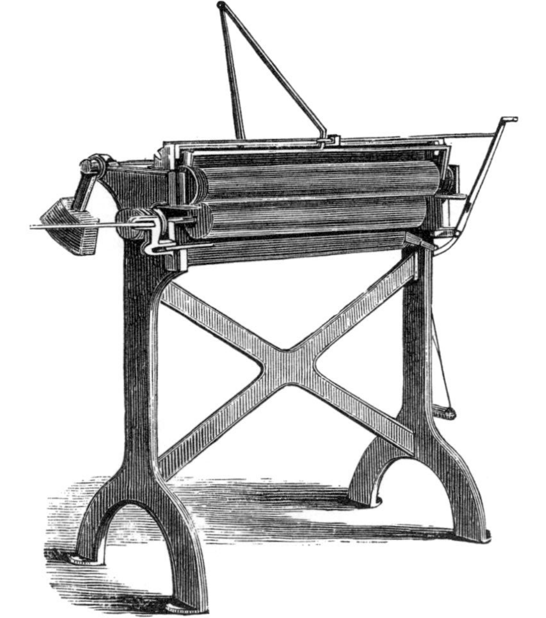

Patent Hand Press Self-Inking Machine.

By attaching this machine to a Washington or Smith Hand Press the pressman inks the form by the ordinary operation of the press, and gives at the same time a more perfect distribution. It is much more simple in its construction, regular in its movements, and easy to put up than any machine heretofore in use for the purpose.

Sizes and Prices.

Foolscap	$135.00.
Medium	145.00.
Super Royal	155.00.
Nos. 1 & 2	170.00.
" 3 & 4	185.00.
Boxing and Carting	5.00.

Terms of Payment—Cash at manufactory in New-York.

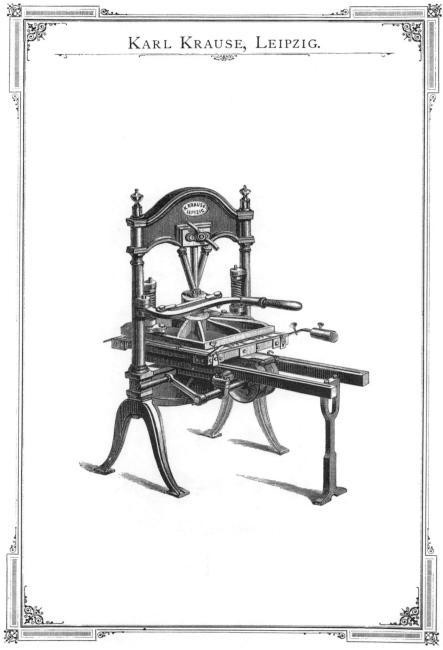

Imperial Press manufactured by Cope & Sherwin in London. Circa 1828.

KARL KRAUSE, LEIPZIG.

K. KRAUSE LEIPZIG

Circa 1860

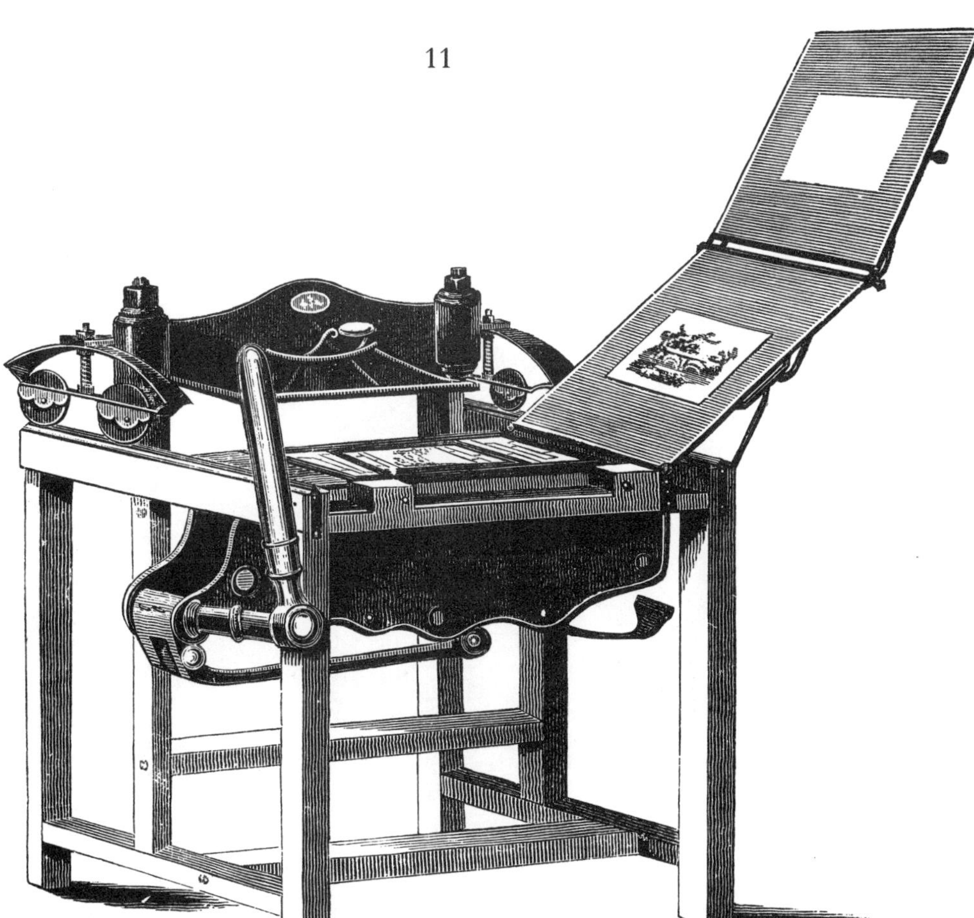

The Ruthven Press patented in 1813 by John Ruthven of Edinburgh, Scotland.
Manufactured and sold in the United States by Adam Ramage.

The Smith Press patented by Peter Smith in 1821 and manufactured by R. Hoe & Co.

Patent Smith Printing Press.

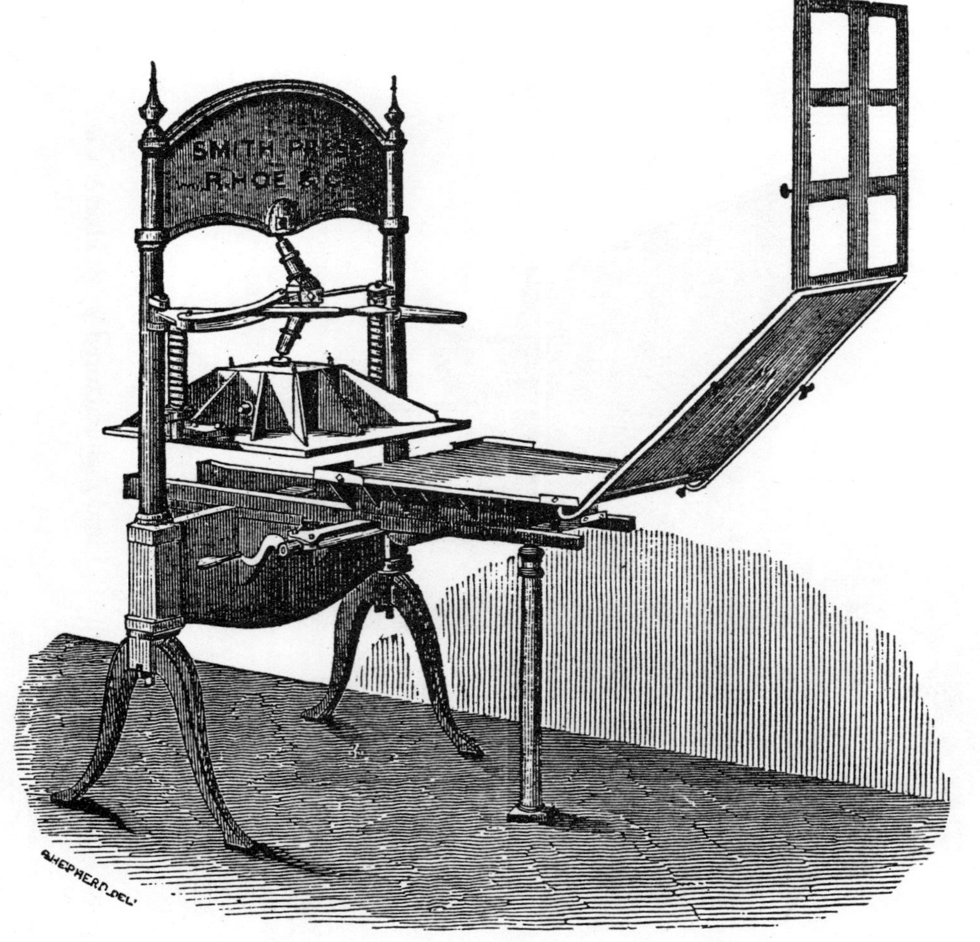

DIRECTIONS FOR PUTTING UP THE WASHINGTON AND SMITH HAND PRESSES.

It will be necessary to observe that all the connecting parts are marked, or indented by points; if these are carefully observed the press may be put together without difficulty.

After setting the frame upon its legs, and putting on the ribs and bed, lay the platen on the bed, placing under it two bearers about type high. Then put the springs in their places, and the nuts over them, and pass the suspending rods through them, observing to place the rods so that the number of indentations on them correspond with those on the platen. Give the nuts two or three turns, then run in the bed, so as to bring the platen under the rods, and screw them fast to the platen, after which put in the bar-handle, standard and lever, (or wedge and knees if a Smith Press.)

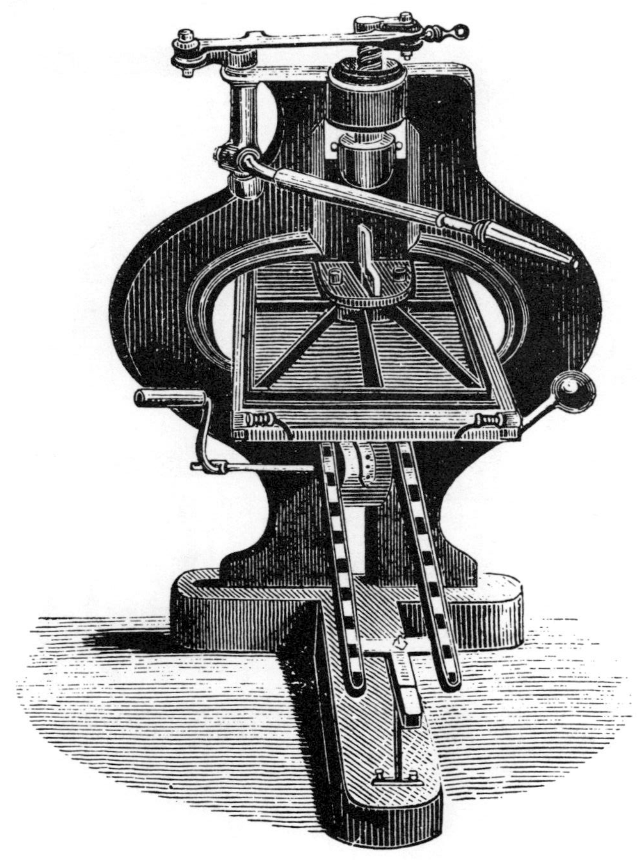

The Stanhope Press. The first all metal hand press was built by Lord Stanhope in England. Circa 1810.

George Medhurst's Press, one of the first ones to use a 'torsion toggle', a mechanism that was used by several manufacturers. Circa 1820

The Stansbury Press patented by Rev. Abraham Stansbury in 1821 and Manufactured by Isaac Adams, R. Hoe & Co. and Cincinnati Type Foundry.

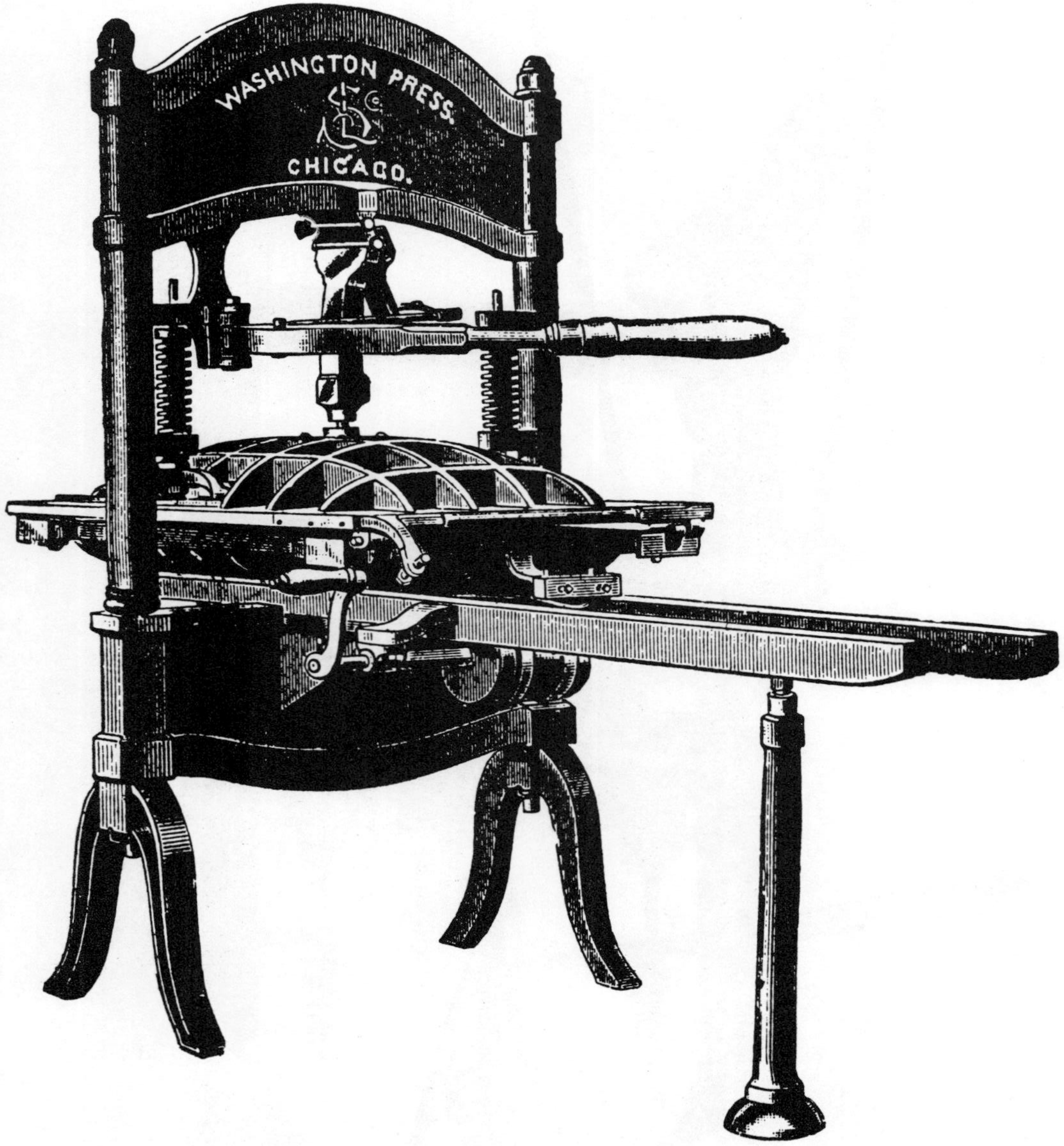

The Washington Press. Manufactured by Shniedewend & Lee Co. Chicago. Circa 1884

Reliance Proof Press, a Washington style hand press manufactured by Paul Shniedewend & Company in Chicago. Circa 1896

The Wells Hand Press. Introduced two major changes in design: the use of a toggle replacing the screw and a counterweight to return the platen to the upper position. Circa 1816.

The Wells Press manufactured by John Wells of Hartford, Connecticut. On this model the weight was eliminated and replaced by springs and a different toggle. Circa 1819.

Cylinder Presses

The needs of the printing industry have been multi-lateral ever since the early nineteenth century. In the 1830's, while hand presses were still being manufactured and improved upon, the cylinder press was making rapid headway in Europe, primarily in England and Germany.

The bed and platen press had become quite popular for the medium-size printing establishment and served as an intermediary between the hand press and the cylinder press. The bed and platen press provided a stopgap between the two machines, as it did not require as much mechanical skill to run it as the cylinder press, yet provided faster production. The bed and platen press used the same principles as the hand press but with the addition of automatic inking. This press was a stepping stone towards faster production since it was capable of producing 500 to 1,000 sheets per hour with two persons working the press. With the advent of steam power, the bed and platen press could be converted from either hand or horsepower. Electric motors were not introduced until 1884.

Larger establishments, naturally, began to ask for faster presses to meet the demands of their business. The cylinder press with its output of up to 1,500 sheets per hour was their answer. Printers who had outgrown the hand press readily accepted the cylinder press. By mid-century the cylinder press had come into its own in the United States.

The three basic styles of cylinder presses each found their own applications. The Country cylinder press was made to order for small newspapers; the Job and News cylinder press was made for the shop doing both commercial and newspaper work. The Two-Revolution press was made for printers producing quality work requiring good register for color. Printing illustrations and engravings required a press with heavy construction as the Two-Revolution press.

The cylinder press progressed into four types of design:

1. The Drum Cylinder, whose circumference was twice the length of the bed, allowing the bed to return with one revolution of the drum.
2. The Stop Cylinder, that would make one impression and then stop while the bed returned.
3. The Two-Revolution Cylinder, that would make one impression at every other revolution of the cylinder.
4. The Reversing Cylinder, that traveled with the bed.

Many different companies manufactured the cylinder press in the 1800's. Each model incorporated many improvements and advancements, such as using grippers, invented by Napier in 1869, instead of string or tapes. Delivering the sheets in the press after printing varied with each design. At first all the cylinder presses delivered the sheets in back of the press with or without tapes. Most used long fingered racks that would "fly" the sheet with printed side down. Then some manufacturers developed a delivery mechanism that delivered the sheets to the front of the press with tapes, printed side up, so the sheets could be inspected while being printed. Some presses could be converted to deliver this way or to deliver the sheet using the fly method, printed side down for easier back up printing.

Other cylinder presses had novel inking rollers and ink distribution. As soon as the mechanics of the cylinder press were proven, innovative ideas came along such as printing two colors at one time, automatic feeding, etc. The most practical and welcome development was the perfecting or printing of both sides of the paper with one pass through the press. R. Hoe & Co. made a perfecting press in 1871. These presses had a problem with set-off until better drying inks were introduced.

There are probably no cylinder presses from the nineteenth century still in use today. However, the cylinder press played such a major role in the development of the printing industry that it is important to show as many illustrations of this type of press as possible. About 200 different cylinder presses from over 30 manufacturers are illustrated here, but each one of the presses is a little different. Often refinements in the ink systems were the selling points when a printer made a decision to select a new press. The number of form rollers, the type of fountain for better inking power, as well as the distributor ductor and oscillating rollers of the inking system were all special aspects of various cylinder presses. Air springs and air cylinders were other major improvements that made them desirable.

R. Hoe and Company was the most prolific manufacturer of cylinder presses, although Koenig and Bauer, a German company, made the first cylinder press in 1811. Hoe was manufacturing presses at that time, but didn't produce a cylinder press until 1830. The R. Hoe and Co. had one of the longest manufacturing histories, producing printing presses from about 1805 to 1969. The C.B. Cottrell and Sons Co. was another press manufacturer that started in the 1800's and continued in operation well into the 20th century. Although they were taken over by Harris and then by Heidelberg, web offset presses manufactured today are still known as Cottrell.

As in other industries, many owners of printing press factories got their experience working for other companies. In the case of printing press manufacturers, the Hoe Company was the leader. A.B. Taylor was a foreman at Hoe. Later Andrew Campbell was a foreman at the A.B. Taylor Printing Press and Machine Co. Taylor tried unsuccessfully to develop an automatically fed cylinder press. As late as the end of the 19th century, 95% of the presses were still fed by hand.

Hoe developed the idea of a continuously revolving drum with cam-operated stops for positioning the paper, and using coiled springs at each end of the bed for cushioning. Later A.B. Taylor used an air plunger and cylinder for the same purpose.

The need to increase output for newspapers resulted in the development of two feeding positions for one press, thus doubling production. This type of press then brought about the development of a two-color cylinder press. This press was in great demand because it generated greater output of printed material, and was largely responsible for the rapid growth of the printing industry in the nineteenth century.

Acme Country Newspaper Press

No. 64 FEDERAL ST., BOSTON, MASS.

PRICE LIST.

REGULAR COUNTRY.

Size, 28x40	Inside Bearers,	$ 900
" 30x43	" "	950
" 31x46	" "	1,000

COMPLETE COUNTRY.

Size, 30x43	Inside Bearers,	$1,100
" 32x46	" "	1,200
" 34x50	" "	1,300
" 37x50	" "	1,400

COMBINATION PRESS.

Size, 30x41	Inside Bearers,	$1,500
" 32x44	" "	1,600
" 34x48	" "	1,800

BOOK AND JOB PRESS.

Size, 30x41	Inside Bearers,	$2,000
" 32x44	" "	2,200
" 34x48	" "	2,500

These prices include Blanket, Wrenches Mould, Extra Roller Stocks, and Cone Pulleys for steam machine.

THE ALLEN ROTARY JOB PRESS.

ENLARGED, AND IMPROVED IN DISTRIBUTION AND REGISTER.

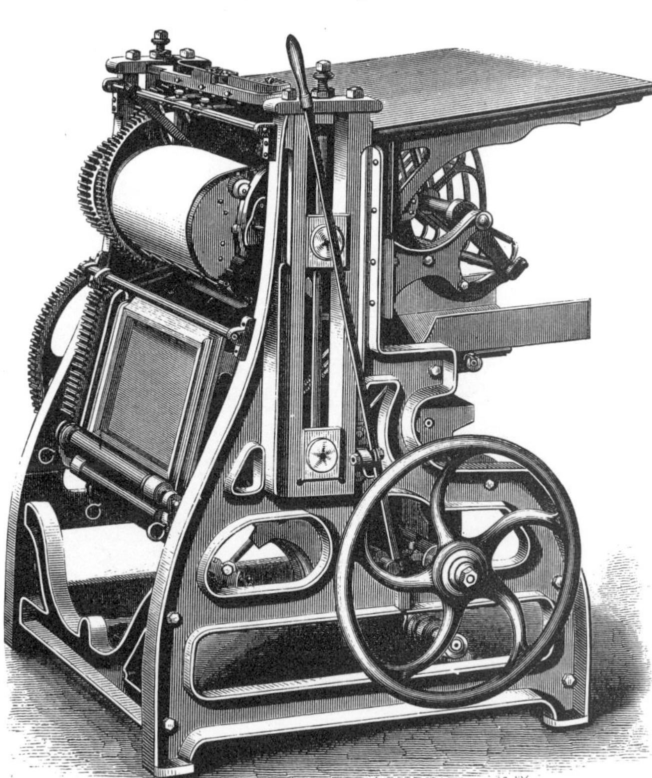

Manufactured by the ALLEN MANUF'G CO., Norwich, Conn.

The capacity of this Press is from 2,000 to 3,000 impressions per hour; it is really only limited by the ability of the feeder. We especially claim it to be a profitable Press, saving fully $600 per annum over other Job Presses, wherever there is work enough to keep it running. It is now **unsurpassed** in DISTRIBUTION and REGISTER. In strength and perfection of its mechanism it will compare favorably with the best Press in the market.

Prints a Form 8 by 14, and will carry a Sheet 14 by 17 Inches.

TESTIMONIALS.

OFFICE OF THE CONGRESSIONAL PRINTER,
Washington, February 7th, 1873.

I take pleasure in saying that the Allen Rotary Press fully merits my expectations. It does its work expeditiously and well, and is the best jobber in the office by far. It does the work of fully three Gordon Presses, with the feeding expense of one. I shall add another as soon as I find place for it. Your respectfully, A. M. CLAPP, Cong. Printer.

BUFFALO, N. Y., June 6th, 1872.

We are very much pleased with the Rotary Press sent us about three months since. We were able to do the work of three Gordon Presses within three days after starting it; and any of our feeders can readily feed up to this mark, and beyond it. We regard it as indispensable, and hope soon that we can dispose of some of the job presses we have, when we shall desire one or two more of your presses. We heartily commend it to the trade. Yours respectfully, WARREN JOHNSON & CO.

PRICE $800 --- Counter-Shaft, Hangers, and Cone-Pulley included.

WM. G. ELY, Gen'l Agent, Norwich, Conn.

Circa 1883

THE
ADAMS HAND CYLINDER PRESS
SPEED, 300 TO 400 PER HOUR.
Each Press complete with Felt Blanket, Inking Apparatus, Roller Frame, one Cast Roller, and one extra Roller Core
J. MANZ & CO.

Brothers Seth & Isaac Adams started manufacturing presses in Boston in the 1830's.
R. Hoe & Co. bought them out in 1859.

Adams hand powered, patented by Seth Adams in 1830.
Later manufactured by R. Hoe & Co.

The Babcock Printing Press Mfg. Co.

THE "REGULAR."

"Perfect Inking" Cut and Color Press.

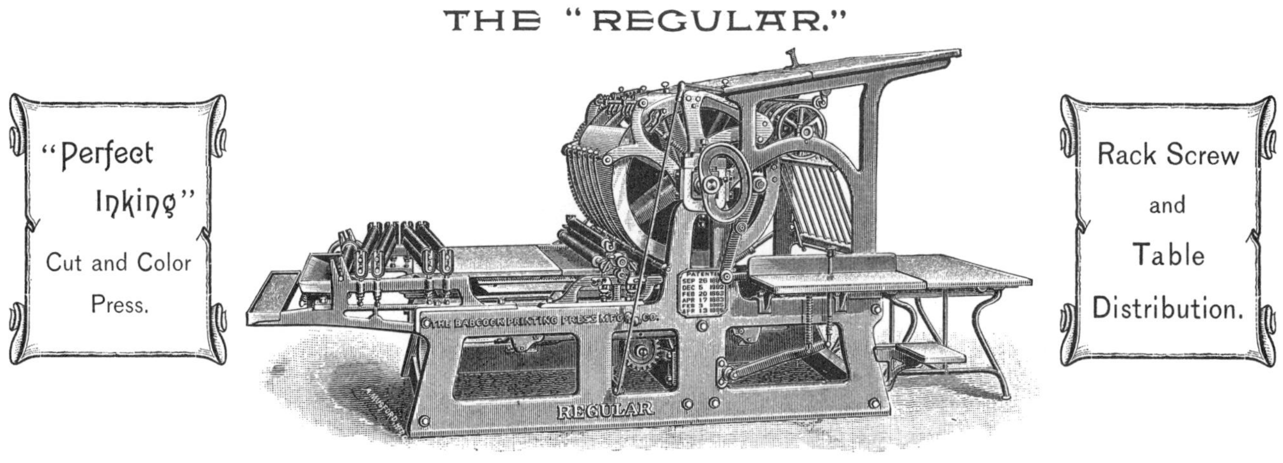

Rack Screw and Table Distribution.

Main Office and Works: NEW LONDON, CONN.

New York Office: 26 & 27 Tribune Building.

MANUFACTURERS OF

Drum Cylinder, Stop Cylinder, Lithographic and Two-Revolution Presses,

NEW LONDON, CONN.

NEW YORK OFFICE, 26 and 27 TRIBUNE BUILDING.

BARNHART BROS. & SPINDLER, 115 and 117 Fifth Avenue, CHICAGO, ILL., GENERAL WESTERN AGENTS.

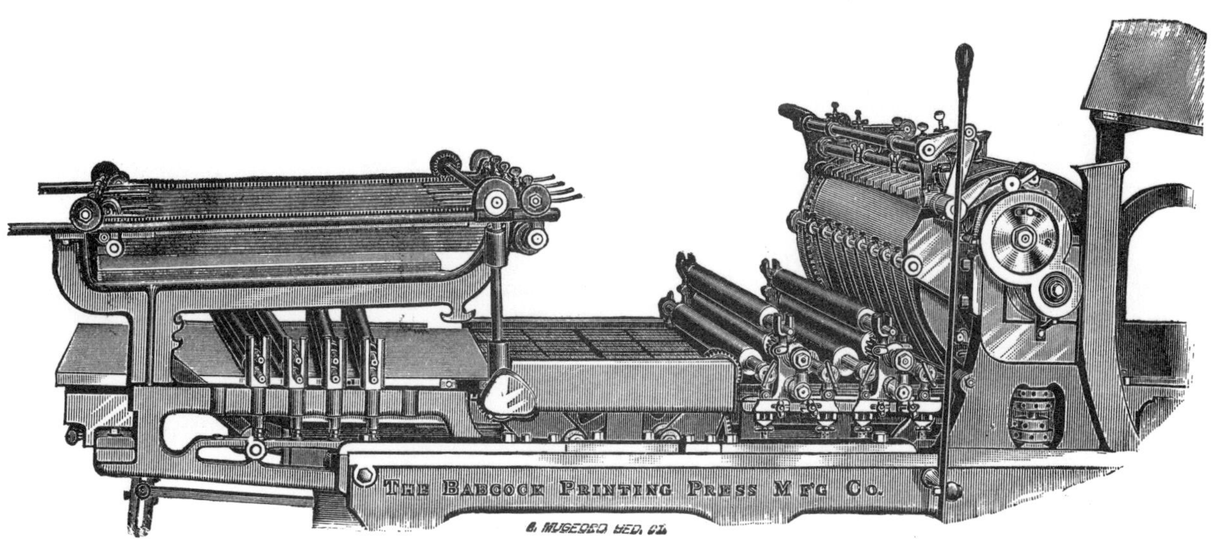

Babcock "Country" – 2 roller, air springs, rack and cam distribution, tapeless delivery.
Circa 1880

Babcock "Country" (Reliance) – Slight variation with ink fountain and gear guards.

Babcock "Standard" – 2 roller, air springs, rack and cam distribution, tapeless delivery.
Late style.

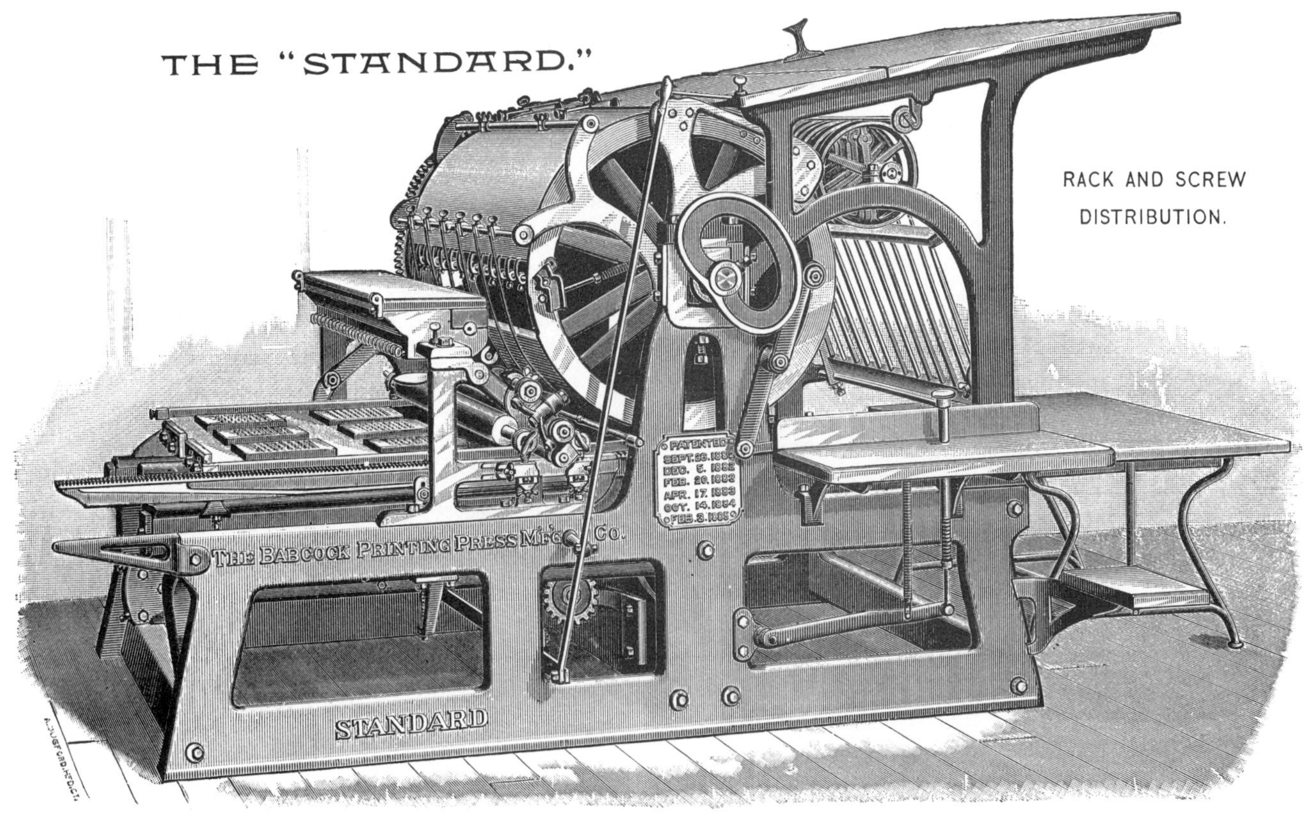

"HIGH FOUNTAIN" BOOK AND JOB PRESS.

Babcock "Standard" – 2 roller, air springs, rack and cam distribution, tape delivery, back-up.

From the Warren, Pa., Ledger, of Nov. 20, 1885.

There may be a better press than the "STANDARD" built by the Babcock Printing Press Mfg. Co., of New London, Conn., but we have not seen it. The No. 6 "STANDARD" recently placed in our office, by the above company, is entirely satisfactory. It runs without jar over 1,800 impressions per hour; a 1,500 motion is slow. Two thousand can be made easily without injury to the machinery.

From Fuller & Stowe Co., 49 Lyons St., Grand Rapids, Mich., March 3, 1886.

BABCOCK PRINTING PRESS MFG. CO.: *Gentlemen*,—Your favor of the 27th came to hand, and same day your new vibrating attachment. We consider it a great improvement over the old style. We are much pleased with the operation of the machine, and shall add another of your make as soon as our work will warrant it.

Yours truly, FULLER & STOWE CO.

Office of the Times, Lima, Ohio, Dec. 1, 1886.

BABCOCK PRINTING PRESS MFG. CO.:—*Gentlemen*,—Some months ago we bought from Messrs. Barnhart Bros. & Spindler, of Chicago, one of your "STANDARD" Presses, which has been in constant use in our office ever since, and gives perfect satisfaction. We have used presses of many styles, but never operated one that embraced so many good features as your "STANDARD" series. It is a first-class machine in every respect, and yet so simple as to be easily operated and capable of doing the finest kind of work. Our press (a No. 2) is capable of running as many sheets per hour as the feeder can place properly. In fact, it is just the press we were looking for, and we would not exchange it for any other press in the market.

Very respectfully yours,

O. B. SELPRIDGE, Manager *The Times Co.*

BABCOCK PRINTING PRESS MFG. CO., MAIN OFFICE AND WORKS, New London, Conn.

Babcock "Dispatch" – Single feed, 4 roller, rack, screw and table distribution, tape delivery.

THE BABCOCK PRINTING PRESS MANUFACTURING CO.

MAIN OFFICE AND WORKS, NEW LONDON, CONN.

THE "DISPATCH"—DOUBLE-FEED.

Circa 1892

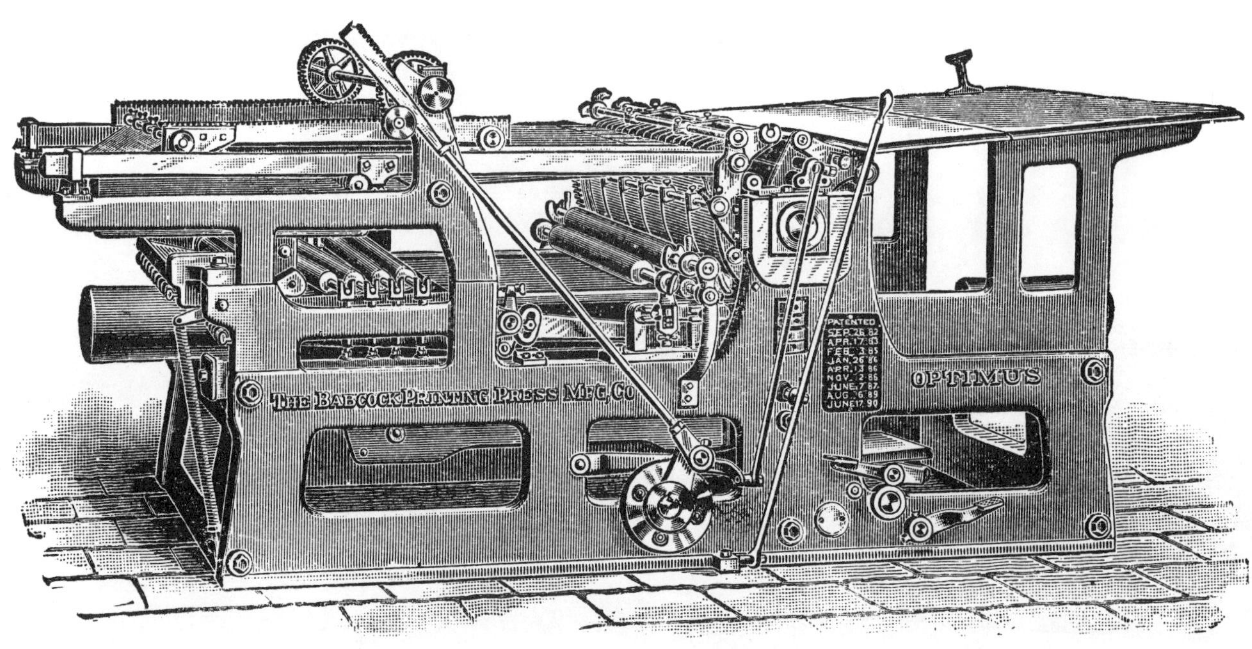

Babcock "Pony Optimus" – Two revolution, 2 roller, rack, cam and table distribution, air springs and front delivery

The Babcock Printing Press Manuf'g Co.

THE "OPTIMUS."

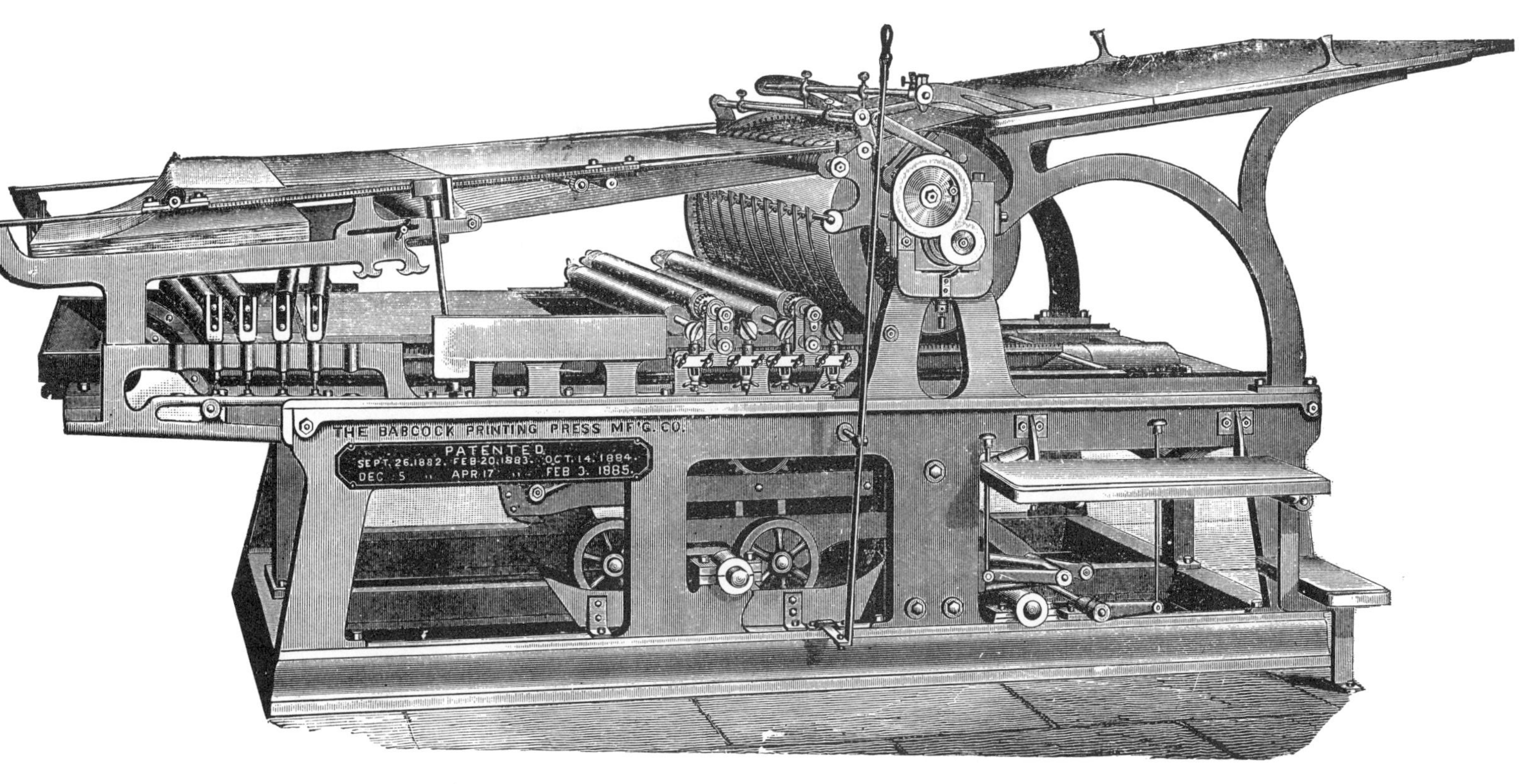

Babcock "Optimus" – Two Revolution (old style) 4 roller, air springs, rack, screw and table distribution, front delivery.

Babcock "Optimus" – Two Revolution, later style.

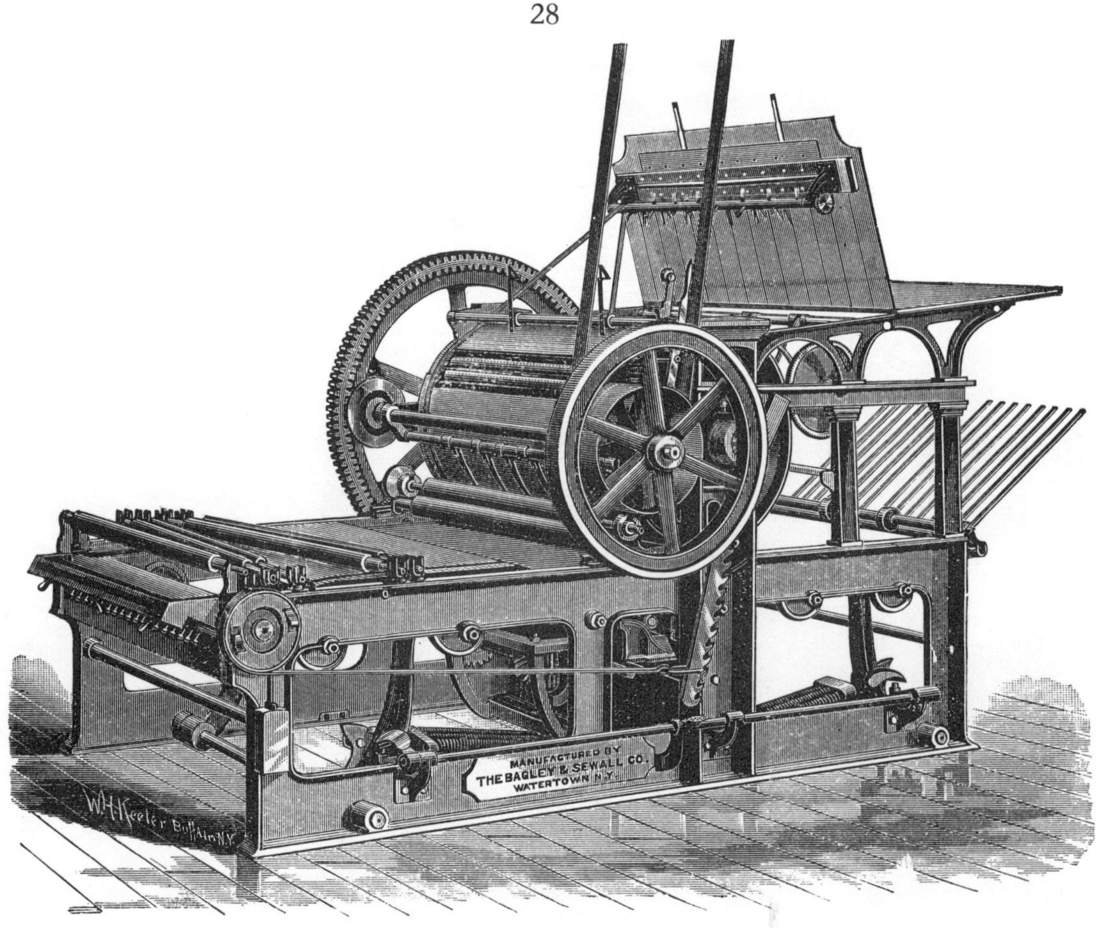

Bagley & Sewall "Complete" – 2 roller, wire springs, screw vibrator and table distribution, brush delivery. Manufactured by The Bagley & Sewall Co. of Watertown, N.Y.

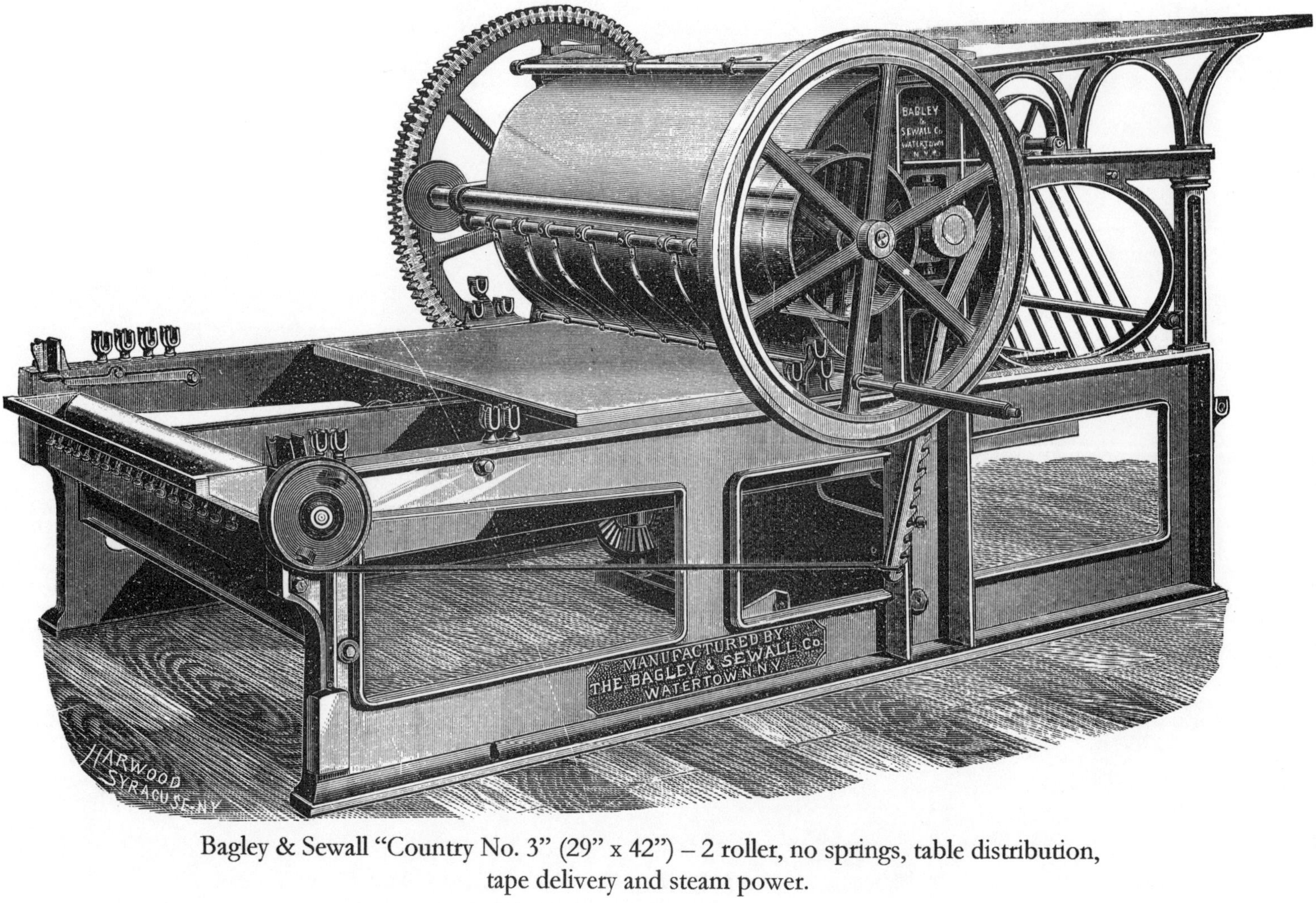

Bagley & Sewall "Country No. 3" (29" x 42") – 2 roller, no springs, table distribution, tape delivery and steam power.

Bagley & Sewall "Country No. 5" (34 x 50") – 2 roller, no springs, table distribution, tape delivery, hand and steam power.

STOP CYLINDER PRESS.

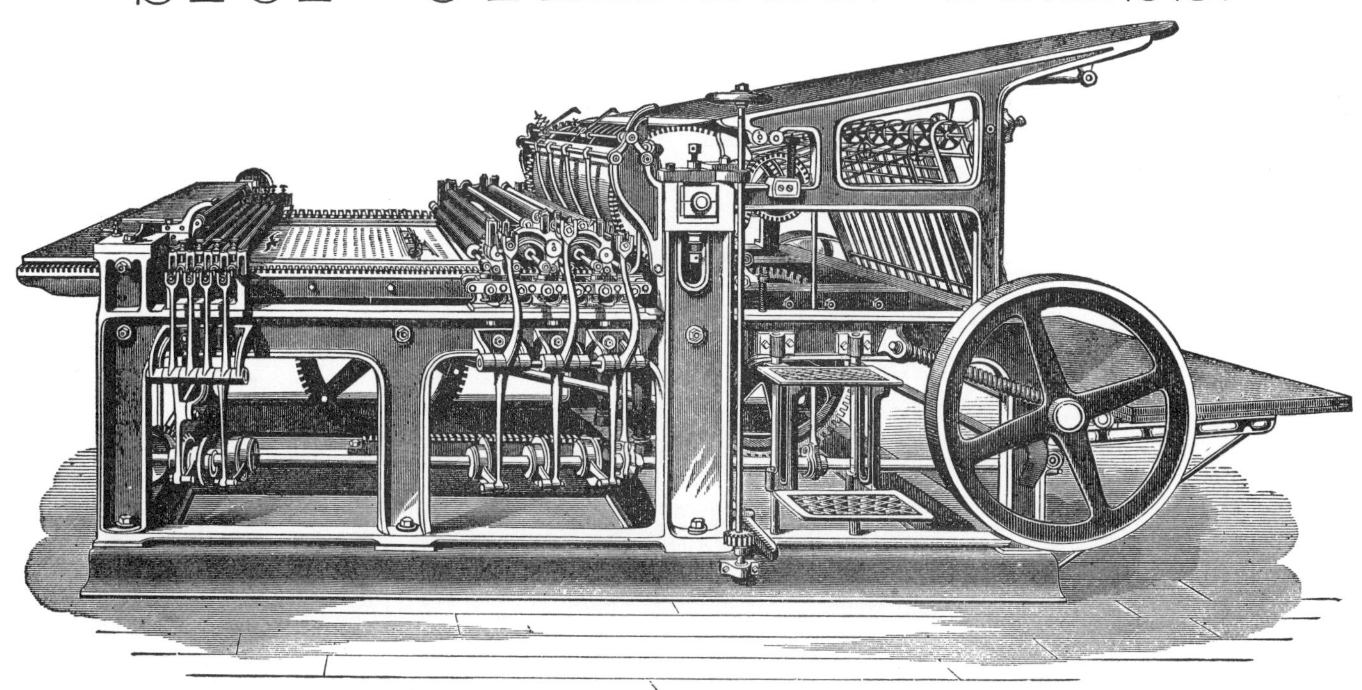

UNEQUALED FOR FINE AND FAST WORK, COMPLETE DISTRIBUTION, THOROUGH ROLLING, CLEAR IMPRESSION, AND PERFECT REGISTER.

The prices on these PRESSES have been much REDUCED, and will be furnished parties on application stating terms on which they wish to purchase.

Unidentified used Stop Cylinder Press being sold in 1875.

Illustrated Catalogue.

Campbell Press Works.

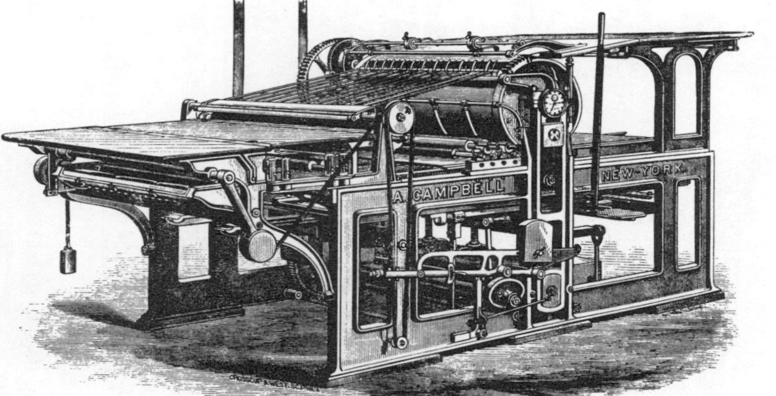

THE CAMPBELL

PRINTING PRESS AND MANUFACTURING COMPANY,

PROPRIETORS.

OFFICE,

No. 39 Beekman Street, New York.

MANUFACTORY,

Wythe Avenue, Hewes and Penn Streets, Brooklyn, E. D., N.Y.

CAMPBELL'S COMBINATION BOOK SERIES.

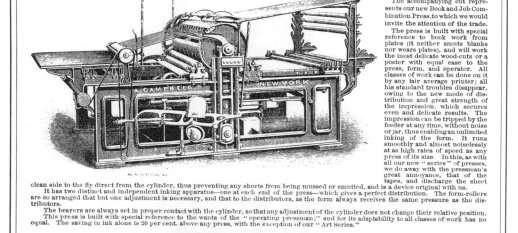

The accompanying cut represents our new Book and Job Combination Press, to which we would invite the attention of the trade.

The press is built with special reference to book work from plates (it neither smuts blanks nor wears plates), and will work the most delicate wood-cuts or a poster with equal ease to the press, form, and operator. All classes of work can be done on it by any fair average printer; all his standard troubles disappear, owing to the new mode of distribution and great strength of the impression, which secures even and delicate results. The impression can be tripped by the feeder at any time, without noise or jar, thus enabling an unlimited inking of the form. It runs smoothly and almost noiselessly at as high rates of speed as any press of its size. In this, as with all our new "series" of presses, we do away with the pressman's great annoyance, that of the tapes, and discharge the sheet clean side to the fly direct from the cylinder, thus preventing any sheets from being mussed or smutted, and is a device original with us.

It has two distinct and independent inking apparatus—one at each end of the press—which gives a perfect distribution. The form-rollers are so arranged that but one adjustment is necessary, and that to the distributors, as the form always receives the same pressure as the distributors.

The bearers are always set in proper contact with the cylinder, so that any adjustment of the cylinder does not change their relative position.

This press is built with special reference to the wants of the "operating pressman;" and for its adaptability to all classes of work has no equal. The saving in ink alone is 20 per cent. above any press, with the exception of our "Art Series."

SIZES, PRICES, etc.,

No.	Size of Bed.	Size of Form.	No. Rollers.	Speed per Hour.	Price.	No.	Size of Bed.	Size of Form.	No. Rollers.	Speed per Hour.	Price.
1	37x52	32x47	4	800 to 1800	$5,000	3	28x41	24x38	4	800 to 2000	$3,800
2	32x50	28x45	4	800 to 1900	4,400	4	27x36	22x32	4	800 to 2200	3,200

CAMPBELL'S COMBINATION BOOK AND JOB SERIES.

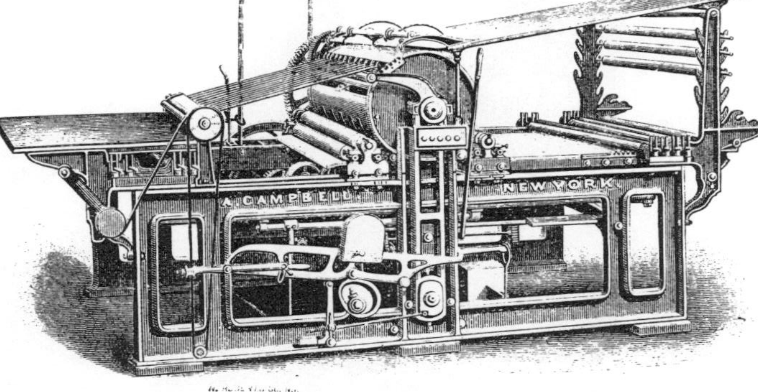

This cut represents our new Job and Book Press, which is acknowledged to be without a competitor for its excellency and rapidity of work.

It has two rollers over the form, with an arrangement for tripping the impression, which allows unlimited inking of the form.

It is especially adapted to general job office work, having no tapes, and discharging the sheet direct from the cylinder, with the clean side to the fly, thereby preventing the smutting of sheets when large colored surfaces are exposed.

It has our unrivalled patent combination distribution, which, together with the table distribution, original with us, makes it perfect.

The speed is greater than any other press of its size, with the same number of rollers, though it runs with less noise and without any jar whatever.

SIZES, PRICES, etc.,

No.	Size of Bed.	Size of Form.	Rollers.	Speed per Hour.	Price.	No.	Size of Bed.	Size of Form.	Rollers.	Speed per Hour.	Price.
1	41x56	36x53	2	1500	$4,000	4	31x46	28x42	2	1800	$3,000
2	37x52	32x48	2	1600	3,500	5	30x41	24x37	2	1900	2,700
3	34x50	29x46	2	1700	3,200	6	27x36	21x32	2	2000	2,400

OFFICE---39 Beekman Street, New York. A. CAMPBELL.

Circa 1873

Campbell "Country" Press. Andrew Campbell was the first American to engage in country press manufacturing from 1867 to 1876.

CAMPBELL'S COUNTRY PRESS,

WITH RACK AND SCREW AND TABLE DISTRIBUTION, TYMPAN NIPPER, AND REEL RODS IN THE CYLINDER.

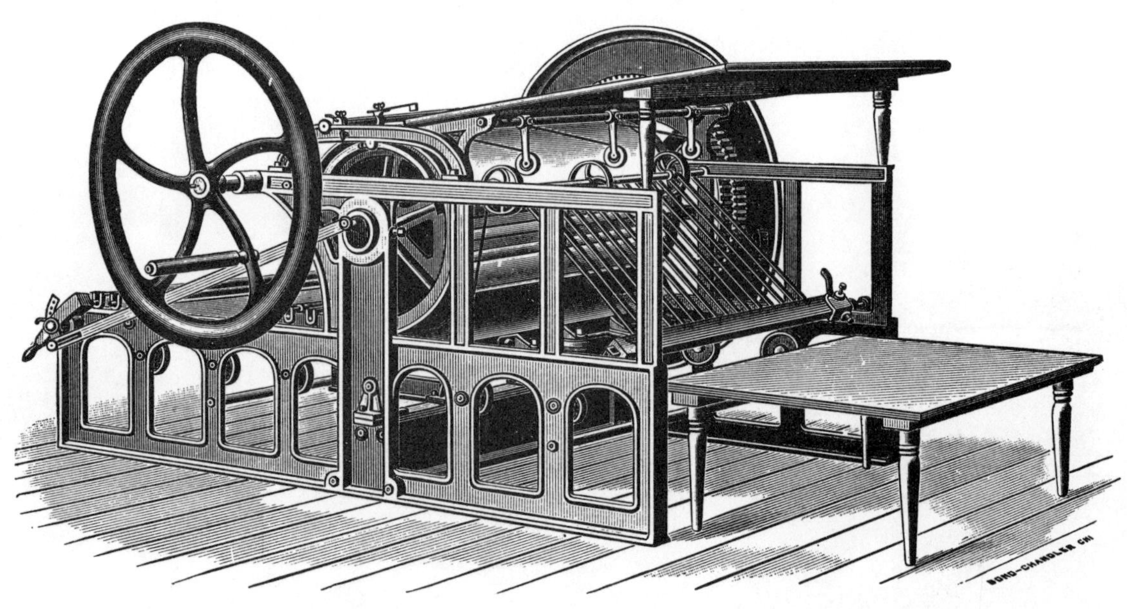

The Campbell "Country Press" was a hand powered drum cylinder press designed for the country newspaper field. Circa 1861.

Campbell "Country" Improved Box frame – 2 roller, no springs, table distribution, tape delivery, hand and steam power.

Campbell "Country" Hand Cylinder – 2 roller, no springs, table distribution, tape delivery, hand power.

Campbell Oscillating Country Press.

Campbell "Country" Oscillator -- 2 roller, no springs, vibrator and table distribution, front delivery. Sheet was fed under the cylinder. 29 x 46" cost $775 & 33 x 48" cost $875. Speeds up to 1200 impressions per hour. Circa 1880.

Campbell "Complete" Old Style frame – 2 roller, wire springs, screw and table distribution, tapeless delivery.

Of the two smaller sizes of the "Country" and "Complete" we make a special pattern of frame, as they are more especially designed for jobbing work, and in very many instances take the place of small platen jobbing presses.

They are constructed to gauges, as are all our other machines; are quiet in operation and easily handled; and in view of their ultimate adoption by all jobbing houses, we have placed them at the following reduced prices:

ERRATA.

COMPLETE PRESS.

No. 6.	**Size of Bed, 23 × 28**	**Size of Form, 18½ × 24**	**No. Rollers, 2**	**Speed per Hour, 800 to 1,600**	**Price, $1,280**
7.	**" 20 × 25**	**" 16 × 21**	**" 3**	**" 800 to 1,600**	**" 1,200**

COUNTRY PRESS.

WITH RACK AND SCREW AND TABLE DISTRIBUTION, BOXING AND SHIPPING.

No. 6.	**Size of Bed, 23 × 28**	**Size of Form, 18½ × 24**	**No. Rollers, 2**	**Speed per Hour, 1,400**	**Price, $900**
7.	**" 20 × 25**	**" 16 × 21**	**" 3**	**" 1,400**	**" 800**
	Steam Fixtures, extra				**50**

Campbell "Complete" Improved box frame – 2 roller, wire springs, screw and table distribution, tapeless delivery.

CAMPBELL'S COMPLETE PRESS.

No.	Size of Bed	Size of Form	No. Rollers	Speed per Hour
No. 0.	Size of Bed, 36×52	Size of Form, 32 ×47	No. Rollers, 2	Speed per Hour, 800 to 900
1.	" 32×50	" 28½×46	" 2	" 800 to 1,200
2.	" 32×48	" 28½×44	" 2	" 800 to 1,200
3.	" 31×46	" 27½×42	" 2	" 800 to 1,200
4.	" 26×41	" 23 ×37	" 4	" 800 to 1,200
5.	" 25×31	" 21 ×27	" 4	" 800 to 1,400

Campbell Two-Revolution "Country" Press – 2 roller, wire springs under bed, table distribution, front delivery, hand or steam power. Circa 1881.

THE CAMPBELL PRINTING PRESS AND MANUFACTURING COMPANY.

THE IMPROVED
CAMPBELL TWO-REVOLUTION PRESSES.

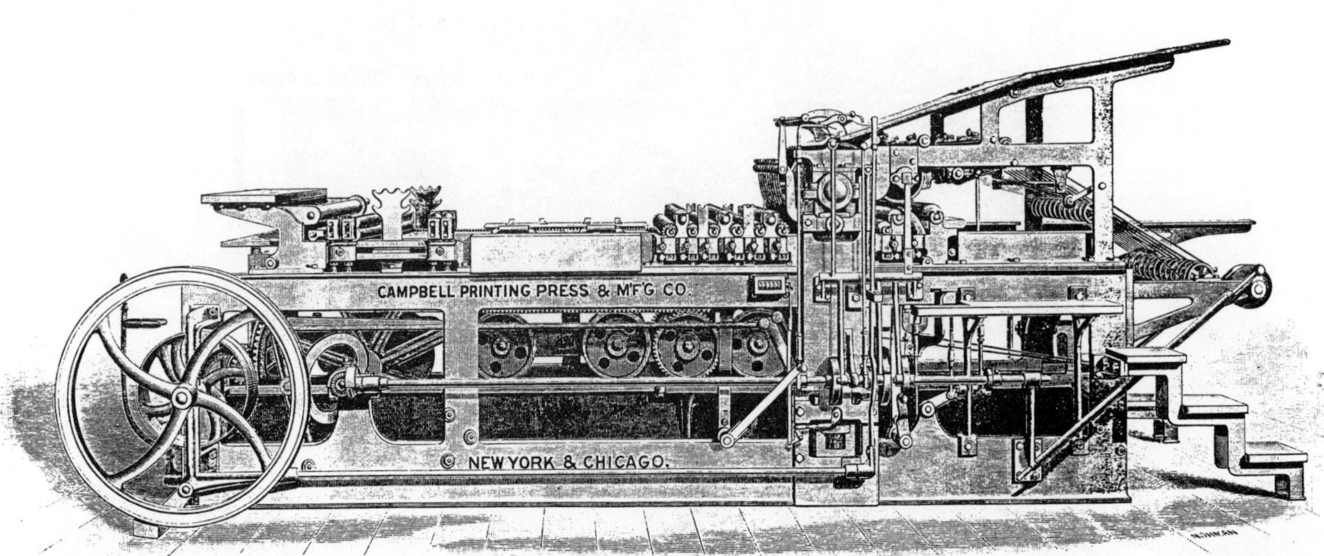

Campbell's Celebrated Cylinder Presses,

OVER 600 OF WHICH ARE NOW IN USE.

Circa 1871

CAMPBELL'S COMBINATION PRESS.

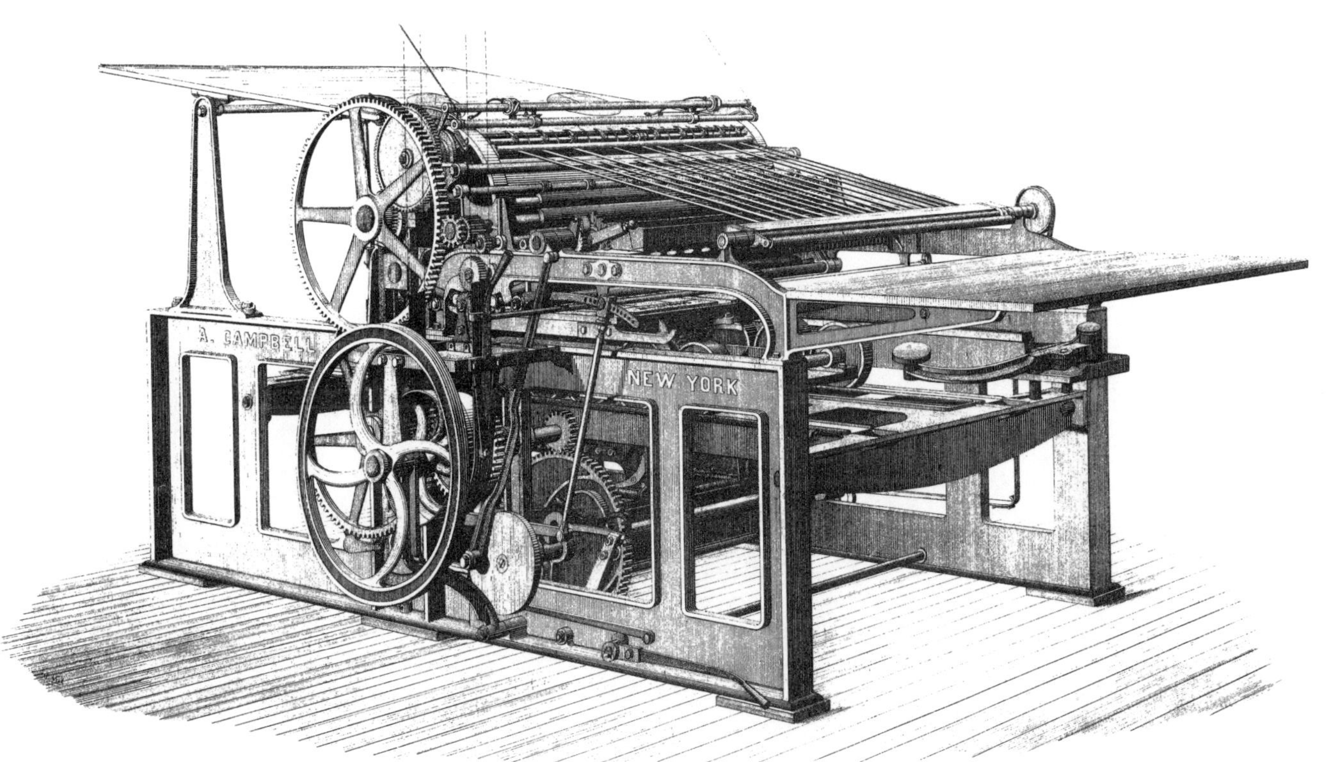

NEWSPAPER AND JOB SERIES.

Circa 1871

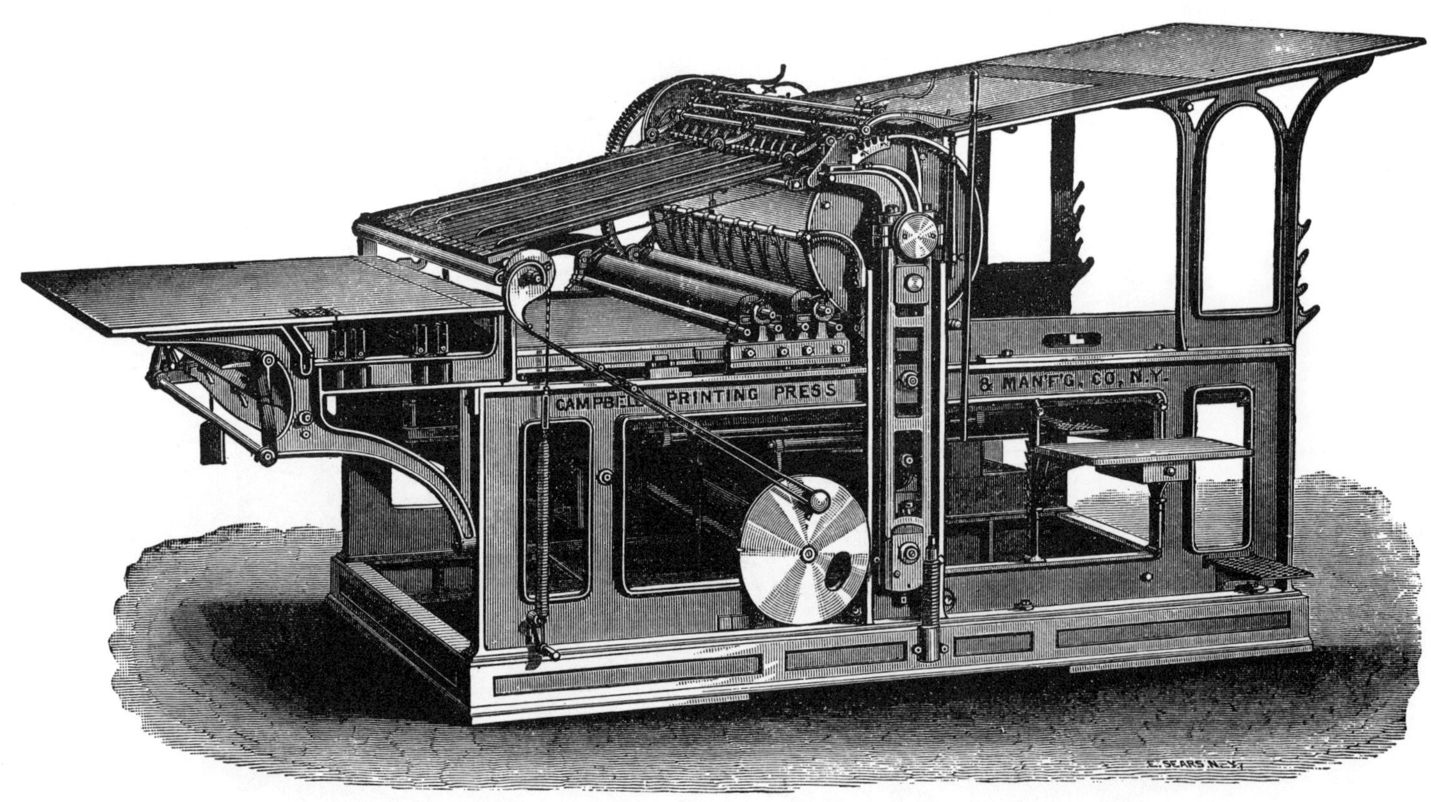

Campbell Two-Revolution Job and Book Press – 4 roller, wire springs, combination and table distribution, front delivery, impression trip.

Campbell Job and Book Oscillator Press – 4 roller, no springs, vibrator and table distribution, front delivery, impression trip.

Campbell Two-Revolution Job and Book Press – New style fly cam, 4 roller, wire springs, combination and table distribution, front delivery, impression trip.

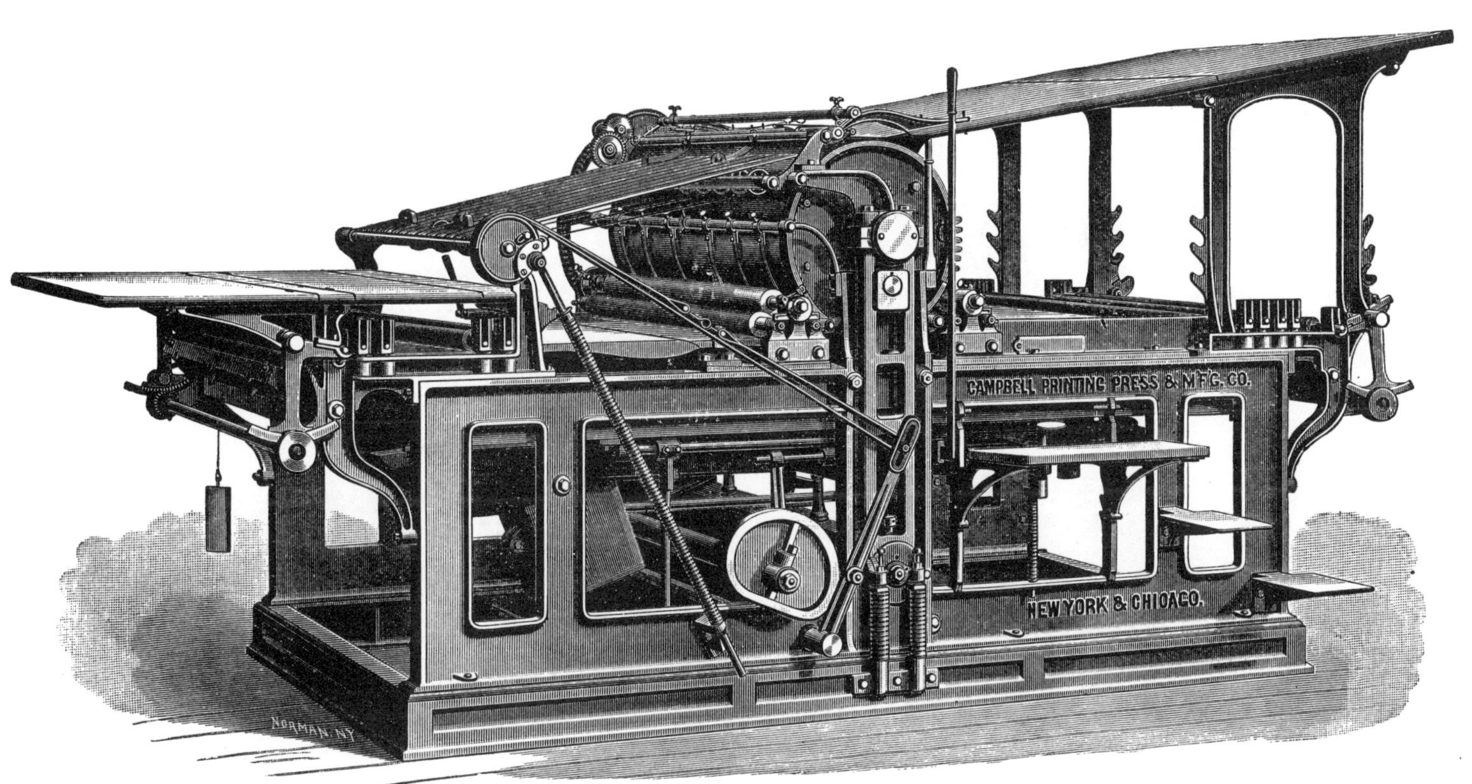

Campbell Two-Revolution Book Press – Double Ender – 4 roller, wire springs, combination and table distribution, front delivery, impression trip.

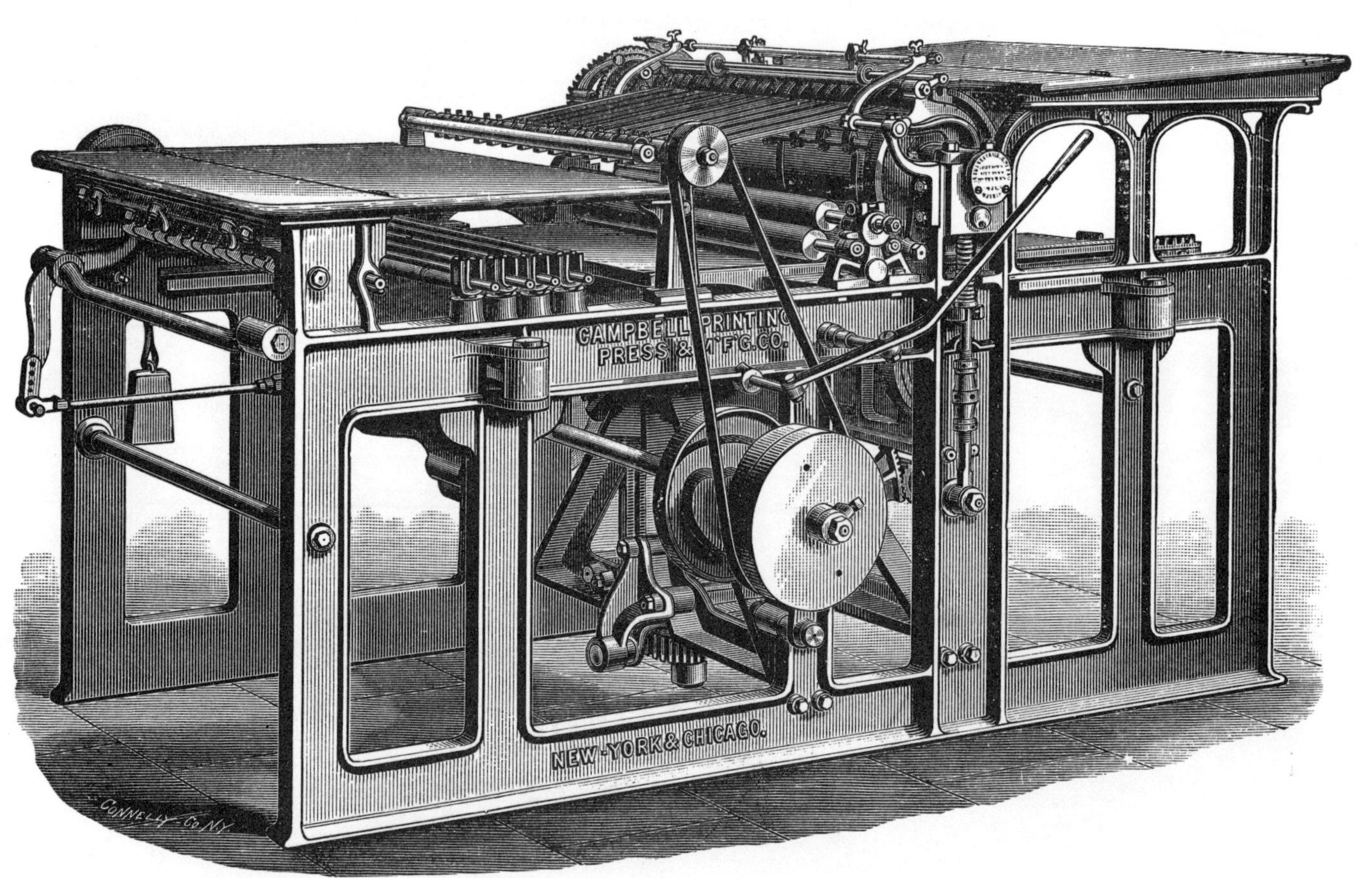

Campbell "Pony No. 7" Two-Revolution – 2 roller, combination vibrator and table distribution, front delivery. 23 x 28" press sold for $2000 in 1887.

Campbell "Intermediate" Two-Revolution – 2 roller, wire springs, combination vibrator and table distribution, front delivery.

Campbell's Combination—Art Series.

FOUR ROLLERS AND DOUBLE FOUNTAIN.

WHEN this press is in operation it is automatic in all its movements, the sheet itself being the agent through which the press is made to print. It never prints on the tympan, therefore cannot waste sheets by offset; it takes ink always for the next sheet to be printed, and cannot take more, and consequently cannot over-ink the work. The fly operates only when the sheet is fed; by this means we avoid offset by the empty fly slamming. A badly fed sheet is thrown out white, about three inches of the edge being out of the pile on the fly board, thus avoiding white sheets going to the bindery — only properly fed and printed sheets being counted. With the ordinary points or to the guides, the register is governed by the feeder — if fed perfect the register is perfect.

This press is without springs; is easily handled; does not require to be backed up; has no tapes; discharges the sheet clean side to the fly; very easy on the rollers; does not injure the plates as much as an ordinary hand-press; runs on 40 per cent. less ink than any press built, except our "Book Series;" saves from 8 to 10 per cent. of paper; does not require waste sheets to be run through to get up color; and runs almost noiseless.

This press has thus far done not only THE FINEST WORK IN THIS COUNTRY, but, in the same hands and on the same work, it has turned out TWICE AS MUCH WORK IN THE SAME TIME, and DONE IT BETTER than any of its competitors. In the hands of good and honest workmen, it not only *will* do, but it *has* already done, BETTER WORK WITHOUT AN OVERLAY than can be done on an Adams or a hand-press WITH THE MOST CAREFUL PREPARATION; thus demonstrating our *dictum* at the outset of our career, namely, that *if a press be properly constructed, the tedious and expensive work of overlaying wood-cuts can be almost entirely dispensed with.* It has worked large sheets of cuts and type, indiscriminately mixed in the form, at a single impression, WHICH CANNOT BE DONE BY ANY OTHER PRESS YET BUILT.

No.	Size of Bed	Size of Form	Speed per hour
No. 1.	37×51	32×46	800 to 1,100
2.	" 31×46	" 26×42	" 800 to 1,300
3.	" 28×41	" 23×36	" 800 to 1,500

With these presses are furnished cone-pulleys, counter-shaft and hangers, wrenches, two roller-moulds, two sets of roller-stocks, and boxing and shipping.

CAMPBELL'S COMBINATION—BOOK SERIES.

FOUR ROLLERS AND DOUBLE FOUNTAIN.

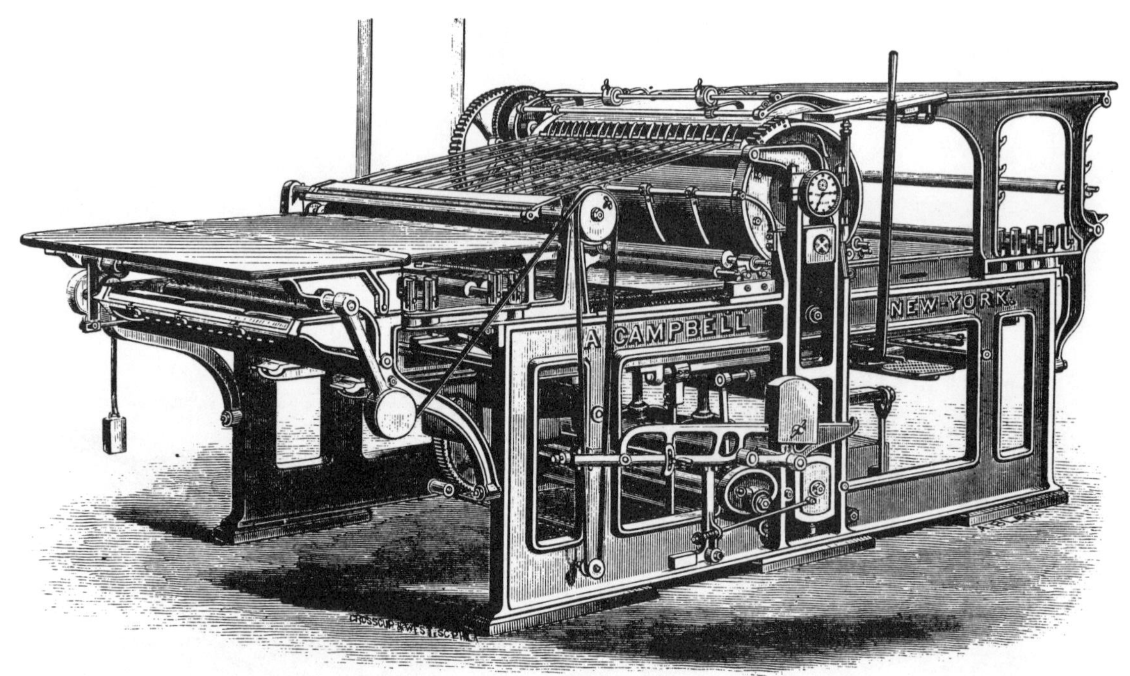

WE HAVE CONSTRUCTED THIS PRESS WITH A VIEW TO ITS ULTIMATE ADOPTION BY ALL BOOK PRINTERS AND PUBLISHERS.

CAMPBELL'S COMBINATION—JOB AND BOOK SERIES.

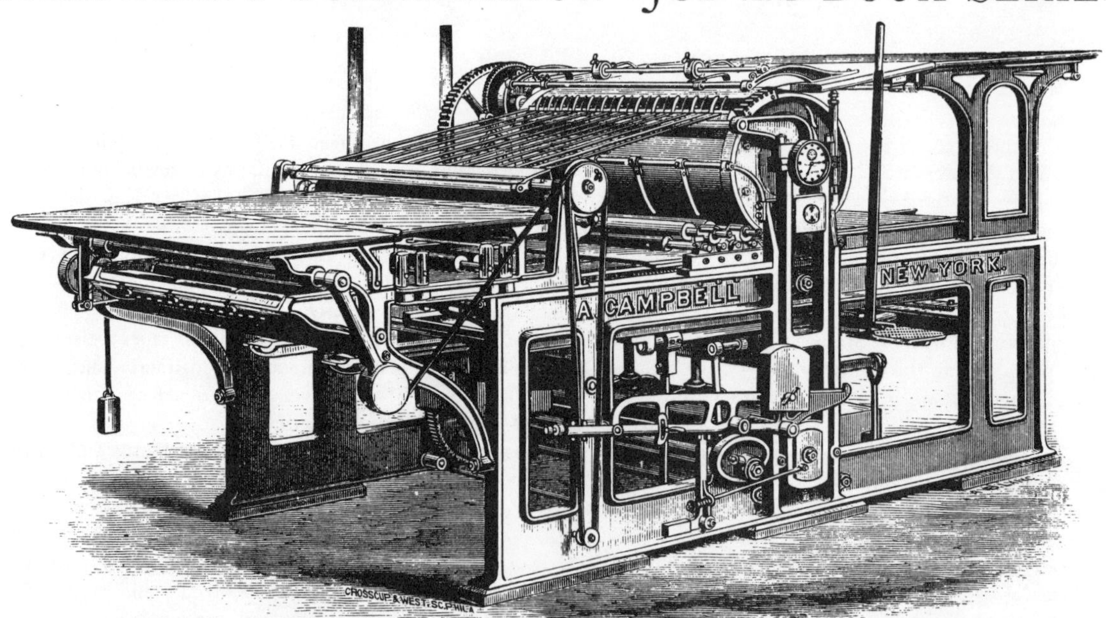

THE above cut represents our Job and Book Series. This press is constructed with table distribution, and is designed, as its name indicates, with special reference to the easy and rapid change of forms for general job and book work. The form rollers are on the Combination principle, under which head you will find a description.

Of all the presses we build, we find this the best adapted for *all* kinds of work. For making alterations and corrections in the form it has no equal. It is the easiest to handle and most accessible of any press in the market. The *bed* is as handy as an imposing stone. Every feature has been most carefully studied with a view to make it what it is, *the best, quickest, and most convenient Job and Book Press in the world.*

Campbell Two-Revolution Job and News Press – 2 roller, wire springs, rack and screw distribution, rear tape delivery.

CAMPBELL'S COMBINATION—JOB AND NEWS SERIES.

TWO ROLLERS.

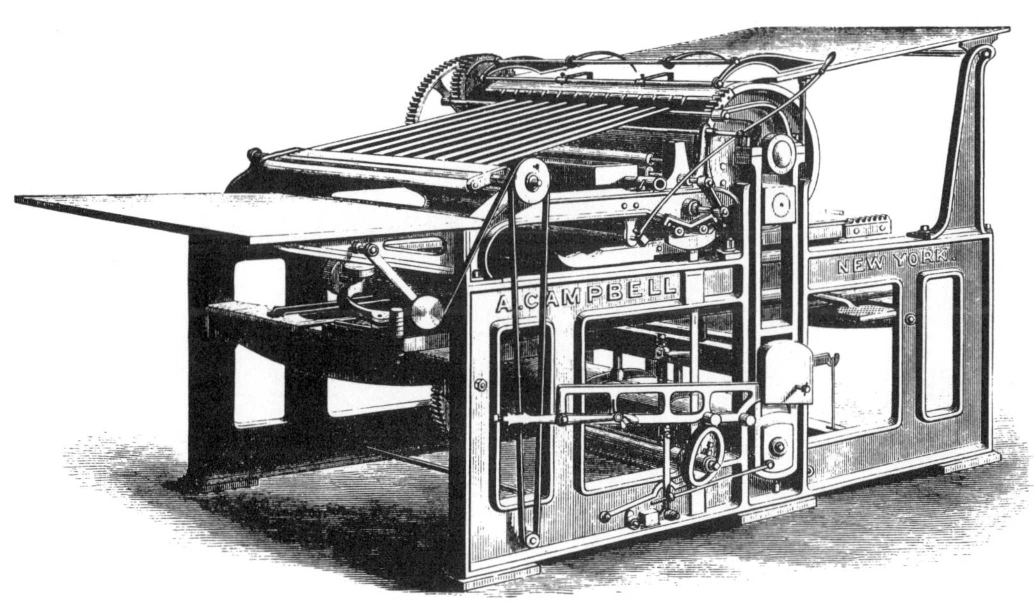

THE engraving upon this page shows all the press, as nearly as possible; but to be understood it must be seen.

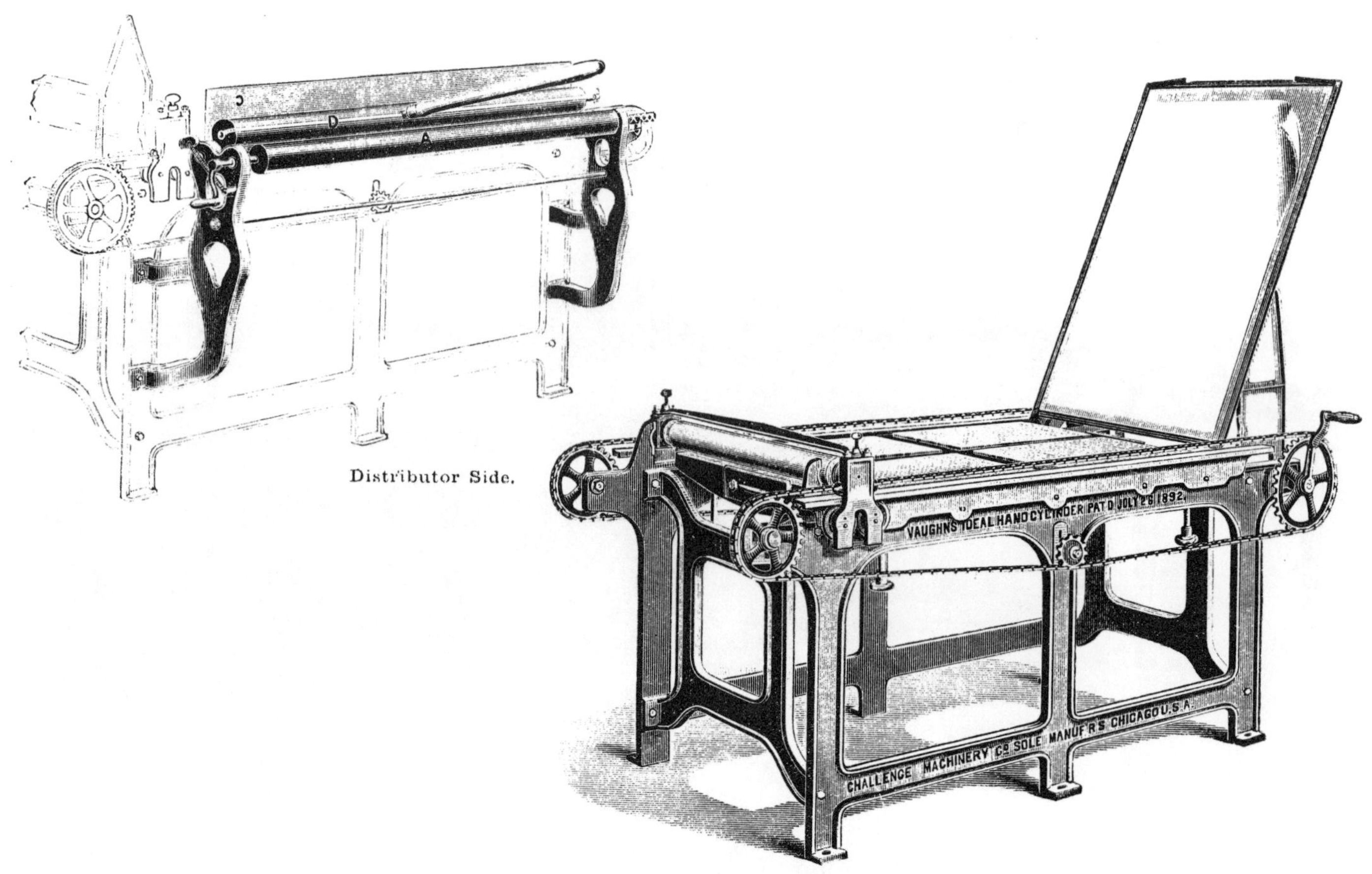

Vaughn "Ideal" Hand Cylinder Press. Circa 1892

Challenge "Country" Cylinder – hand power, by Challenge Machinery Co. of Chicago.

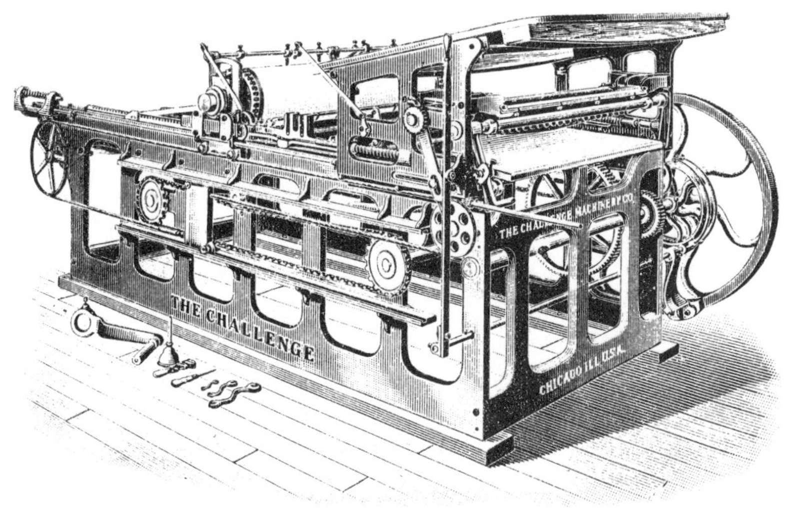

Challenge "Country" Cylinder Press – for power.

CINCINNATI CYLINDER PRESS

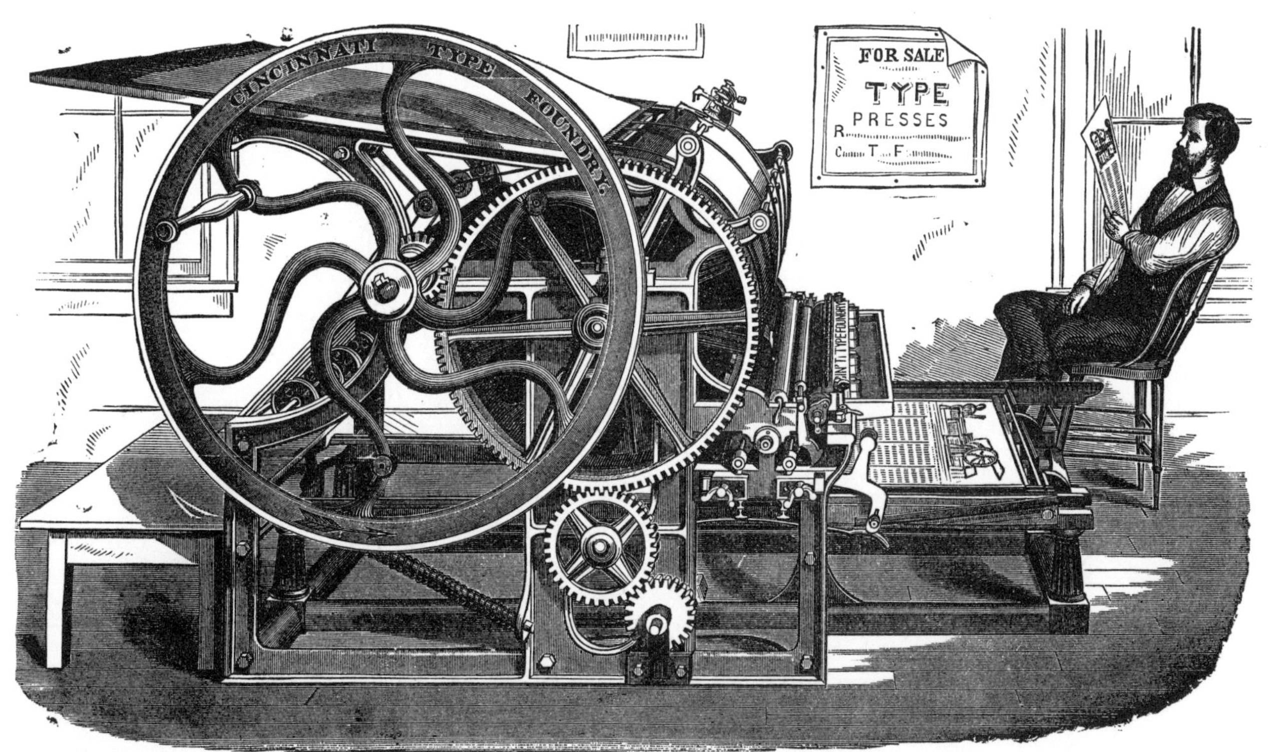

THE CHEAPEST RACK AND SCREW DISTRIBUTION NEWSPAPER PRESS EVER MADE.

GEM, Bed 28x40, $1,200. **DOUBLE SUPER ROYAL, Bed 31x46, $1,350.** **MAMMOTH, Bed 34x52, $1,750.**

Circa 1868

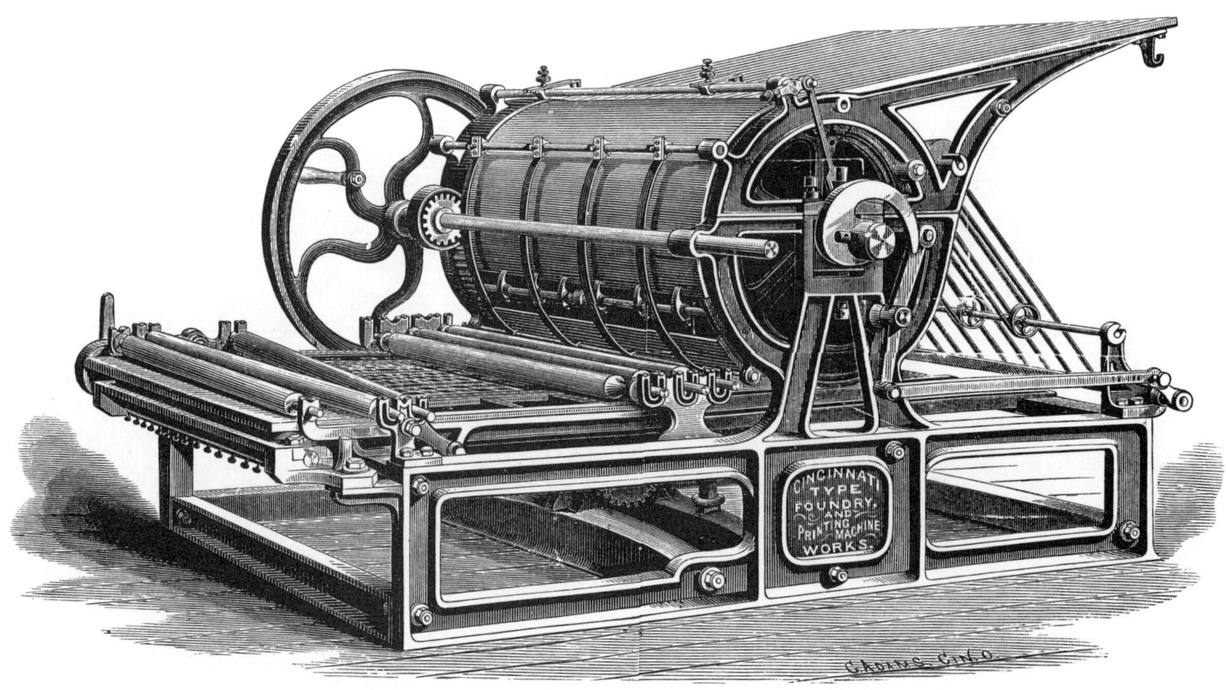

Cincinnati "Country" Press – 3 roller, table distribution, tape delivery, wire springs under the bed, hand power.

Cincinnati Country Cylinder.

RACK AND SCREW DISTRIBUTION.

SIZES:

28x40, 31x46, & 34x52 Inches.

This press was introduced by us in 1859, and many of them were sold between that time and 1880, but of late the table distribution presses have largely superseded them, being more simple in construction, lower in price, and more satisfactory in inexperienced hands. We still have some demand for these rack and screw distribution presses, chiefly from printers who have had experience with them, and we still build 7, 8, 9 and 10-column sizes to order. Prices given on application.

Second-hand presses of this pattern often find their way back to us, are rebuilt and made good as new, sell for moderate prices, and give entire satisfaction to all who have them in use.

CINCINNATI TYPE FOUNDRY,

CHAS. WELLS, Treas. No. 201 Vine St.

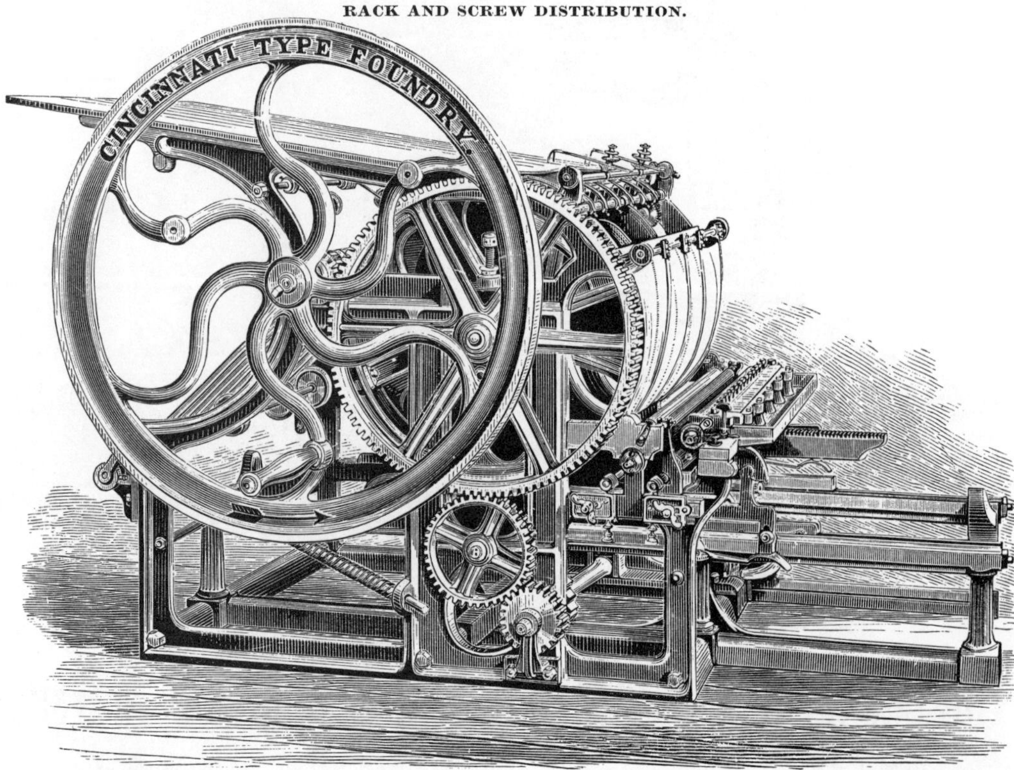

HALF-MEDIUM

CYLINDER PRESS

Size, $17x21\frac{1}{2}$ between bearers.

This press is of the same series as the large press, cut of which is shown on the preceding page. It has tapeless delivery, noiseless nipper motion, open fountain, removable distributing cylinder, and all modern improvements, and is still a simple, strong, rapid press, fully equal to the capacity of the best feeder to supply sheets to.

FOR PRICE, SEE PRICE LIST.

Circa 1880

DRUM CYLINDER PRESSES

The above cut represents our first-class Drum Cylinders, 22x28 and 22x37 inches. They have tapeless delivery, and all the latest improvements, and are heavy, strong, rapid machines.

While belonging to the same series as the presses shown on pages 224 and 225, each has a different form of inking apparatus, the whole series of presses being so constructed as to serve the buyer with the inking arrangement that best suits his notions and his work. As either character of inking can be fitted to either press.

Persons who contemplate putting in fine, rapid, first-class machines are invited to correspond with us, tell us size of bed wanted, kind of work to be done, kind of inking apparatus preferred, and terms wanted.

CINCINNATI TYPE FOUNDRY,

Circa 1880

THE ARMY PRESS.

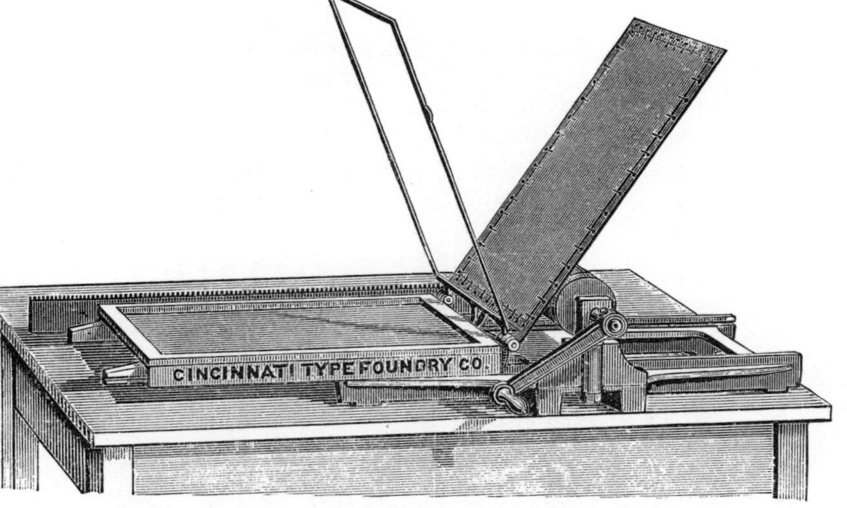

This is the cheapest reliable device we know of for printing a country paper of small circulation. We made it about 1862 for use in camps, where lightness and simplicity were the great desiderata. When the occasion which called them into existence was at an end, we dropped them from our list of manufactures, but printers who had seen and used them would not give them up, and there was a moderate call for them for many years. When finally convinced of the worthiness of this, our neglected child, we changed the sizes to fit standard newspaper measures, and now offer them, with confidence, to customers who do not wish to invest much money in what may be a mere experiment. Should the enterprise increase so as to demand better, more expensive apparatus, our patrons will always find us ready to exchange on fair terms.

It resembles the modern common Hand Press in having *ways*, *bed*, *tympan* and *frisket*. In place of a *platen* and *levers*, it has a *cylinder*, by the rotation of which the bed is moved and the impression is given at each motion, back or forth. The tympan is covered with the best gum cloth. The frisket is covered with paper, same as other Hand Presses. The form is inked by hand. The impression is adjusted by screws under the bearings of the cylinder. The sheet is worked folded, and turned, taking four impressions to complete each paper. The pressman can work from 200 to 300 impressions per hour and do good newspaper work. There is nothing wonderful about this kind of newspaper work except the cheapness of the outfit for it. Where it is desirable to start on a very economical scale, commencing with a small circulation, this outfit does admirably.

Each press is furnished with two chases, six Hempel patent quoins, roller frame and cast roller, oiler and wrench. No table is included—any strong table answers the purpose.

The Army Press should not be confounded with the Adams Cottage Press. The latter has no frisket, the former has; the latter has a loose cylinder, while, in the Army, the bed and cylinder are firmly geared together, and there are other important differences.

Circa 1860

Cincinnati Country Cylinder.

TABLE DISTRIBUTION.

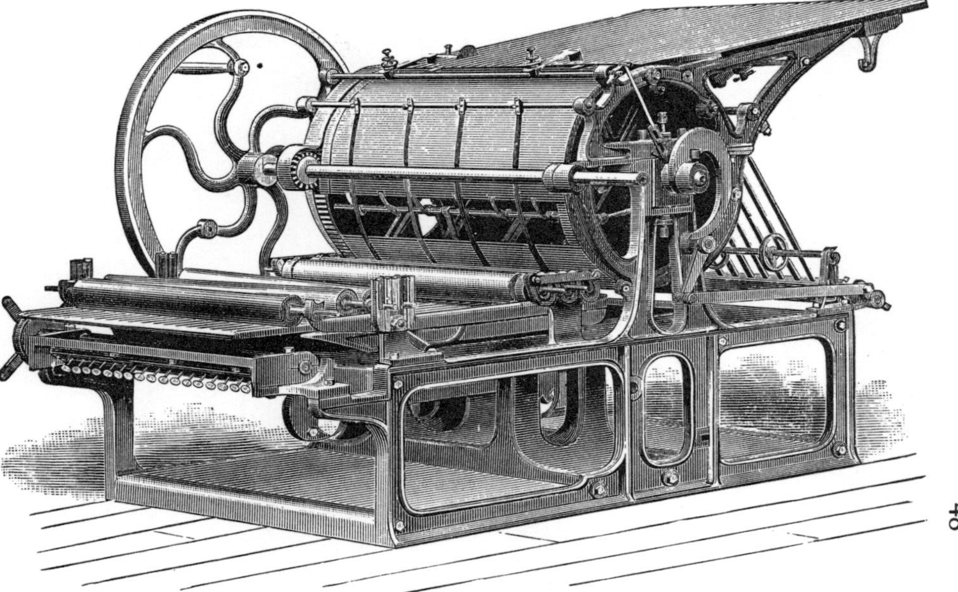

This is by far the simplest form of power press ever introduced. It can be set up and run by anybody with capacity to run a hand press; has cut gear, steel bed shoes, and steel tracks; does its work easily, quietly, and rapidly, and *does not get out of order*.

The rollers are all alike and interchangeable, and, for this reason, very economical, as, when form rollers become damaged, old, or hard, they can be used as distributors or fountain rollers for a long time, leaving only the best rollers for the form. The fly being fastened by thumb screws, is taken off in an instant, and leaves the bed accessible from three sides.

Late improvements have materially strengthened these presses, and make them capable of largely increased speed. Several of the seven-column folio presses are now in use in city job offices, doing fine work at a speed of from 1200 to 1800 per hour.

The old size of Country Press, 31x46, is no longer made by us. It was an eight-column press when wider columns were in vogue, and it is discarded because it is larger than necessary for an eight-column press, and yet not large enough to print a nine-column paper conveniently, and will not print a six-column quarto at all. In comparing prices, *remember* that our No. 5 Press fills all legitimate uses of a 31x46, and rates the same.

Correspondents should state size of press and terms of purchase desired by them. Also ask for fresh prices.

PRESS No. 3.
7-Column Folio.

Size bed	28×40 in.
Largest form covered by two rollers	24×36 in.
Room occupied on floor	52×78 in.
Height to top of cylinder	52 in.
Weight, boxed	5,400 lbs.
Speed by hand	700 per hour.
Speed by power	1,400 per hour.
Price, with Hand Wheel	**$900 00**
Boxing	**25 00**

PRESS No. 5.
8-Column Folio or 5-Column Quarto.

Size bed	29×43 in.
Largest form covered by two rollers	24×39 in.
Room occupied on floor	55×80 in.
Height to top of cylinder	53 in.
Weight, boxed	5,800 lbs.
Speed by hand	650 per hour.
Speed by power	1,200 per hour.
Price, with Hand Wheel	**$1,000 00**
Boxing	**30 00**

STOP CYLINDER PRESS.

PATENTED.

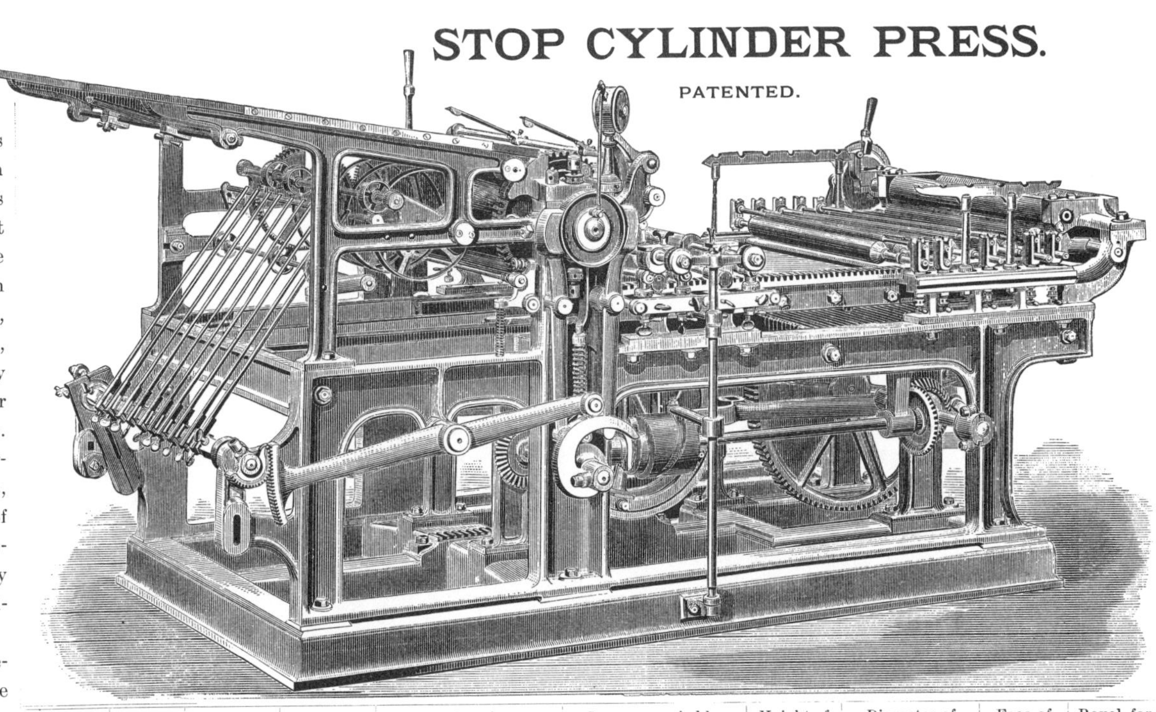

This press is adapted to the very finest kinds of wood-cut, book and color printing. The register is perfect; speed equal to drum presses of any size. Each press is provided with our new patent guide, which is fastened to the cylinder, and does away with the tongues. They run quietly, smoothly, without bed-springs, or the need of them, and occupy far less room than large cylinder presses of the same capacity. The price includes the counter-shaft, hangers, driving pulleys, two cone pulleys, two sets of stocks, roller moulds, and shipping. For setting up, we only charge our patrons actual traveling expenses.

The above cut shows the delivery with tapes, but we make presses with and without them, as preferred by the purchaser.

Other sizes made to order.

CINCINNATI TYPE FOUNDRY,
No. 201 Vine Street.

CHAS. WELLS, Treas.

Bed inside Bearers.	Matter printed.	No. of Ink Rollers.	Weight of Machine.	Size of Ground Frame.	Space occupied by the Machine.	Height of Machine.	Diameter of Driving Pulleys.	Face of Pulleys.	Revol. for 1 impression.
18¼×24	14½×20	4	4,000 lbs.	5 ft. 4 in.×3 ft. 4 in.	8 ft. 11 in.×4 ft. 9 in.	4 ft. 2 in.	14 in.	2½ in.	5
23 ×28	19 ×24	4	6,500 "	7 " 3 " ×3 " 9 "	11 " 2 " ×5 " 3 "	4 " 6 "	16 "	3½ "	5
25¼×35	21½×31	4	8,500 "	8 " 6 " ×4 " 5 "	12 " 1 " ×5 " 7 "	4 " 10 "	20 "	4½ "	4
32 ×46	27 ×42	5	11,000 "	10 " 3 " ×5 " 6 "	13 " 10 " ×7 " 9 "	5 " 8 "	24 "	5½ "	4½
38 ×52	32 ×48	6	16,000 "	12 " 0 " ×6 " 1 "	17 " 3 " ×9 " 3 "	6 " 5 "	26 "	5½ "	5

New Double Stop Cylinder Jobber.

THIS PRESS has a large cylinder, with a stop at each half turn; it has two printing surfaces, and when both are made ready and used, four rollers pass twice over the whole form, and the work is done with considerable speed. When only one surface is made ready, four rollers pass four times over the form, at each impression, giving the most perfect inking, and by feeding one set of nippers with fine paper, and the other with set-off sheets, the work is kept perfectly clean, no matter how heavy the inking. The sheet is delivered by a new devise, perfectly effective, without fly or tapes, and a set-off is impossible.

The distribution is both table and cylindrical, with four vibrating rollers, and effectual for the stiffest ink. Register absolutely perfect. For work of great delicacy, or fine Show Cards in colors, requiring large quantities of ink, and several impressions, the press has no equal short of double the price.

PRICE, INCLUDING COUNTER SHAFT, AND TWO FIVE-SPEED CONE PULLEYS, FOUR CHASES AND ONE MOULD, **$1,250.**

CINCINNATI TYPE FOUNDRY,

CHAS. WELLS, TREAS.

201 VINE STREET, CINCINNATI, OHIO.

Circa 1875

EXTRA HEAVY, FIRST-CLASS
CYLINDER PRESSES

Sizes and Prices given on application.

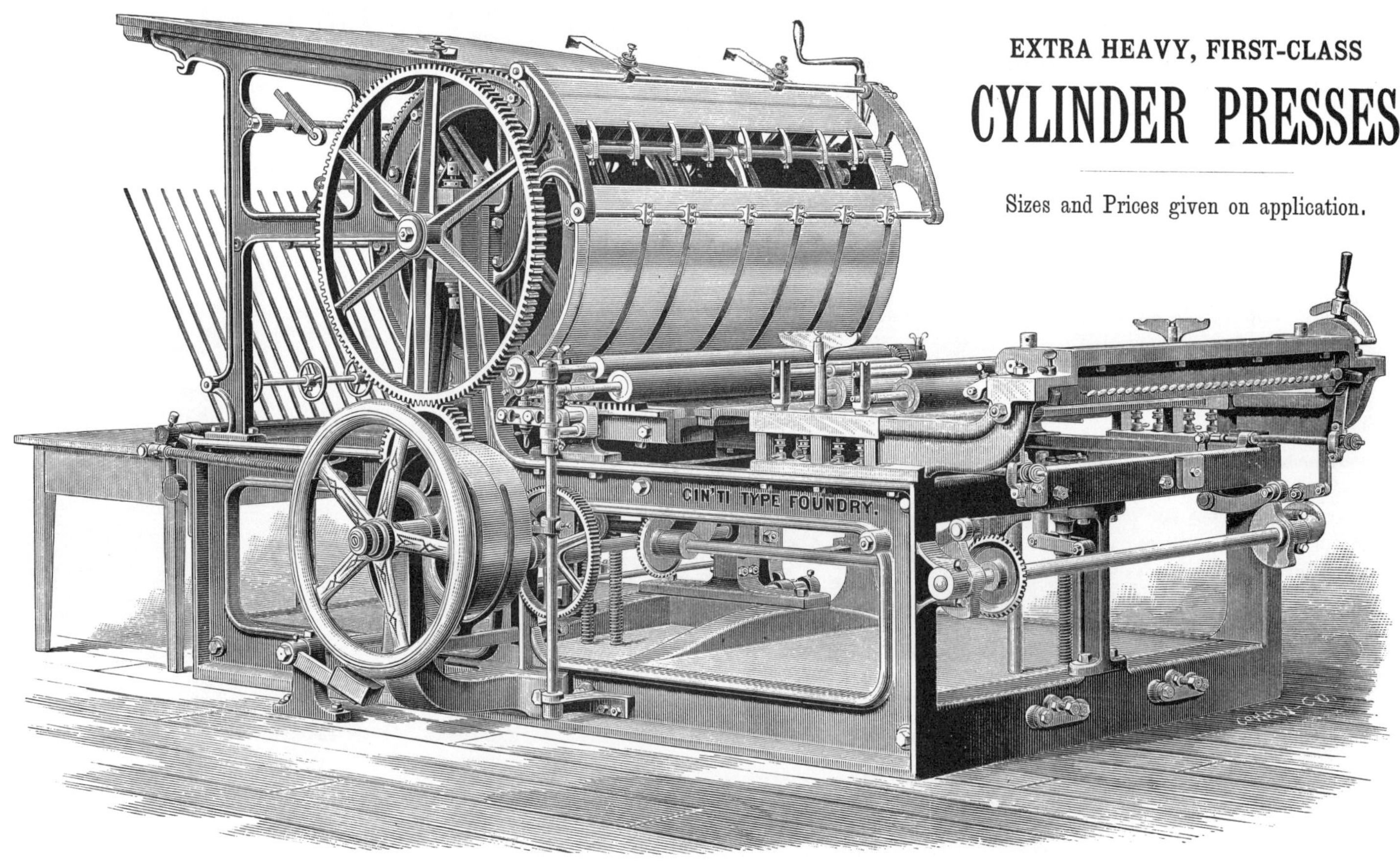

This machine is built on purpose to print flour and other bags, either in one or many colors at one impression. The bed is 22x37 inches, and has capacity for the largest paper bag made. It has conveniences for two feeders to work at once, so that small bags may be fed double. The bed motion is very short, the construction strong, and great speed may be attained.

It also has our patent color distribution, and the inks are fed on from separate boxes placed in the fountain, the quantity fed being entirely at the disposal of the pressman. Its whole management is exceedingly simple, and it is a solid, durable machine.

References can be given to a number of the largest bag manufacturers in the Union, who have them in use. Prices on application.

The same press, with ordinary table and cylinder distribution, for either two or four rollers, instead of the patent chromatic distribution, is admirably adapted for fine work on any long, narrow forms suited to its capacity, high speed being always attainable, and it is particularly recommended for coupon tickets, long programmes, etc.

CINCINNATI TYPE FOUNDRY,

CHAS. WELLS, Treas. **No. 201 Vine Street.**

Chromatic Cylinder Press.

PATENTED.

SIZE OF BED, 22x37 INCHES. WITH TAPELESS DELIVERY.

Cottrell & Babcock "Country" – 2 roller, rack and cam distribution, tapeless delivery, hinged roller frame.

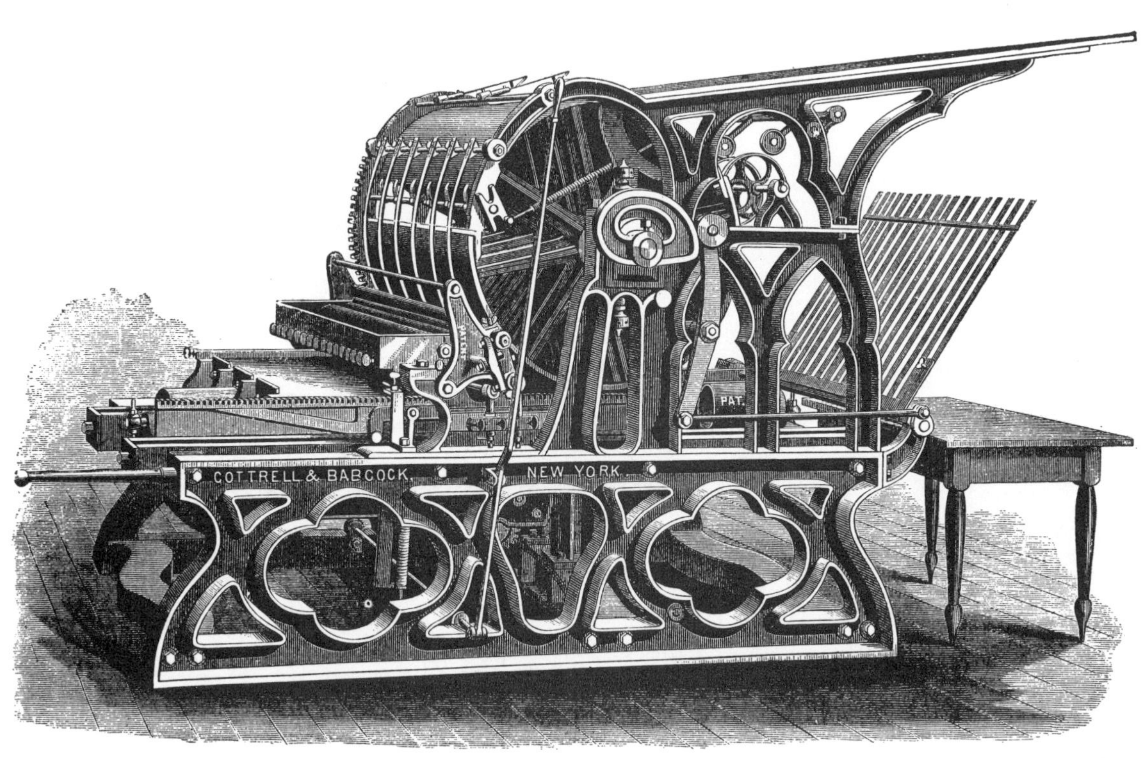

Cottrell & Babcock Job and News Intermediate Drum – 2 roller, rack and screw distribution, tapeless delivery, hinged roller frame. Circa 1875.

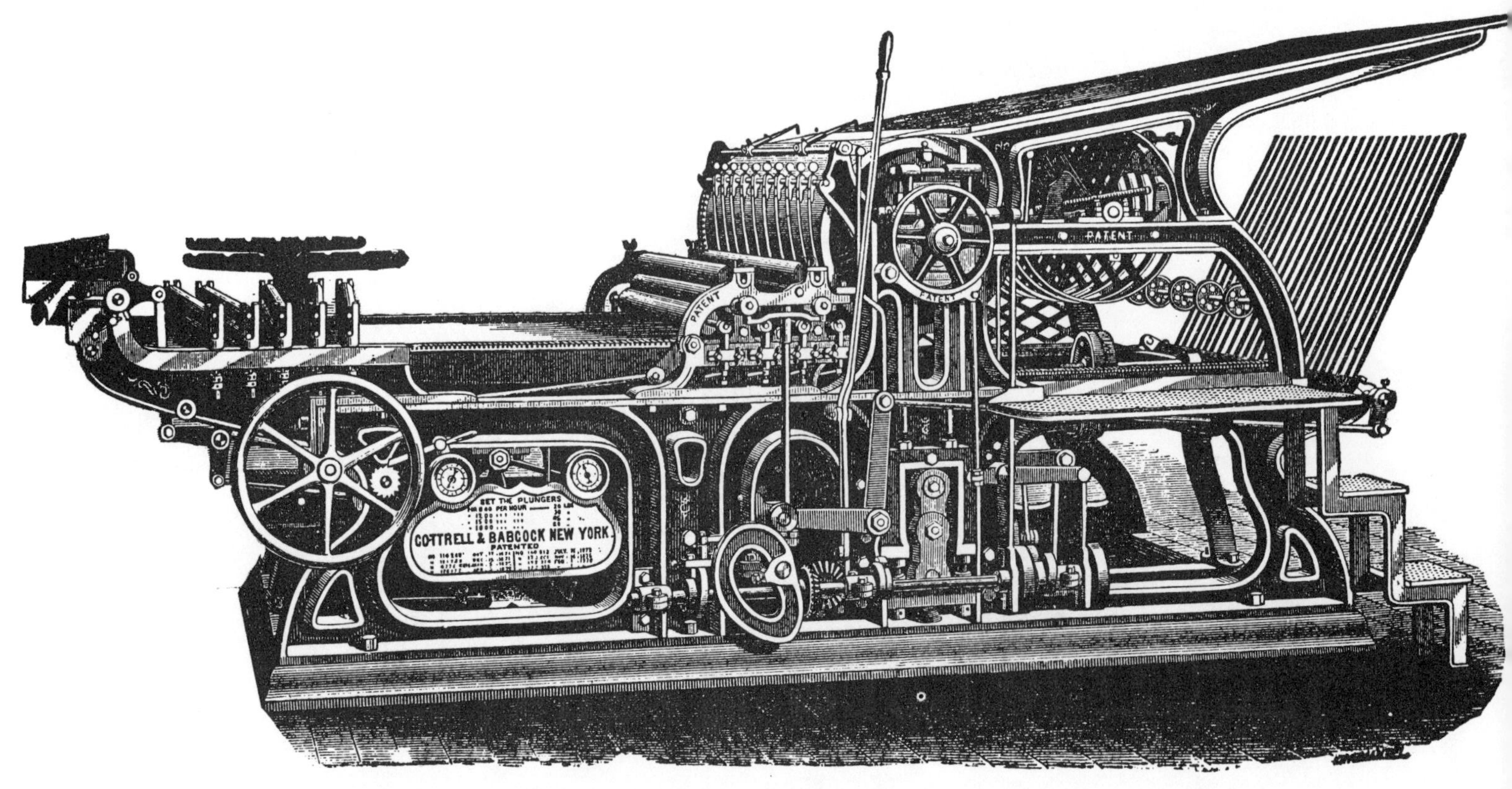

Cottrell & Babcock "Two Revolution" – 4 roller, rack cam and table distribution, tapeless delivery, air springs, hinged roller frame.
The plate under the gauges reads: Set the plungers for 800 per hour – 20 lbs., 1200 per hour – 30 lbs., 1500 per hour – 45 lbs., 1800 per hour – 60 lbs. Circa 1876.

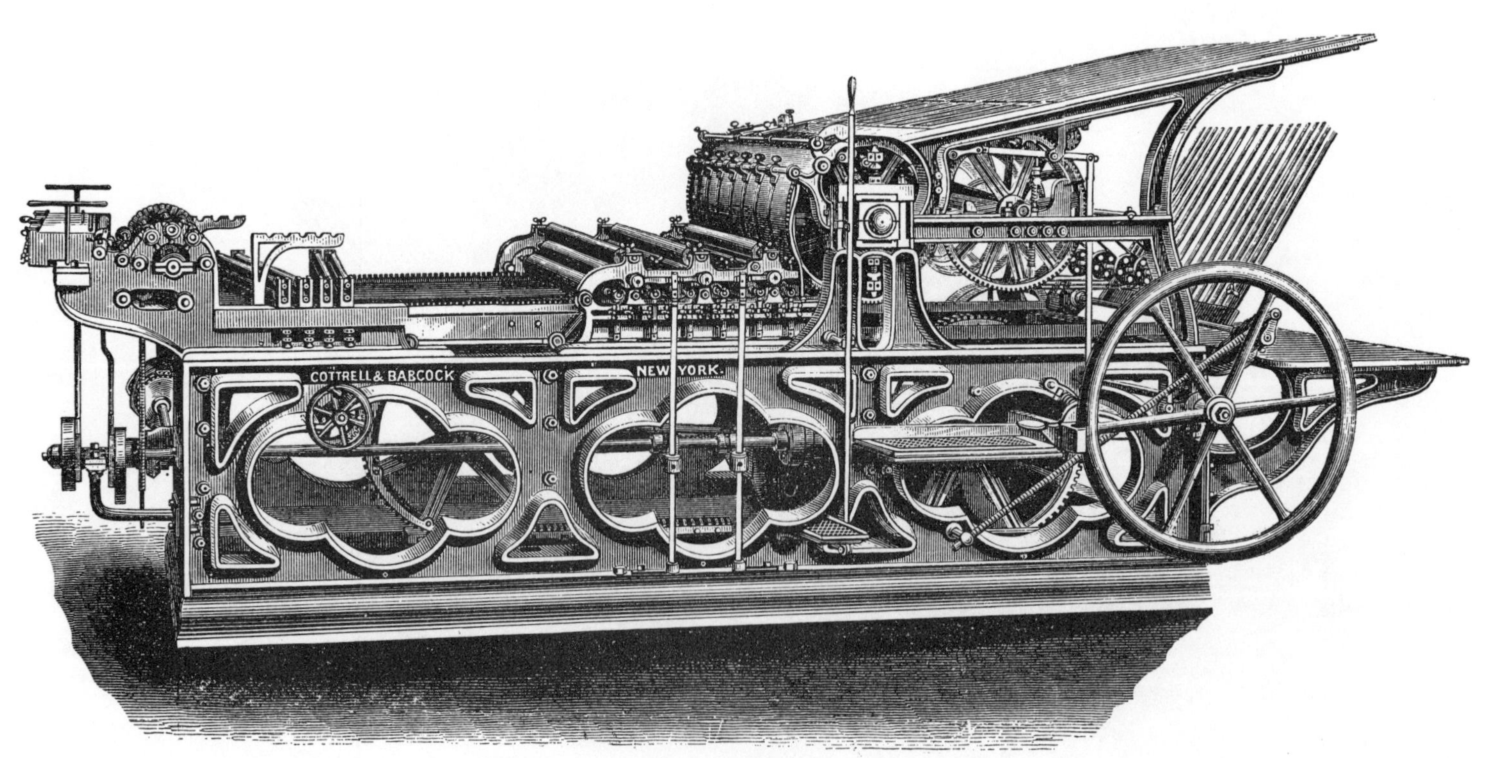

Cottrell & Babcock "Stop Cylinder" – 6 roller, rack, cam and table distribution, front fountain, rear tapeless delivery, hinged roller frame.

C. B. COTTRELL & CO.,

(SUCCESSORS TO COTTRELL & BABCOCK)

PRINTING PRESS MANUFACTURERS.

We invite the attention of the Trade to our late **Improvements in Printing Machinery.** The Superiority of the **AIR SPRING** is no longer disputed by competitors. With this improvement we attain a rate of speed at **Least One-Third Faster** than is possible in a Press using the Wire Spring.

The **Hinged Roller Frame** saves both time and Rollers, as by this means the Rollers can be handled in **seven-eighths less time** than on any other Press, and it entirely obviates the necessity of resetting them every time they are handled. The *Delivery Without Tapes, Geared Sliders and Friction Attachment for Controlling the Momentum of the Cylinder,* are among our many valuable patented improvements.

THE WESTERN STATIONER AND PRINTER.

Our Celebrated Two-Revolution Presses are to be found in operation in all the leading offices of Chicago.

We desire to call Special Attention to our **Patent Air-Spring Country Press.** *This Press will do Book Work, Job Work or Newspaper Work with equal facility. The register is perfect. It will run faster with power and easier by hand, and is, all things considered, the cheapest Country Press in the market. Send for Illustrated Catalogue.*

8 SPRUCE ST., NEW YORK. C. B. COTTRELL & CO., 112 MONROE ST., CHICAGO.

Circa 1880

C.B. Cottrell & Sons "Two Revolution" – 2 roller, rack and cam distribution, rear tapeless delivery, air springs, impression trip and back-up.

C.B. Cottrell & Sons "First Class" Drum – 2 roller, rack and cam distribution, rear tape delivery, box frame base.

C.B. Cottrell & Sons "First Class" Extra Heavy Drum – 2 roller, air springs, tapeless delivery. Circa 1870.

C.B. Cottrell & Sons "First Class" Extra Heavy Drum – 2 roller, rack and cam distribution, tapeless delivery, air springs, hinged roller frame. Circa 1875.

C.B. Cottrell & Sons "First Class" Drum – 2 roller, air springs, rack and cam distribution, tapeless delivery, box frame base.

C.B. Cottrell & Sons "Monarch" – 2 roller, rack cam and table distribution, tapeless delivery, front fountain, air springs, hinged roller frame, back-up motion.

C.B. Cottrell & Sons "Monarch" – 2 roller, rack and cam distribution, tapeless delivery, hinged roller frame, back-up motion.

C.B. Cottrell & Sons "Triumph" Country – 2 roller, rack, cam and table distribution, front fountain, tapeless delivery, air springs, hinged roller frame

C.B. Cottrell & Sons "Paragon" Job and News – 2 roller, rack cam and table distribution, front fountain, tapeless delivery, air springs,hinged roller frame.

C.B. Cottrell & Sons "Two Revolution" – 2 roller pony, rack and cam table distribution, rear tapeless delivery, air springs, hinged roller frame, impression trip and back-up.

C.B. Cottrell & Sons "Two Revolution" – 2 roller pony, rack and cam table distribution, rear tapeless delivery, air springs, hinged roller frame, impression trip and back-up.

C.B. Cottrell & Sons "Two Revolution" – 4 roller pony, rack, cam and table distribution, rear tapeless delivery, front ink fountain, hinged roller frame, impression trip and back-up.

COTTRELL COUNTRY CYLINDER PRESS.—PRICES ON APPLICATION.

Circa 1882

The above engraving represents our new Front Delivery. This unquestionably the most important improvement in Printing Machinery that has been made for many years. It delivers the sheet printed side up in full view of the Pressman. No part of the printed matter being touched by anything, thus avoiding all possibility of smut, no matter what the quantity or quality of ink it may be found necessary to carry. In addition to this, it leaves the front and back of the Press free of access at all times; there being no Fly, Strings, Tapes or obstructions of any kind, and as it lays the Printed Sheets almost as straight as when they come from the mill, it will be admitted that the percentage of waste is reduced to the minimum. It delivers the sheets at fast or slow speed equally well; it does not require to be set for different size sheets. Circa 1885

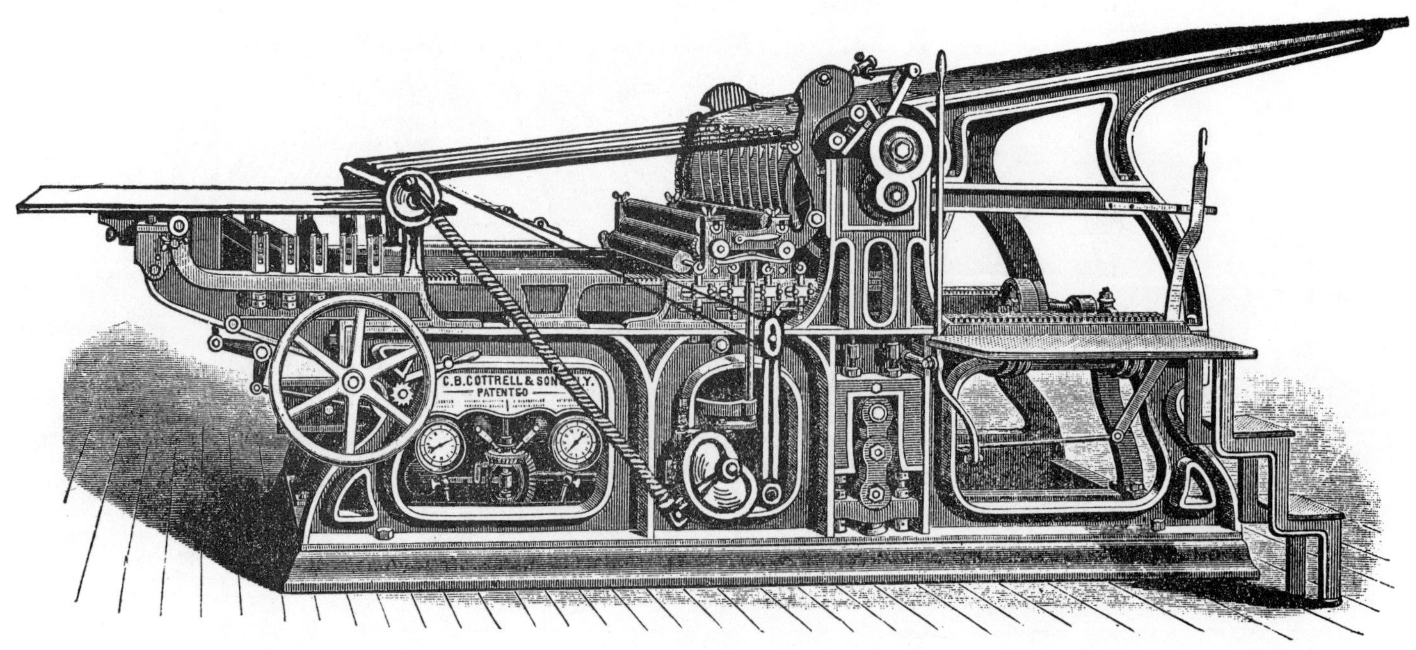

C.B. Cottrell & Sons "Two Revolution" – 4 roller, rack, cam and table distribution, front ink fountain, air springs, flange frame. Campbell front delivery added.

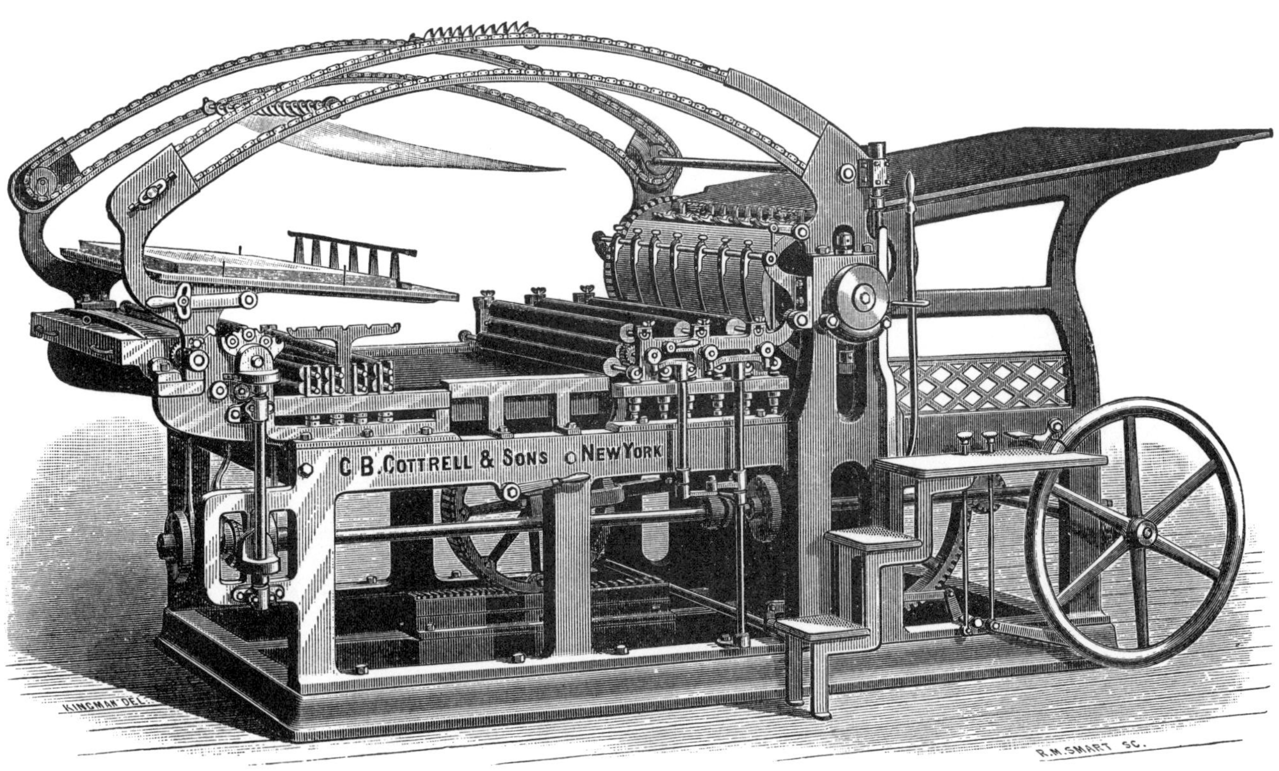

C.B. Cottrell & Sons "Stop Cylinder" – 6 roller, rack, cam and table distribution, hinged roller frame, impression trip and back-up motion. Cottrell was the first press with front-delivery of the sheet printed side up with a chain. Circa 1895

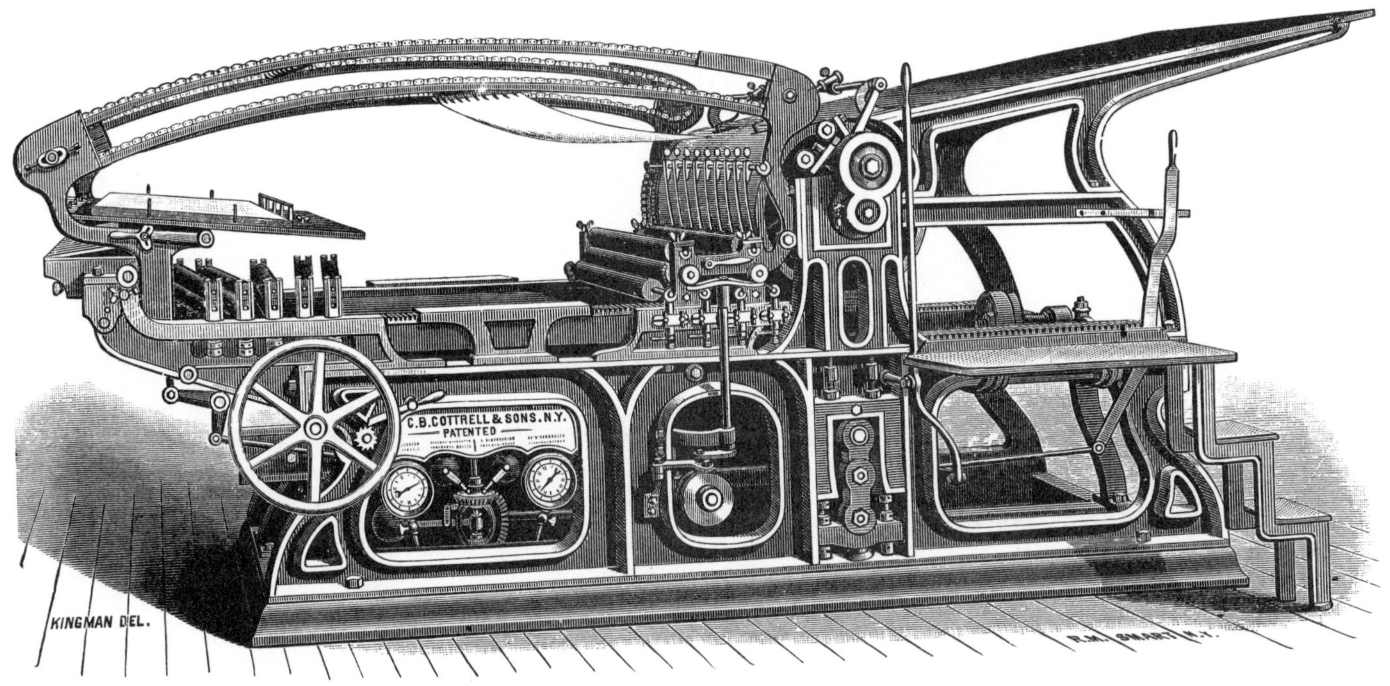

Front Delivery Press. Delivers the sheet printed side up in full view of the pressman, lays sheet straight, with no flys, strings, tapes or obstructions of any kind. Manufactured by C.B. Cottrell & Sons, New York City & Chicago. Circa 1886

C.B. Cottrell & Sons "Two Revolution" – hand-fed flatbed cylinder press, equipped with a convertible sheet delivery, set to deliver sheets printed side up with tapes or change to regular fly delivery.

Two-cylinder Flatbed Perfecting Press printed both sides of the sheet at one cycle. It made use of a Cottrell development, the shifting tympan which was designed to prevent setoff. Circa 1895.

The Cox "Country Press" with a folder by the rear delivery. Circa 1886.

The Cox "Art" Stop Cylinder Press. Circa 1885.

CRANSTON'S
NEW AND IMPROVED TWO ROLLER
COUNTRY PRESS.

HAND or STEAM POWER.

THE "BEST MADE" COUNTRY PRESS IN THE MARKET.

THE ONLY "FIRST CLASS" COUNTRY PRESS IN THE MARKET.

The above cut represents our New and Improved Newspaper, Book and Job Press. It has Steel Shoes, Steel Track and Rollers, and all wearing parts are of Steel. All our Gears are accurately cut, which insures absolutely positive register.

SIZE AND PRICE.

Size of Bed 32 x 48 Inside Bearers, Price $1400.
Hand Power. - - - - - - - - - - 40.

Blankets, Wrenches, extra set of Stocks, including Steam Fixtures, Boxed and Shipped on Cars or Steamer.

We are prepared to furnish two sizes of our popular First Class Drum Cylinder Printing Presses, 25 x 36 & 32 x 48.

J. H. CRANSTON & CO.,
NORWICH, CONN.

Circa 1880

J. H. CRANSTON'S

FIRST-CLASS PATENT IMPROVED

TWO ROLLER PRESS

For Fine Book, Newspaper and General Job Work.

ACCURATE REGISTER.
PERFECT DISTRIBUTION.
NOISELESS IN OPERATION.
FAULTLESS BUNTER MOTION

OFFICE

48 and 50 DUANE STREET, NEW YORK.

FACTORY, NORWICH, CONNECTICUT.

SEND FOR CIRCULAR.

Circa 1880

THE "CRANSTON"

PATENT IMPROVED

Two-Revolution Printing Presses.

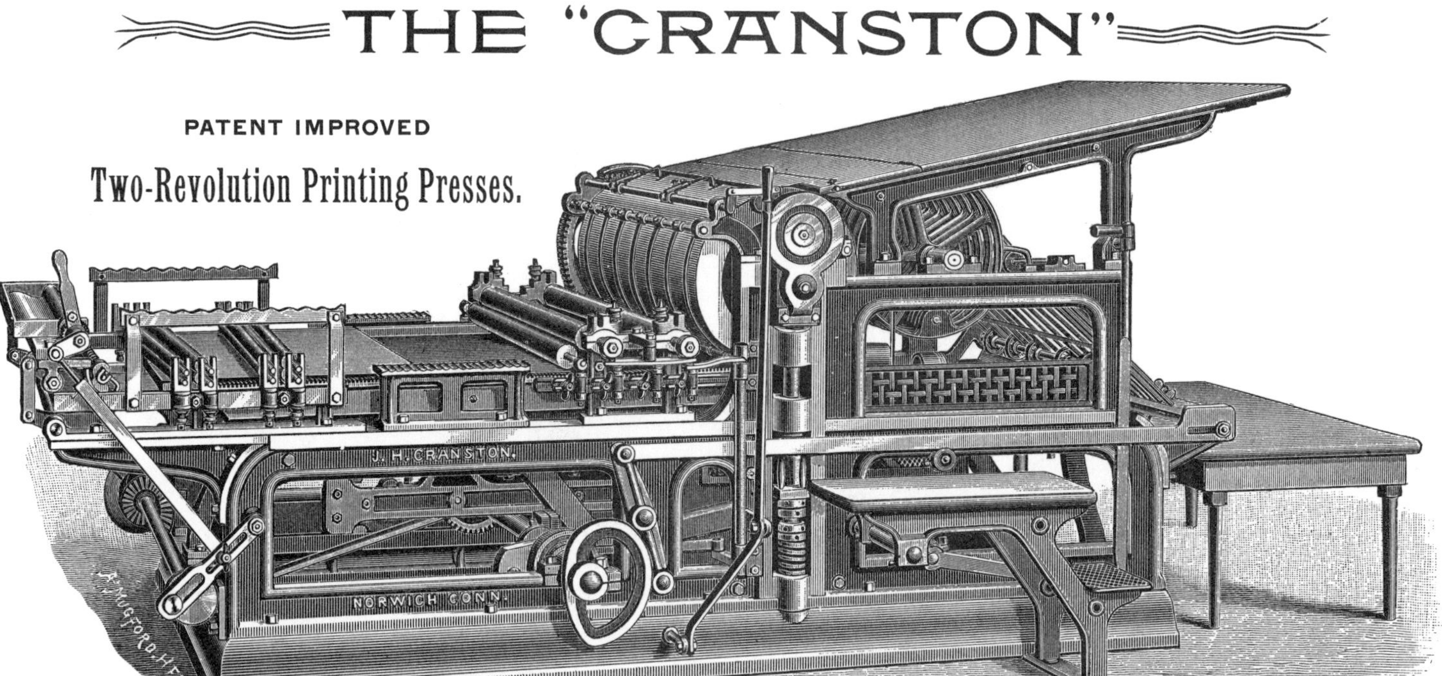

No Presses have ever been made to excel them in point of convenience, finish and durability.
They can be fully depended upon, having proved their merits under varied trials.

J. H. CRANSTON, - - - Manufacturer, - - - NORWICH, CONN.

Cranston "Commercial" Patent Improved Drum – 2 roller, rack and cam distribution, tapeless delivery, air springs, back-up

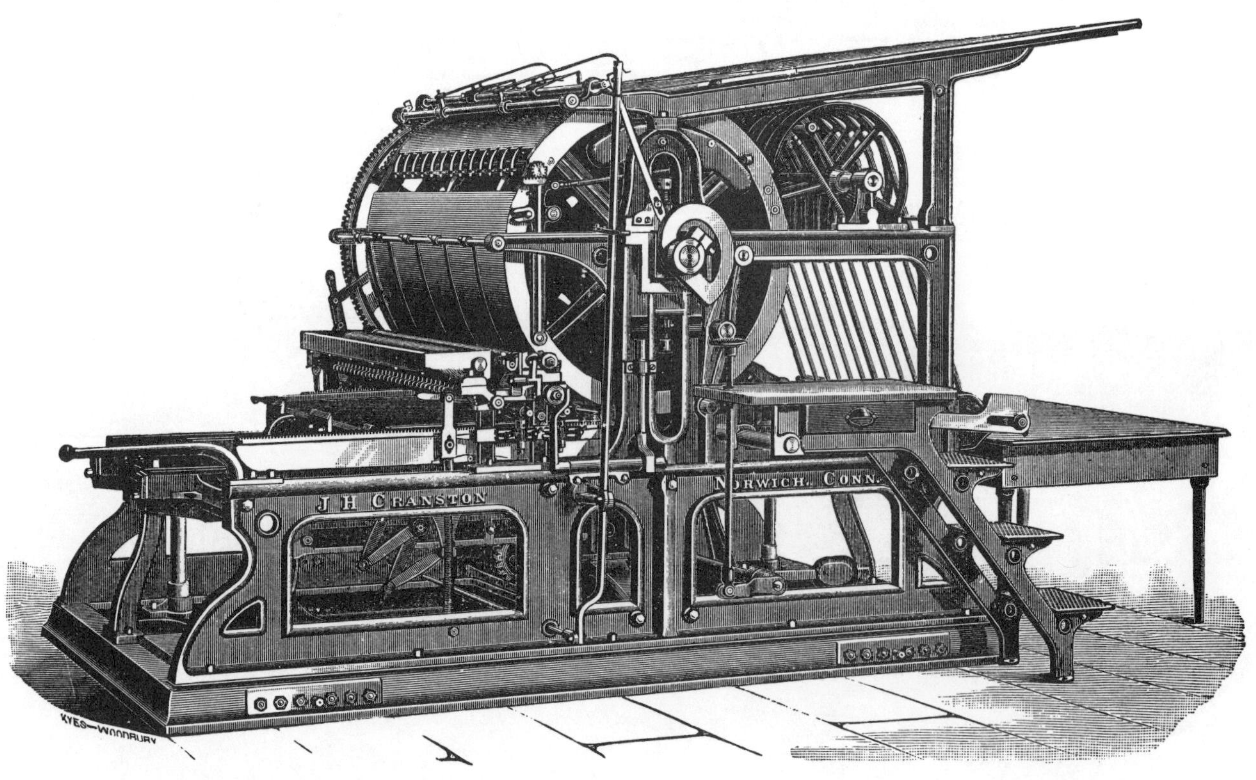

Cranston "Improved First-Class Drum" – 2 roller, rack and cam distribution, tapeless delivery, wire springs, back-up motion. Steam power. Circa 1880.

Cranston Two-Revolution – 2 roller, rack and cam distribution, rear tapeless delivery, air springs, impression trip and back-up.

Cranston "Victor" Two-Revolution – 4 roller, rack, cam and table distribution, rear tapeless delivery, air springs and back-up.

Cranston "Newspaper Drum" – 2 roller, rack and cam distribution, rear tapeless delivery, air springs. Manufactured by Cranston and sold by American Type Founders.
Circa 1893

GORDON'S
FRANKLIN CYLINDER JOBBER.

SIZE INSIDE OF CHASE--14 x 22 3-4 INCHES.

Circa 1865

HARRILD AND SONS'
REGISTERED "BREMNER" PRINTING-MACHINE,
"FLEET" WORKS, LONDON,—E.C.
Circa 1873

"FAIRHAVEN" COUNTRY NEWSPAPER PRESS.

Manufactured by the
BOSTON AND FAIRHAVEN IRON WORKS,
FAIRHAVEN, MASS.

Simple in Construction,
Runs with Great Ease and Smoothness,
Nicely Adapted for Job Work,
Easily Managed.
Good Distribution and Register,
Runs either by Hand or Steam,
Strong and Durable,
And not easily put out of Order.

Fully meeting the wants of Printers wishing to print a handsome Newspaper or Job and Poster Work.

SIZES AND PRICES:

Bed 31×46.....*$1,000* *Boxing*............*$25*
Bed 28×40..... *900* " *25*

Full and complete instructions furnished for setting up.

For full particulars and testimonials, address

JOB C. TRIPP, Treas.,
Fairhaven, Mass.

W H I T L O C K ' S

HAND AND STEAM POWER PRINTING PRESSES.

SIZES AND PRICES:

Bed, inside Bearers 33×48	$1,100	Bed, inside Bearers, 28×40	$900
Boxing	50	Boxing	50
Steam Fixtures	50	Steam Fixtures	50
Weight	5,500 lbs.	Weight	4,000 lbs.
Speed by Hand, 600 per hour, by Steam, 1200.		Speed by Hand, 800 per hour, by Steam, 1500.	

For further information, address

THE WHITLOCK MACHINE WORKS,
Birmingham, Conn.

Circa 1875

THE COUNTRY NEWSPAPER PRESS

MANUFACTURED BY THE

BOSTON AND FAIRHAVEN IRON WORKS, FAIRHAVEN, MASS.

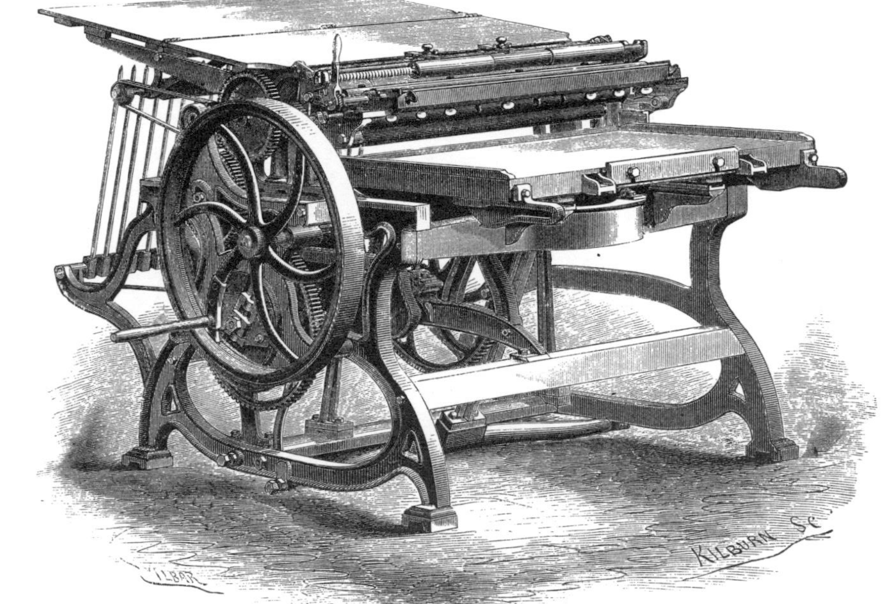

These presses are designed for Country Newspaper, Book and Job work, and are giving excellent satisfaction wherever they are used. The material and workmanship are of the first quality, they run either by hand or power with great ease, and will turn off from 800 to 1000 impressions per hour. For beauty of workmanship, speed, ease and economy in running, and freedom from jar or noise they are much the cheapest presses in market.

SIZES AND PRICES:

Bed 31×46 inches within Bearers..........$950.......**Boxing and Carting**..........$25.
Bed 28×40 " " .... 825........ " " .... 25.
Bed 24×32 " " .... 700........ " " .... 20.

Among those using these machines we are pleased to refer printers in want of presses to the following parties:

Shippensburg, Pa., July 7, 1869.

Having had one of your Newspaper Printing Presses in use in the News office for almost a year, we feel no hesitancy whatever in recommending it to the trade or profession. Parties are invited to address us at any time for any particulars concerning the Press, or such other information they may desire. The Press is cheap, substantially made, and produces work equal to any of the higher priced presses. It is also fast and runs with but little power.

D. K. & J. C. WAGNER.

F. A. ROOT, Atchison, Kansas.
BLOSSOM & EASTERBROOK, Hingham, Mass.
BOYLE BROTHERS & REED, Mauch Chunk, Pa.
HARVEY SICKLER, Pub. "Wyoming Democrat," Tunkhannock, Pa.
A. H. BYINGTON & CO., Norwalk, Conn.
M. M. OSBORN, Rahway, N. J.
NEWS PUBLISHING CO., Schenevus, N. Y.

AMERICAN PAPER CUTTERS.

Length of Knife 28 inches..........$125.

Orders promptly executed. For further particulars and testimonials address

JOB C. TRIPP, Treasurer,
Fairhaven, Mass.

Circa 1873

THE FAIRHAVEN

Is ESPECIALLY DESIGNED for COUNTRY NEWSPAPER, BOOK AND JOB WORK.

It can be run either by Hand or Steam Power, giving from 800 to 1,200 impressions per hour.

Numerous testimonials from all parts of the country confirm our claims that ***the FAIRHAVEN runs with great ease, economy, and freedom from jar or noise; has an excellent ink distribution and adjustment; great convenience in changing forms,*** and all the adjustments are so arranged that it is easily kept in perfect running order, and fully meets the wants of those wishing to print a handsome Newspaper, or for Job, Poster and Book Work. Each Press furnished complete with Blanket, two sets Roller Cores, extra Roller Wheels, Wrenches and Gauges. One set of rollers is sent with the composition on, ready to run.

A SAMPLE TESTIMONIAL:

Ever since I graduated, nearly twenty years ago, I have looked forward to the time when I could own a Fairhaven Cylinder Press. During all these years I have owned and operated several other makes of presses, but not until February of the present year was my wish gratified. When I purchased this office I found a Fairhaven Press among the material, and without any previous knowledge of the press, I put on the forms, and with the help of a boy, got off a 35 quire edition in 55 minutes. The beauty of it is, the press is so simple in its construction that any one, with no knowledge of cylinder presses, can operate it as easily and successfully as a Washington hand press. I consider it as the best adapted for country newspaper work, and for simplicity, convenience and utility, it stands at the "top of the column."—W. E. CHURCHILL, Mohawk, N. Y., May 25, 1888.

SIZES AND PRICES

No. 3—Bed 28 x 42 in. inside bearers, prints 25 x 39, price..............$750
(Size, 5½x6½ feet; weight, boxed, 3,800 lbs.; partial boxing, $10.00.)

No. 4—Bed 31 x 46 in. inside bearers, prints 27 x 43, price..............$900
(Size, 6x7 feet; weight, boxed, 4,500 lbs.; partial boxing, $10.00.)

No. 3 will print an 8-col. folio, or a 5-col. quarto. No. 4 will print a 9-col. folio, or a 6-col. quarto.

The above prices include Fixtures for either Steam or Hand Power.

MANUFACTURED BY **GOLDING & CO.**, FORT HILL SQUARE, BOSTON, MASS.

Full details given in our Press and Tool Catalogue, which is sent free to any address on application. Our complete Catalogue, giving prices and full details of everything needed in a first-class office, including Presses, Tools, Type and Material, sent on receipt of ten cents.

"FAIRHAVEN" COUNTRY NEWSPAPER PRESS.

MANUFACTURED BY THE

Boston and Fairhaven Iron Works, Fairhaven, Mass.

International Exhibition,

PHILADELPHIA, 1876.

The United States Centennial Commission has examined the Report of the Judges, and accepted the following reasons, and decreed an award in conformity therewith:

For strength and durability, simplicity of construction, ease of adjusting rollers and ink fountain, adaptability for newspaper and job work, and general excellence.

"The Improved Fairhaven Press" does excellent work; has a speed of one thousand per hour. The bed is moved by a lever and connecting rod, which holds it firmly in position.

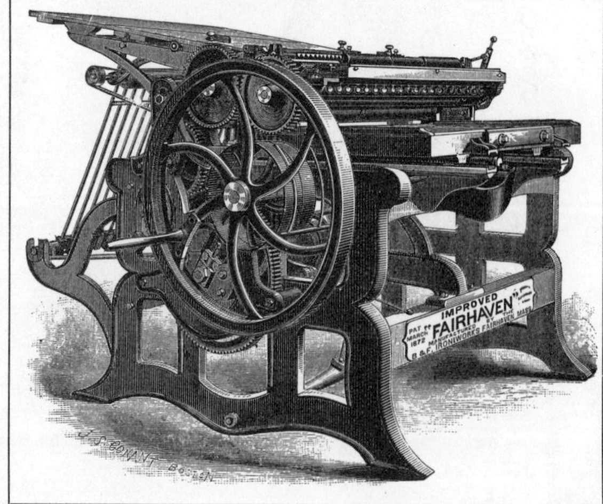

JACOB HEINMILLER,

Of ALBANY, N. Y.,

Says the "Fairhaven" Press is just what it is represented to be, and works like a charm, especially in its

Register and Impression.

I have now run the press every day for over eight months, and not the least part of it has ever been out of order. I can recommend it as a first-class press.

SIZES AND PRICES:—Bed, 31 x 46, - - - $1,000. Bed, 28 x 40, - - - $900.

Boxing, $25.00. Steam Fixtures, $25.00.

The Above two presses look identical with the exception of the nameplates. Each one shows a different manufacturer.

Four Roller Book Printing Machine.

THIS Machine is particularly adapted to fine book and cut work. The bed is impelled by a crank and lever placed below it, which obviates the necessity of bed-springs, and gives to it a slow and uniform motion during the impression, but a quick return movement. The larger sizes have four inking rollers, and also a pointing apparatus, and as the impression cylinder is stationary while the fingers close on the sheet, a perfect register is insured. The fingers never require shifting, whatever the size of the form, and the sheet flyer is so arranged that no tapes are used on the press; this makes it very convenient for job work.

Sizes, Prices and Capacities.

No.	Size of Bed inside of Bearers.	Size of Matter printed.	No. of Inking Rollers passing over Form.	Size of Foundation Frame.	Height from floor to highest point of feed-board.	Weight boxed.	Price.
1	13 × 16 in.	9½ × 12 in.	2	24 × 43 in.	40 in.	1,800 lbs.	$1,050.00
2	16 × 22 "	12 × 18 "	3	32 × 54 "	52 "	2,500 "	1,750.00
3	23 × 28 "	19 × 24 "	4	42 × 71 "	80 "	5,000 "	3,000.00
4	25 × 33 "	21 × 29 "	4	47 × 71 "	82 "	6,000 "	3,350.00
5	25 × 38 "	21 × 34 "	4	52 × 71 "	82 "	7,000 "	3,650.00
6	28 × 41 "	24 × 37 "	4	57 × 89 "	68 "	8,000 "	4,025.00

Circa 1860

R. HOE & CO.'S PATENT

RAILWAY COUPON TICKET PRINTING AND NUMBERING MACHINE

This machine is a simple modification of the well-known Cylinder Press. The form and numbering wheels are put on a traveling bed, and receive their ink from the same rollers. The impression cylinder gears into the bed, turning forward and backward with it. Instead of fingers, it is furnished with cords, that run round in the spaces between the coupons. The feed-table delivers the paper under the cords, by which it is carried down and the body of the ticket is printed; then the motion of the cylinder is reversed, the ticket changes its position, and is presented to the numbering wheels. In its course down and up, the ticket passes under the prickers, and is finally deposited in a receptacle, printed side upward, under the eye of the attendant. A numbering plate is arranged for each different spacing of coupons, so that no time is lost in adjusting the wheels. Local tickets can be printed in strips, and cut up afterward. The machine will print 27 inches of matter, and will run with ease 1,500 sheets per hour.

For additional information and particulars apply to

R. HOE & COMPANY,

Printing Press, Machine, and Saw Manufacturers,

31 Gold Street, New York.

Circa 1871

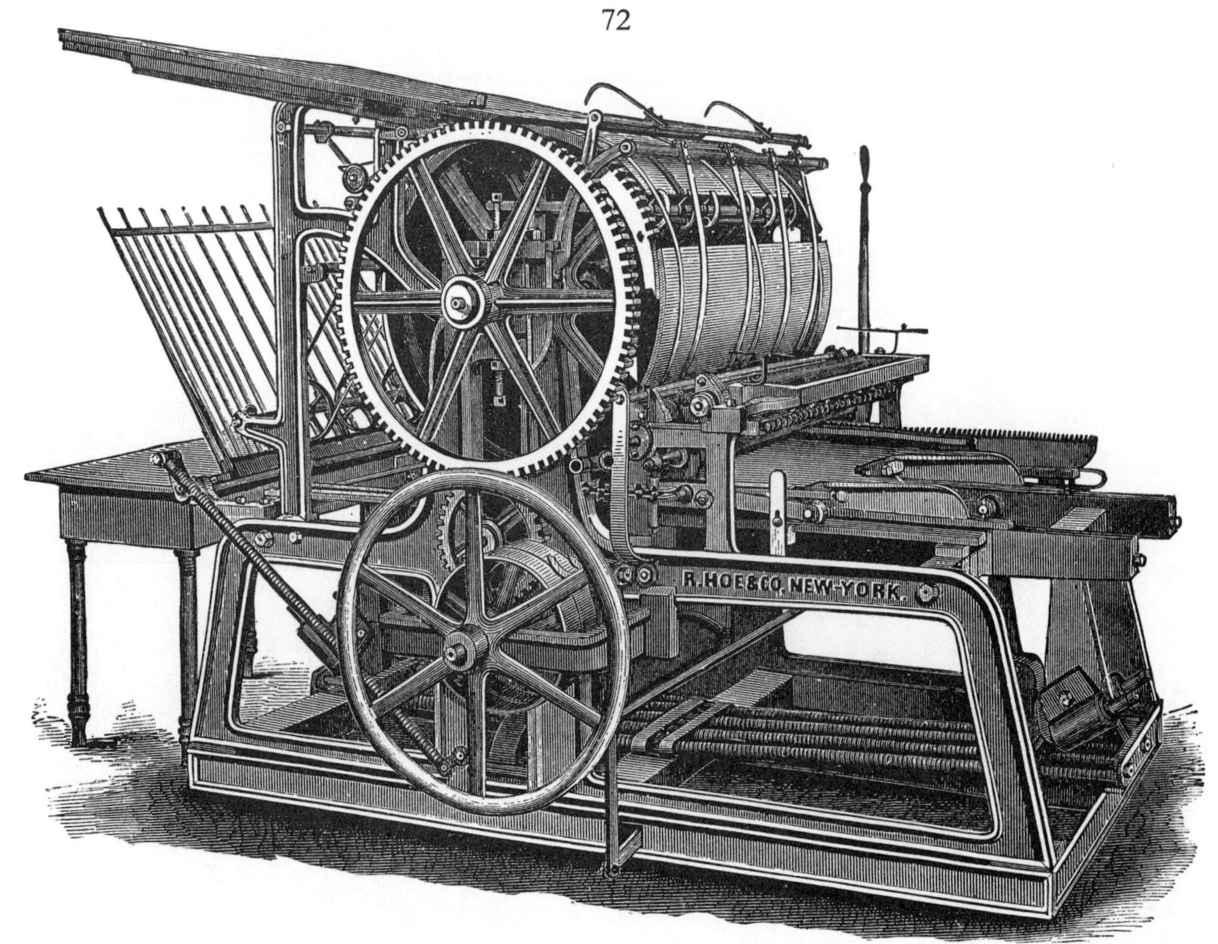

Hoe Drum (old Style) – 2 roller, rack and screw distribution, tape delivery, wire springs in base. Circa 1830.

Hoe Three Revolution Press. Circa 1844.

R. HOE & CO.'S STOP CYLINDER WOOD-CUT PRESS.

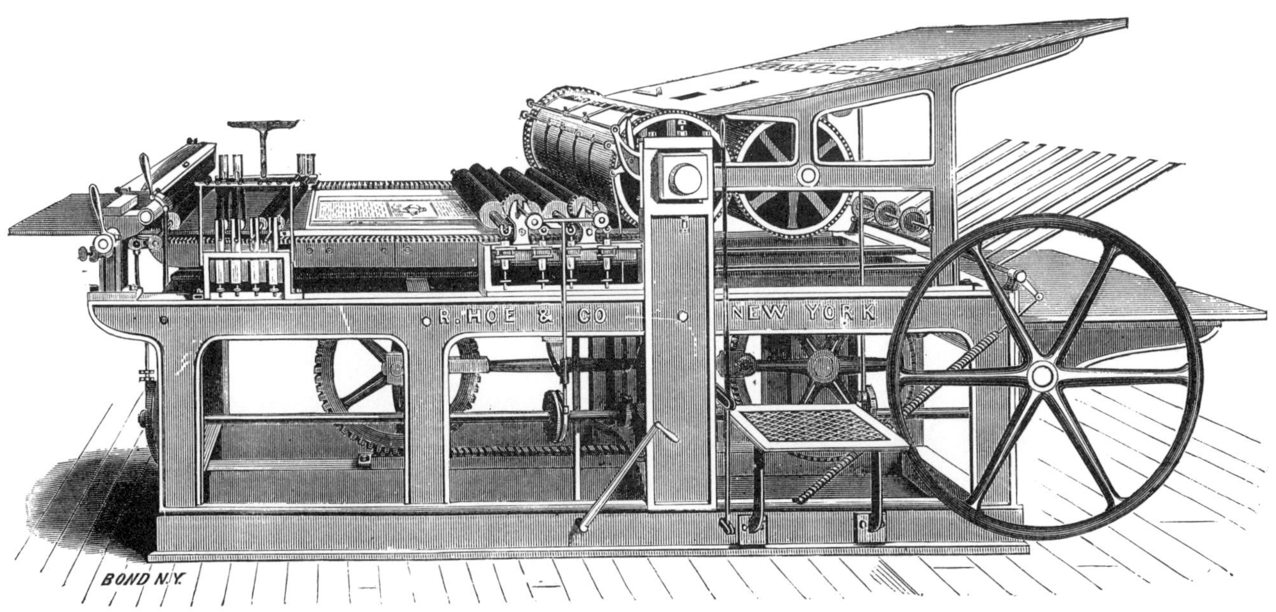

This machine is of a new pattern, and designed for the finest kind of Book, Wood-cut, and Color printing. The distribution is either by an inking table or vibrating cylinder, as may be desired, and the number of form rollers, from two to ten, according to size. The bed is driven by a crank, without bed-springs, and without the slightest jar. The impression cylinder is stationary during the return of the bed, and the fingers close on the sheet before the register points are withdrawn; the cylinder then revolves, and, as it gears directly into the bed, perfect register is obtained. The fingers never require shifting, whatever the size of the form, and no tapes are used. When so ordered, the bed is arranged to be run either once or twice, thus passing the form under the inking rollers either two or four times to each impression, as may be required.

ILLUSTRATED CATALOGUES SENT ON APPLICATION.

R. HOE & CO., New York.

Circa 1871

Hoe "Intermediate" Stop Cylinder – 4 roller, rack, cam and table distribution, rear tapeless delivery.

Hoe Three-Revolution Old Style Frame – 2 roller, rack and screw distribution, tape delivery, air springs, folder attached.

Hoe Three-Revolution single small cylinder – 2 roller, rack and screw distribution, tape delivery, air springs, box frame.

Hoe "News Cylinder" Pioneer Large Cylinder – 2 roller, rack and screw distribution, tape delivery, hand power.

Hoe "News and Job Cylinder" – 2 roller, rack and screw distribution, tapeless delivery, air springs.

Hoe Drum "Job and News" – 2 roller, rack and screw distribution, tapeless delivery, air springs, box frame.

Hoe Drum "Job and News" – 2 roller, rack and screw distribution, tape delivery, wire springs.

Hoe Drum Cylinder “Half Medium” (bed 17” x 21”) – 2 roller, rack and screw distribution, tape delivery, wire springs under bed.

Bed and Platen Press. Manufactured by Seth Adams & Co. from 1853 to 1859. Patented by Isaac Adams. R. Hoe & Co. purchased Adams. Circa 1860.

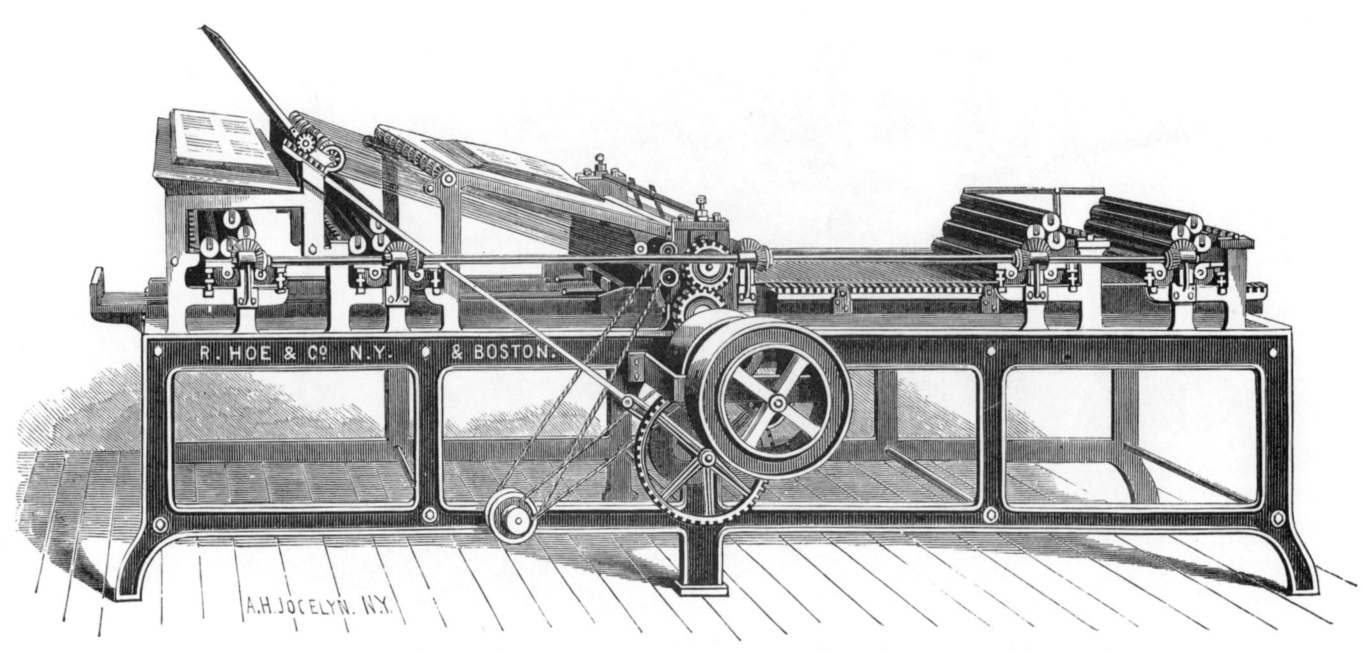

R. Hoe & Co. Two Color Printing Machine. Circa 1860.

Two-Color Printing Machine.

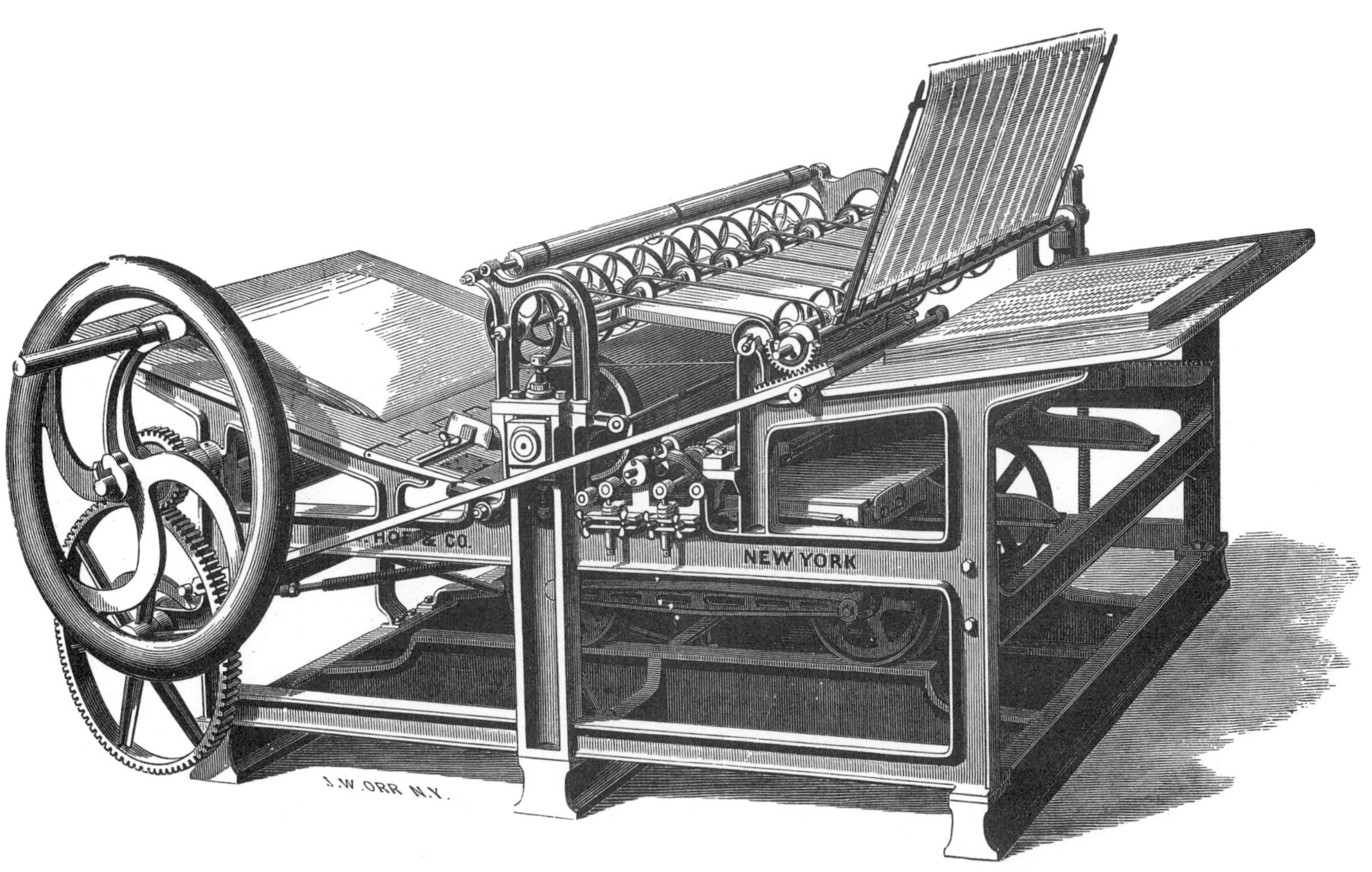

R. Hoe & Co. Railway Stop Cylinder Newspaper Printing Machine. Circa 1867.

Hoe Two Revolution – 4 roller, rack, cam and table distribution,
rear tapeless delivery, wire springs.

Single Large-Cylinder Hand Printing Machine

This Press is similar to our "Single Large Cylinder", but it is somewhat lighter, and more simple in construction. It is intended to supply newspapers of moderate circulation with a plain but first-rate machine on which also general job work can be done. It is designed to run either by hand or steam power. With one man at the wheel, it will work off eight hundred impressions per hour; and, by applying steam power, its speed may be increased from twenty-five to fifty percent. It has two form rollers, which go over the whole form. Ca. 1873

R. HOE & COMPANY'S

Hand Stop-Cylinder Printing Machine

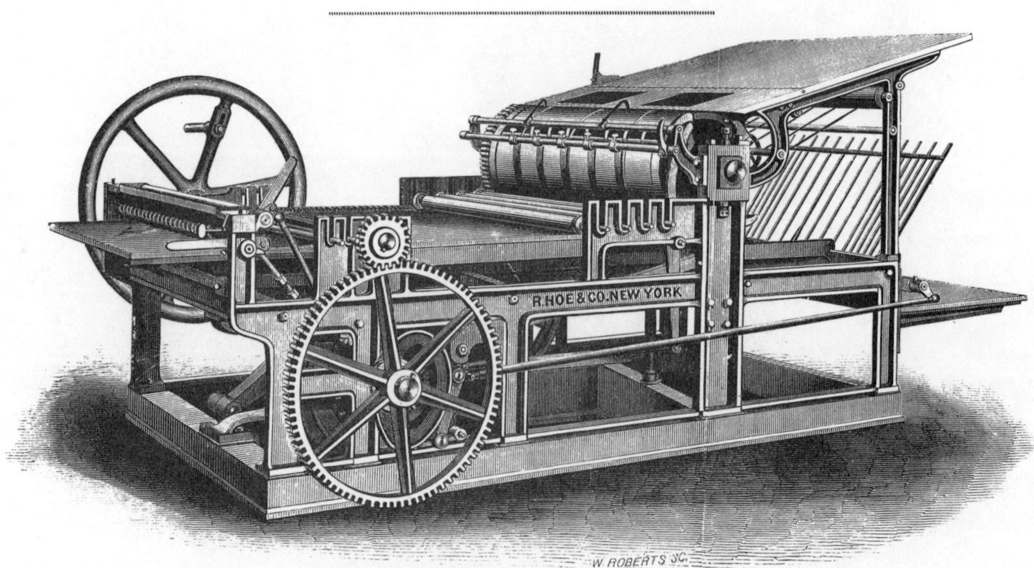

This machine in its general design is similar to our well-known Stop-Cylinder Press, but is lighter in all its parts, so as to be easily driven by hand. It will print satisfactorily all kinds of newspapers and ordinary book work at the rate of seven or eight hundred impressions an hour by hand, or one thousand by steam power. The bed is driven by a crank, so that there is no jar at either end. Circa 1873

Single Small Cylinder Printing Machine.

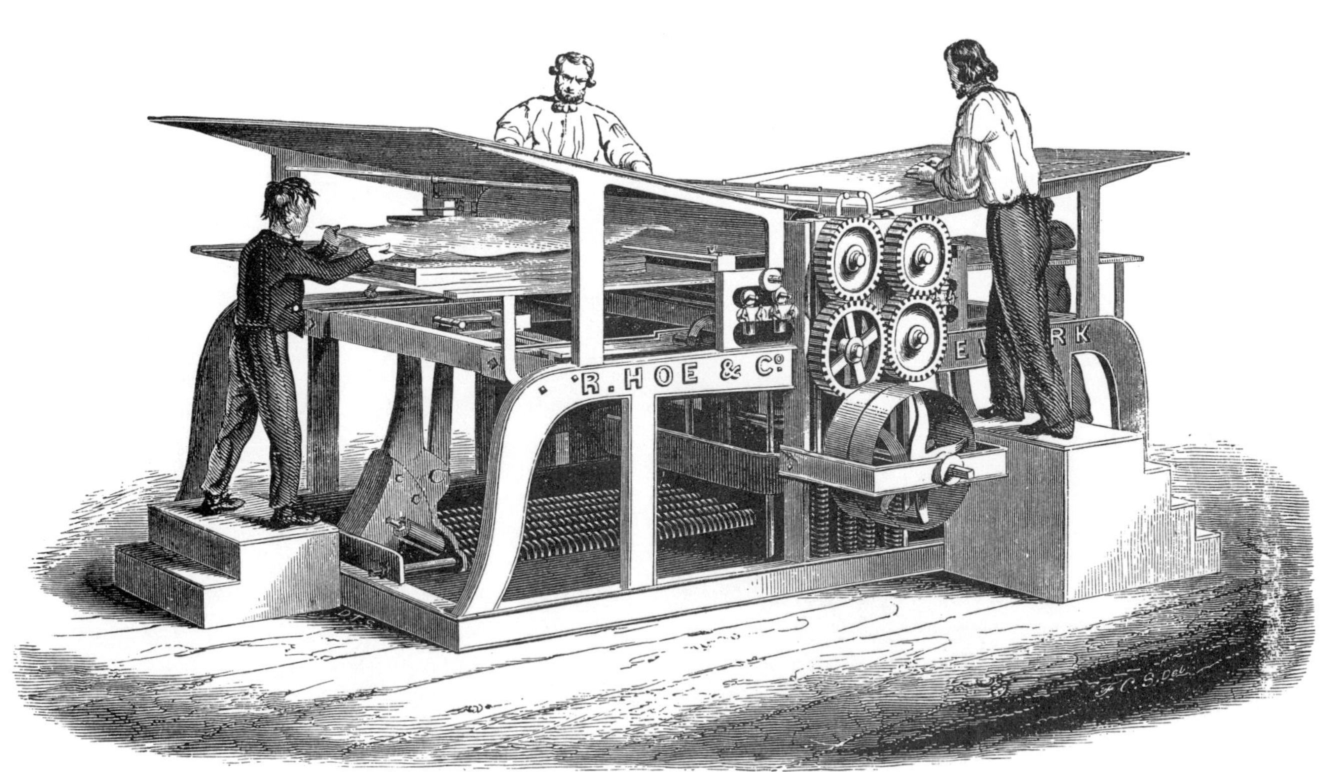

Double Cylinder Printing Machine.

Hoe "Double Cylinder" old style – 2 rollers at each end,
rack and screw distribution, tape delivery.

Hoe "Double Cylinder" new style box frame – 2 rollers at each end,
rack and screw distribution, tape delivery.

The American Power Press Manufacturing Company.

PRINCIPAL DEPOT, 36 DEY STREET, N. Y.

A. ROBERTSON, PRESIDENT.
JOHN HENRY, TREASURER.
E. S. CONDIT, SECRETARY.

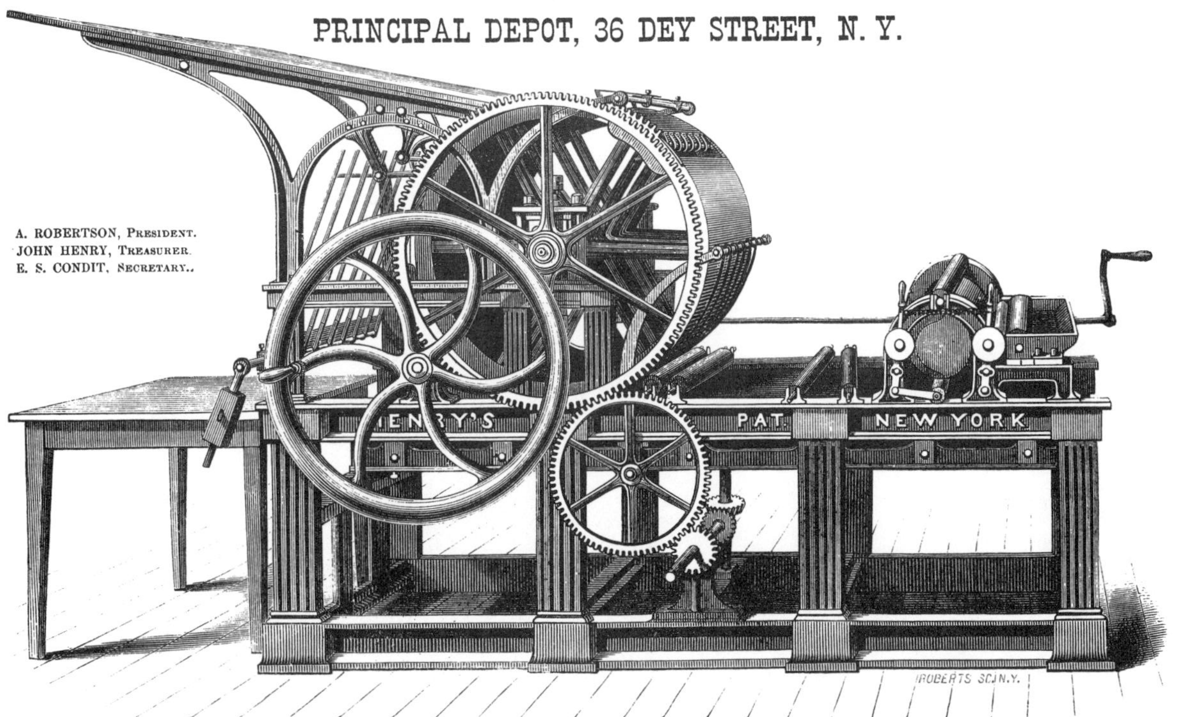

HENRY'S PATENT COUNTRY NEWSPAPER, BOOK AND JOB PRESS.

Size 32X48—for largest class Country Paper; Price $1,000; Boxing and Shipping, $50.

TWO ROLLER MOULDS, RUBBER BLANKET, EXTRA ROLLER STOCKS AND WRENCHES GO WITH EACH PRESS.

Circa 1869

WE STAND ON MERIT ALONE.

THE HUBER

CRANK MOVEMENT

IMPROVED TWO-REVOLUTION

JOB AND BOOK PRESS.

DOUBLE ROLLING. ∴ SINGLE END. ∴ SIX FOUR-INCH FACE TRACKS. ∴ BOX FRAME.
NO SPRINGS. ∴ FRONT OR BACK DELIVERY.

UNEQUALED BY ANY TWO-REVOLUTION PRESS IN **Impression, Register, Distribution, Speed and Life.**

The Huber Presses are used by the representative houses of this country, who will substantiate all we claim for them. Send for descriptive circulars of our Sheet Perfecting Book Press, Two-Color Press, Two-Revolution Job and Book "Crank Movement" Press, Two-Revolution Job and Book "Air-Spring" Press, and Two-Revolution "Mustang" Rapid Jobber "Crank Movement."

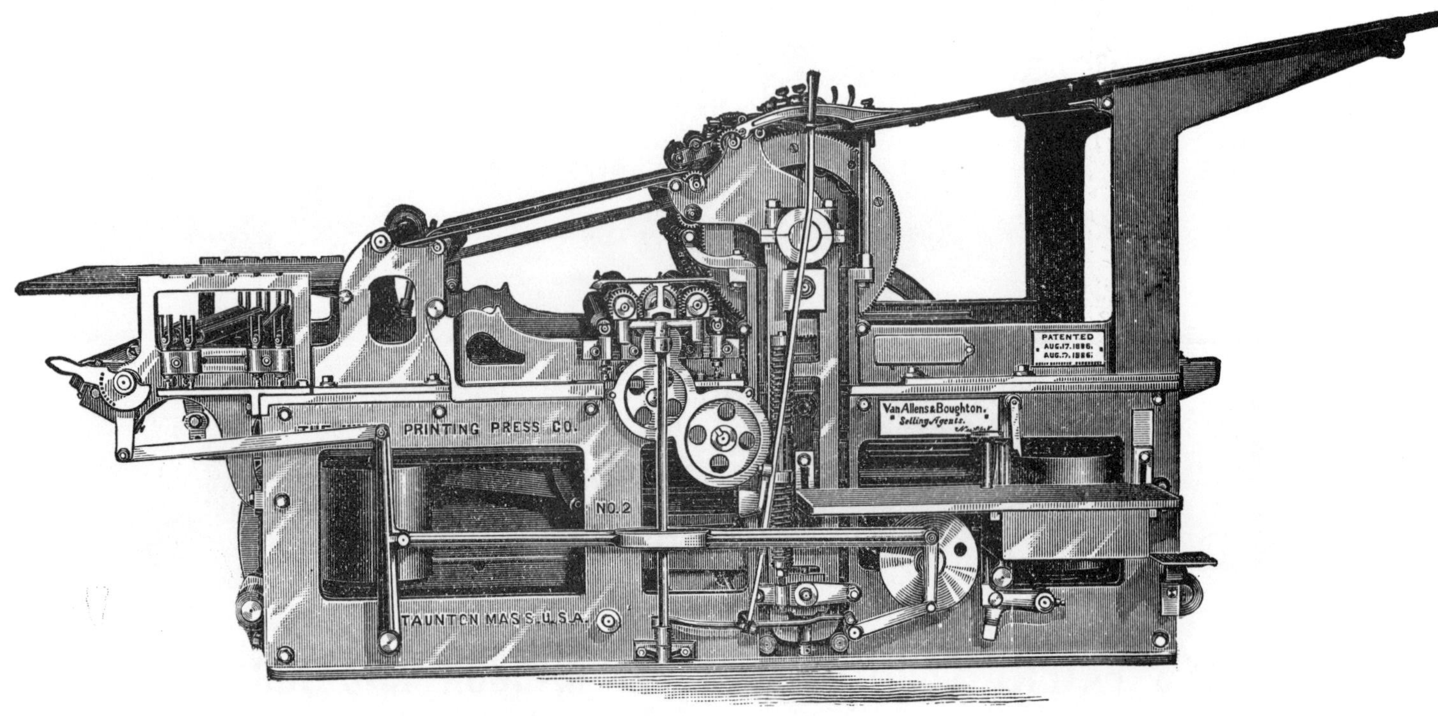

Huber Two-Revolution – 4 roller, rack, cam and table distribution,
front fly delivery, and impression trip.

Huber "Pony" Two-Revolution – 2 roller, rack, cam and table distribution, front delivery.

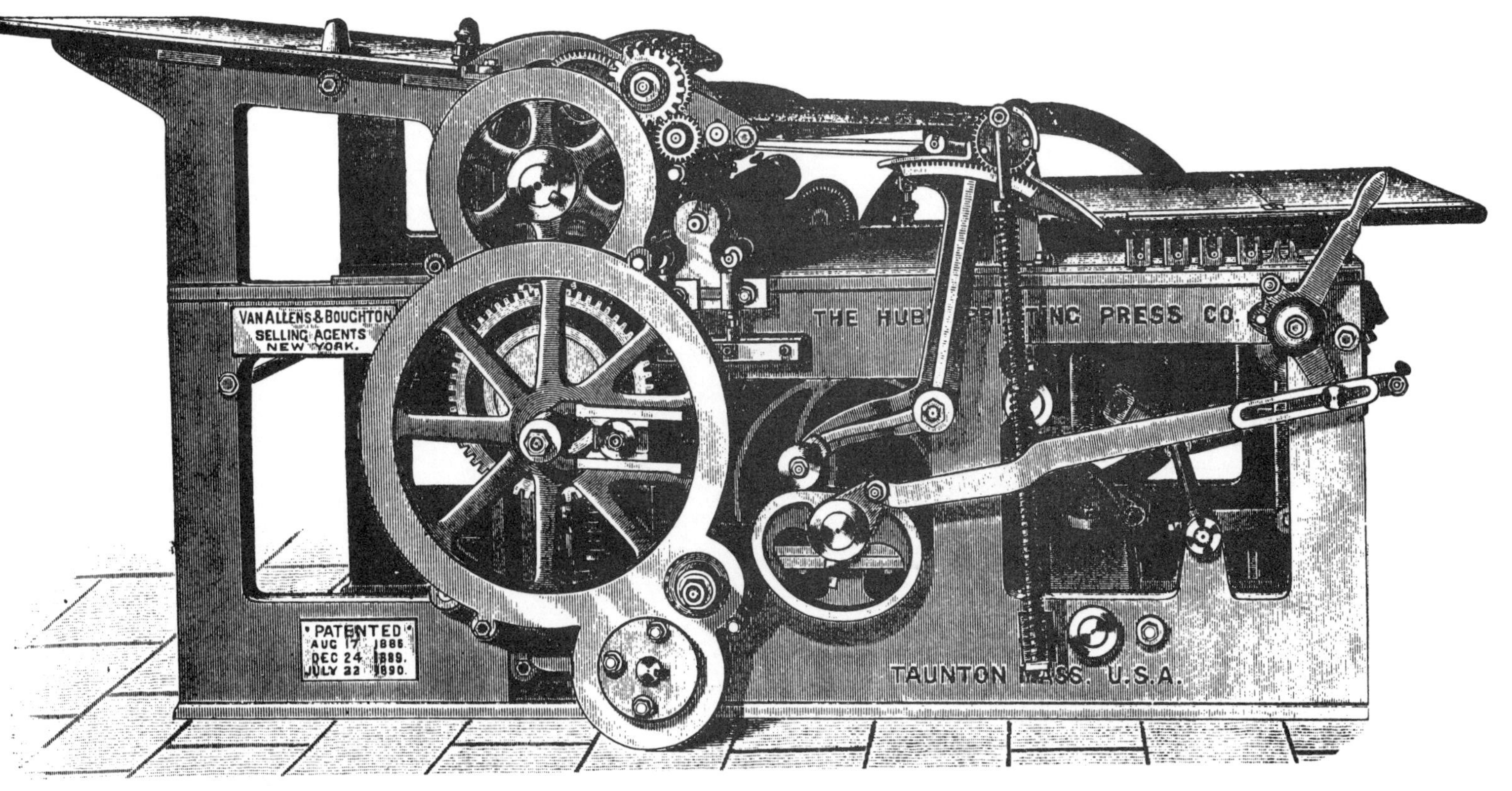

Huber crank movement two-revolution hand-fed cylinder press with front delivery and a 28 x 35" bed. The bed and cylinder driven by a crank with no springs required to reverse the motion of the bed. Circa 1890.

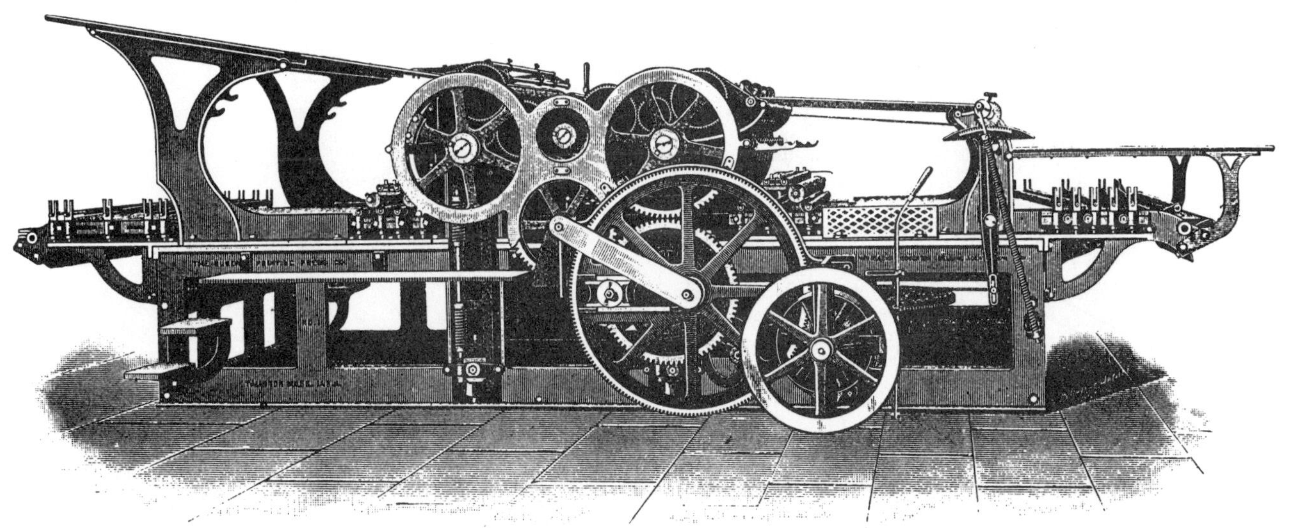

Huber 2-Color Press with front delivery, four form rollers to each bed. Available in three sizes; 33 x 50", 33 x 55" and 42 x 58". Circa 1894.

Typographic and Lithographic Machinery.

H. JULLIEN, BRUSSELS, BELGIUM.

STOP CYLINDER PRINTING PRESS.

This machine is solid and of elegant appearance, and built with the greatest care. It is fitted with all our latest improvements, and possesses the following features:

The space occupied is less than that of any other press of the same size.

The fly is so located that the turner (when the press is driven by hand) can look after the fly.

The hollowed axle of the carriage (patent) allows the use of a straight connecting rod, which insures an even and regular movement of the bed.

The cylinder is driven or stopped by means of a straight rod acted on directly by cams without the use of any intermediate piece.

This feature presents a very smooth starting of the cylinder and keeps it steady during the feeding time.

The teeth of the rack and cylinder gear are cut out of the solid. The wheels under the bed and the racks are helicoidal; this gives a very smooth movement to the bed, and prevents any slur.

The machine is fitted with front gauges, which hold the paper till the grippers close; an automatic fly delivery; an improved system of points; special brackets for placing the distributing rollers either straight or obliquely; a supplementary delivery table for the reception of card or other small sized work without the use of tapes.

Sizes.	Size of Paper.	Size of Bed.	Prices.	Sizes.	Size of Paper.	Size of Bed.	Prices.
Propatria,	14 x 18 in.	17 x 20 in.	$360 00	Double carré,	26 x 36½ in.	31 x 40 in.	$800 00
Coquille,	17½ x 22 "	21½ x 25½ "	440 00	Double raisin,	29 x 39½ "	32 x 43 "	900 00
Grand raisin,	19½ x 25½ "	23½ x 28½ "	540 00	Double jésus,	30 x 44 "	34½ x 47½ "	1000 00
Grand jésus,	22 x 30 "	27½ x 32½ "	600 00	Double colombier,	34 x 51 "	39 x 55 "	1300 00
Grand colombier,	26 x 34 "	28½ x 36½ "	720 00				

N. B.—The railway movement of the Double jésus machine is fitted with six wheels and that of the Double colombier machine with eight wheels. The Double carré size and above, are fitted with double racks on the bed and two wheels on the cylinder, and with an adjustable supply of ink without disturbing the screws of the fountain.

Circa 1892

HAND CYLINDER PRESS.

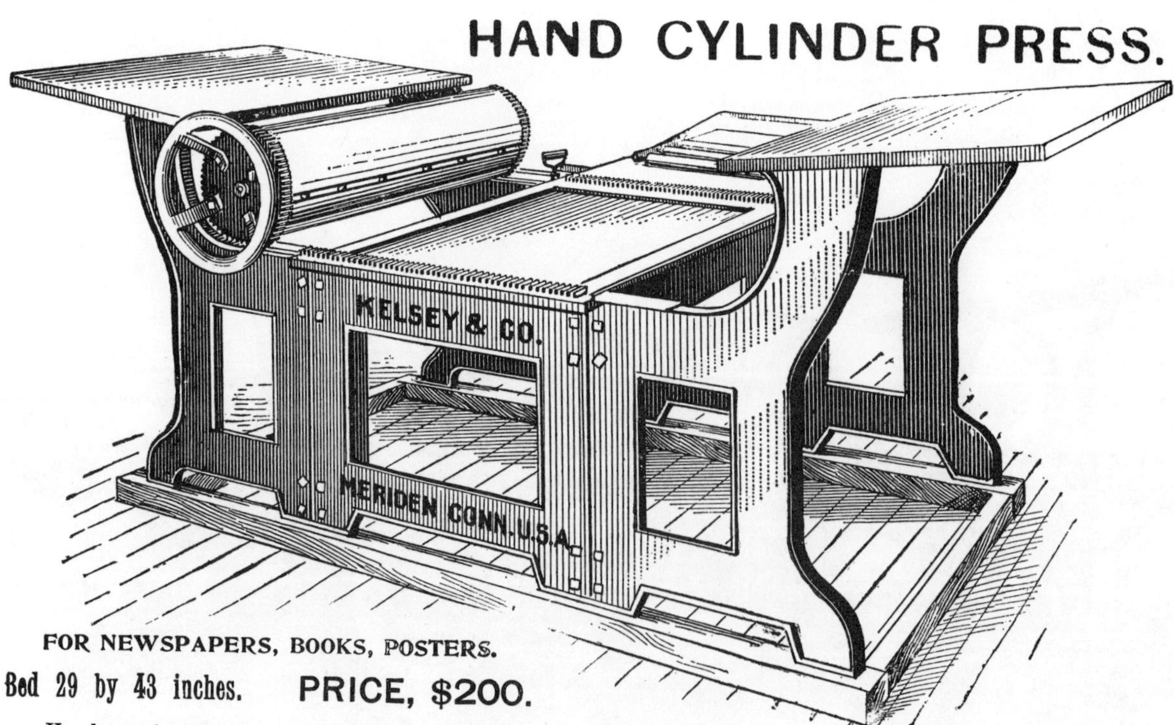

FOR NEWSPAPERS, BOOKS, POSTERS.

Bed 29 by 43 inches. **PRICE, $200.**

Handsome in appearance, easy to work, does excellent printing. Three rollers, carriage covering full form, cut gearing, good regulation of impression. Two chases, ink rollers, roller mold, with each machine. Shipping weight about 1.400 lbs. Price $200. Or with good newspaper outfit $500.

Circa 1899

The Kidder Pony Cylinder Press.

Built by the KIDDER PRESS MANUFACTURING CO., Boston, Mass.

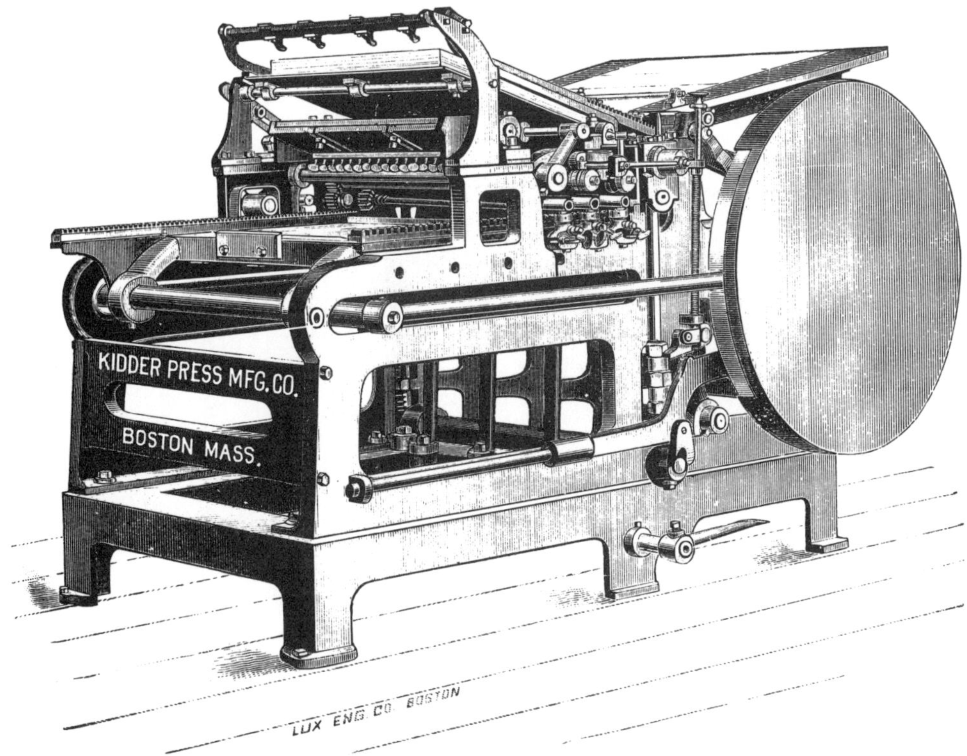

THIS machine is a new design for job work.

We make the following claims for this press:

It is the simplest and most durable in use.

It will do the finest possible three-roller presswork to exact hair-line register. The register is exact at any attainable speed.

The bed is driven by a direct crank similar to a horizontal steam engine. The machine moves past its centres and reverses the bed at each end of the stroke without jar or noise and without the least necessity for air or wire springs, bumpers or other devices. A smoothness of motion is imparted that insures the greatest possible nicety in printing and durability in the machine. Very slight effort is required in turning the machine over the centres, as there are no hard points. The cylinder is geared direct to the bed and reverses with it. The grippers back up to receive the sheet and at the moment of closing the cylinder and bed are *stationary*, the cranks being on the centres insuring the absolute hairline register of the best stop cylinder machines. No tapes, delivery cylinder or fly are required. The sheet is drawn straight from the cylinder in front and deposited in the pile printed side up, close to the eye of the feeder.

No possibility of blur or smut in heavy color work. Speed, 3000 impressions per hour. Please send for our new illustrated and descriptive catalogue printed on this machine.

Circa 1889

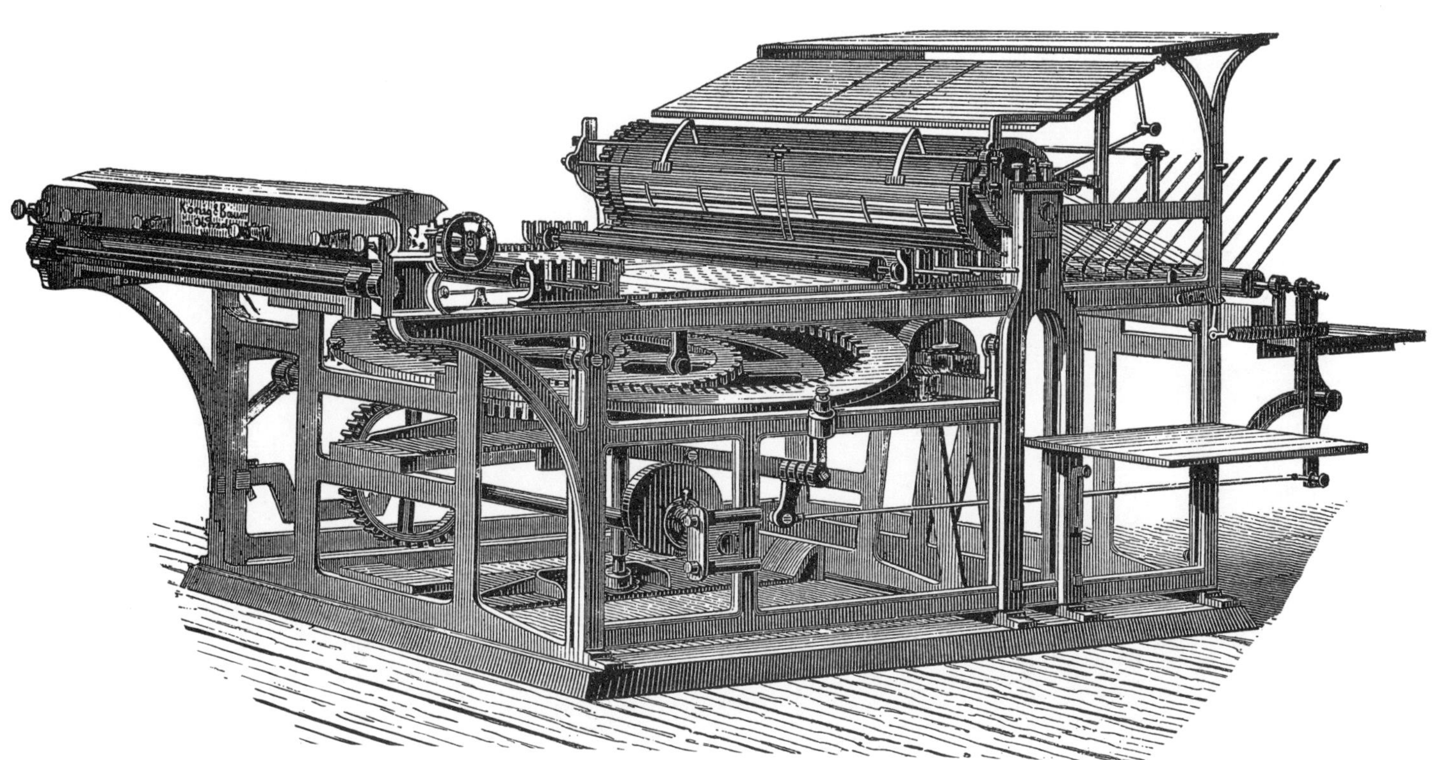

Koenig & Bauer Circular Motion Press, manufactured in Germany. Circa 1840

IMPROVED STOP CYLINDER PRESS

Capable of running 500 to 800 by hand, and 800 to 1,100 impressions per hour by steam.

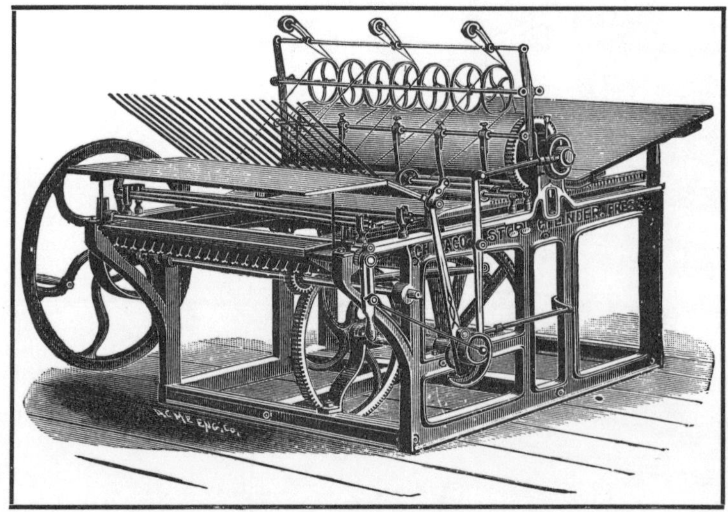

Size 32x47 nine column folio or 6 column Quarto; Price complete $650.

This press has lately been improved by putting in regular tracks, and is provided with wire bumper. The ink table has been lengthened six inches, thereby giving greater distribution. The ink fountain is the same in character as on first-class presses. The form rollers have adjustable bearers, set with thumb screws. For particulars address

BARNHART BROS. & SPINDLER.

For sale by Minnesota Type Foundry Co., St. Paul, Minn.; Great Western Type Foundry, Kansas City, Mo.; Great Western Type Foundry, Omaha, Neb.; St. Louis Printers' Supply Co., St. Louis, Mo.

Chicago Improved Stop Cylinder Press sold by Barnhart Bros. & Spindler. Circa1889

The first Miehle Press, Serial No. 1, a 38 x 52 ½" two-revolution flat bed cylinder press
Featuring a new bed driving mechanism. Circa 1887

Miehle Two-Revolution – 4 roller, rack, cam and table distribution, front delivery.
S.K. White in Chicago manufactured these presses. Circa 1889.

Miehle "Pony", their smallest flatbed press. Circa 1892.

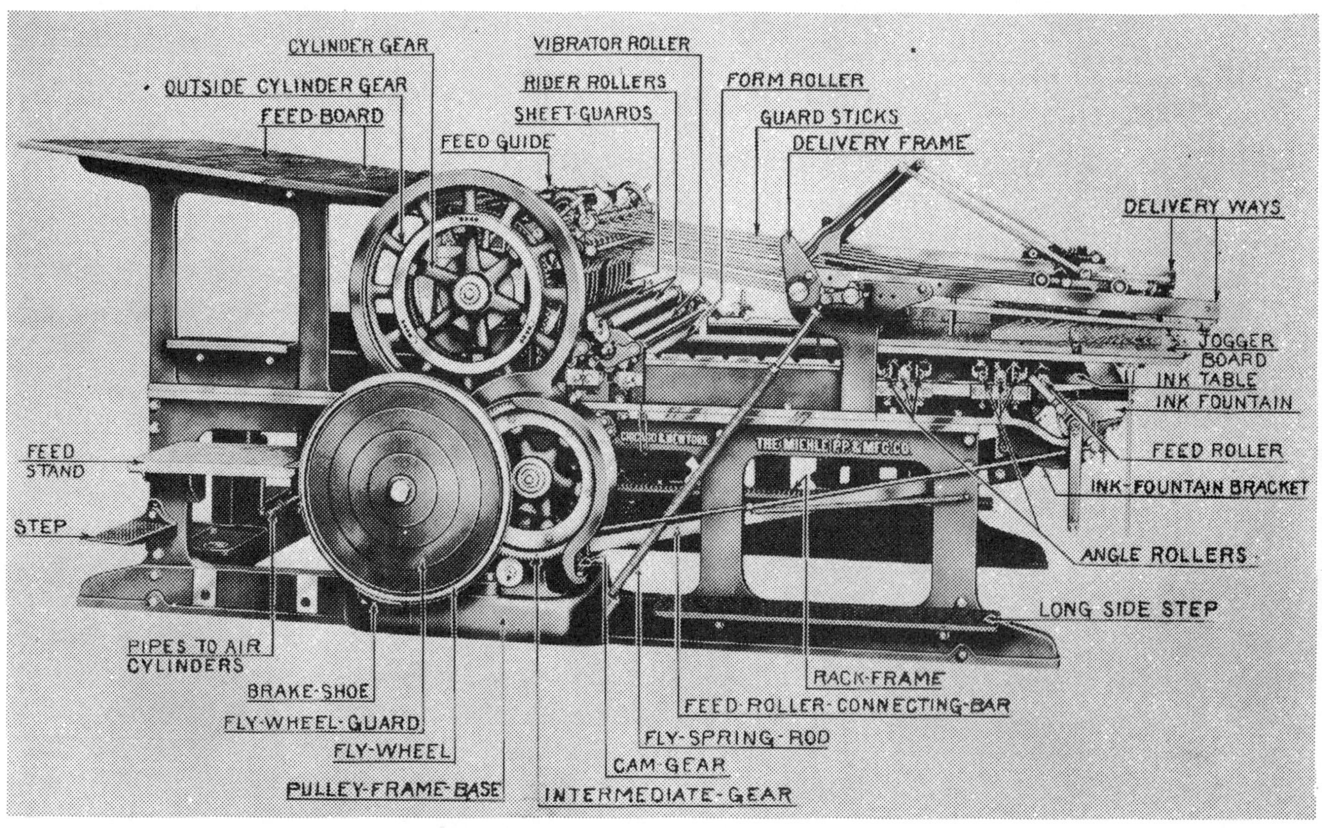

Miehle Two-Revolution Flatbed Cylinder Press made in sizes 22 ½ x 34" to 49 ½ x 73 ½"
with two, three or four form rollers, fly or tape delivery and speeds up to 2500 iph.
Circa 1899

Newbury Cylinder Press, hand power. Circa 1863

The Newbury Country Press. Manufactured by A. & B. Newbury, Coxasackie, New York.

PRINTERS' CIRCULAR.

HUMPHREY, HASLER & CO.'S

Letter-Press Machines,

WITH PATENT FLYERS.

Working with great success.

PATENTED FOR AMERICA.

Nos.	Size inside bearers.	Prices.
1	18x12	$890
2	24x20	1,100
3	29x23	1,280
4	30x25	1,450
5	35x25	1,675
6	40x29	1,900
7	46x34	2,200
8	54x42	2,700

REFERENCES.

LUCAS & SON, Baltimore, (5 presses.)
B. SINGERLY, Harrisburg, Pa.

PATENT EXCELSIOR LITHOGRAPHIC MACHINES.

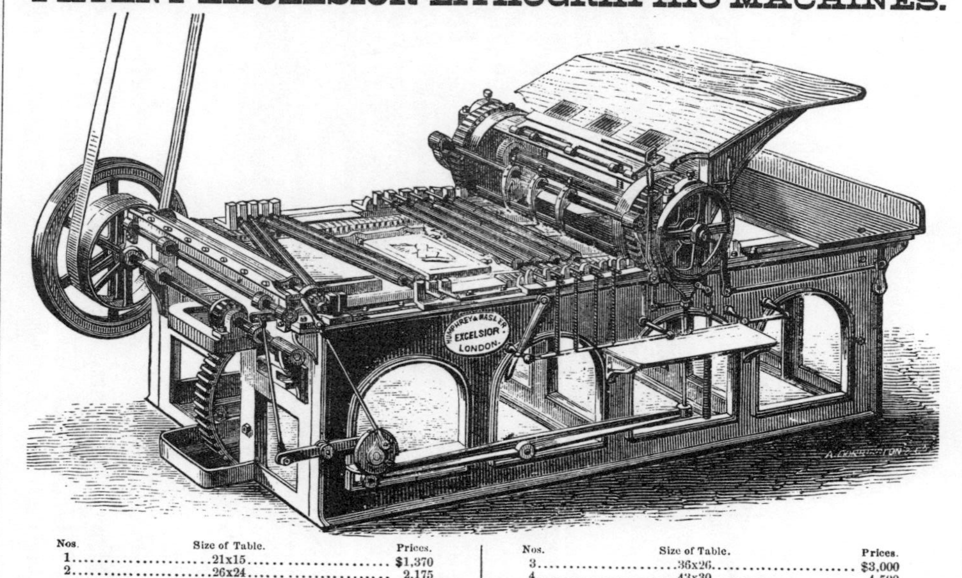

Nos.	Size of Table.	Prices.
1	21x15	$1,370
2	26x24	2,175
3	36x26	$3,000
4	43x30	4,500

The above prices include countershaft, hangers, pulleys, blanket, molds, two sets roller stocks, boxing, and delivered in New York; also, a liberal discount for cash sent with order. All rollers cover a full form.

HUMPHREY, HASLER & CO., 69 Old St., London, E.C.

Circa 1873

HIRD'S

PATENT

PNEUMATIC PAPER DELIVERER,

FOR LETTER PRESS AND LITHOGRAPHIC MACHINES.

The attention of Printers and Lithographers is called to the above important Invention, which has now been thoroughly tested, and proved to be the ONLY PERFECT DELIVERER for Printing Presses.

A. H. begs to inform the Trade that he has perfected an Apparatus for taking the sheets off the cylinder and delivering them to the usual board, thus saving any set-off from the tapes or cylinder, when cylinders are used, and dispensing with the taking-off boy, in those machines having no fly, saving the wages and general inconvenience attending that class of labor.

The Machine cannot easily get out of order, and never fails in taking the sheet off and placing it evenly on the board. It can be adjusted in less than two minutes from the largest to the smallest size sheet, thus making it invaluable for a jobbing office.

The working of it does not interfere with the printer attending to the stone or form, or getting it in or out of the Printing Machine,

THE ADVANTAGES OFFERED ARE AS FOLLOWS:

It is an effectual remedy for the set-off—the great annoyence to printers.
It dispenses with Boy labor, with its attendant inconveniences.
It can be adjusted to suit any size of sheet in one or two minutes.
It does not interfere with the Printer getting at the Form, Stone, Rollers, or any part of the Machine.
It is very simple, effective, and not liable to get out of order.
The Sheets are delivered on the usual board, printed side up, and perfectly straight.
It is an effectual remedy for smearing or finger-marks, however full the Sheet may be.
It requires no additional space.

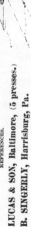

Circa 1880

MONTAGUE'S

PATENT PRINTING AND PAPER CUTTING MACHINERY.

The Only Cylinder Printing Machine

THAT CAN BE FED AND TURNED BY ONE PERSON.

A Boy of Sixteen can do the Work

AT A SPEED OF 1,000 IMPRESSIONS PER HOUR.

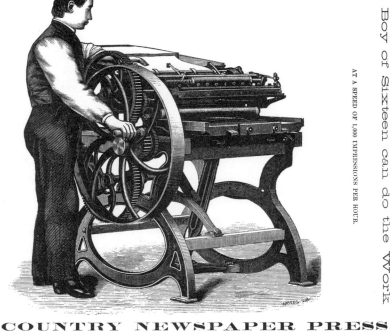

THE COUNTRY NEWSPAPER PRESS.

THIS PRESS require *less power* than any other, and can be easily turned by a boy. It will execute the best of Newspaper Work, and also Fine Book and Job Work. The Rolling and Distribution are superior, and great economy in wear of type is saved over other machines. An exact Illustration on Wood will be given in the May number of this Magazine. Each Press is furnished with a Rubber Blanket, two Setts Roller Stocks, Roller Molds, Ink Fountain, etc. Price $800. The cheapest machine in the market.

Circa 1866

MONTAGUE'S

PATENT PRINTING AND PAPER CUTTING MACHINERY.

The Only Cylinder Printing Machine

THAT CAN BE FED AND TURNED BY ONE PERSON.

A Boy of Sixteen can do the Work

AT A SPEED OF 1,000 IMPRESSIONS PER HOUR.

THE COUNTRY NEWSPAPER PRESS.

THE principle of this machine is the same as that of the Super-Royal press (represented by the above engraving), and it is confidently recommended as the BEST Country Newspaper and Job Press offered to the trade, without regard to price. The press is constructed in the best manner, all the gearing being cut instead of cast, as on other presses, and the machine therefore makes much less noise in operation, and there is no jar: no sacrifice of ink distribution or speed has been made in order to render it possible to operate the press by hand power. Operated by hand the press will print from 800 to 1,200 impressions per hour, and one man or boy can turn it more easily than any other Country Press. It is convenient for Job and Book work, the register is perfect, and rolling and ink distribution superior. The feeder can throw off or suspend the impression at will, a feature possessed by no other cylinder press. The press is complete, and no extra attachments are necessary for the execution of fine job work or delivery of the sheet. It prints a sheet 28x40 inches in size. Price delivered at shop, $800. Boxing, $25.

SUPER-ROYAL JOB & BOOK PRESS.

THE above engraving is a representation of our improved Super-Royal Press, bed 22x32 inches inside bearers. The machine is a universal job and book press, and will execute the finest character of work at a speed of from 1,000 to 1,500 impressions per hour. The press can be operated by hand as well as steam power, can be turned by a boy, and even turned and fed by the same person on short editions (see engraving). In operation the press makes very little noise, and no jar. Great improvements have been made in the construction of this press, and the manufacturers are confident that, both in durability and the execution of work, it will recommend itself and give entire satisfaction to the printer. The following are features of interest, most of which are peculiar to our presses, and are not possessed by any other:

The Machine may be accurately Fed and Turned by one person.
Perfect Register may be obtained.
Superior Rolling and Distributing Apparatus.
The Impression may be suspended at will.

Double or Treble Rolling of the Form may be had.
The Distribution of Ink may be made without taking Impression.
The Impression is very Slow in comparison with the Speed.
Rollers are of One Size, and Interchangeable—no Cloth Rollers used.

The Super-Royal Press occupies a space six feet square, including room for feeder and boy to turn the press. Weight 1,700 lbs. Price delivered at shop, $700. Boxing, $20.

Circa 1866

THE PIONEER PRESS

Circa 1892

COUNTRY PRINTING MACHINERY.

POTTER'S POWER PRINTING PRESSES,

No. 8 SPRUCE STREET, NEW YORK.

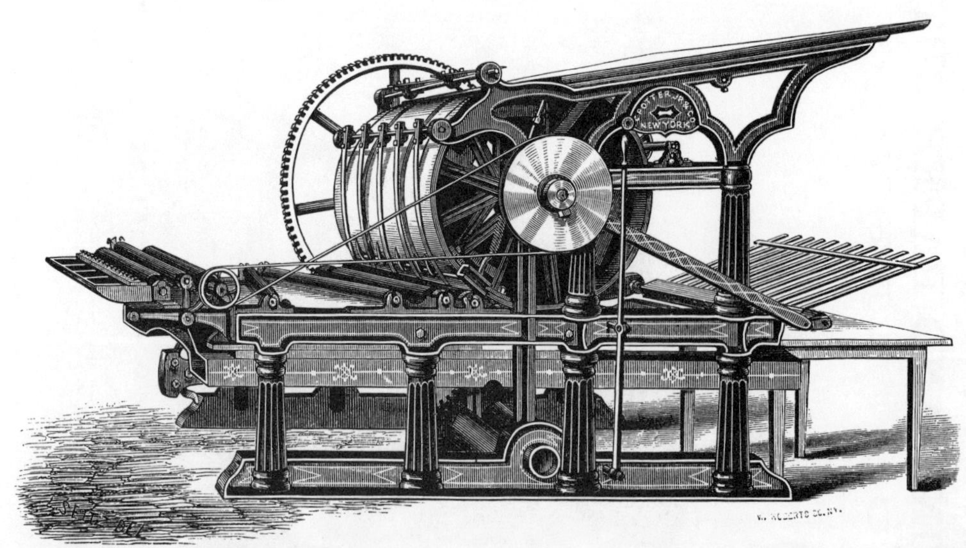

POTTER'S COUNTRY NEWSPAPER & JOB PRESS.

The particular features of this Machine are described on the adjoining page; in connection with which we are pleased to state that they are rapidly becoming popularized, not only with the Country Trade, but also with that of our largest Cities. Their convenience and adaptability to all classes of Printing make them general favorites wherever introduced. The Prices and Styles are as follow:

Country Newspaper and Job Press, 30×46 inside Bearers, with Table Distribution and without Fly .... $1,100.
do do do with Cylindrical and Table Distribution and with Fly .... 1,200.
do do do do with Bunter Springs and Steam Fixtures .. 1,300.
Cone Pulleys, Shafting, and Two Hangers .... $50. Boxing and Shipping .... 50.

Circa 1866

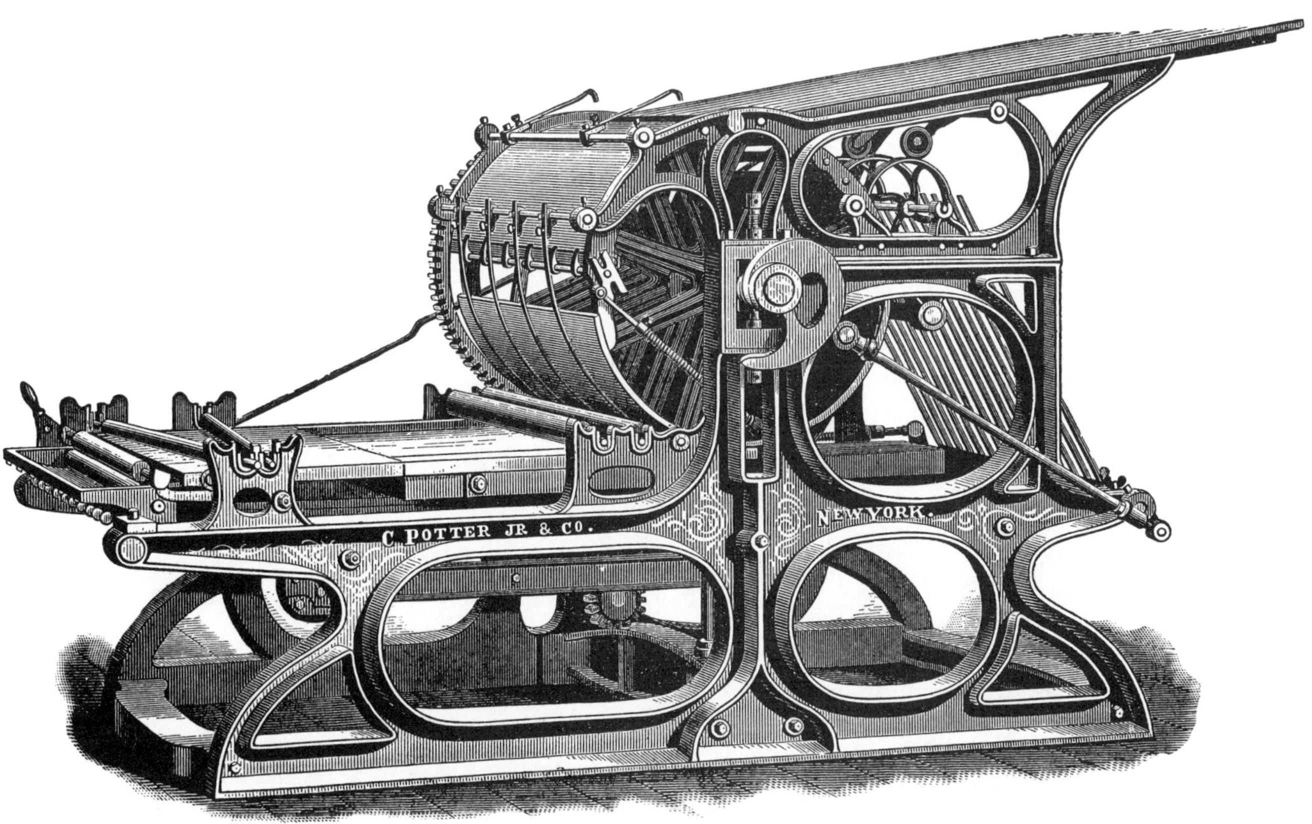

Potter "Country Drum" – 2 roller, table distribution, tape delivery, springs under bed.

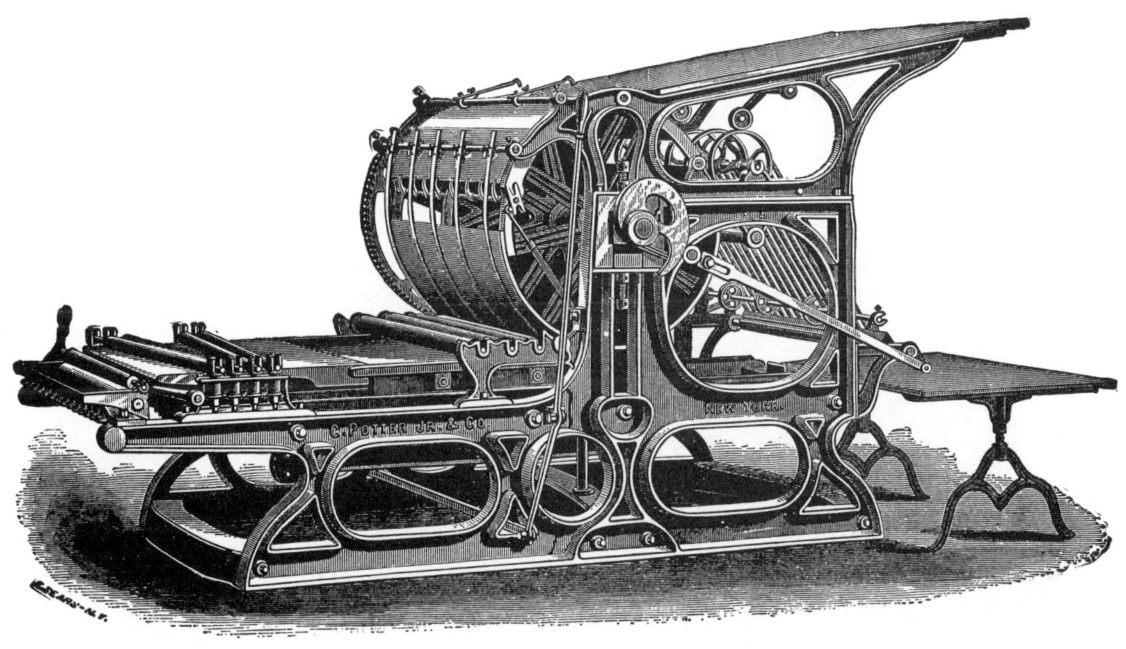

Potter "Country Drum" – 3 roller, table distribution, tape delivery, springs under bed.

THE BEST COUNTRY PRESS EVER MADE FOR THE PRICE.

Potter's Improved Country Presses

FOR NEWSPAPER AND JOB WORK.

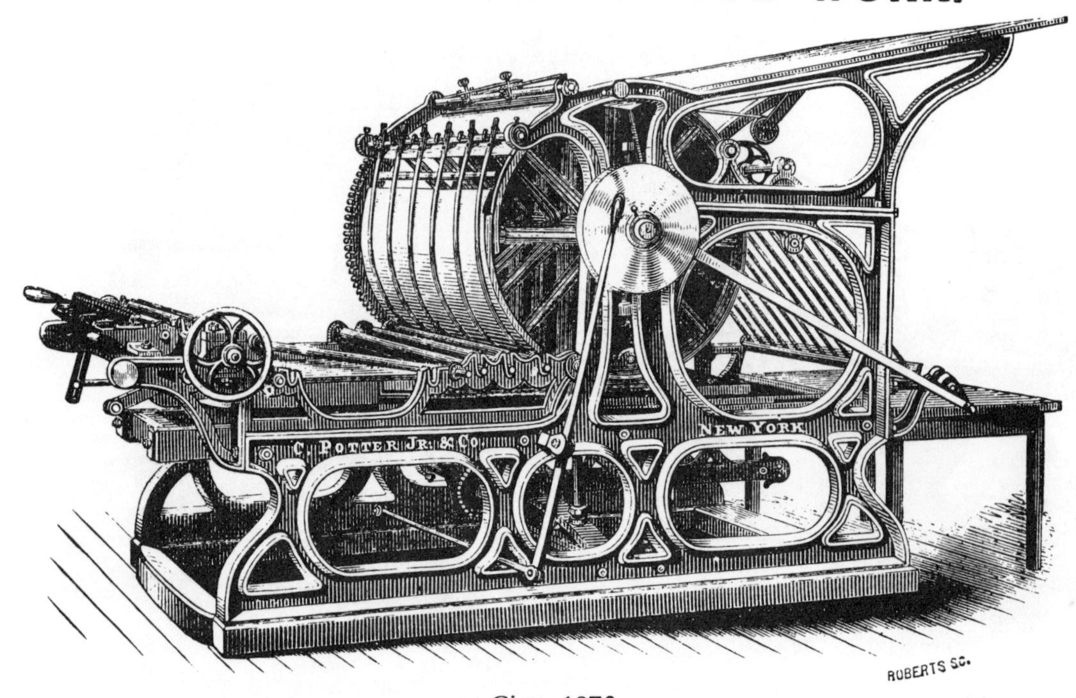

Circa 1873

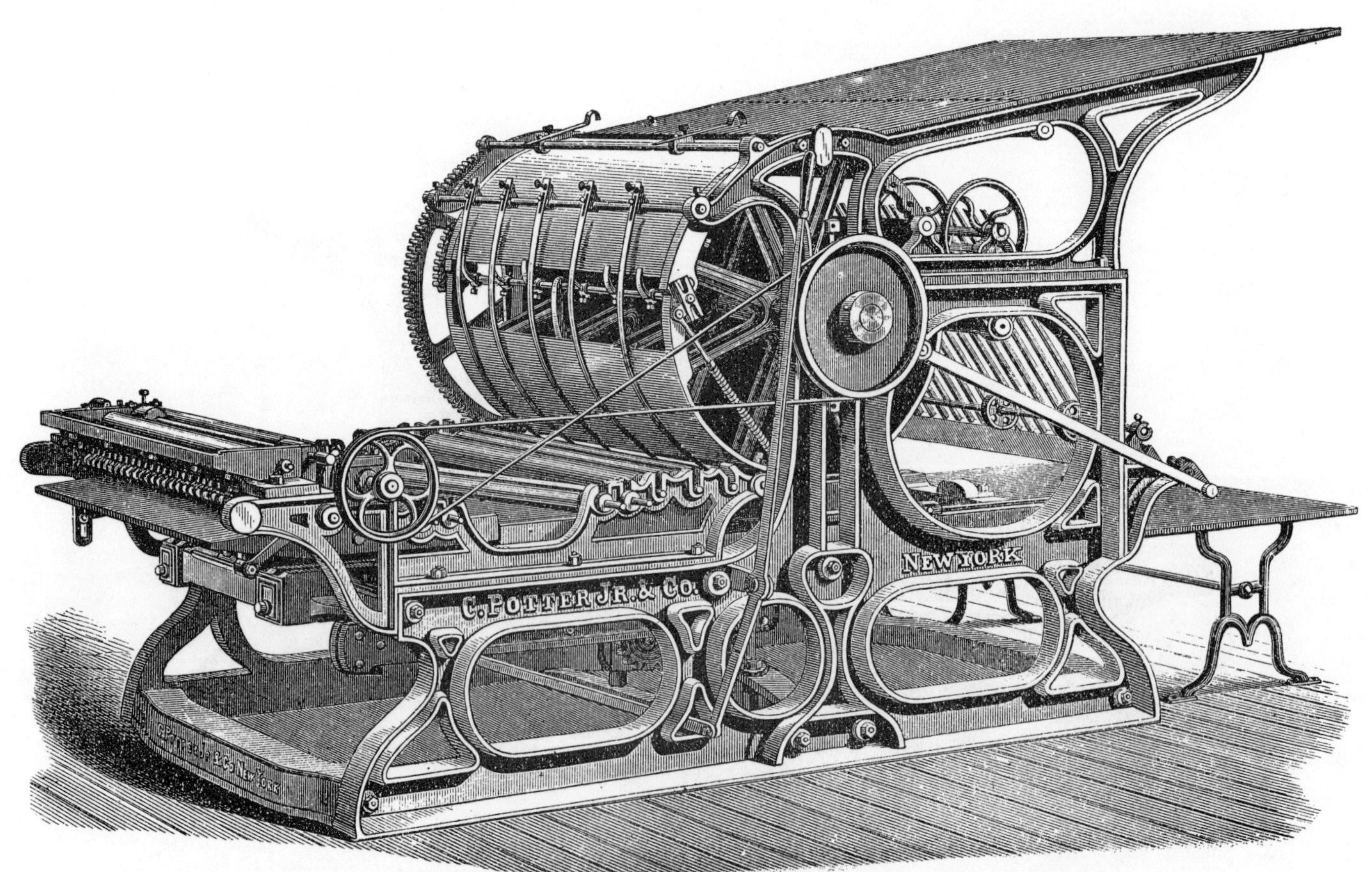

Potter "Improved Country" – 3 roller, belt, cylinder and table distribution,
Wire springs under bed, tape delivery. Circa 1870

POTTER'S POWER PRINTING PRESSES

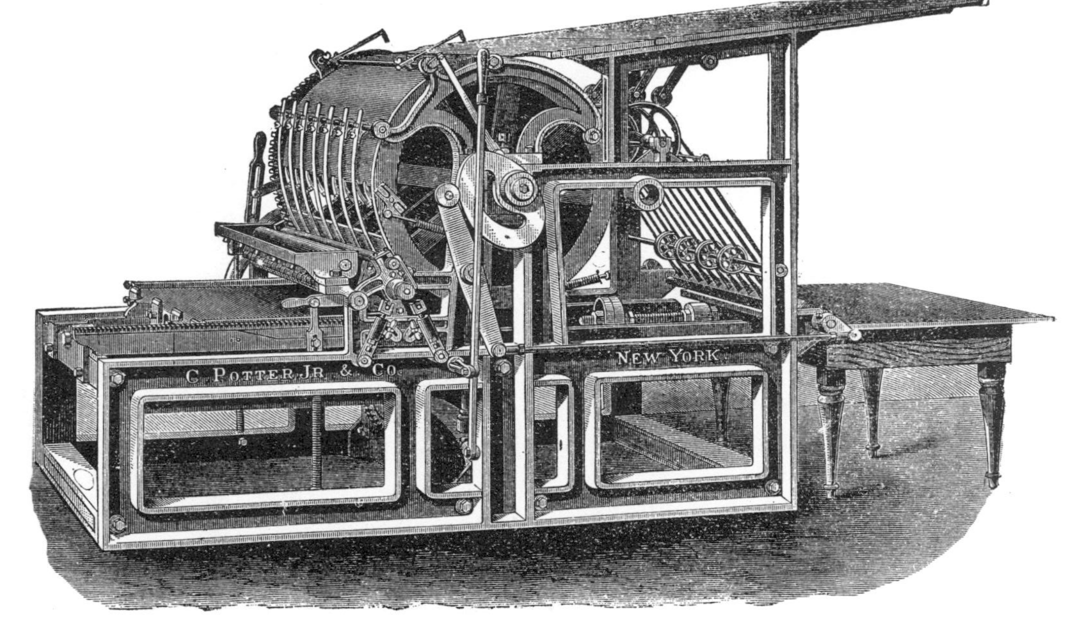

Above we give a cut of our FOUR-ROLLER DRUM CYLINDER PRESS, with Rack and Screw Distribution. We also make them with TABLE or TABLE, RACK AND SCREW Distribution, as may be desired by our customers. Presses for fine colored work, with perfect Register, made a specialty. We believe our presses have a reputation second to none in this or any other country, and we point with feelings of laudable pride to the extensive patronage with which the Craft have favored us, and to one other fact: that, although we have over FOUR HUNDRED OF OUR PRESSES IN USE, there is not to-day a single one of them that is for sale as a second-hand press.

The following are some of the reasons why our presses are preferred before all others:—

First—They are the best. Second—They are the strongest. Third—They are the Heaviest. Fourth—They have Potter's Patent Bunter Spring. Fifth—They are for that reason the smoothest running. Sixth—They are the easiest running. Seventh—They are the fastest running. Eighth—They make the best register. Ninth—They do the best work. Tenth—They are the best presses made on this or any other continent. Eleventh—They are cheaper than any other first-class press. Twelfth—They are warranted fully as above.

FIRST-CLASS PRESSES.

SIZES AND PRICES:

WITH PATENT BUNTER SPRINGS.

No. 0	20×25		$1,275
No. 0 ex.	21×27		1,475
No. 1	24×30		1,700
No. 1	24×30	Extra Heavy	1,800
No. 2	25×35		1,850
No. 2	25×35	Extra Heavy	2,000
No. 3	31×46		2,200
No. 3	31×46	Extra Heavy	2,500
No. 4	32×48		2,400
No. 4	32×50	Extra Heavy	2,700
No. 5	34×52		2,600
No. 5	34×52	Extra Heavy	2,900
No. 6	40×54	Extra Heavy	3,200
No. 7	40×60	Extra Heavy	3,500

COUNTRY PRESSES.

SIZES AND PRICES:

TABLE AND CYLINDRICAL DISTRIBUTION.

No. 3	31×46	Hand Power	$1,200
No. 4	32×50	"	1,300
No. 5	34×52	"	1,700

RACK AND SCREW DISTRIBUTION.

No. 3	31×46	Hand Power	$1,450
No. 4	32×50	"	1,550
No. 5	34×52	"	1,750

For Steam Power, extra, $50.—Boxing and Cartage, $50.

Each Press is furnished with Blanket, Wrenches, two Roller Molds, nine Roller Stocks for Table Press, and six Stocks for Rack and Screw.

Extra Heavy First-Class Presses, Four Rollers Over a Full Form.

No. 1	24×30	$2,200
No. 2	25×35	2,400
No. 3	31×46	$3,100
No. 4	32×50	3,300

Counter Shaft, 2 Hangers, 2 Cone Pulleys, and 1 Driving Pulley, $50.—Boxing and Cartage, No. 0, $25, other sizes, $50.

Each Press is furnished with Rubber Blanket, set of Wrenches, Screw Driver, two Roller Molds, and two sets of Roller Stocks.

C. POTTER, Jr., & COMPANY,

No. 10 SPRUCE STREET, NEW YORK.

TERMS CASH.

C. POTTER, Jr. ALL MACHINERY SHIPPED FROM THE SHOP, AT NORWICH, CONN. J. F. HUBBARD.

Circa 1870

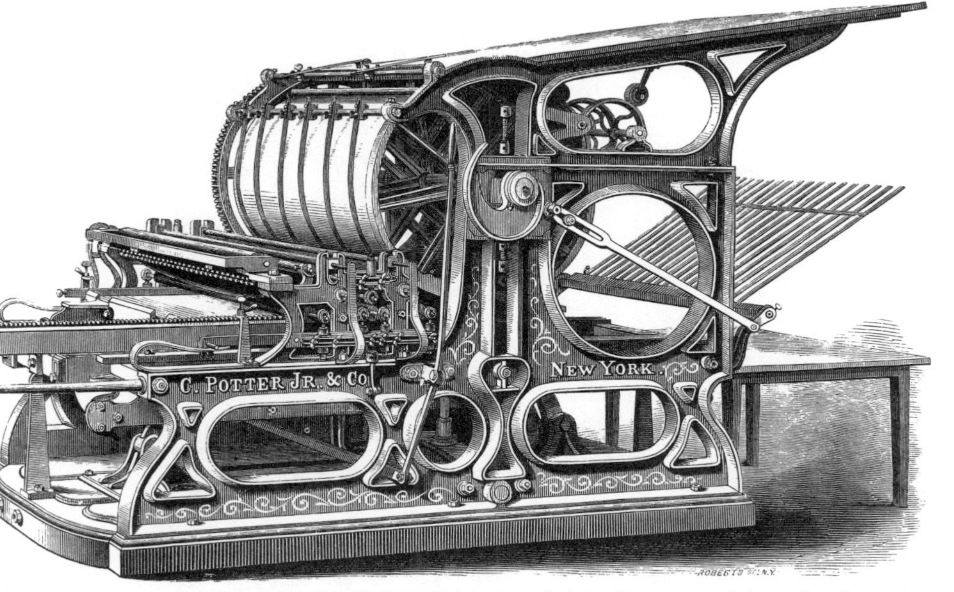

Potter "Country" New Series – 2 roller, rack and screw distribution, tape delivery, air springs. Circa 1886

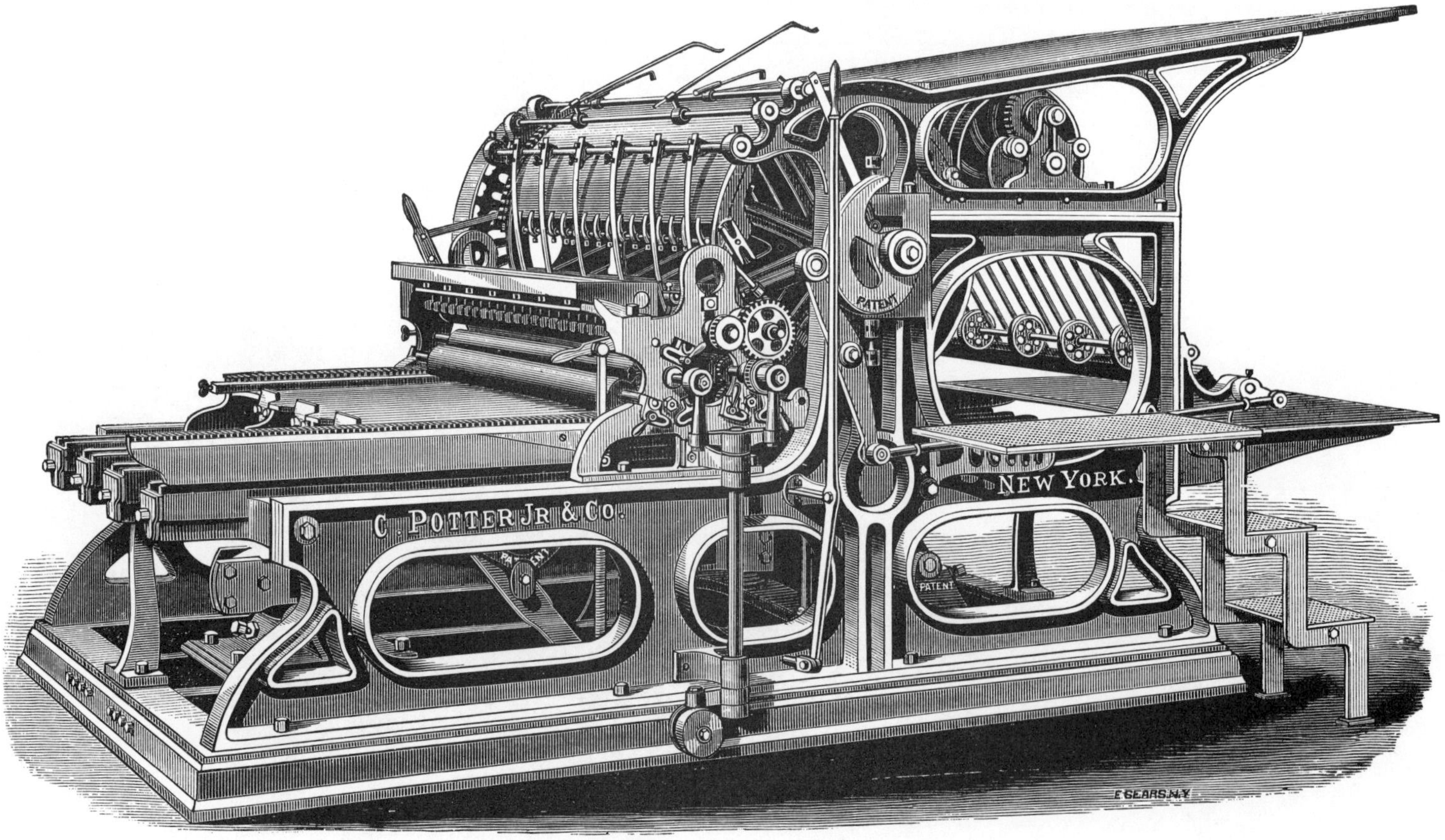

Potter "Combination" slow down – 4 roller, rack and cam distribution, rear tapeless delivery, wire springs.

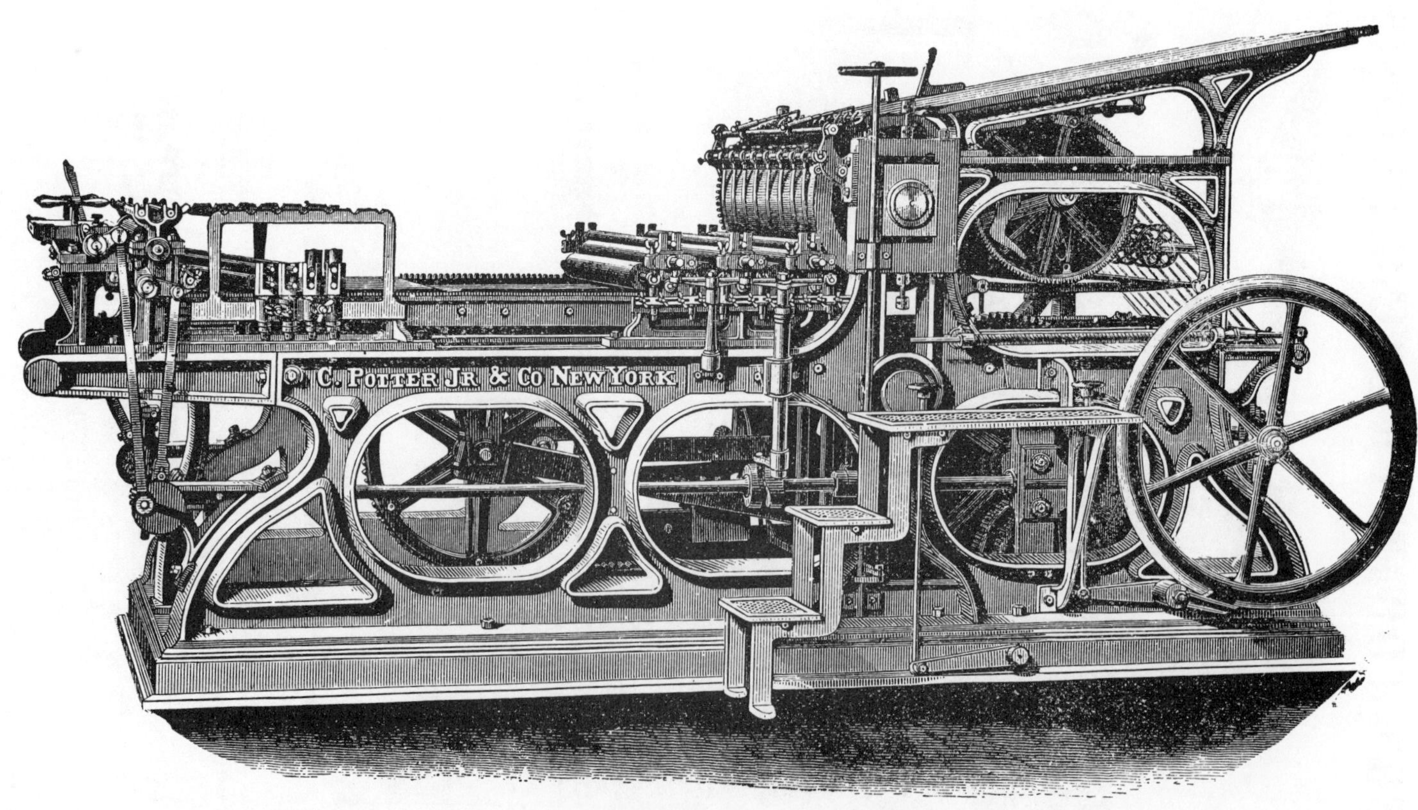

Potter Stop Cylinder – 6 roller, rack, cam and table distribution, rear tapeless delivery, impression trip and back-up.

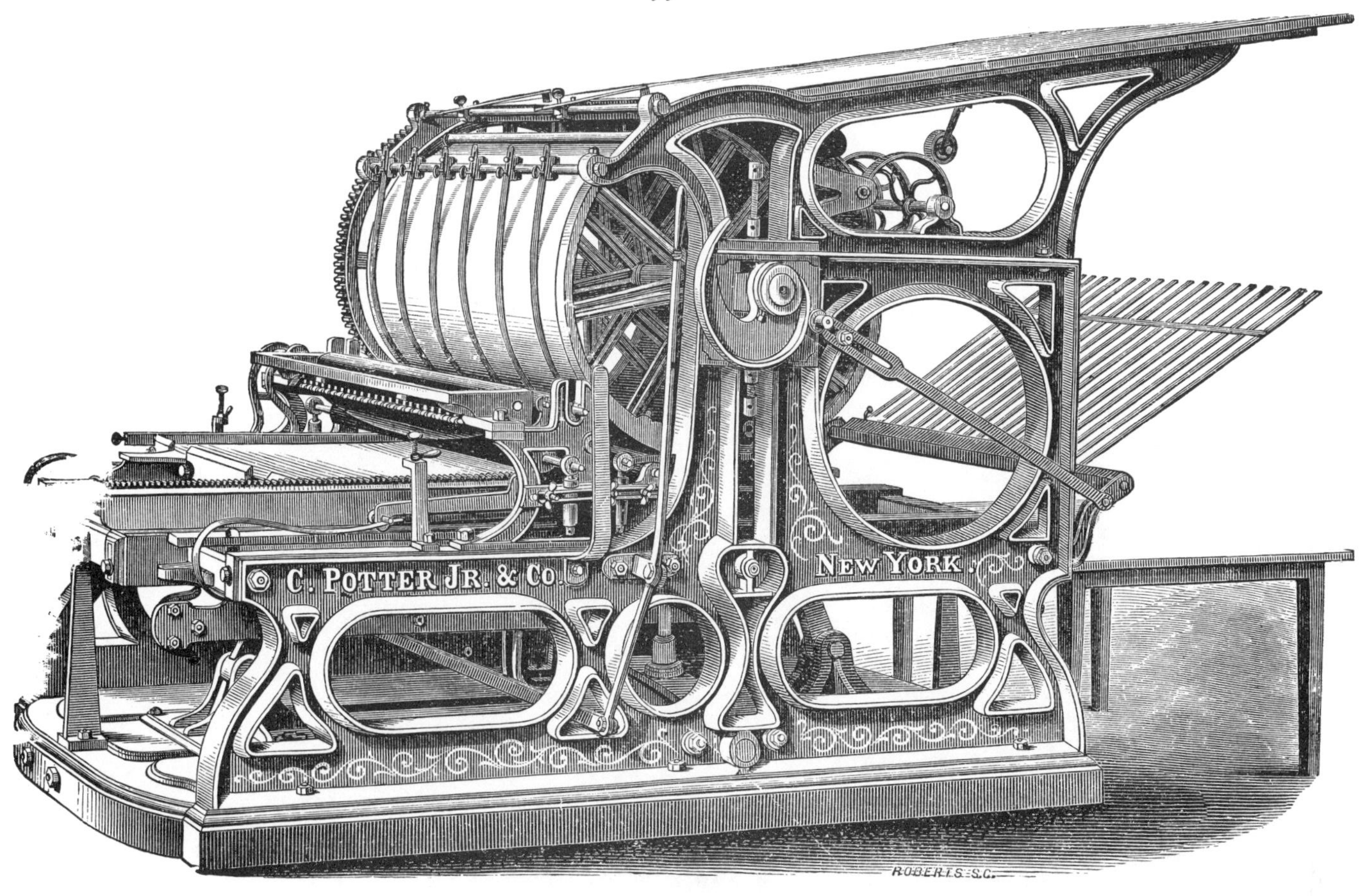

Potter "First-Class" Drum – 2 roller, wire springs in base, rack and screw distribution, tape delivery. Ca. 1880.

Potter "First-Class" Drum – 2 roller, rack and screw distribution, tapeless delivery, air springs and back-up.

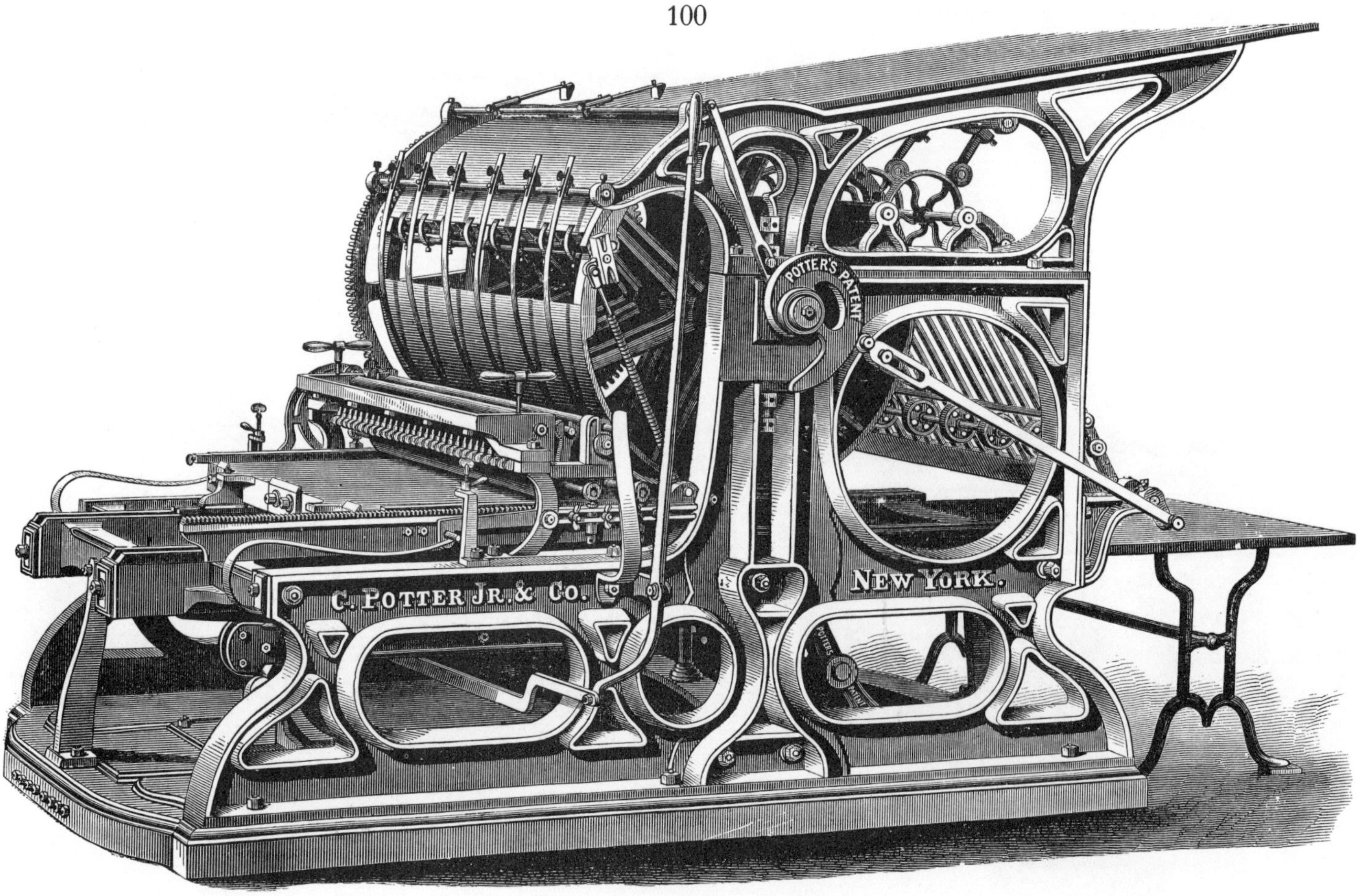

Potter "First-Class" Drum – 2 roller, wire springs in base, rack and screw distribution, tape delivery. Ca. 1880.

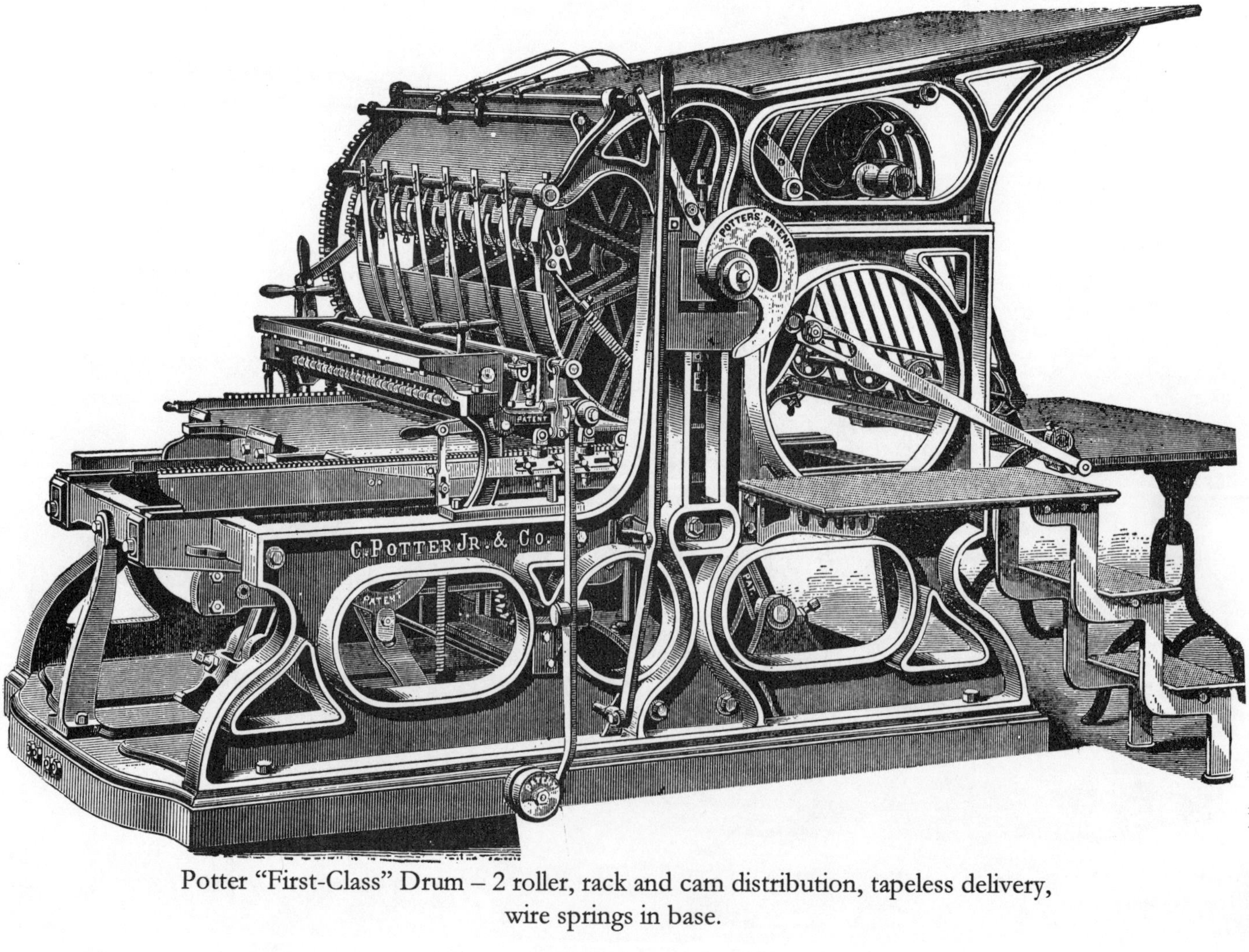

Potter "First-Class" Drum – 2 roller, rack and cam distribution, tapeless delivery, wire springs in base.

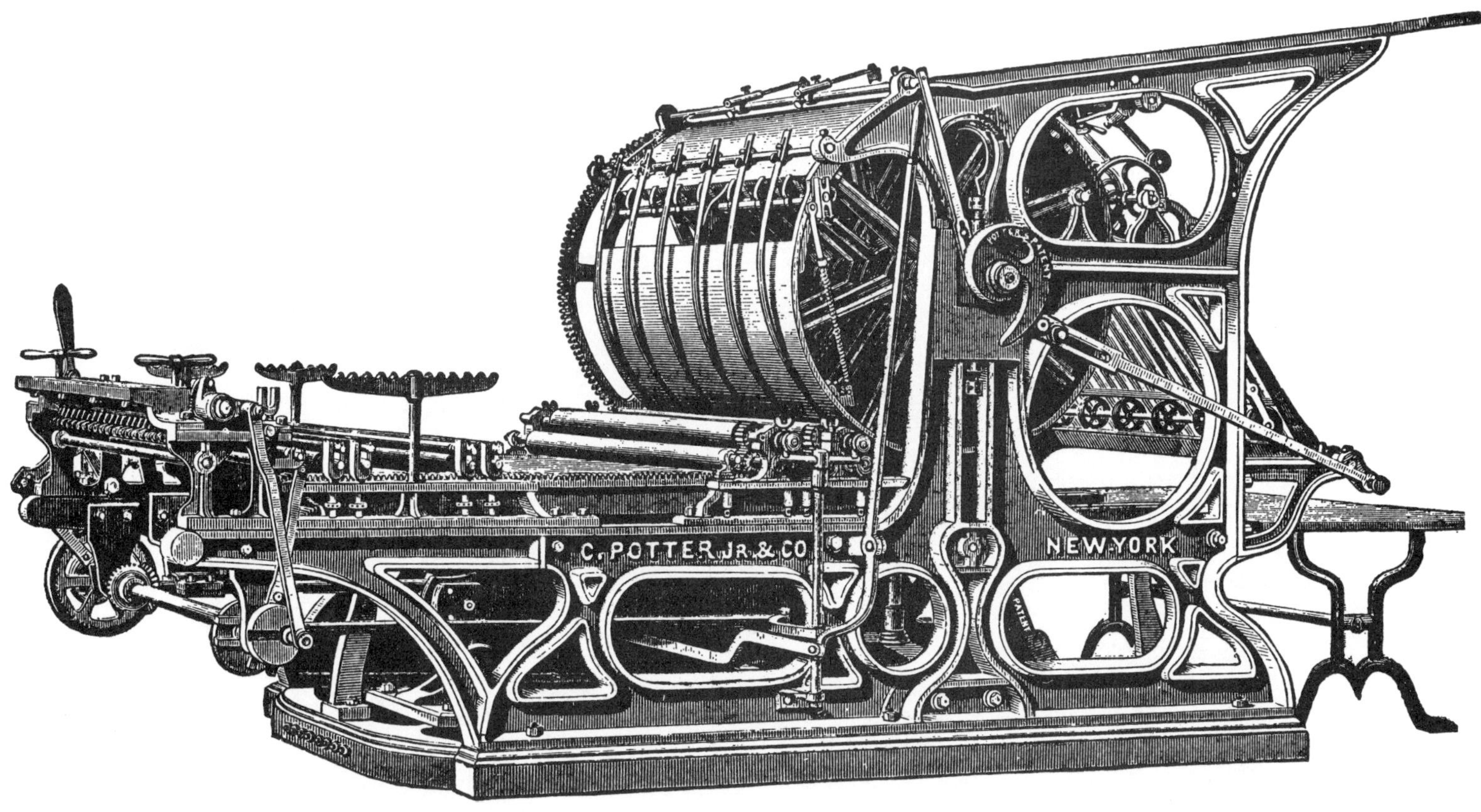

Potter "First-Class" Drum – 4 roller, rack, cam and table distribution, tape delivery, wire springs in base.

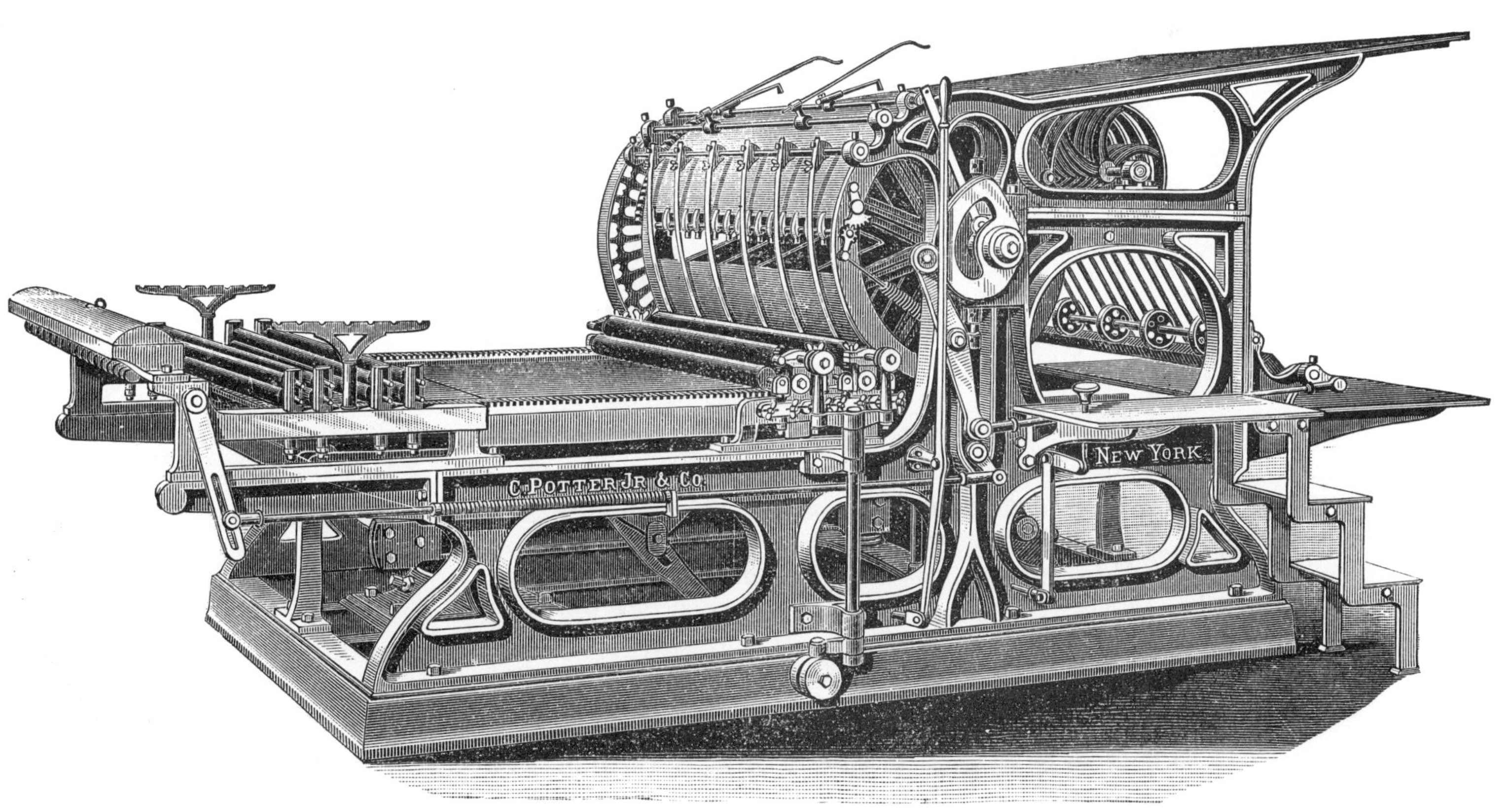

Potter "First-Class" Drum – 4 roller, rack, cam and table distribution, tapeless delivery, wire springs in base.

C. POTTER, JR. & CO.,

— MANUFACTURERS OF —

Web-Perfecting, Lithographic, Two-Revolution,

LARGE CYLINDER and COUNTRY

PRESSES

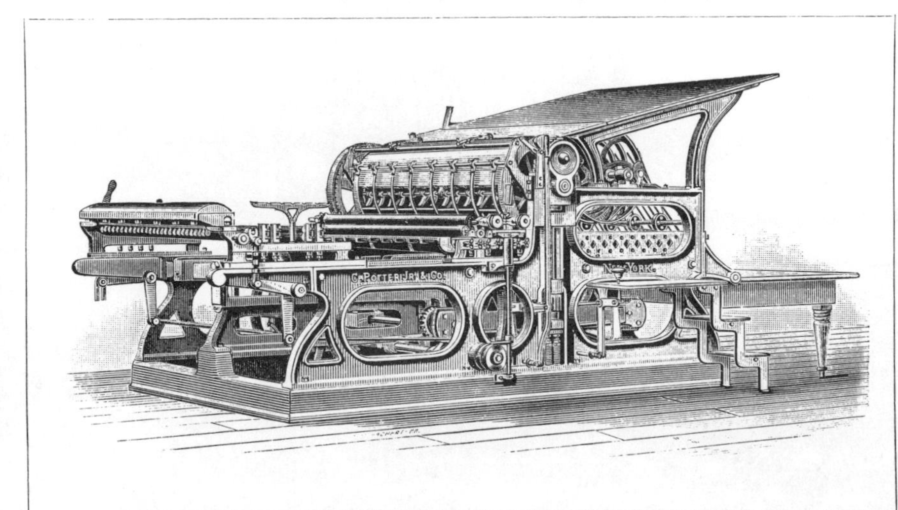

OF LATEST AND MOST IMPROVED STYLES.

OFFICE: Nos. 12 & 14 SPRUCE STREET, NEW YORK.

SEND FOR CATALOGUE.

Circa 1886

C. POTTER, JR. & CO'S

12-14 SPRUCE STREET,
NEW YORK.

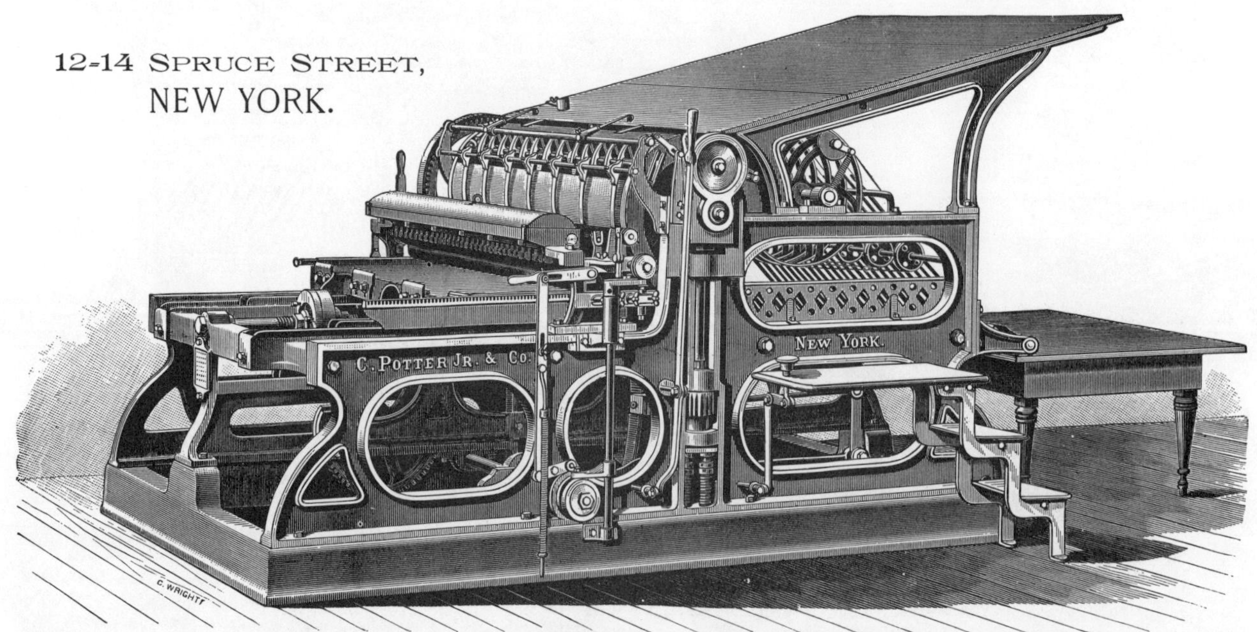

PATENT IMPROVED TWO-REVOLUTION PRESS

WITH patented mechanism for controlling the vertical movement of the impression cylinder. It is extremely powerful, accurately fitted, free from friction and evenly balanced. A patented automatic device is also provided which prevents lost motion, and governs the degree of impression. Its patent reversing mechanism consisting of a cross-belt and spring shifter, is operated by the foot, which places the Press under the immediate control of the feeder. These advantages, with its Sheet Delivery, Hinged Distributer, Caps, Positive Slide Motion, Noiseless Grippers, etc., complete a printing machine that in every respect is equal to the most exacting demands of the times.

The SCOTT LATEST IMPROVED NEWS and JOB DRUM CYLINDER PRINTING PRESS

The above illustration shows our new drum cylinder press which we have designed to meet the demands for the best possible press for newspapers in the smaller cities and towns. It has many features exclusively our own, a full description of which is given on the reverse side of this circular.

PATENTED AND MANUFACTURED BY

WALTER SCOTT & CO.,

DAVID J. SCOTT, General Manager

Main Office and Factory: PLAINFIELD, NEW JERSEY, U. S. A.

CABLE ADDRESS: WALTSCOTT, NEW YORK. CODES USED: ABC (5th EDITION) AND OUR OWN

CHICAGO OFFICE:
Monadnock Block

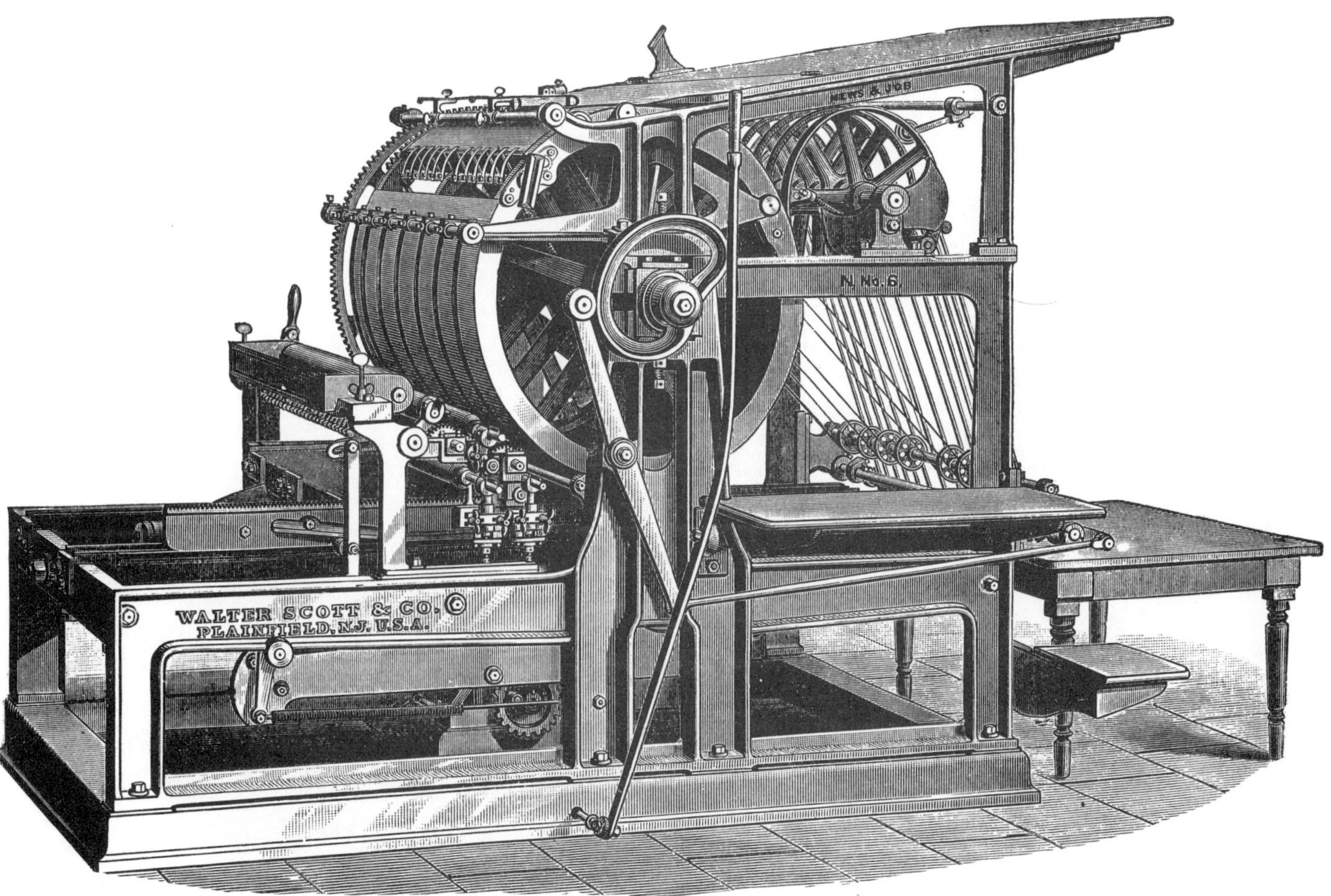

Scott “News and Job” – 2 roller, rack and screw distribution, tape delivery, air springs.

Scott Two-Revolution Printing Machine

Two Revolution, Stop-Cylinder, Single Cylinder, Lithographic and Roll-Feed Perfecting Printing Machines, Paper Folders, Etc.

OSTRANDER & HUKE, 81 and 83 Jackson Street, Chicago, Western Agents.

Circa 1886

The . . . . SCOTT Book and Job Printing Machine.

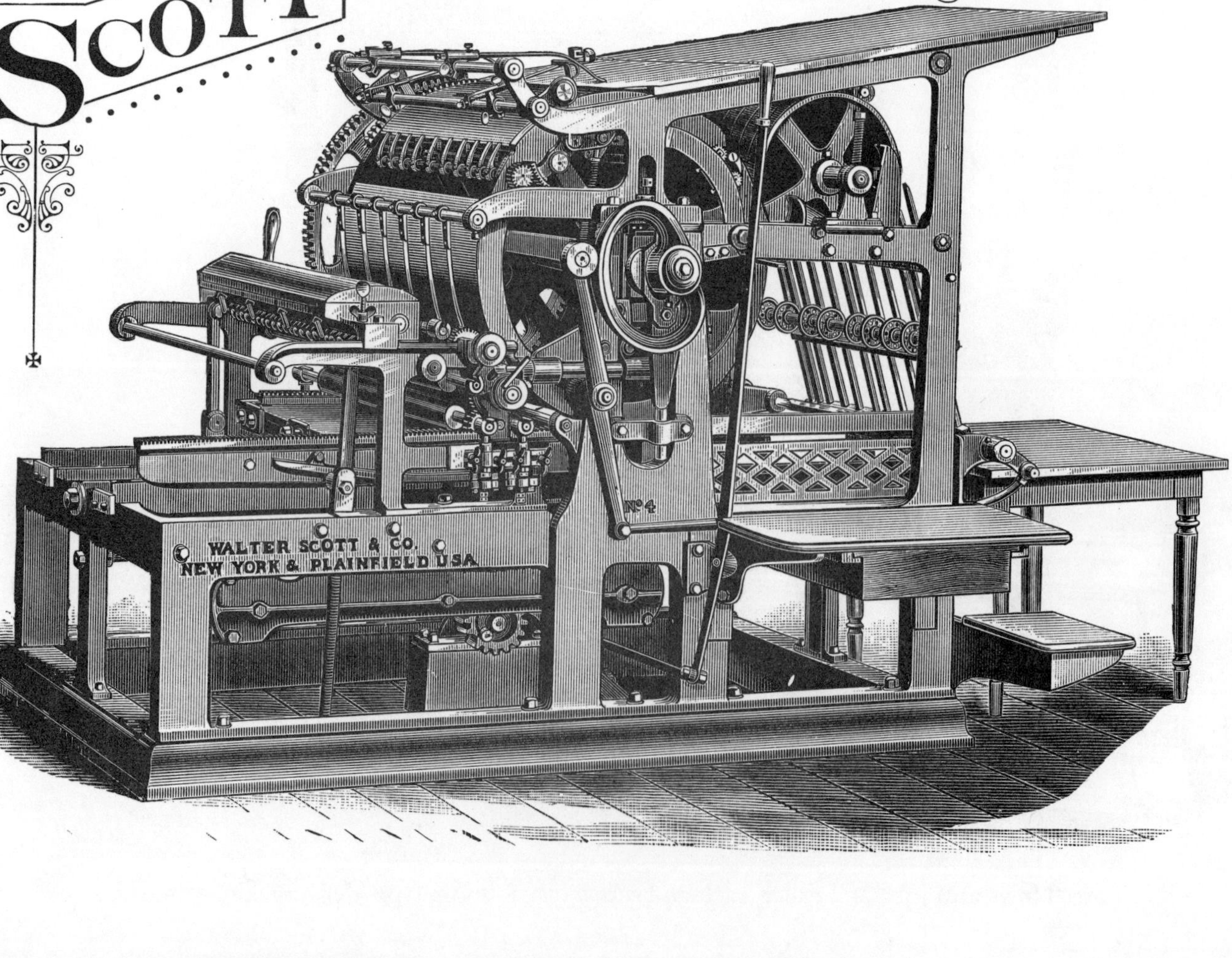

The Scott Stop-Cylinder Printing Machine.

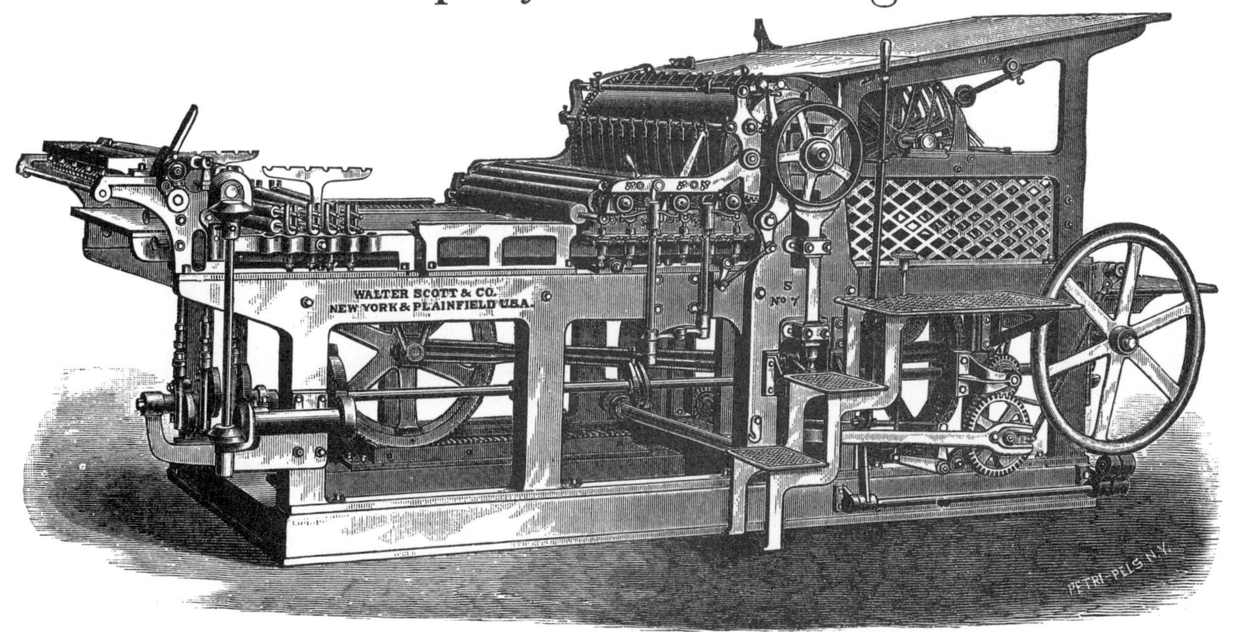

WALTER SCOTT & CO.

PLAINFIELD, N. J.

Plainfield is forty minutes' ride on the Central Railroad of New Jersey. Depot—foot of Liberty Street, New York.

MANUFACTURERS OF

Two-Revolution, Stop-Cylinder, Single-Cylinder, Lithographic and Roll-Feed Perfecting Printing Machines, Paper Folders, etc., etc.

Scott Two-Revolution – 4 roller, rack, cam and table distribution, rear tapeless delivery, air springs, impression trip, hinged roller frame.

The Scott Flat Bed Perfecting Printing Machine

Our Two-Cylinder, Two-Revolution, Flat Bed Perfecting Machine,

WITH TWO FORM ROLLERS TO EACH CYLINDER.

Circa 1892

The Scott Stop-Cylinder Printing Machine.

Class I. H.

Scott Stop-Cylinder Flatbed Press with six form rollers. The bed reversing mechanism occupies the entire area under the feedboard. Circa 1898.

THE A. B. TAYLOR
PRINTING PRESS AND MACHINE CO.

OFFICE AND MANUFACTORY,

Nos. 1, 3, 5, and 7 HAGUE STREET, and 369 PEARL STREET, NEW YORK.

ESTABLISHED IN 1842.

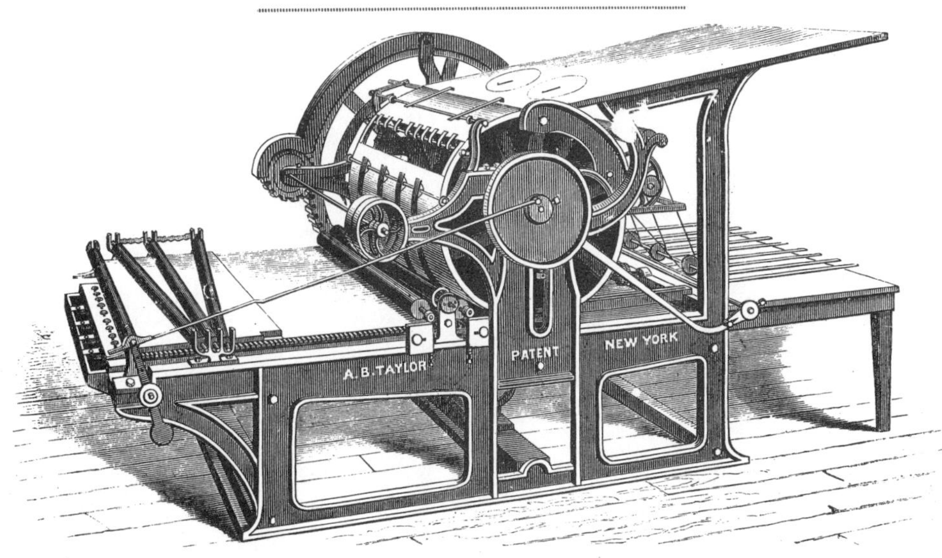

IMPROVED LARGE CYLINDER BOOK AND JOB PRESSES.

These highly improved Printing Machines have advantages of Distribution beyond any others in existence. When steam is impracticable, they can be conveniently run by hand. They are furnished with all the modern improvements, and are particularly designed for the finest quality of work. They have Registering and Sheet Flying apparatus attached, and with each Machine is furnished, included in the price, two sets of Roller Stocks, Blanket, Roller Molds, Counter Shaft, two Hangers, Driving Pulley, two Cone Pulleys, and boxing and shipping or carting and putting up in New York.

SIZES AND PRICES:

No. 1—Bed 56×44 inches.........$3,240	No. 4—Bed 50×31 inches.........$2,750	No. 7—Bed 33×25 inches.........$1,828
No. 2—Bed 54×40 inches......... 3,120	No. 5—Bed 46×31 inches......... 2,470	No. 8—Bed 28×23 inches......... 1,565
No. 3—Bed 52×34 inches......... 2,935	No. 6—Bed 41×29 inches......... 2,320	No. 9—Bed 24×19 inches......... 1,182

Circa 1842

Taylor Double Cylinder Press manufactured by A. B. Taylor Printing Press & Machine Co. of New York City. Circa 1842

Taylor "Chicago" Regular Style – 2 roller, vibrator and table distribution, tapeless delivery, air springs, power.

Taylor's automatic feeder installed on an A. B. Taylor Perfecting Press. The feeder can be seen directly under the suspended delivery board. Circa 1857.

Taylor "Chicago" Late Style – 2 roller, vibrator and table distribution, tapeless delivery, double air springs.

Taylor Drum Cylinder Press

Taylor "Chicago" two-roller hand powered drum cylinder press made in two sizes; 32 x 46" and 33 x 50". This press was designed for the country newspaper market. Circa 1887.

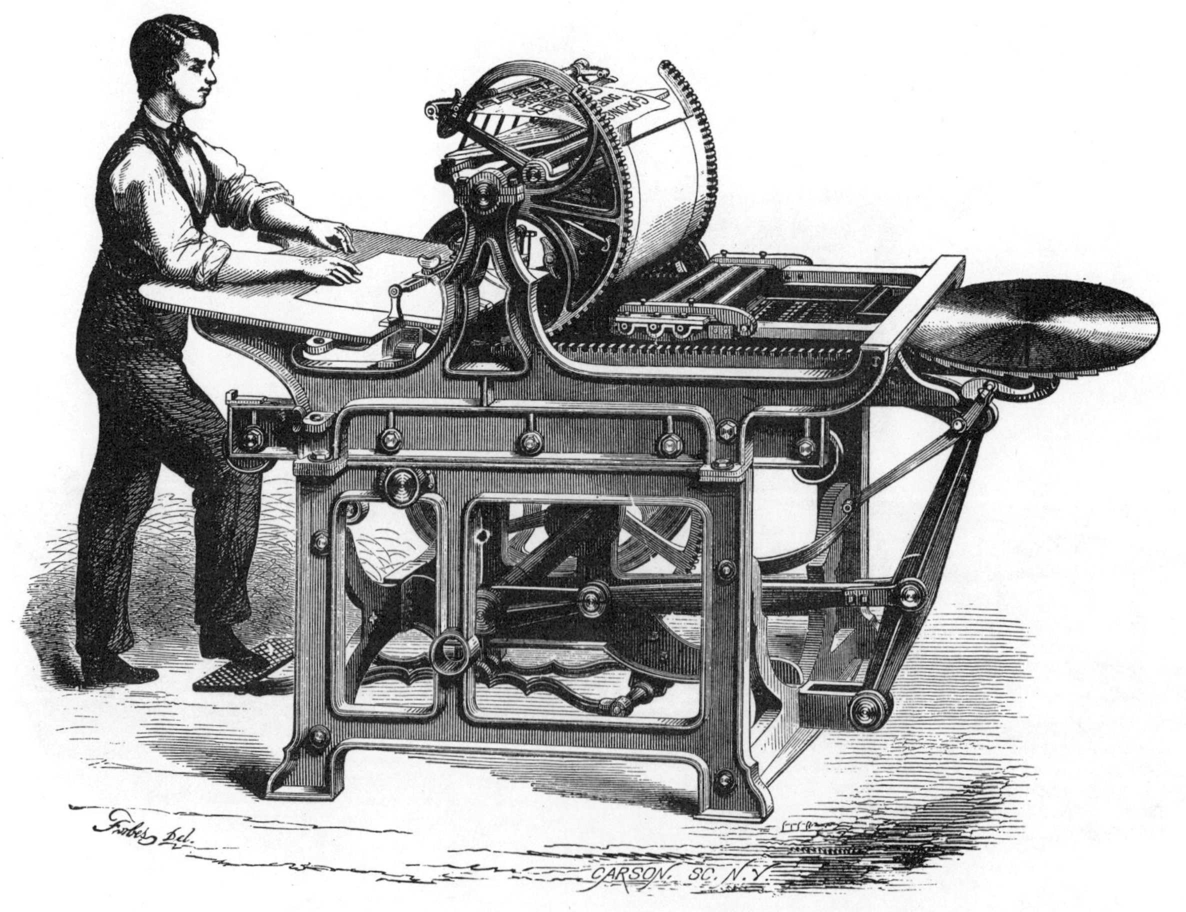

Unidentified, unusual press with a half cylinder. Circa 1865.

THE CELEBRATED

PROUTY ✣ CYLINDER

News, Job and Book Presses.

Write for Terms and Cash Discounts on the Five Roller News and Job Press and the New Eight Roller Combination Book Press.

THESE PRESSES WILL SAVE YOU FROM $500 TO $1,500.

SPLENDID BARGAINS IN WASHINGTON PRESSES AND JOBBERS.

WRITE TO

W. G. WALKER & CO., Sole Proprietors, MADISON, WIS.

Improved Job and Book Rapid Cylinder Press manufactured by George W. Prouty & Co.
in Boston, Massachusetts. Circa 1878

THE WONDERFUL PROUTY PRINTING PRESS

SHIPPED INTO ELEVEN STATES IN PAST THIRTY DAYS.

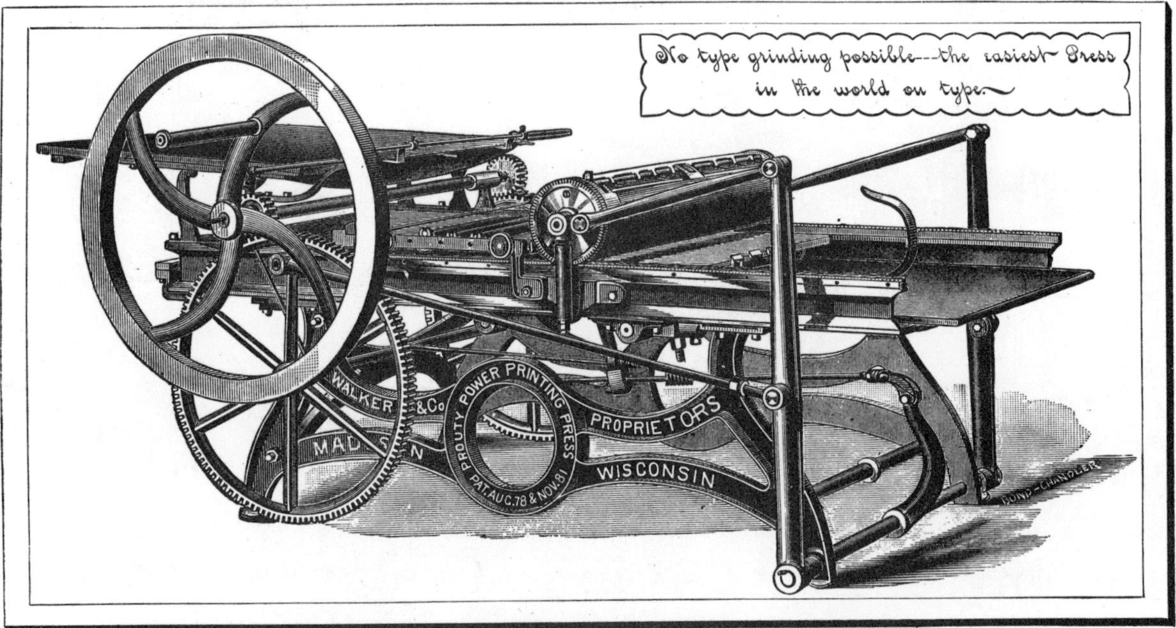

IF YOU EXAMINE A PROUTY YOU WILL BUY IT, AND SO SAVE MONEY.
NO TAPES, PULLEYS OR FLIERS. PERFECT REGISTER AND DISTRIBUTION.

Circa 1863

Prouty "Standard" without gears on ends of cylinder.

Prouty "Monona" Press manufactured by W. G. Walker & Co. in Madison, Wisconsin.

"Monona" Leverless News Press by W. G. Walker & Co.

"Madison King" News Press manufactured by W. G. Walker & Co.

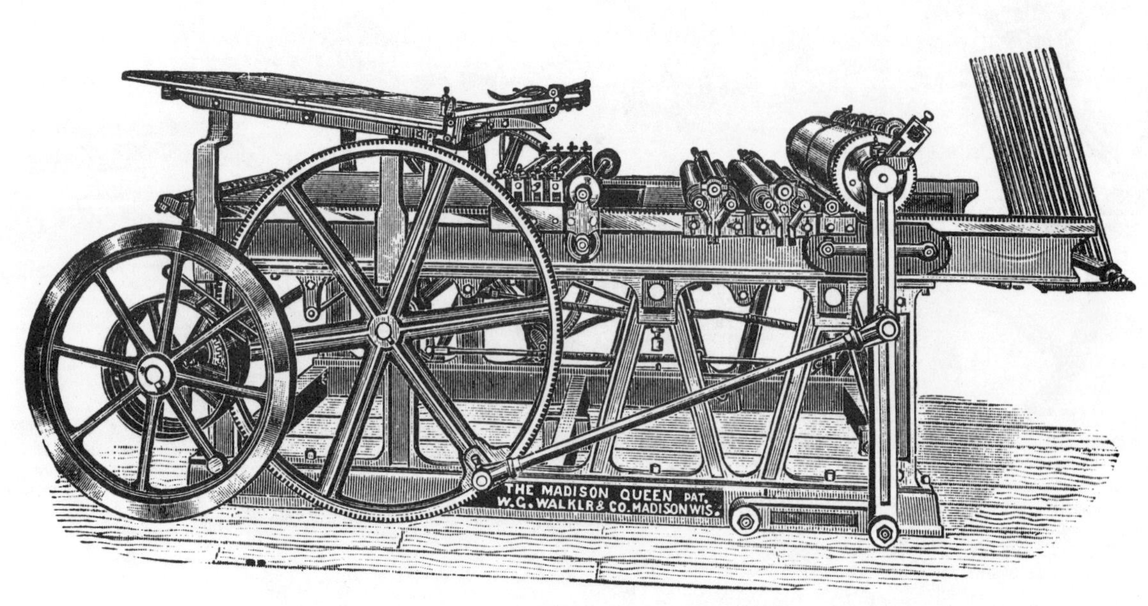

Walker & Co. "Madison Queen" Press.

Prouty "Standard" Newspaper Press.

Prouty "Improved" Job and Book Press with cylinder and inking rollers traveling over a stationary bed, with fly delivery. Circa 1886.

WHITLOCK JOB & BOOK PRESS

AS SHOWN BELOW

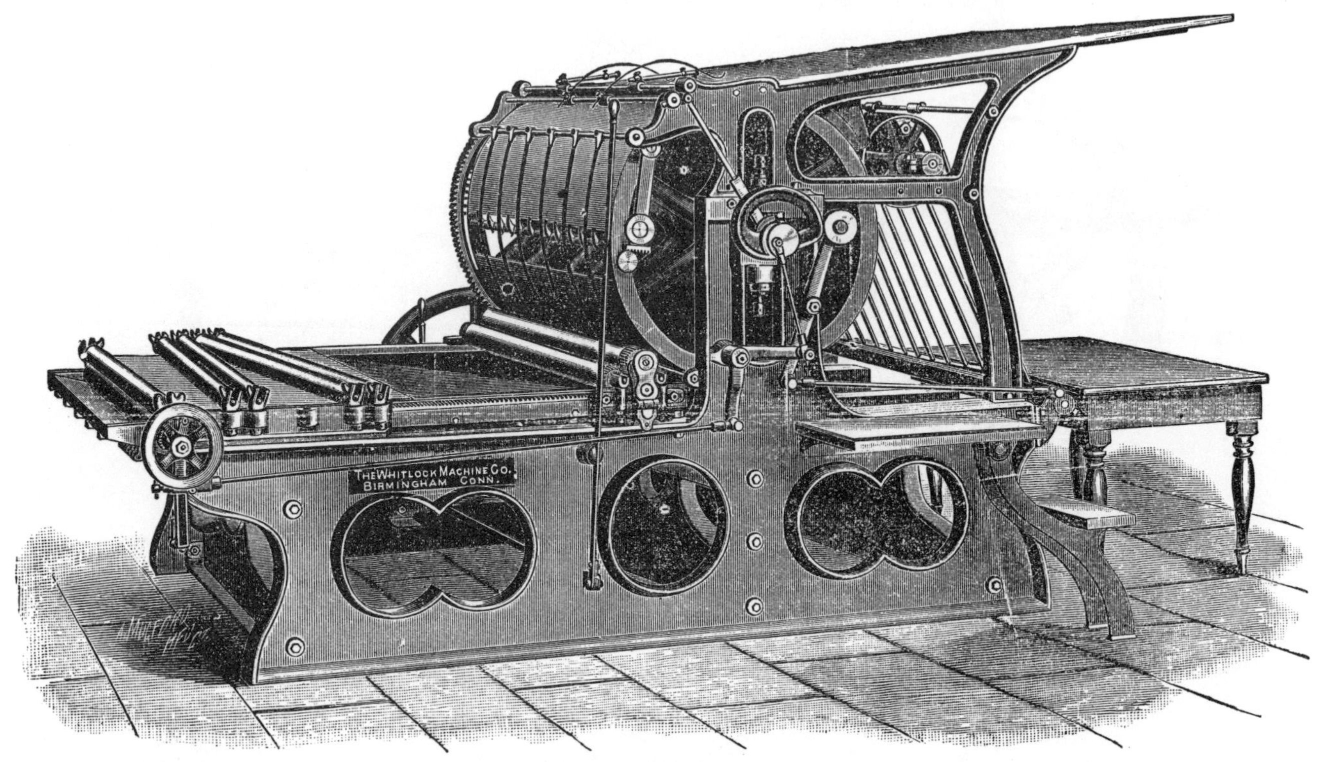

Circa 1890

Whitlock "Country" Drum Press – 2 roller, rack, cam and table distribution, tape delivery.

Whitlock Two-Revolution Napier Motion – 4 roller, rack, screw and table distribution, air springs, front delivery.

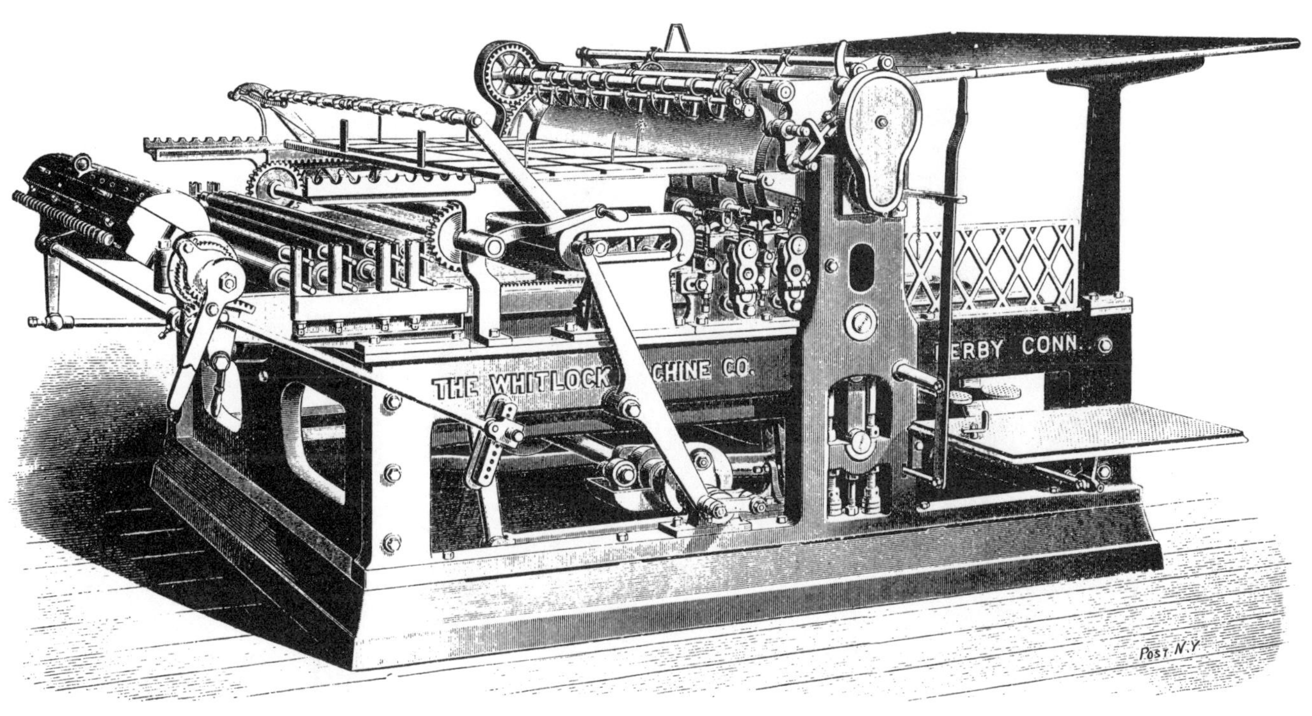

Whitlock Press – long frame, front-delivery, two revolution flatbed cylinder press. Circa 1895

THE "DIAMOND" CYLINDER PRINTING MACHINE,

ADAPTED FOR

BOOKWORK, BROADSIDES, NEWSPAPERS, AND GENERAL JOBBING.

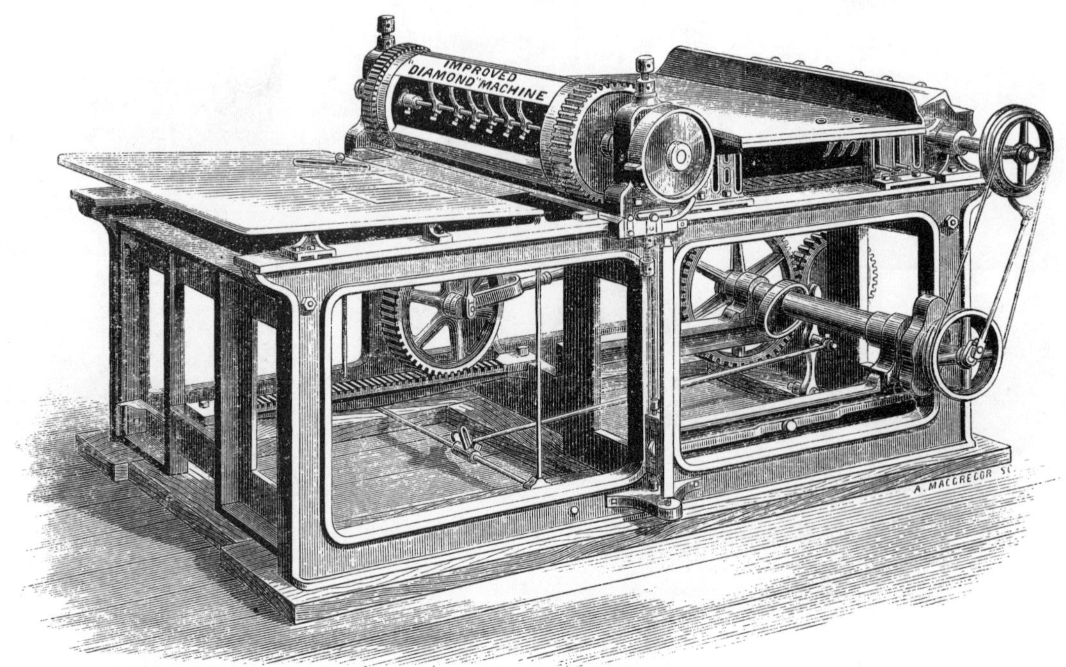

Manufactured by the "Victory" Printing and Folding Machine Manufacturing Company, Limited.

Circa 1873

Unidentified second-hand machine on the market in 1863 at "War Prices".

platen presses

A unique American development of the nineteenth century was the platen press, also referred to as a job press or jobber. The platen press ranged in size from 5 x 8" to 18 x 22" and was used for small job work such as business cards, envelopes, billheads, circulars, and some small newspapers or any work that was not suited for the already established hand or cylinder press.

The basic concept of all the platen presses was a hinged platen and/or bed, one of which/or both came in contact with each other after the form was inked and a sheet of paper had been placed on the tympan. Printing on a hard tympan vastly improved the quality of reproduction. The press could produce 1,000 to 1,500 impressions per hour, and the equipment itself required a low capital investment. These factors resulted in greatly reduced printing costs, bringing printed matter into the financial realm of many more people, thus contributing to the growth of commerce in the United States.

The job press successfully used dry paper, eliminating the time-consuming process of using wetted paper as on the hand press. A foot treadle powered most platen presses, thus freeing the hands to operate the press. Although steam power and then electric motors were added later to these presses, the fact that they could rely on foot power made them very popular on the frontier and any place else where no other power source was available.

The father of the platen press was an American printer, George P. Gordon, who received his first patent in 1850. Although he wasn't the first to design a platen press, his was the most popular. Gordon was a prolific press builder, having over 50 patents to his name. George Gordon called his press the Franklin because he claimed that Benjamin Franklin had given him the idea for the press in a dream.

Since the design of the job press was so basic and fairly simple, it is surprising that almost seventy different manufacturers in the United States produced their own versions. Palmyra, New York, a small town on the Erie Canal and the birthplace of the Mormon Church, boasted of having six different press manufacturers who built 13 advertised presses. Not all inventors of platen presses had their own factory. Several of these designers had their presses built for them by machine shops. Platen presses, each with some of their own improvements and features, were advertised under 125 different press names.

The newer features included the addition of a throw-off, oscillating ink ductors, retractable grippers, rotating and reversible inking disk, inking drums, ink fountains, two and three-color presses. Some presses were very distinct in design and quite ornate. Others looked almost identical to the presses of other manufacturers. In the late 1890's the more progressive press builders were experimenting with improvements such as automatic feed and roll-fed platens. There were at least seven distinct types of platen presses developed in the latter part of the nineteenth century:

1. Alligator Press, brought out in 1851, was Gordon's first press. The platen was stationary set at an angle of 45 degrees. The bed, at rest, was vertical and hinged at the lower end. The form was inked over a curved plate and then the bed was tilted forward to meet the platen. This was a dangerous press, hence the name.
2. Gordon's first patented press had the bed mounted on two legs that were hinged near the floor. The platen, supported by a large shaft, allowed a rotating motion of about 90 degrees. This press originally used a flat or curved ink table, later replaced by the ink disk. This basic style was one used on the majority of platen presses, including the Chandler and Price which is called a Gordon style press. By 1895, after Gordon's patents expired, there were 11 manufacturers producing a Gordon style press.
3. Gordon came out with a new style press in 1872. The platen was hinged at its lower edge and did not open up as far. The bed only traveled about half the distance. This press did have a throw-off, which the earlier model did not have. The new style press utilized a round ink disk. The new style Gordon was never as popular as the old style.
4. The clamshell type press was a lighter and cheaper press. It had a platen that was hinged at the bottom, and met a stationary vertical bed. Because it was a less expensive press, desired by printers just starting out, several manufacturers sold them to printing supply houses that marketed them under their company name.
5. Several companies manufactured another type of press similar to the clamshell. It had a stationery bed but utilized a platen that was fastened to long legs, which pivoted at the bottom of the press.
6. The Universal press, patented by Merritt Gally in 1863, used a large metal drum that was positioned under an ink fountain to supply the form rollers instead of using an ink disk. The press was very heavy, slower and more expensive than the Gordon. But with the superior ink distribution system and the stationary vertical bed that met the platen at a parallel position, it was capable of producing the finest work, and put the Universal in a class by itself. Gally had the press manufactured by several different plants over the course of many years. After it was manufactured at the Colt's Armory, it was called the Colt's Armory Press.
7. The Ruggles press was a design popular for a relatively short time before the Gordon. The Ruggles press had a cylindrical stationary bed frame. The rollers were inked on the round frame and the platen was pushed against the bed.

One of the most important developments to the platen press was the throw-off, which gave the printer the ability to keep the impression from being transferred to the tympan when no paper was being fed. Even though the throw-off was patented in the early 1850's it was not used in many presses until the 1870's, when the patent expired and that feature entered the public domain. The Liberty, one of the first presses of the 1870's to use a throw-off, was unusual as the ink disk was found on the back of the press.

By the end of the nineteenth century there was not a printing establishment in the country that did not have at least one platen press. Even today many printing plants still have a job press for imprinting, numbering or die cutting. The platen press continues to be very popular with both private press and hobby printers.

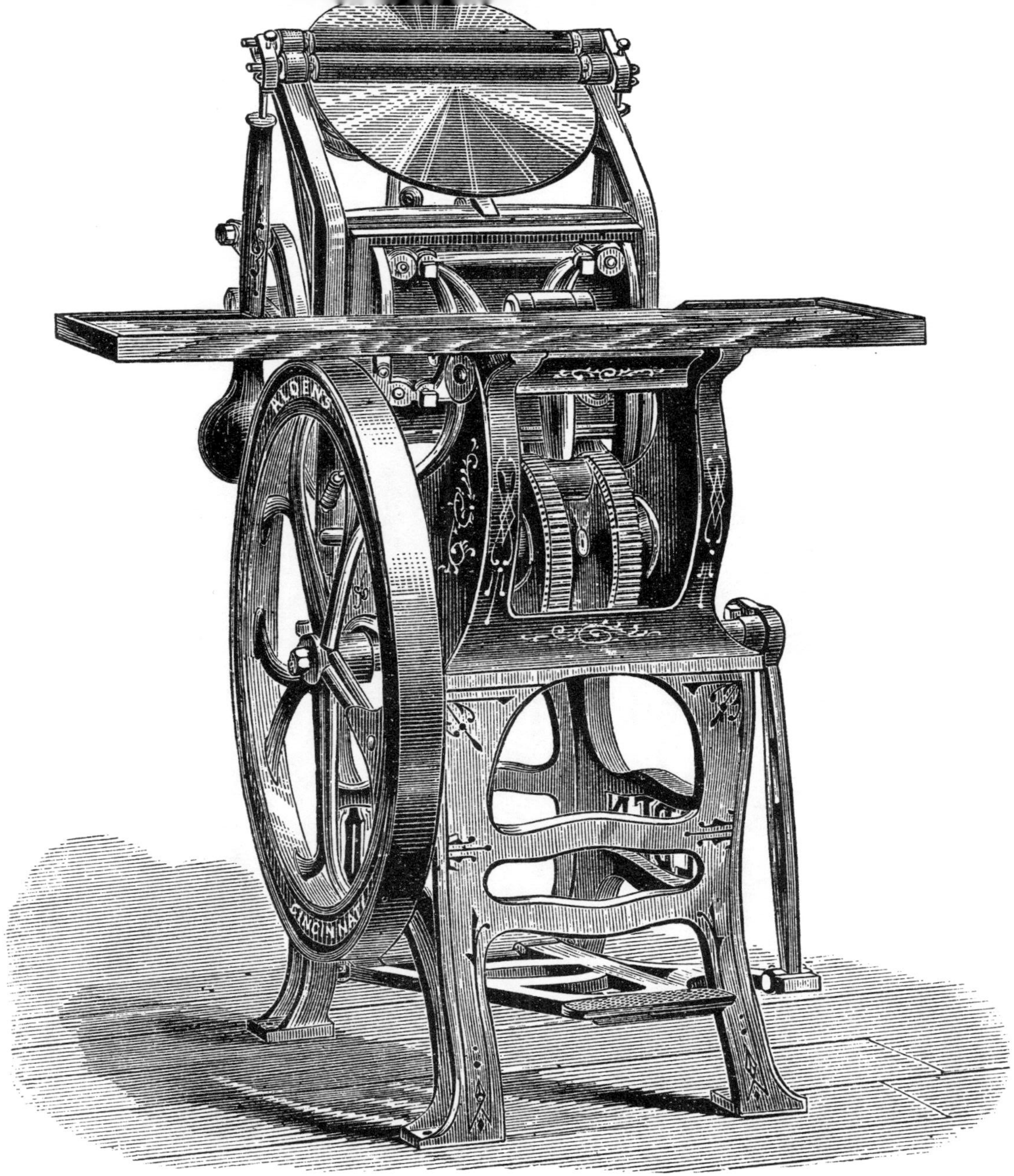

"THE ALDEN PRESS."

Sold by Edwin Alden & Bros.of Cincinnati, Ohio. Circa 1885.
Looks identical to the Model Press by J. W. Daughaday & Co.

THE PROGRESS PRESS

$50.00 CHEAPER

Than any Other Eighth Medium Press.

STRONG AND DURABLE.

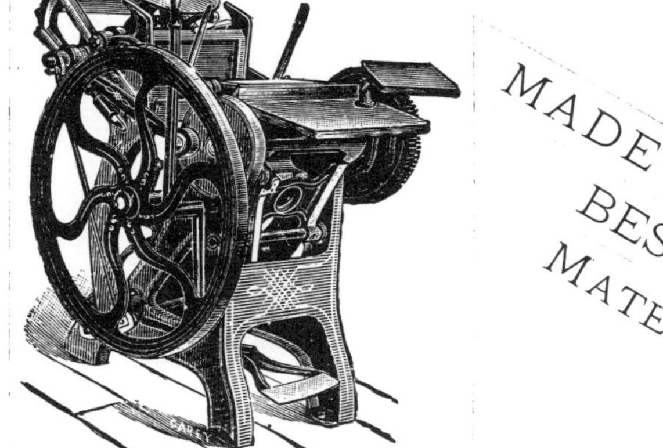

MADE OF BEST MATERIAL.

Size, 8x12 inches, with Throw-off, - - $175.00.

Roller Mould, Stocks and Wrenches Included.

The above cut represents the old reliable and ever popular **OLD STYLE GORDON,** made in a new and more attractive form and improved by the addition of an IMPRESSION THROW-OFF, and an increase in size of platen and bed.
Material and workmanship guaranteed.

BENTON, WALDO & CO.,

MILWAUKEE, WIS. ∴ ∵ ∴ ∵ SAINT PAUL, MINN.

Circa 1885

THE NATIONAL JOB PRINTING PRESS.

Manufactured by the Allen Manufacturing Co., Norwich, Conn.

This new Press is especially adapted to the wants of printers who work for profit. It combines rapidity and excellent quality of work, is as quickly made ready as any of the popular presses of to-day. It has a thorough distribution of ink, and gives a square impression, with a slight dwell. The platen comes to a rest while the paper is being fed, and its motions are so nicely arranged that it operates more rapidly without strain than any of the bed and platen presses in the market.

Size of Platen, 7 by 11 inches.

PRICE, $250.

STEAM FIXTURES, $20. BOXING, $6.

Circa 1873

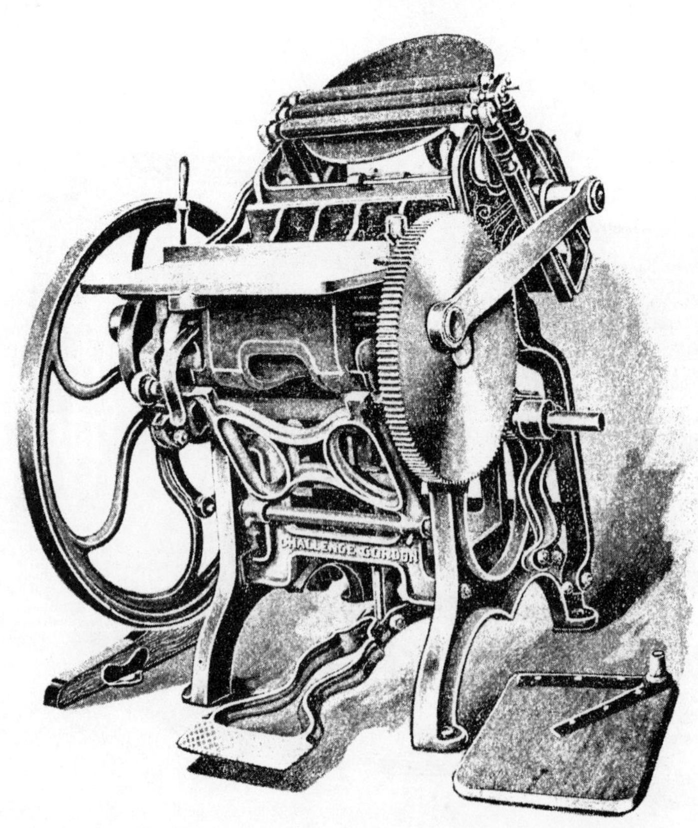

Challenge Gordon, late style with throw-off, manufactured by Challenge Machine Co.
Circa 1894

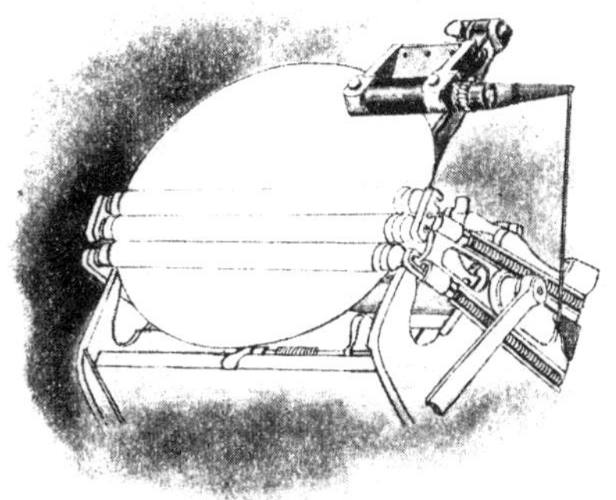

Challenge Buckeye Fountain

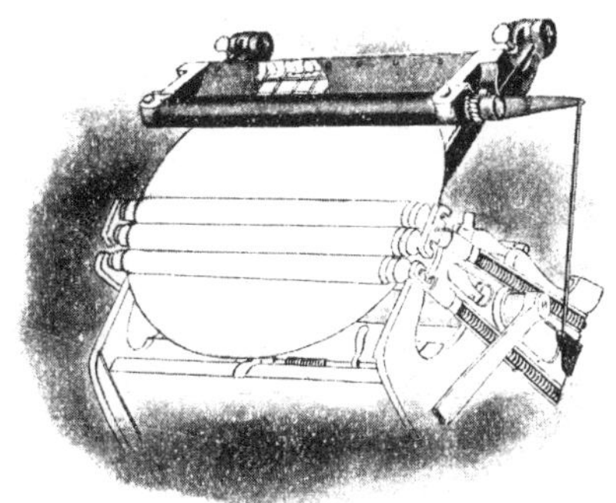

Challenge Long Fountain

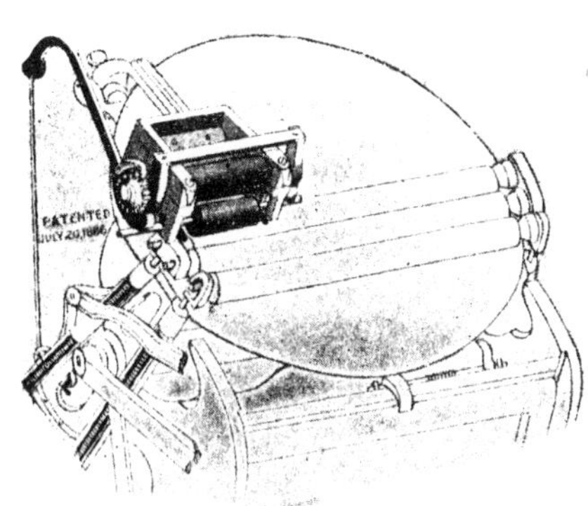

Challenge Pony Fountain

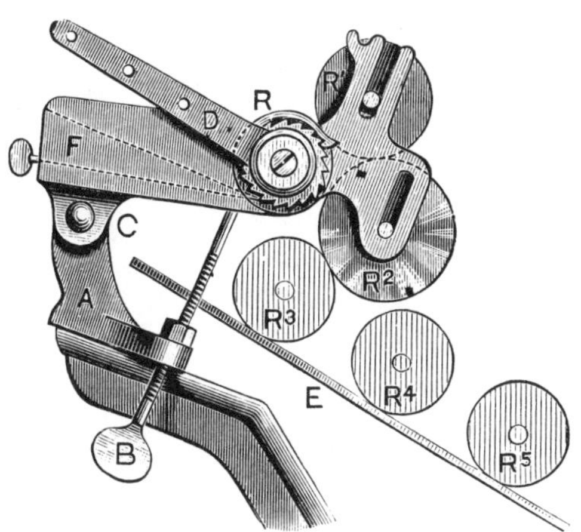

Challenge Long Fountain

Patented 1886

CHANDLER & PRICE,

MANUFACTURERS OF

Printing Presses and Printing Machinery

OFFICE AND WORKS—EAST PROSPECT STREET AND C. & P. R. R. CROSSING,

CLEVELAND, OHIO.

MAKERS OF THE

CHANDLER
· · & · ·
PRICE

OLD · STYLE

Gordon ∴ ∴ Presses

FIVE SIZES,

7 x 11, 8 x 12, 10 x 15,
14 x 20, 14½ x 22.

Ask Your Dealer for Them.

ALSO MAKE

OVERHEAD FIXTURES,

Common Screw, Yankee, and Buckeye

COMPOSING STICKS,

JOB AND PROOF

Roller Frames,

LAMP HOLDERS,

Galley Rests,

Shooting Sticks,

ETC.

ALL THE BEST!

THE CHANDLER & PRICE OLD STYLE GORDON PRESS.

SPECIAL FEATURES:

Steel Shaft and Steel Side Arms, forged from solid bar, without seam or weld.
The Most Positive and Practical Throw-off yet introduced.
Best Material Used. Most Carefully Finished.

We have recently greatly improved these Presses, enlarging and strengthening the parts, and so arranging the disk and roller carriers as to give greatly increased distribution, and we believe it is unequaled in this respect by any press now made.

The Most Durable and hence the Most Economical Press for the Printer.

We never have had to take a Press back!
Every one is giving Entire Satisfaction.

IMPRESSION THROW-OFF. DEPRESSIBLE GRIPPERS.
HARDENED TOOL-STEEL CAM ROLLERS.

EIGHTH MEDIUM,	7 x 11,	with Throw-off and Depressible Grippers	$150.00
" "	8 x 12,	" " "	165.00
QUARTO MEDIUM,	10 x 15,	" " "	250.00
HALF MEDIUM,	14 x 20,	" " "	400.00
" "	14½ x 22,	" " "	450.00
STEAM FIXTURES			15.00
CHANDLER & PRICE FOUNTAIN, for either size Press			20.00
BUCKEYE FOUNTAIN			10.00

With each Press there are three Chases, one Brayer, two sets of Roller Stocks, two Wrenches, and one Roller Mold. No charge for boxing and shipping.

We Challenge Comparison. All our Goods Guaranteed in every respect.

Write to your Dealer for Prices and Terms.

CHANDLER & PRICE, East Prospect and C. & P. R. R. Crossing, CLEVELAND, OHIO.

N. B.—None genuine without name of CHANDLER & PRICE, CLEVELAND, OHIO, cast upon the rocker.

Circa 1886

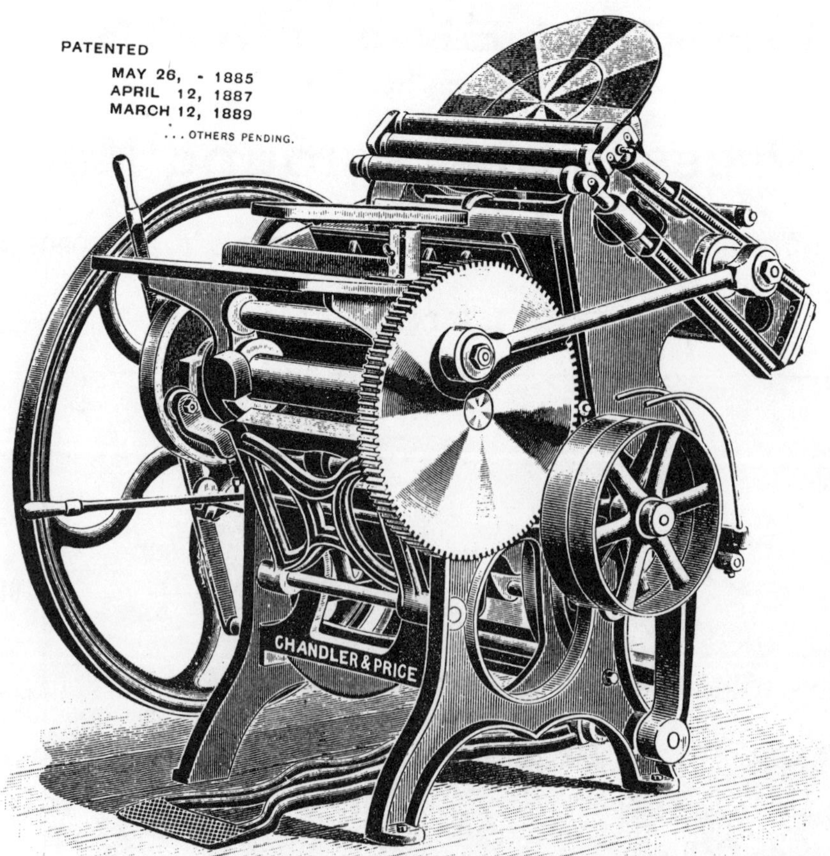

Old style 12 x 18" Chandler & Price Gordon with double inking disk, pulley, belt shifter, impression throw-off. The horizontal clutch lever also served as a brake. Circa 1889

CINCINNATI PRINTING MACHINERY.

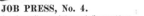

NONPAREIL JOB PRESS, No. 4.

The cut above represents the large size, the smaller ones being so similar as not to require special illustration. The frame and bed are, in every case, one solid piece of iron, to which the working parts are attached. The Machines are very strong and compact, occupying less room than any other of same capacity. They are very manageable and reliable for any kind of work, distribute the stiffest ink, and take the heaviest impression ever required.

No. 1. The smallest occupies a space 2¾×3 feet on the floor, is 3⅗ feet high, and weighs 550 pounds, runs very easily by foot, measures 6×12 inches inside of chase, with screws, and costs $250. Boxing $6.

No. 2. Stands on 2⅔×3⅗ feet, is 4 feet high, and weighs 860 pounds, runs by foot, measures 10×15 inches inside of chase, and costs $400. Boxing $8.

No. 3. Is complete with fountain, stands on floor 3¼×3¾ feet, is 4½ feet high, and weighs 1,500 pounds, runs by treadle on small jobs or moderate speeds, but has also a crank for heavy or fast work. Size 15½×18½ inches inside of chase, costs $550. Boxing $10.

No. 4. Is similar to No. 3, runs by crank, stands on floor 4×4½ feet, is 4½ feet high, 15½×24½ inches inside of chase, weighs 1,775 pounds, and costs $650. Boxing $12. Pulleys for steam are extra.

GUILLOTINE PAPER CUTTER.

A new and powerful machine, claiming superiority over all others in the market; it is peculiarly excellent as a power machine, but may easily be run by hand.

The knife has an oscillating as well as a sliding motion, and makes a clean, true cut, with but little or no inclination to gouge or draw the paper under the clamp.

The knife-bar descends to a given point, and rises immediately, without reversing the motion of the machine.

When run by power, the paper is placed in position and clamped down, the machine started, the cut made, knife returns to place, and machine stops automatically. It is of the best materials and workmanship, and fully warranted to give satisfaction.

PRICE:—To cut 28 inches, $600; to cut 32 inches, $700. Larger sizes to order.

Sizes and Prices of Cylinder Presses.

MAMMOTH.—Size of Bed, inside bearers, 34×52 inches. Largest form printed, 31½×48 inches. Room occupied on floor, 8¾×6½ feet. Hight to top of cylinder, 4½ feet. Weight, 5,500 pounds. Price $2,000. Boxing $50.

DOUBLE SUPER-ROYAL.—Bed, inside bearers, 31×46 inches. Largest form printed, 27×42 inches. Room occupied on floor, 7½×6 feet. Hight to top of cylinder, 4 feet. Weight, 4,500 pounds. Price $1,500. Boxing $40.

THE GEM.—This is a new size, which at its greatest extent prints a 7-column newspaper, but is much more convenient for job-work than the larger sizes, running easier and faster. —Bed, inside bearers, 28×40 inches. Largest form printed, 24×36 inches. Room occupied on floor, 7×5½ feet. Hight to top of cylinder, 3¾ feet. Weighs 3,500 pounds. Price $1,350. Boxing $40. Pulleys for steam, extra.

CINCINNATI CYLINDER PRESS.

This Machine is a modification of the old and well-tested Drum Cylinder Press, retaining all its principles of action, so modified as to render it comparatively light and cheap, while in strength and stiffness it is equal, if not superior, to the original model. This end is chiefly attained by reducing the number of pieces in the frame, and casting large sections solid. The whole frame of the Press, from the bed to the floor on which it rests, is one solid piece of iron. If the floor be level, no secondary platform is needed on which to place the Press, no can the frame spring or weave every time the floor is bent by some unusual weight, thus avoiding one very fruitful source of difficulty in machine-printing.

It runs smoothly and almost without noise, takes but little room, and is very convenient to the operator; the register is perfect, and the Machines adapted to hand or power turning; and the manufacturers offer them, not as the lowest-priced Presses in the market, but as thoroughly reliable and well-made machines, which they can warrant satisfactory.

For further particulars and testimonials send to

CINCINNATI TYPE-FOUNDRY AND PRINTING MACHINE WORKS,
201 Vine Street, Cincinnati, Ohio.

Manufacturers and Dealers in Printing-Machines, Type, Cases, Cabinets, Sticks, Galleys, and every article used in the Printing Business.

Circa 1868

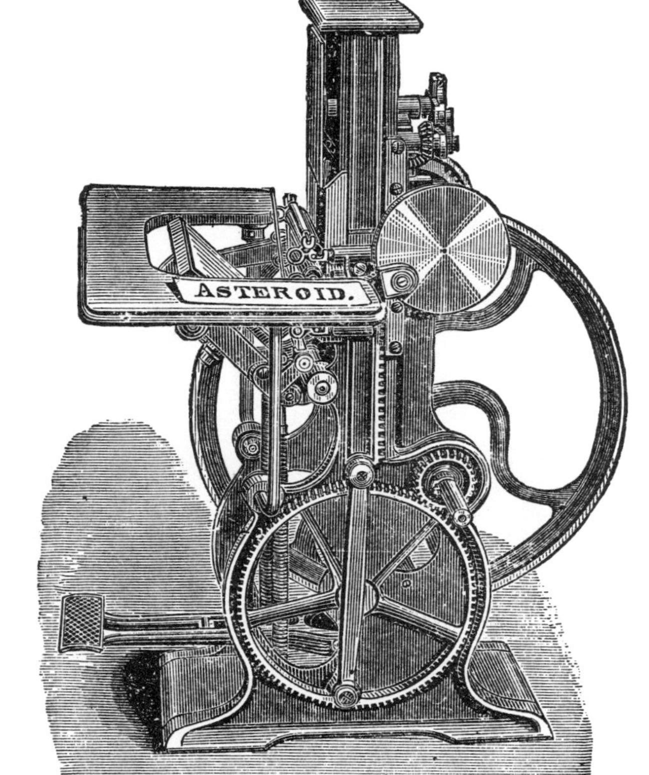

The Asteroid Jobber manufactured by Cincinnati Type Foundry. Circa 1875

NONPAREIL JOB PRESS,

WITH RECEDING BED.

Nonpareil Presses have perpendicular bed in front of feeder. The platen is moved back and forth by a crank motion, vibrating between the type and feeder, never absolutely stopping, but by a motion peculiar to those presses moving slowly and opening wide when under the feeder's hands, so that he has ample time and convenience to feed in and remove the sheet. They have three rollers over the full form, and disk distribution. The smaller sizes (9x12, 10x15, 12x17) have the bed adjusted to a wedge, the withdrawal of which draws the bed back from BOTH, or EITHER, the rollers or platen, enabling the pressman to distribute without rolling, to roll repeatedly to each impression, or to print a dirty form clean of ink without removing the rollers—advantages possessed by no other disk-distributing press. In other presses, you may save a sheet improperly placed by cutting off the impression, but you are apt to spoil it after all by printing the next impression on a doubly-inked form. In the presses of this construction also, the impression, though adjusted by four screws in front of the platen, may be evenly increased or diminished by a single screw in the wedge like a hand press.

SIZES:

9x12 and 12x17 Inches, inside chase.

FOR PRICES, SEE PRICE LIST.

Circa 1870

RELIABLE JOB PRESS.

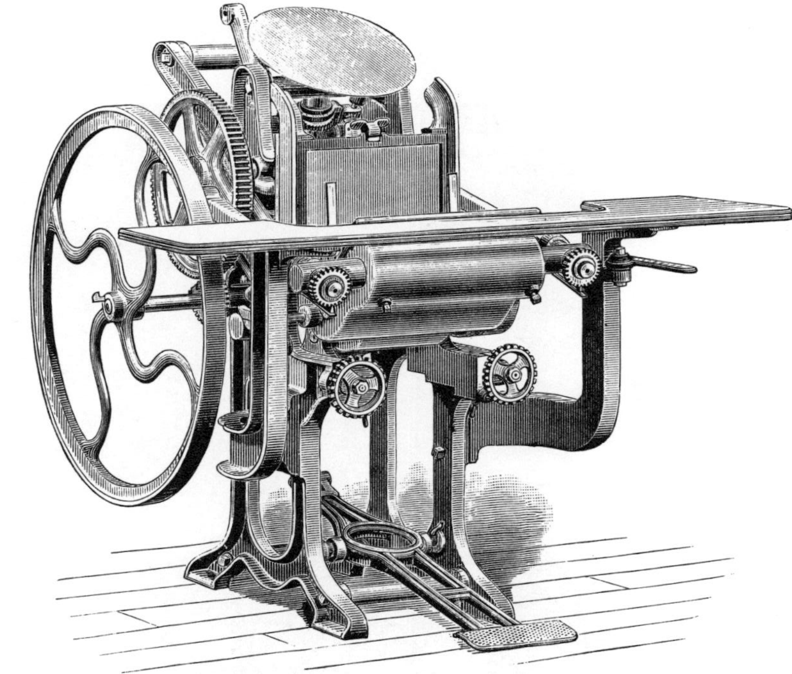

This press is what its name indicates, a very simple, strong machine, runs easily, with fair speed, does the best of work, and can be safely trusted in the most inexperienced hands.

Three rollers pass over the entire form.

The impression adjustment is extremely simple and very effective.

Its simplicity renders a description of the cut unnecessary.

THE BEST LOW-PRICED PRESS MADE.

It is sold on a warrantee of complete satisfaction, and at a price far below that of any press of equal excellence.

Each press is furnished with four cast rollers and two chases; or roller-mould instead of cast rollers, at the option of the purchaser.

Circa 1888

Nonpareil Jobber with receding bed disk manufactured by Cincinnati Type Foundry. Circa 1886.

Nonpareil Jobber manufactured by Cincinnati Type Foundry.

NONPAREIL NEWSPAPER AND JOB PRESS.

For Prices, see Price List.

This massive piece of machinery moves with wonderful ease. It is an admirable machine for large job work or small book forms, and is especially adapted to a seven-column newspaper, one page at the time. One man works on the Jobber less laboriously than he can on the hand press, although he there has the help of a roller boy; thus, it not only doubles the speed, but does so with about half the labor. A hand-wheel can be furnished, if desired, but our opinion is that, when two boys are employed on the press, they had both better work on the treadle, the foot-board of which is made long for that purpose.

In quality of work—register, evenness of impression and color—it has no superior.

In economy, in the use of other material, one page only being printed at the time, considerably less type is needed, and hand press, inking apparatus, chases, roller-mould, and hand-roller may be omitted from cost of outfit. Still, the saving on all these articles does not make up for the cost of the Jobber, and it is only when the paper is run in connection with a job office that great economy in first cost is discernable. Then it saves the usually indispensable half-medium job press, and reduces the cost of the combined news and jobbing outfit about $250, besides the first mentioned advantages and its great superiority over the usual job press in point of size.

CINCINNATI TYPE FOUNDRY,

No. 201 Vine Street.

THE LATEST!

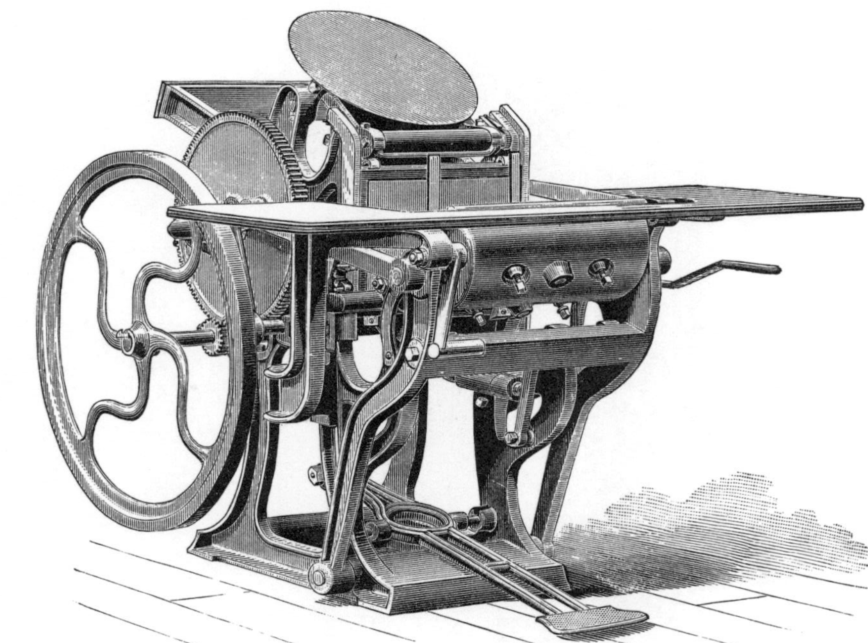

A NEW SIZE—10x15 INCHES.

It has all the PERFECTIONS of the well-known

NONPAREIL PRESS

BESIDES

A LONG AND COMPLETE FOUNTAIN UNDER THE DISK.

Conveniences in Making Ready, Easy Action, and all the other Special Features of the Nonpareil have been retained.

FOR PRICES, SEE PRICE LIST.

NONPAREIL JOBBER.

SMALL SIZE.

Cincinnati Type Foundry Co. 201 Vine Street.

NONPAREIL JOBBER.

—:o:—

Best Foot Jobber Extant.

—o—

SIMPLE,

EASY TO MANAGE,

LIGHT TO TREAD, AND

STRONG TO WORK

Works One or Many Colors at One Impression.

—o—

7x12	***$250***
10x16	***450***
15x19	***600***
15x25	***700***

—o—

Cincinnati Type Foundry Company.

CHAS. WELLS, Treas'r,

G. S. NEWCOMB & CO., Sole Agents, Cleveland, O.

Circa 1875

Nonpareil Chromatic Press, old style, manufactured by Cincinnati Type Foundry.

Nonpareil Chromatic Press, new style, manufactured by Cincinnati Type Foundry.

THE COMPLETE ROTARY

POWER PRESS.

[DUMMER'S PATENT ALLOWED.]

This Press is called the Complete Rotary Power Press, since it has the least reciprocating movements of any oscillating press that has ever been offered to the public. The motion of the inking rolls is not only continuous and in one direction, but it is caused with the least expense of power, as the latter is applied the most directly possible through the whole distance travelled by the rolls. By moving the inking rolls as done in this press, all the parts of the press may be condensed into the least possible space, as the ink-plate may be placed at the rear of the bed and parallel with it, not only to occupy less space for itself but to be revolved simply and directly from the crank shaft.

This circular printed on the Complete Rotary Power Press by an amateur.

Circa 1878

It is claimed that this press is superior to all other rotary power presses, since it is most

Compact, occupying the least possible space for the reasons given above, and as may be readily seen from the cuts.

Easily Run, since there are few moving parts and connections, and the power is directly and continuously applied, there being absolutely NO RECIPROCATING MOVEMENT to the inking rolls or plate.

Substantial, since there need be no small connections and attachments, and on account of the compactness of the press it may be solidly built.

Durable and easily kept in order, as the rotary parts are few and may be substantially made, and if broken, others are easily substituted.

Inexpensive, being of so few and simple parts, it may be thoroughly constructed with the least possible cost.

Convenient, since all the movements are simple, direct and quickly understood. As it is of the least possible weight to have the required strength, it is readily packed, moved, set up and worked, with the least labor, and in the smallest space.

The first cut gives a front view of this press set on an iron stand containing a cabinet of drawers and with treadle, all complete, ready for use. The second cut gives a rear view of the press to illustrate the position of the ink plate and press as it may be placed for working on any suitable table or box.

Only one size—chase $6\frac{1}{2}$ by $9\frac{1}{2}$ inside—is now ready. Other sizes are being built and will be offered as soon as possible.

PRICES

Press with Iron Stand, Cabinet of Drawers, Chase, all complete, ready for working $85.00
Press with Treadle, Chase and Box upon which the Press may be worked; all complete 70.00

COLUMBIAN Rotary Press

Size inside of chase, 6 x 9 inches.

PRICE, $85.00.

Weight, 417 pounds. Boxing, $3.00 extra.

SIMPLE, STRONGLY BUILT.

Perfect rest to platen. Perfect distribution.
The cheapest thorough-made Press in existence.
Two Chases, two Rollers and two Wrenches with each Press.

Manufactured by Curtis & Mitchell of Boston from 1878 to 1891.

COLUMBIAN ROTARY PRESS.

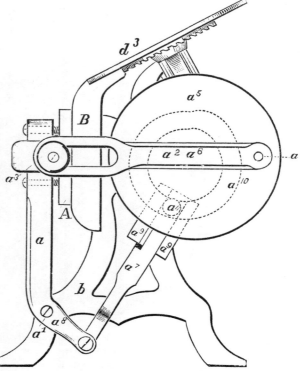

FOR the construction of the COLUMBIAN ROTARY PRESS due regard is paid to mechanical principles and the employment of the best material. It gives a firm and even impression without the possibility of spring or *slur*. Has a large distributing surface, and is the strongest and best press of its size ever put upon the market. The accompanying cut gives a side elevation, and the following is a description of its mechanism:—

A is the platen, and B the bed. The platen A is adjustably secured upon the platen-frame a, which is fulcrumed at a^1 to the main frame b. The platen-frame is moved toward and from the bed by the slotted connecting-rods $a2$ $a2$. The ends $a3$ of the platen-frame each enter one of the slots in the rods $a2$, and these rods are each secured by wrist-pin $a4$ to one of the crank-wheels $a5$, which are fast upon and revolve with the shaft a^6. This shaft $a6$ is driven as is usual in this class of presses.

In addition to this mechanism for moving the platen-frame a toward and from the bed B, a connecting-rod, a^7, is jointed to the projecting end a^8 of the platen-frame. This rod slides in ways a^9, properly secured to the main frame b, and is actuated by the cam a^{10}, which, for compactness, is formed on the inner face of the crank-wheel $a5$. A wrist-pin, a^{11}, projecting from the upper end of the rod a^7, enters the cam-groove a^{10}, and consequently the rod a^7 is moved endwise by the cam a^{10} when shaft a^6 revolves; and this motion of the rod a^7 rocks the platen-frame a upon its fulcrum a^1, and thus moves its upper end, which bears the platen, toward and from the bed.

Circa 1888

Columbian 5 x 8" Job Press manufactured by Curtis & Mitchell. Circa 1885.

Excelsior Card and Job Presses

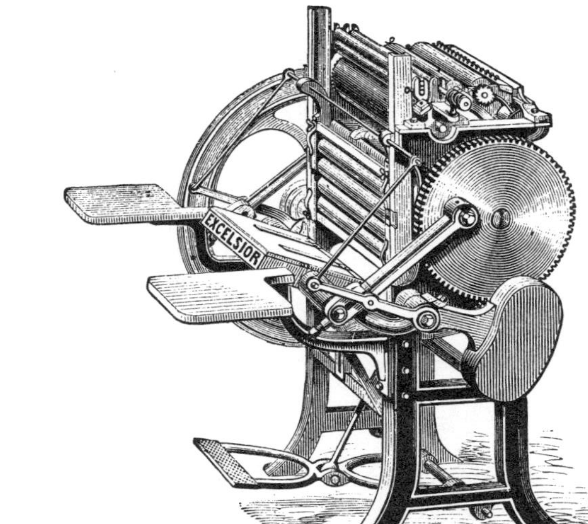

DESCRIPTION
OF THE
Excelsior Card and Job Presses.

THE BED—Is vertical and faces the operator. It is fitted to the frame of the press.

THE PLATEN—Vibrates on a centre at its lower side, to receive the impression from the position in which it receives the sheet. The sheet is relieved from the type by fingers, acted on by a spring.

DISTRIBUTION—In which the rotary cylinder with vibrating roller is used, the motion of which is positive, being driven with gear.

	Impressions per hour.
Eighth Medium Excelsior	500 to 2,000
Quarto and Half Medium	500 to 1,200

THE NET CASH PRICES ARE:

EIGHTH MEDIUM EXCELSIOR, 7 by 11 inches inside of chase, with two Rollers in frame, $250. Boxing, $6.

QUARTO MEDIUM EXCELSIOR, 10 by 15 inches inside of chase, with four Rollers in frame, $425. With Fountain, $25 extra. With Steam Fixtures, $30 extra. Boxing, $8.

HALF MEDIUM EXCELSIOR, 13 by 19 inches inside of chase, with four Rollers in frame, $550. With Fountain, $25 extra. Steam Fixtures, $30 extra. Double Geared, $600. Boxing, $12. One Roller Mold, two Sets of Roller Stocks, three Chases, one Wrench, go with each Press.

These Presses will all be proved and properly boxed and delivered to the order of the purchaser in any part of New York City.

WILLIAM BRAIDWOOD, Manufacturer and Patentee,

FACTORY, 15 HARLEM R. R. BUILDING,

WHITE STREET, COR. CENTRE, NEW YORK.

Circa 1870

.....OUR NEW AND LATEST.....

IMPROVED

GORDON PRESS

Strongest, Easiest Running and Best Job Press

IN THE WORLD

Steel Shafts, Steel Draw Bar Arms,

Dwell on Impression.

PERFECTLY NOISELESS.

OCCUPIES LITTLE SPACE.

MOVEMENT PERFECTION.

This Press, so long and favorably known to the printing trade as the Latest Improved Gordon, embodies many movements and principles not contained in the Old Style Gordon or any other job press.

There is a long dwell on the impression to give the paper time to absorb the ink, and this gives a clearer and better impression with less power than when given quickly as in other presses.

The bed and platen are heavily ribbed, and parts are made heavy and strong where strength only is required.

All parts are interchangeable, so that in case of an accident new parts can be immediately supplied to fit. In fact, this style supersedes all other presses.

DAMON & PEETS, 44 BEEKMAN STREET, NEW YORK.

Circa 1893

Favorite Jobber manufactured by Damon & Peets from 1887 to 1894.

Prize Medal Awarded at the Paris Exposition.

MODEL PRINTING PRESS

No. 3.—Size inside of Chase, 7 x 10 inches. Price, $100.00.
No. 4.—Size inside of Chase, 8 x 13 inches. Price, $175.00.

——o——

Two Chases, Roller-mould, Set of Ink-rollers, Extra Set of Roller-stocks, Hand-roller, Wrenches and Oiler included with each Press. Boxing, $5 extra.

——o——

Model Job Press manufactured by J. W. Daughaday & Co. from 1877 - 1885.

In business from 1860 to 1877. Succeeded by F. M. Weiler and Liberty Machine Works.

Circa 1866

BALTIMORE JOBBER,

GIVE IT A TRIAL.

ALL SIZED PRESSES. CATALOGUES FREE.

Easiest running.
Strong as any.
The most durable.
Costs less for repairs.
Will do as good work.
Last but not least.
Cheapest First-class Press.

Jobber No. 5.	**Jobber No. 6.**	**Jobber No. 7.**
Chase, 8x12 inches.	Chase, 10x15 inches.	Chase, 12x17 inches.
Nickeled, with throw-off.	Nickeled, with throw-off.	Nickeled, with throw-off.
- - - - - $175.00.	- - - - - - $250.00	- - - - - - $300.00.
Plain, without throw-off.	Plain, without throw-off.	Plain, without throw-off.
- - - - - $150.00.	- - - - - - $225.00	- - - - - - $275.00.

For sale by

BALTIMORE TYPE FOUNDRY

Chas. J. Cary & Co., Baltimore, Md.

Manufactured by J.F.W. Dorman of Baltimore. Circa 1885.

Eclipse Jobber with throw-off, manufactured by J.F.W. Dorman. Circa 1890

Aldine Job Press manufactured by Dokum & Sons of New York City. Circa 1878.

MANUFACTURED BY BOSTON AND FAIRHAVEN IRON WORKS, FAIRHAVEN, MASS.

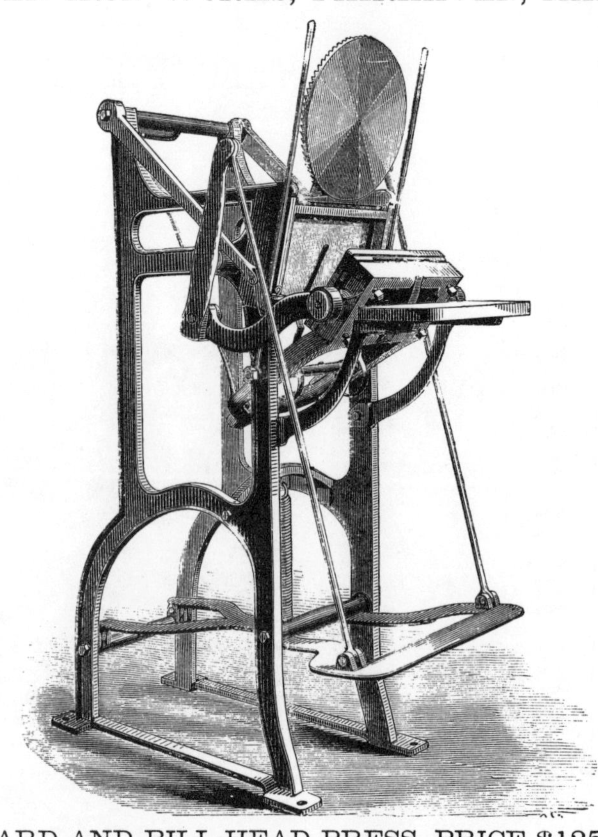

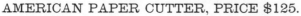

AMERICAN PAPER CUTTER, PRICE $125. CARD AND BILL-HEAD PRESS, PRICE $125.

These Machines are manufactured from the best materials in a thorough and workmanlike manner, and will be found reliable in every way, doing as good work as many of the highest priced machines. Several years' constant use in many offices confirm us in all we claim for them. We have placed them at a price which will enable every country printing office to have them. For further particulars and testimonials address

Circa 1872

M. GALLY'S
Universal Printing Press

The Universal Press.

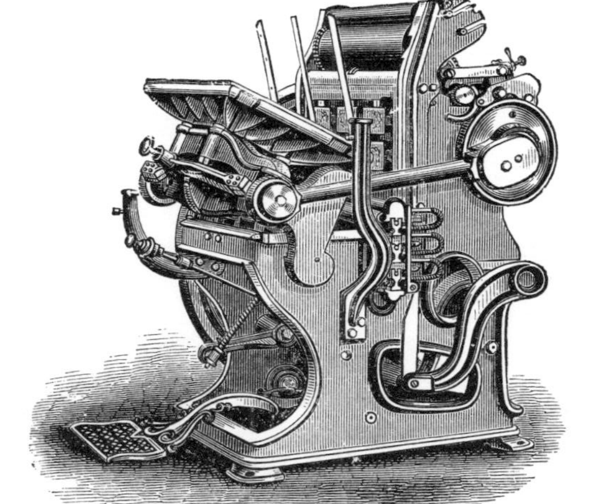

Greatly Improved.

The inventor and patentee has now the entire control of the Universal Press Business and is sparing no pains or expense in making it decidedly the Best Job Press in the world.

THE machines are built at the "Colt's Armory," by the manufacturers of the celebrated Colt's Revolvers, etc., and their world-wide reputation is sufficient guarantee for the quality of the "UNIVERSAL," when it is understood that they are no longer restricted as to the quality of material or finish. The Platen Bridge (formerly of cast iron) has now entirely through it a SHAFT OF STEEL, which renders breakage impossible. The Adjuster Bar, (formerly of cast iron,) is now made of STEEL. Two strong springs are now used to draw back the platen instead of one, so that if one gives out the other will carry the press safely in its movements, until the damaged one can be replaced. NEW STYLE CAMS are placed on the half medium size, which increase the speed at least three hundred impressions per hour, with perfect steadiness of motion. The presses are made to run easily by treadle, when steam cannot be applied. The distribution of ink may be varied to suit the character of the work, reaching, if desired, ten times that of any other job press. The impression can be instantly adjusted to any form without turning the platen screws or packing up with paper. The form may be rolled on or not, or given any number of rollings desired. The impression may be thrown off at will.

Among all the presses sold by the inventor for nearly a year, since he took the business into his own hands, he can only record one slight breakage, and not the cost of a single cent for repairs. This is the most remarkable record for job presses ever known.

PRICE LIST:

HALF MEDIUM, 13x19 inches inside of chase, (platen 14x22 inches,) - $400.00
Boxing, $10.00. Ink Fountain, $25.00. Steam Fixtures, $15.00.

QUARTO MEDIUM, 10x15 inches inside of chase, - - - - - - $300.00
Boxing, $7.00. Ink Fountain, $25.00. Steam Fixtures, $15.00.

EIGHTH MEDIUM, - - - - - - - - - - - - - - $225.00
Boxing, $6.00. Ink Fountain, $25.00. Steam Fixtures, $15.00.

Office and Salesroom, 39 Park Row, New York.

Circa 1880

New Universal Press manufactured by Merritt Gally. Circa 1888.

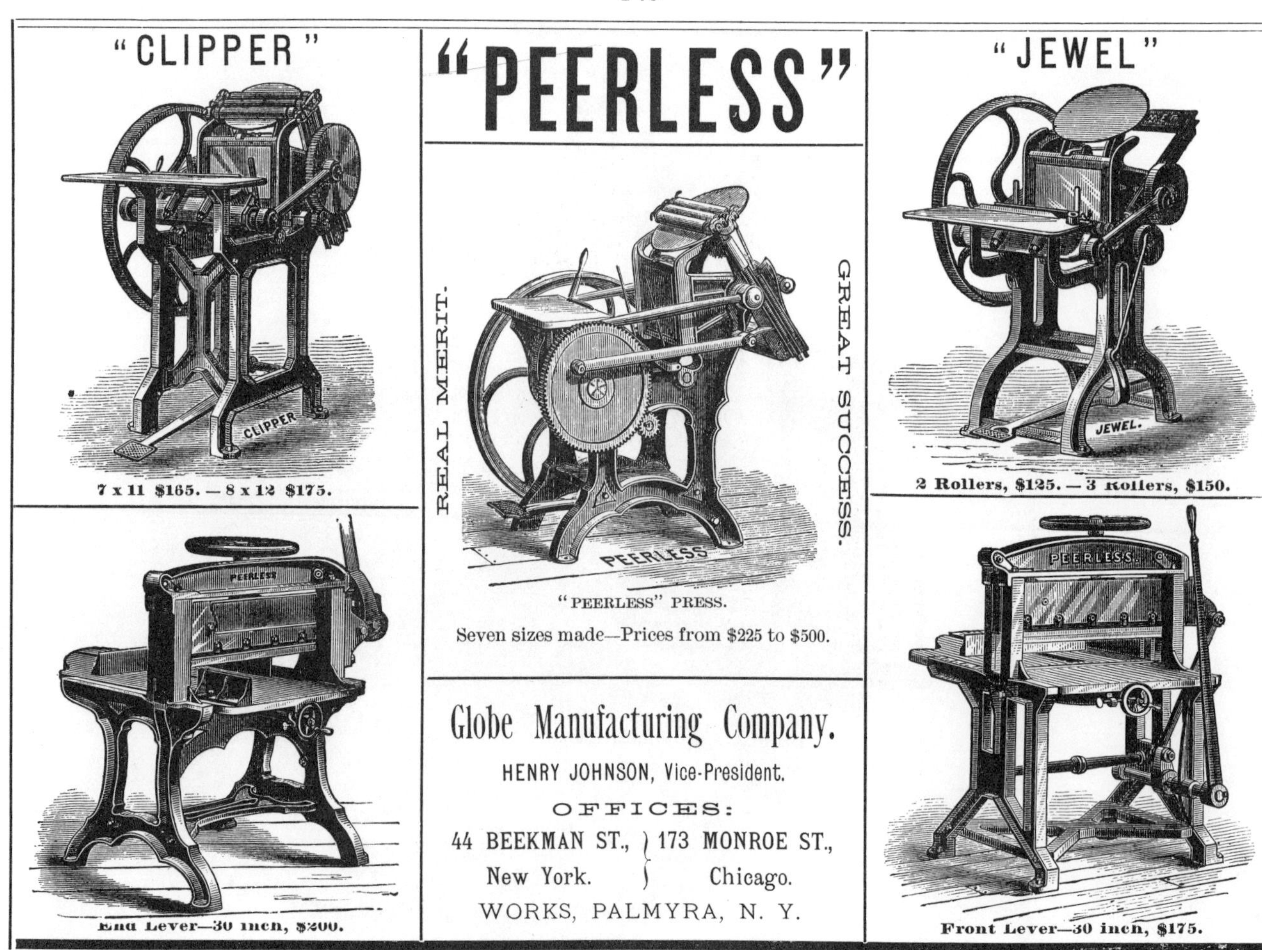

Circa 1881

The Clipper originally manufactured by Globe Manufacturing Co. of Palmyra, N.Y. and later by J. M. Jones Co. also of Palmyra. Circa 1885.

Peerless Press manufactured by Globe Manufacturing Co., of Palmyra, N. Y. Circa 1896.

THE PEARL

Is the Strongest, Lightest Running and Most Rapid Job Press manufactured.

FOR twelve years the Pearl has been the favorite among the printers of the United States. Its nicely balanced motion and dwell of impression, together with its perfect construction and low cost, make it the most economical Press for all kinds of small work.

SIZES AND PRICES.

No. 1,	5 x 8 inches inside chase,	- -	$ 70.00
No. 3,	7 x 11 " " "	- - -	110.00
No. 5,	9 x 14 " "	with throw-off,	180.00

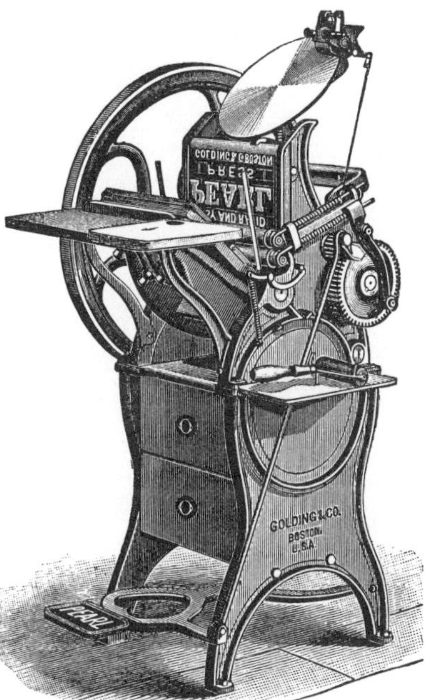

DEALERS WHO SELL THE PEARL.

BARNHART BROS. & SPINDLER, 115 and 117 Fifth Avenue, Chicago, Ill.

BENTON, WALDO & CO., 292 East Water Street, Milwaukee, Wis.

BENTON, WALDO & CO., 311 Robert Street, St. Paul, Minn.

CENTRAL TYPE FOUNDRY, Fourth and Elm Streets, St. Louis, Mo.

L. GRAHAM & SON, 99 and 101 Gravier Street, New Orleans, La.

GREAT WESTERN TYPE FOUNDRY, 324 West Sixth Street, Kansas City, Mo.

R. W. HARTNETT & BROS., 52 and 54 North Sixth Street, Philadelphia, Pa.

N. C. HAWKS, 320 Battery Street, San Francisco, Cal.

MARDER, LUSE & CO., 139 and 141 Monroe Street, Chicago, Ill.

MARDER, LUSE & CO., 14 and 16 Second Street, Minneapolis, Minn.

TATUM & BOWEN, 423 Clay Street, San Francisco, Cal.

Send postal for Press and Tool Catalogue.

GOLDING & CO., MANUFACTURERS.

Fort Hill Square, BOSTON, MASS.

Circa 1880

THE PEARL PRESS

ON WOOD STAND.

For cut of press as now built, see page 14. This cut shows the manner of mounting on wood stand.

Manufactured by Golding & Co. of Boston. Circa 1886.

Pearl Press, No. 14, with and without throw-off. Circa 1896.

The GOLDING JOBBER

Is by long odds the best Job Press now in the market. This is no idle claim, but is a POSITIVE FACT, and the press will prove it if given a trial. We are positive about this,

BECAUSE

We build the press and know what we are talking about.

It has a solid frame, and as a result all the bearings are kept in line, even though the press does not rest evenly on the floor.

On other presses the bolts may work loose and materially affect the bearings.

It can be easily run at a faster speed than any other press, and with less vibration.

It is noiseless and will not "pound" when printing a full form.

The Automatic Brayer Fountain gives a perfect ink supply, a result not attained by any other press with a disc.

The impression can be adjusted in a moment.

It is impossible to "slur" a job if the tympan is put on smoothly.

Where three rollers are used, ALL OF THEM will clear a full form, and as an aid, the Duplex Distributor, under the bed, can be used.

It is a MODERN press, and was not brought over in the Ark.

Modern printers need modern time and labor saving tools, and

BECAUSE

ALL WHO USE THE IMPROVED GOLDING JOBBER WILL SUBSTANTIATE THE ABOVE CLAIMS.

SIZES AND PRICES:

No. 6.— 8 x 12 inches inside chase $200

No. 7.—10 x 15 inches inside chase 275

No. 8.—12 x 18 inches inside chase 350

We also build two sizes of the Fairhaven Cylinder, three of the Pearl and nine ot the Official Presses, and furnish Complete Outfits. Send to us for anything you want. Press and Tool Catalogue sent free on application. Complete Catalogue, Ten Cents.

GOLDING & CO. { 177 to 199 FORT HILL SQUARE, 19 to 27 PURCHASE STREET, } **Boston, Mass.**

Official Press manufactured by Golding & Co. Circa 1885

THE FRANKLIN PRESSES *have been Greatly Improved in Strength and Beauty, and are not Inferior, in any Respect, to any Press Manufactured.*

THE great feature of the **Franklin Job Press** is, that the Pressman may stand directly in front of the Rocking Platen and the Press, to drive and feed the Press, and be enabled, without changing his position, to see the face of the Rocking Platen, the face of the Form, the Ink Distributing surface, and the Inking Rollers, thereby enabling the Operator to detect any imperfection in the working of the Press. *Patented.*

The Platen, when receiving the impression, is securely locked or bolted to its stationary position. This allows the Form to be printed "out of the center," if desired. *Patented.*

Four screws, to which the Platen is attached, regulate the Impression. ***Register perfect.***

☞ The Operator cannot be injured, however careless.

These Presses will all be built with the latest improvements, and of the latest style introduced by the Inventor.

☞ In the Quarto and Half Medium, in combination with the Ink Distributing Table above the Form, are used a Cylinder, a Vibrating Feed Roller, and a Fountain, below the Form.

George P. Gordon of New York City made Franklin Presses. Circa 1883.

Gordon new style with throw-off.

GORDON'S

IMPROVED FRANKLIN PRESSES.

OFFICE—96 FULTON STREET, NEW YORK.

IMPROVED FRANKLIN JOB AND CARD PRESSES.

THE FRANKLIN PRESSES HAVE BEEN GREATLY IMPROVED IN STRENGTH, SIMPLICITY, AND BEAUTY, AND ARE NOT INFERIOR IN ANY RESPECT TO ANY JOB PRESSES MANUFACTURED.

Circa 1866

The Gordon Press Works,

ESTABLISHED FORTY YEARS.

SOLE MANUFACTURERS OF THE

NEW AND OLD STYLE

GORDON'S FRANKLIN

PRINTING PRESSES.

NEW STYLE.

Our well-known New Style is built in five sizes, viz: 13x19, 11x17, 10x15, 9x13 and 8x12 (inside the chase).

We are now also making the Old or Original Style Franklin Press with a "Throw-Off" and other improvements, and of a class of workmanship heretofore unequaled. Sizes, 13x19, 10x15 and 8x12 (inside the chase).

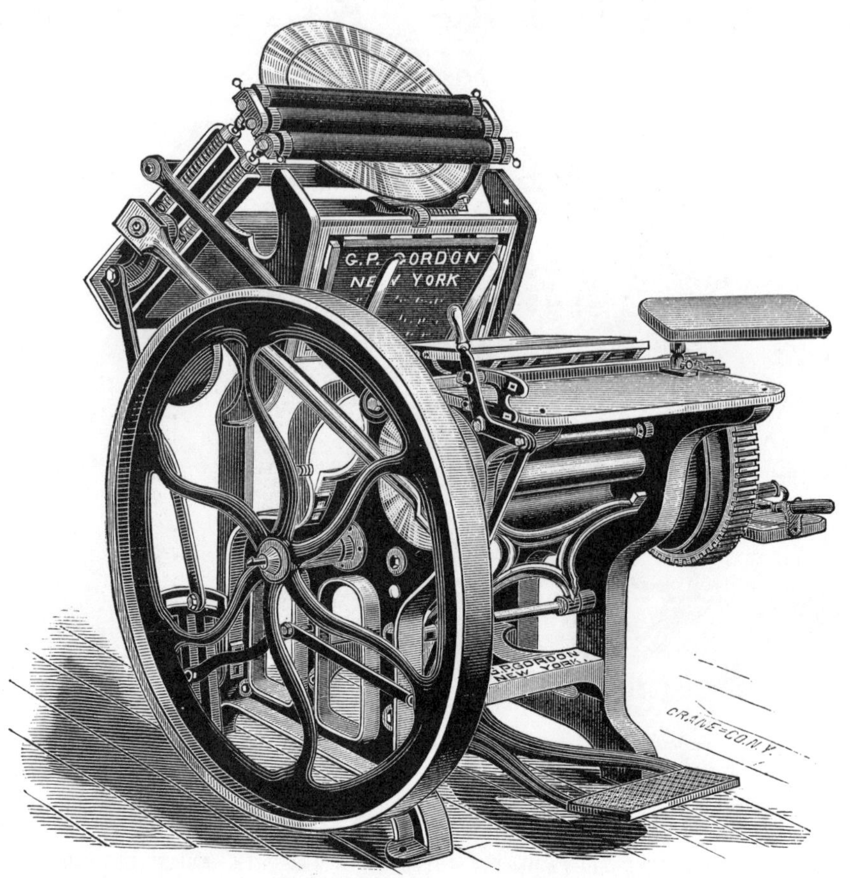

George P. Gordon, old style with throw-off

Gordon, old style with out throw-off.

Gordon, new style with throw-off.

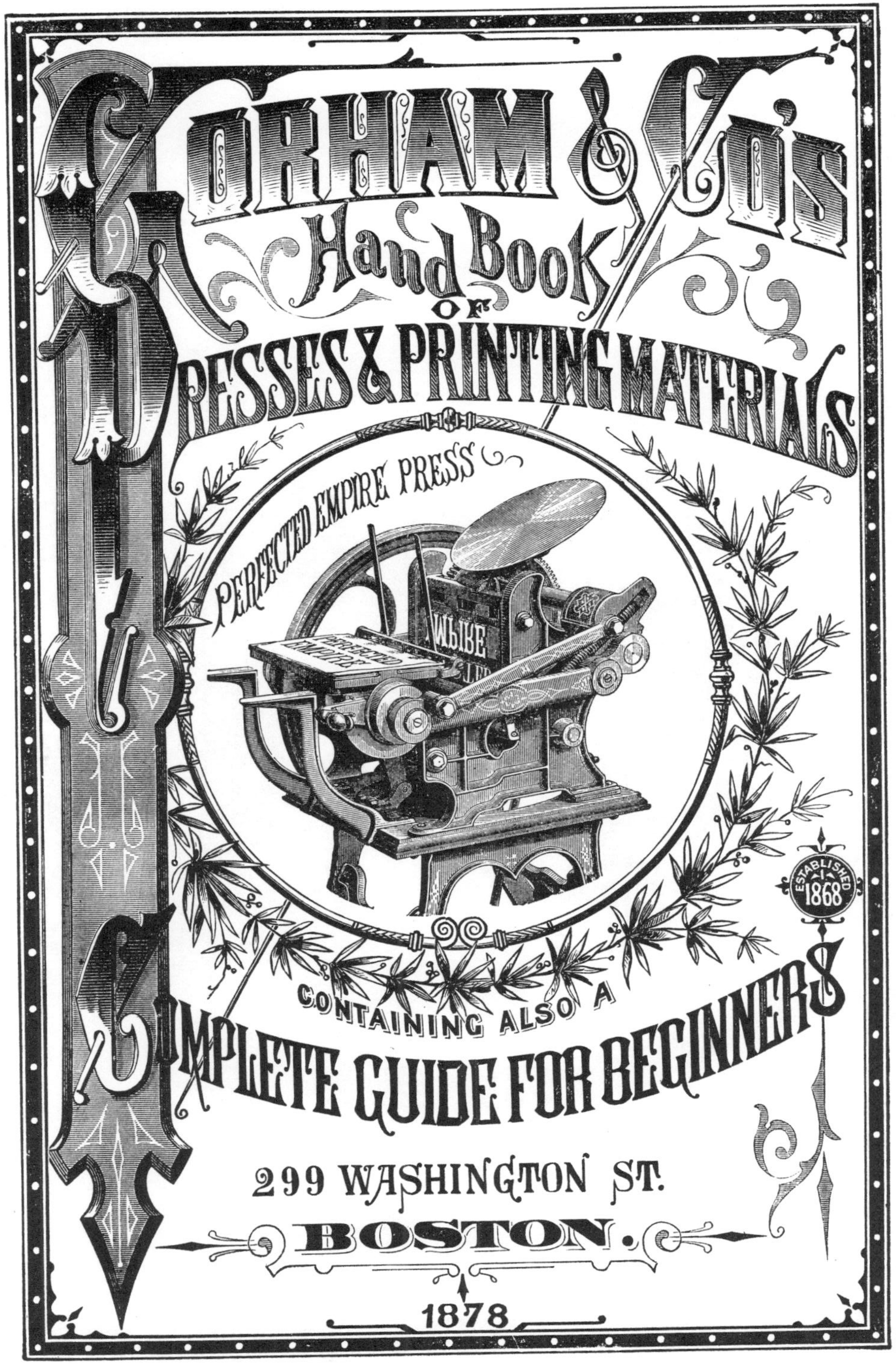

Gorham & Co's
Hand Book
of
Presses & Printing Materials
Perfected Empire Press
Established 1868
Containing also a
Complete Guide for Beginners
299 Washington St.
Boston.
1878

Do your own Printing
Alert Rotary
Alert Rotary 1000 per hour

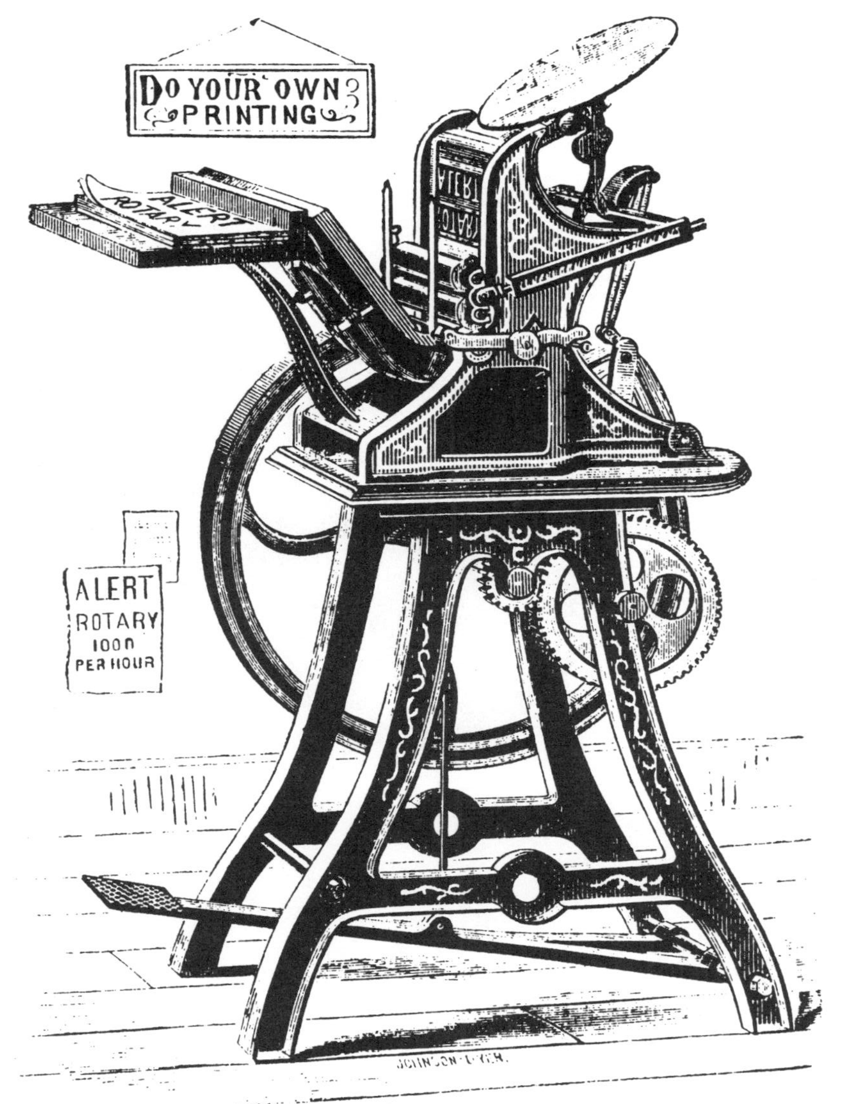

Alert Rotary Press manufactured by W.B. Gorham & Co. Circa 1878

IMPROVED EMPIRE ROTARY PRESS

Patent allowed December, 1874.

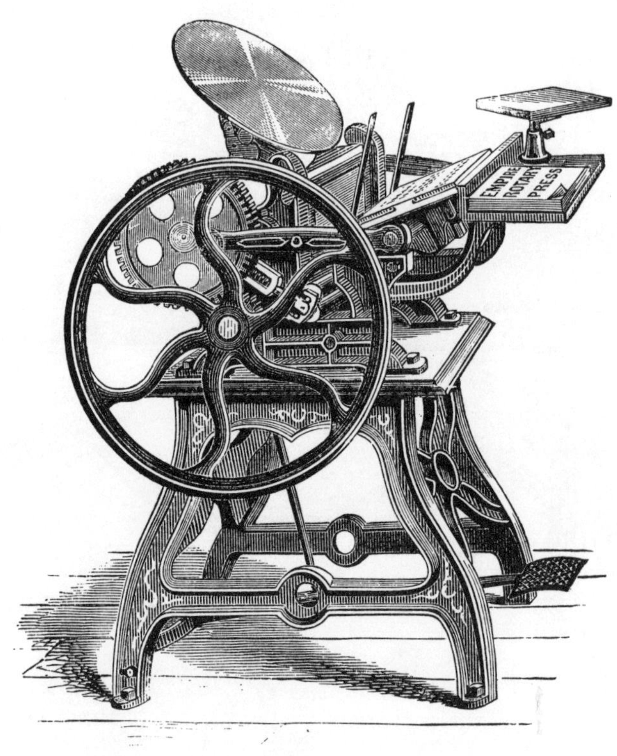

Weight of Improved Empire Rotary Press about 450 lbs.

Size inside Chase, 8 x 12. - - Price, $125.00.

Circa 1878

PERFECTED EMPIRE PRESS.

HAS A THROW OFF!

IS EASY TO FEED!

Weight of Perfected Empire Rotary Press about 525 lbs.

Size inside Chase, 8 x 12. - - - Price, $150.00.

UNIVERSAL PRINTING MACHINE.

MANUFACTURED BY

HAMILTON & McNEAL, Rochester, New York.

"The Strongest,
"Most Durable,
"Most Compact,
"and Simple
"of Presses."

Thorough Distribution.
Square Impression.
Impression Adjuster.
Impression Throw-off.
Roller Throw-off.
Changeable F...

Circa 1872

UNIVERSAL PRINTING MACHINE,

MANUFACTURED BY

HAMILTON & McNEAL,

ROCHESTER, N. Y.

"The Strongest,
Most Durable,
Most Compact,
and Simple
of Presses."

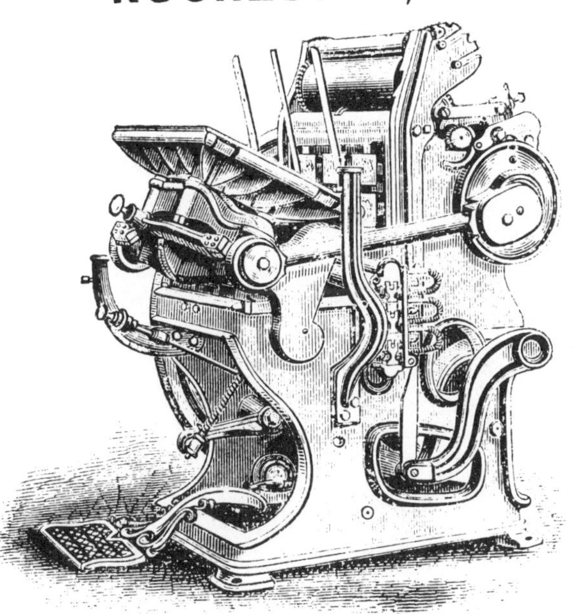

Thorough Distribution,
Square Impression,
Impression Adjuster,
Impression Throw-off,
Roller Throw-off,
Perfect Ink Fountain.

Circa 1873

—THE—

NEW YORK JOB PRESS

Are very Strong and Durable.

Simplicity and Strength.

They Run Easy.

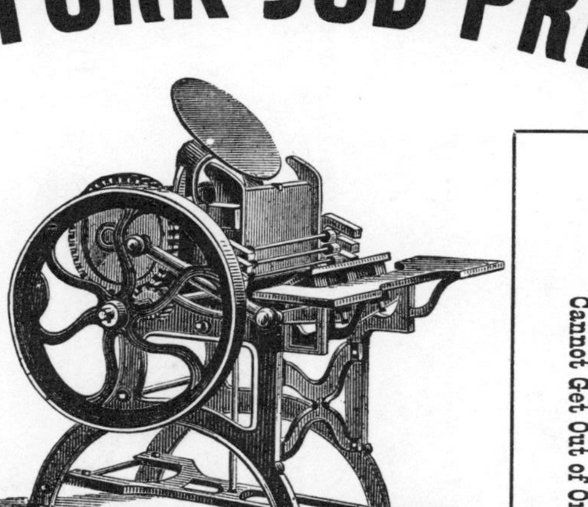

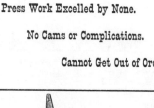

Press Work Excelled by None.

No Cams or Complications.

Cannot Get Out of Order.

A LARGE PAYMENT IS TAKEN IN ADVERTISING.

Why pay a large sum for a Press when here is one JUST AS GOOD, sold on very advantageous terms and with a large payment in advertising.

THE NEW YORK JOB PRESSES

Have now been in the market for Five Years and have been greatly improved and strengthened. Printers are fast becoming convinced of their merits and they are meeting with the greatest success.

The **New York Job Presses** are built in only two sizes.

The EIGHTH-MEDIUM is 9x12 inside the chase. The QUARTER-MEDIUM is 10x15 inside the chase. Three Chases, six Roller Stocks, Roller Mould and Wrenches, accompanying each Press.

For full particulars address the Manufacturer,

M. L. GUMP.

Warehouse, 60 Ann Street, N. Y.

Circa 1877

YORKSTON JOB PRINTING PRESSES.

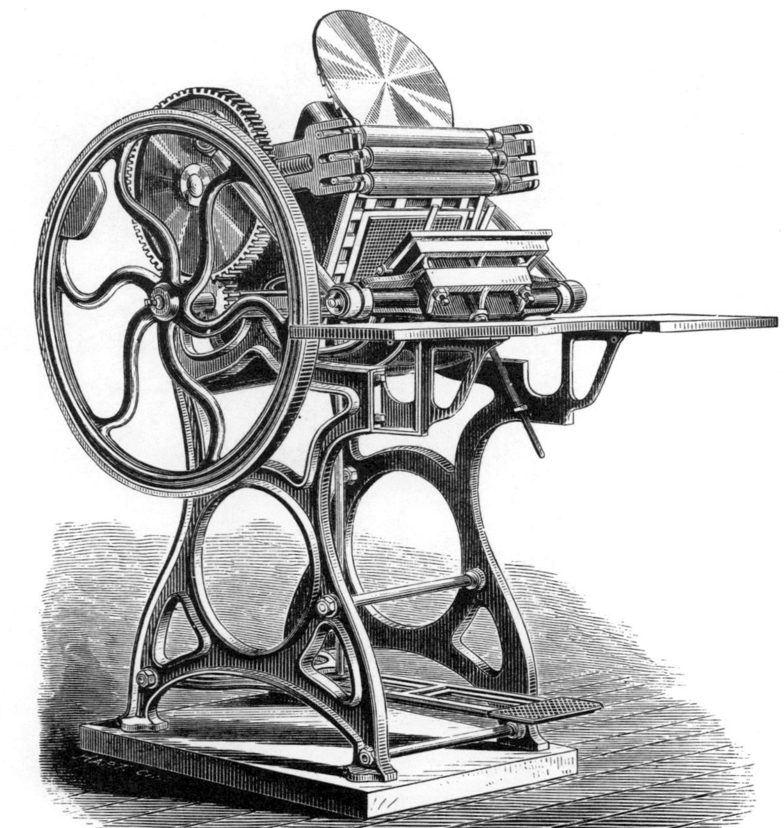

Manufactured by M.L. Gump of New York City. Circa 1874

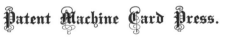

Patent Machine Card Press.

THIS machine is worked either by crank or treadle, and will print from 1,000 to 1,500 cards per hour, in the best manner. The bed is placed vertically, and the impression is given by a cam which brings it forward against the platen.

A Mould, two sets of Roller Stocks, and three Chases are furnished with each press.

Size of Chase inside, 5 × 6¼ inches.

Price, $250.

Boxing and Carting, $5.

Driving Pulley, Fast and Loose Pulleys, Counter-shaft, Hangers and two Cone Pulleys, for steam power, extra, $50.

TERMS OF PAYMENT—Cash at manufactory in New-York.

Circa 1860

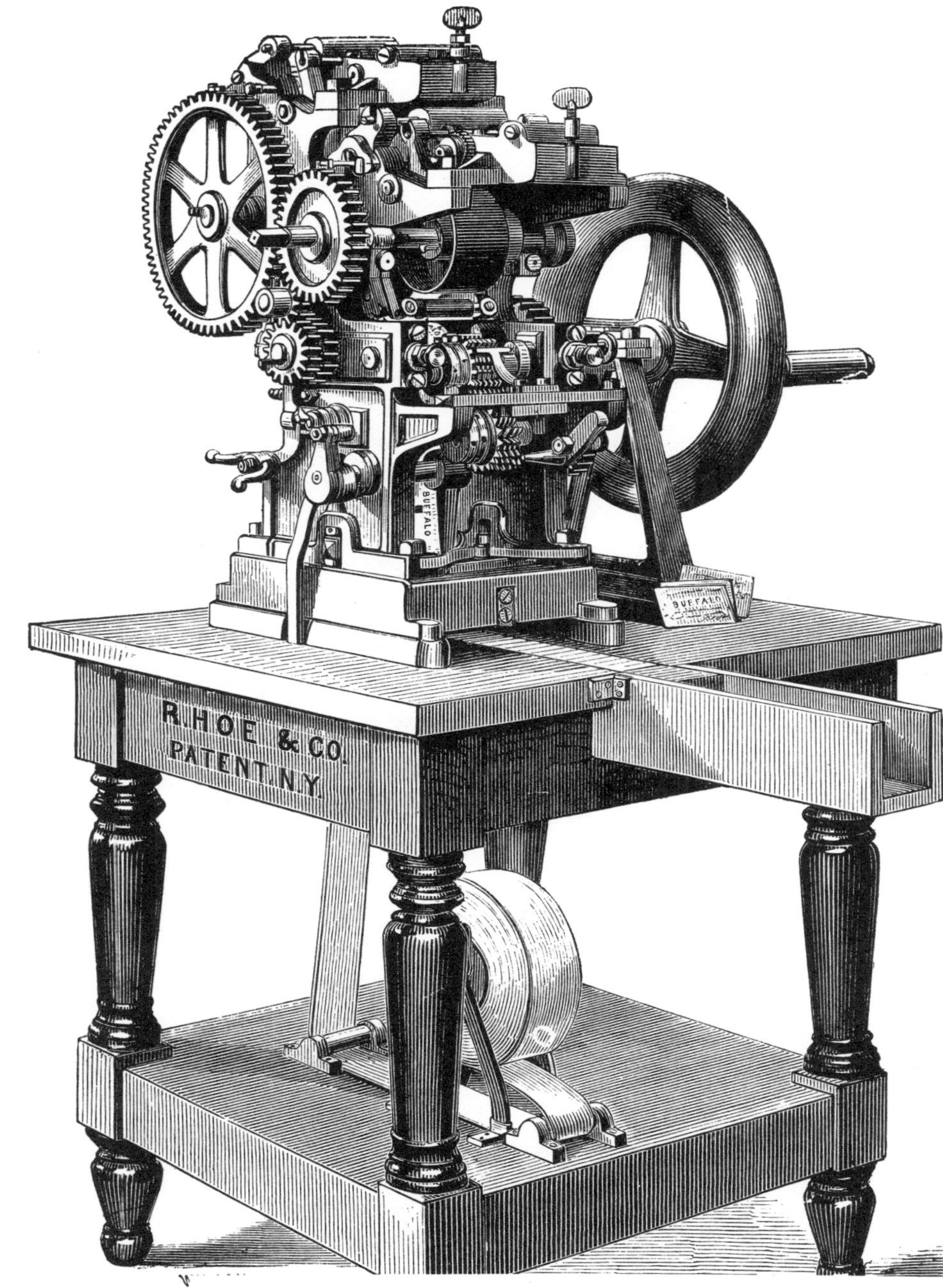

R. Hoe & Co.'s Railway Ticket Machine. Circa 1866

Dauntless Job Press manufactured by P.J. Jennings of New York City. Circa 1885.

As an honest, substantial, low-priced press, it has no superior. It is called "The Dauntless," and P. J. Jennings, of 235 East Forty-first street, New York, is the sole manufacturer. These presses are strongly built, and are guaranteed to do the finest quality of work, and will print a full form with ease. Their simplicity is one of the greatest points in their favor — being free from cams and other intricate machinery, which cause friction and loss of motion. They can be run at a high rate of speed without injury. The bed and platen are true, strong and rigid, and there is no danger of springing or slurring, however heavy the impression may be. They have a very simple throw-off, by means of which the platen may be thrown back instantly.

Circa 1899

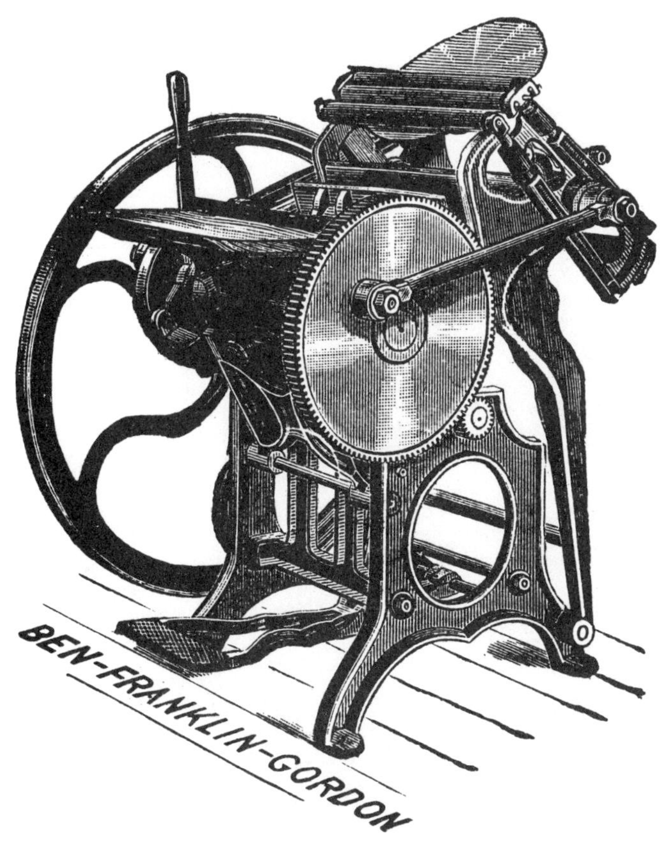

Ben-Franklin-Gordon with 3 rollers and throw-off.
Manufactured by Johnson-Peerless Works, Palmyra, N.Y. Circa 1892.

Ben-Franklin-Gordon 14 x 20". Circa 1895.

BEN-FRANKLIN JOB PRESS

BETTER KNOWN AS THE

OLD STYLE GORDON.

SIZES AND PRICES:

	WITHOUT THROW-OFF	WITH THROW-OFF	BOXING
BEN-FRANKLIN JOB PRESS, 7x11 Inside of Chase,	$140.00	$150.00	$6.00
BEN-FRANKLIN JOB PRESS, 8x12 Inside of Chase,	150.00	—	6.00
BEN-FRANKLIN JOB PRESS, 10x15 Inside of Chase,	250.00	270.00	7.00
BEN-FRANKLIN JOB PRESS, 13x19 Inside of Chase,	350.00	385.00	10.00

FOUNTAIN EXTRA—7x11, $20.00; 8x12, $20.00; 10x15, $22.50; 13x19, $25.00. STEAM FIXTURES, for either size, $15.00.

MARDER, LUSE & CO., 139-141 Monroe Street, CHICAGO.
14-16 Second Street, South, MINNEAPOLIS, MINN.

Made by Johnson Peerless Works, Palmyra, N.Y. Circa 1888.

THE LATEST IMPROVED "GLOBE"

JOB PRINTING PRESSES.

FIRST AND ONLY

EVER GIVEN A

JOB PRINTING PRESS.

Made by J.M. Jones, Palmyra, N.Y. Circa 1875.

THE STAR JOB PRESS

C. H. JONES, Agent.

Western Depot, No. 188 Monroe Street, CHICAGO, ILL.

Manufactured and invented by J. M. JONES, Palmyra, N. Y.

POINTS OF SUPERIORITY:----Great Strength; Unequaled Simplicity; Ease of Running; Manner of Adjusting the Impression; Perfect Ink Distribution, Etc.

THE ONLY PRESS BUILT THAT IS WARRANTED FOR TWO YEARS AGAINST BREAKAGE BY WEAR OR DEFECTIVE MATERIAL.

PRICES THIRTY FIVE PER CENT BELOW EVERY OTHER PRESS EQUALLY AS GOOD.

EXAMINE THESE SIZES AND PRICES:

					Price delivered at Depot in Chicago.
HALF MEDIUM,	13 1-2x19 3-4	at Factory $325	Boxing $8 00	Freight to Chicago $9 25	$342 25
QUARTO "	10 1-2x15 1-5	" 250	" 6 00	" " 7 50	263 50
EIGHTH "	7 1-2x11 1-2	" 165	" 5 00	" " 5 50	175 50

Steam Fixtures $15.00. Including Six Stocks, Roller Mould, Wrenches and Brayer. Fountain $20.00.

What Our Customers Say of the Press:

SOUTH BEND, IND., June 30, 1876.

MR. C. H. JONES:

Dear Sir—The Star Press purchased of you has now been in use in my office over five months and I am entirely satisfied, yes, more am pleased with it. While it is much lower in price than the Gordon and other standard treadle job presses, it is not inferior to them in neatness adjustability and speed, and when it comes to throwing off the impression it "lays over all" of them, since throw off is in the right place and if anything happens that you do not wish to complete the impression, the motion to throw off is as simple as "rolling off a log." I consider it an invaluable acquisition to any office.

E. M. HALL.

MR. C. H. JONES: COTTONWOOD FALLS, KAN.

Dear Sir—I have printed every thing on it, from a sale-bill—filling the chase—to a two-line script card. In the bill I used eighteen-line wood type. I admit that was crowding it too much, but it was equal to the occasion.

W. A. MORGAN.

MR. C. H. JONES: CHARLESTON, S. C.

Dear Sir—The Half-Medium Press has given us perfect satisfaction. We have printed jobs on it ranging in size, from a visiting card up. It runs easily. We have a lad in the office, fourteen years of age, who can run it as well as any one, and prefers working it to a smaller press we have.

ALEXANDER & McTURLOUS.

Circa 1878

WASHINGTON JOBBER.

THIS Press is in use in hundreds of offices and is well adapted to all kinds of job work. It is strongly and perfectly built and is fully equal for speed to any other job press. Built in three sizes, 7 × 10, 8 × 12 and 8 × 14 inches inside chase.

Manufactured by J.M. Jones, Palmyra, N.Y. Circa 1885

THE JONES GORDON JOB PRINTING PRESS

Is not an Old Style Gordon, but has several Important Changes and Improvements which make it quite a different Machine.

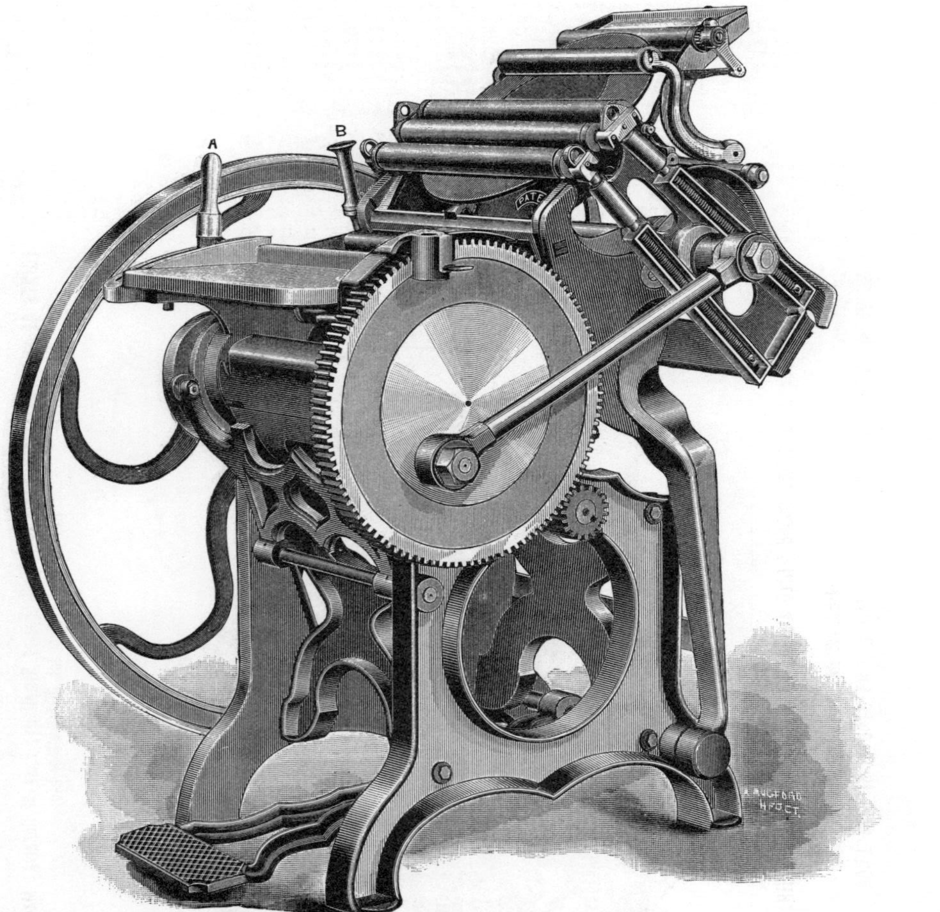

A VERY IMPORTANT FEATURE in these presses is that **the whole Impression may be INSTANTLY CHANGED**—either increased or diminished—**without stopping the press.** When the impression screws are properly set, it is seldom, if ever, necessary to move them, as all adjustments are made by means of the hand wheel, marked ***"B"*** in cut.

Another important feature is, that when the impression is thrown off by means of the lever ***"A"*** a simple device causes the movement of parts that prevents the ink rollers from touching the form, and the press may be run indefinitely for the distribution of ink.

Another feature of considerable importance in saving time and patience is the self-locking Chase Hook and Form Starter. When the chase is put in place on the bed, it is locked without touching any lever, pad, screw or any part of the press. When the form is to be removed, it is only necessary to press forward the pad, marked "patent," which causes the chase hook to raise and the form to move forward so as to be convenient for lifting out.

When the platen is in a convenient position for setting the grippers, they may be brought down on the platen for that purpose. The ink roller carriages are provided with loops to be used for putting in or removing the rollers.

The Duplex Fountain is a great advance over anything heretofore used for the distribution of ink on a disk press A separate distributing roller moves down and back twice, or four times, over the upper part of the disk, each impression. The disk is double and is constantly changing, any part of the main disk only stopping at the same place every hundredth impression.

The press is very heavy, strongly braced and substantially built. The Impression Arms are of steel, forged from one piece without weld. Manufactured by

JOHN M. JONES & CO., PALMYRA, N.Y.

Circa 1890

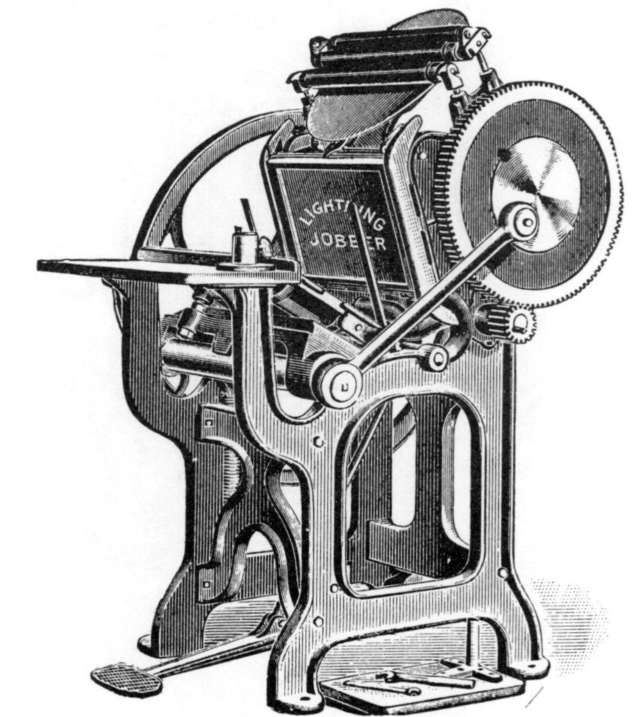

Lightning Jobber, old style, manufactured by J.M. Jones & Co. Circa 1896.

Star Jobber manufactured by J.M. Jones & Co. from 1875 to 1889.

New Star Jobber manufactured by J.M. Jones & Co.

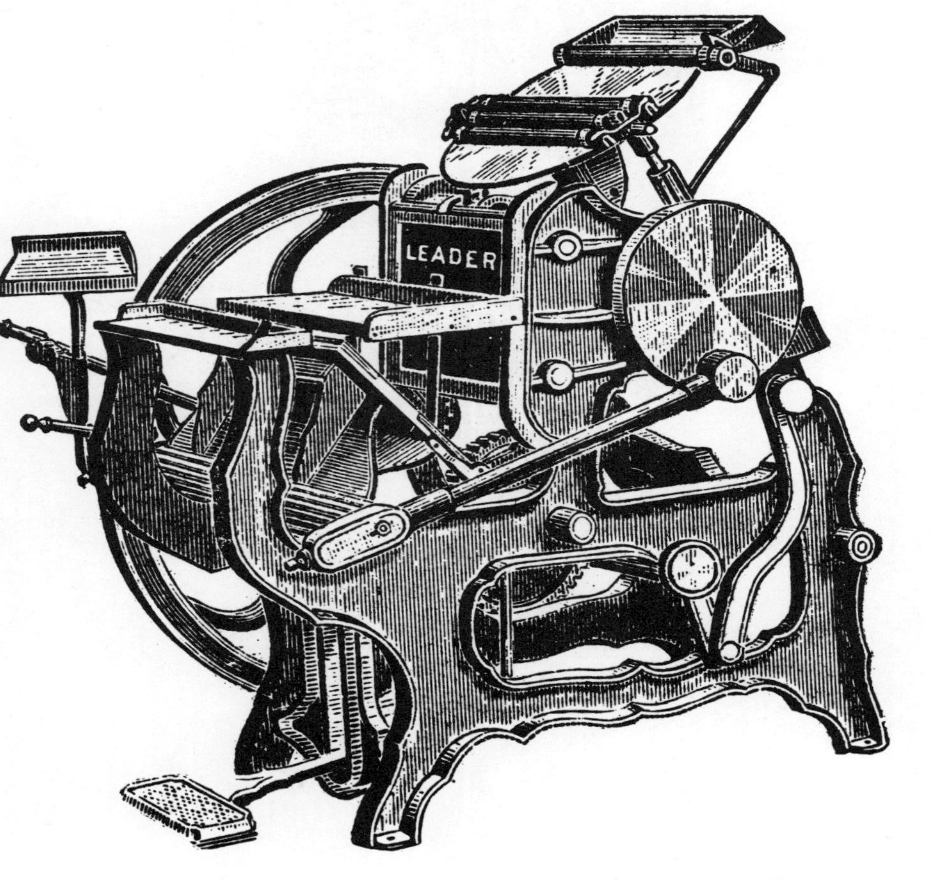

Leader Job Press manufactured by J.M. Jones. Circa 1882.

New Era, old style Gordon manufactured by J.M. Jones. Circa 1894.

KELLOGG'S

NEW STYLE IMPROVED NEWBURY BLANK AND CARD PRESS,

Patented by A. & B. NEWBURY, July 5, 1859, and A. N. KELLOGG, Jan. 6, 1863.

PRINTS a form 6¾ by 11¾, or will print a sheet about 14 by 18, by working and turning. Is capable of printing 1,000 to 1,600 per hour. Will do superior work. Price, boxed, with Table and latest improvements, $150. Terms Cash.

With each Press are sent two Chases, with Sidesticks, two pairs Roller Stocks, Roller Mold, three Friskets, Wrenches, and a Rubber Blanket—the whole carefully boxed.

The Press is shipped almost ready for operation, but for the convenience of purchasers Directions for setting it up and operating are forwarded with each Press.

☞ Eastern purchasers charged only with transportation from New York—Western, from Chicago.

REFERENCES.

C. A. Reed.......Red Hook, N. Y.
A. Clapp.............Dryden, "
W. A. Smith ....Otsego, "
John Jackson..........Calais, Me.
Thos. E. Ash .....Newport, R. I.
E. Cornman & Son....Carlisle, Pa.
G. F. Weaver....Harrisburgh, "
Miller & Irwin.........Mercer, "
Wm. McWilliams.Kittanning, "
L. D. Reynolds.Washington, D. C.
S. W. Smith..........Warsaw, Mo.
D. W. Phillips .....Albion, Mich.
Nims & Beach....Lexington, "
F. D. Austin........Allegan, "
Miller & Underwood.Cha'ston, Ill.
R. H. Ruggles........Mendota, "
Wm. Wagner.........Freeport, "
James Shoaff..........Decatur, "
Wm. Parker ....Winona, "
E. A. Snively........Galesburg, "

H. L. Goodall............Cairo, Ill.
Edwin Dyson........Rushville, "
N. E. Stevens...........Paxton, "
Sapp & Richardson.Woodstock, "
Wm. Hill ....Baraboo, Wis.
O. W. Smith.....Manitowoc, "
E. B. Bolens ......Janesville, "
I. F. Mack, Jr.....Brodhead, "
D. Blumenthal ..Watertown, "
John Hotchkiss...Fox Lake, "
John Ulrich.......La Crosse, "
H. E. Beals............Omro, "
Beers & Eaton........Lyons, Iowa.
Andy Felt...........Nashua, "
T. C. Medary & Co.Lansing, "
C.W.Andrews & Co.Mechanicsv'e"
Ethell & Helm........Muncie, Ind.
Matthias & Schnurr.Galion, Ohio.
Francis Brooks....Defiance, "

Of this Press we offer but one recommendation, as follows:—
"We almost worship it."—H. E. BEALS, Omro, Wis.

ADDRESS

A. N. KELLOGG,
99 and 101 Washington St., Chicago.

Circa 1868

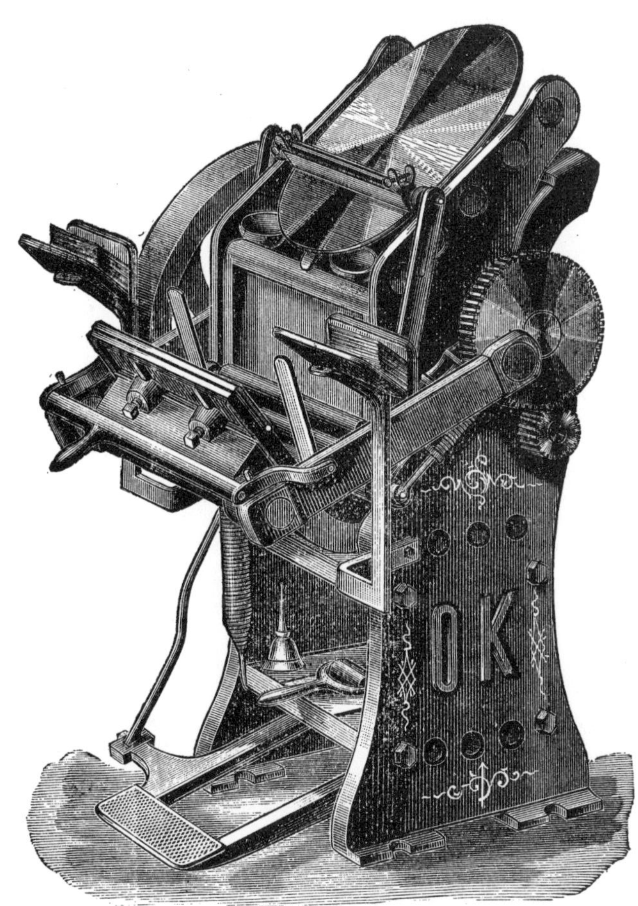

THE O.K. JOB PRINTING PRESS.

Best In The World.

Heavy, Fast, Durable, Powerful, AND HAS MANY IMPROVEMENTS.

PATENTED.

Price Only $100. *Boxed And Shipped Free.*

Complete with CHASE, 3 ROLLERS, &c.

CHASE 9 by 13 INCHES, INSIDE.

Shipping weight about 600 lbs.

Is your patronage increasing? If so hasten to order an O. K. as its capacity will please you.

The O.K. Job Printing Press was made by W.A. Kelsey & Co. from 1886 to 1898.

THE EXCELSIOR JOBBER.

ROTARY power Machine for faster work, in private or job offices. Carries two rollers, revolving ink-plate, and gives very thorough distribution. It is extremely simple in all its arrangements, having precisely the same regulation of impression, patent Chase, and Grippers, as all other Excelsior Presses. Balance-wheel about 100 pounds weight. Solid Iron Stand. The power is given by a compound lever, having connection with a rocking Platen, giving powerful, steady, easy, and rapid action. Good dwell on the impression,—which is necessary to good work—and rest for feeding. No side arms to obstruct feeding of large sheets. Built of the best materials in the most substantial manner, and warranted to do perfect work. It is a Press for *work*, has all its gears and levers inside of frame, out of dust and danger, and is built to do good and long service. Its price is below anything of equal merit.

An Automatic Card Dropper is arranged on each press without extra charge, for which other press builders charge extra. It consists of a Gauge for feeding cards, tags, tickets, etc., on which is arranged an ingenious device which trips it at each impression, dropping the card into a box beneath the Press, and again resuming its position to take another card. The printer has simply to *feed* the cards. This probably doubles the speed, giving from 2000 to 3000 impressions per hour.

Size of Chase 8 1-4 by 12 1-4 inches. Weight, boxed, about 475 pounds. Price $115.00. Fitted with power fixtures, pulleys, $6.00 extra. Boxing and shipping. $4.00 extra.

Each Press set up complete when shipped, ready for use the moment it is unpacked. It is accompanied by Rollers, Patent Chase, Ink Table, Feed Table Bracket, Wrench, and Cabinet Drawer under the Press.

☞ If desired, the ordinary open Chase may be used on the jobber, and it will be so fitted if ordered.

Does ANYBODY ask for a better proof of WHICH Press is best to buy for Amateur use, than the verdict of SEVEN Centennial Judges, who saw the Excelsior work day after day beside others, and tested it fully?

OUR TERMS OF PAYMENT.

☞ *Please give them careful attention, and save needless correspondence.*

All list prices are *net;* no discounts. Terms are cash in every case. Orders should be accompanied by cash in *Registered Letters*, or by *P. O. Money Orders on West Meriden*, Connecticut, as our Money Order Department is in the *West* division of the City; or by *Bank Draft*. Either is safe. If desired, we send *C. O. D.* when order is over $10, but one-third of bill *must* accompany order, as a guarantee that goods will be taken. Return charges on C. O. D. charged to customer always. Goods ordered by freight cannot be C. O. D., but must be fully paid for when ordered. Write address and shipping directions on every order, giving same fully and plainly.

W. A. KELSEY & CO., Meriden, Conn.

* * * Postage Stamps accepted to any amount, as we use them largely. Canada Stamps also taken.

A SPECIMEN OF EXCELSIOR PRESS WORK is the handsome Note Circular sent out with this Catalogue. It was printed on a No. 2½ Press, by an Amateur, a boy in our office.

Circa 1880

THE EXCELSIOR ROTARY JOB PRESS.

IMPROVED AND PERFECTED.

$90.00 COMPLETE.

CHASE 8¼x12¼

HEAVY, STRONG, DURABLE. RUNS EASY STILL AND FAST.

Manufactured by

W. A. KELSEY & CO.,

MERIDEN, CONN.

Circa 1882

THE NEW STAR JOBBER.

★ ★ ★ ★

$60 **$60**

CHEAPEST *PRESS* AND BEST *PRESS* IN THE WORLD.

SPEED 3500.

Chase 7 by 11 inches.

FILLS THE DEMAND FOR A Good Small Jobber AT LOW PRICE.

One or more needed in every office.

"It's a Little Money Maker."

Runs like lightning. Does excellent work. Costs little to buy and little to run. Easy by foot, or with one-quarter horse power. Small electric motor readily attached by any electrician.

This beautiful machine is the invention of the famous designer of printing presses, George W. Prouty. Our company acquired Mr. Prouty's rights, at large cost, and has given the public an excellent little Prouty Jobber at the lowest price ever offered on a good machine.

The engraving explains itself. The design is beautifully simple. A rocking platen, rigidly constructed, carried by compound leverage, with dwell on impression, quick return, and a rest for feeding. No throw-off is needed. running is so light and control so easy. Very still running. No side arms to obstruct work.

PRICE $60. Boxed and shipped to any address, and fully warranted. Ink Fountain, if desired, $10. Extra Chases, $1.50 each. Extra Ink Rollers, $1.10 each. Power Fixtures, $10.

CARD KICKER. For $12 extra our Patent Attachment is added to Press, which kicks off the card, from the platen, after printing. This Kicker is a wonderful help to speedy printing, as the operator only has to feed cards, tags, labels, etc., leaving the hands freer. Each card or tag is thrown into a box conveniently placed at side of the press.

This company owns the trade mark "Star" for printing presses, by succession rights, from 1870, and no other printing machine can be lawfully made as a "Star Press."

THIS IS OUR "WAVE BORDER." FONT OF 30 INCHES, $1.00.

Circa 1899

THE NEW STAR JOBBER

$150 ONLY

CHEAPEST AND BEST PRESS IN THE WORLD

Speed 2000. Chase 7 x 11 Inches.

Fills the demand for a Good, Small Jobber at Low Price

One or More Needed in Every Office.

COMPLETE OUTFIT, $220.

Star Job Press, 7 x 11 inches,	**$150.00**
Furniture and Quoins,	2.50
Black and Colored Inks,	2.50
Ten Fonts of Type,	39.00
Type Cases,	15.75
Leads, Bodkin and Tweezers,	1.50
Gauge Pins,	.50
Mallet, Planer Can of Oil,	.90
Composing Stick,	1.50
Can of Cleaning Preparation,	.35
Lead Cutting Machine,	3.00
Rules, Dashes, etc.,	2.50
This makes a good all-around printing office for a small investment.	**$220.00**

RUNS LIKE LIGHTNING. Does excellent work. Costs little to buy and little to run. Easy by foot or one-quarter horse power.

This beautiful machine is the invention of the famous designer of printing presses, George W. Prouty. Our Company acquired Mr. Prouty's rights at large cost, and has given the public an excellent little Prouty Jobber at the lowest price ever offered on a good machine.

The engraving explains itself. The design is beautifully simple. A rocking platen, rigidly constructed, carried by compound leverage, with dwell on impression, quick return and a rest for feeding. No throw-off is needed, running is so light and control is so easy.

PRICE $150, F. O. B. Meriden, boxed and shipped to any address, and fully warranted. Ink fountain, if desired, $12. Extra chases, $1.80 each. Extra ink rollers, $1.80 each. Power Fixtures, $12.50 extra. Weight, boxed, 500 pounds.

This Company owns the trade mark, "Star," for printing presses, by succession rights, from 1870, and no other printing machine can be lawfully made as a "Star Press."

THE KELSEY PRESS COMPANY,

MERIDEN, CONNECTICUT, U S. A.

Note the same press with different prices.

THE UNION ROTARY JOB PRESS

$125.00

CHASE, 10 X 14

BEST IN WORLD

Powerful Impression.
Perfect Ink Distribution.
Easy Adjustments.

PRICE, $125

Complete with Three Rollers, Chase, Wrench.

Also 1 Extra Chase, Heavy Pattern.

Impression Throw-off,
No Extra Charge.

Boxed for Shipping,
No Extra Charge.

Shipping Weight, 750 lbs.

Power Fixtures, if required, $10 extra.

Roller Mold, $2.50.

A Good Combination of Best Mechanical Principles. Compound Toggle Levers.

Complete Outfit, $180.

A full and excellent selection for general printing.

Union Job Press,	$125.00
Furniture and Quoins,	2.50
Ten Fonts Type,	30.00
Type Cases, Cabinet,	10.00
Black and Colored Inks,	2.00
Leads, Bodkin, &c.,	2.50
Composing Stick,	1.00
Rule and Lead Cutter,	5.00
Dashes, Rules, &c.,	2.00
	$180.00

EXTRA ROLLERS, $1.20 each. CHASES, $1.75 each. INK FOUNTAIN, complete, readily attached ,$10.00.
(Fountains only required by those having long runs. May be ordered with press or can be bought afterward.)

Increasing business demands better facilities or you don't keep up with the times. Buy a Union Press, up-to-date, with speed of 1000 to 3000 per hour. It has all the improvements; depressible grippers; spring chase lock; handy boxes over chase for gauges, pins, paste, etc.; adjustable feed boards; roller racks under press; ink plate for hand roller, and a tool box.

The peerless movement, compound toggle leverage, the most powerful direct action. Three rollers over full form. Quick regulation of impression, and roller adjustment. There is a positive dwell on impression and a long rest for feeding. CHASE, 10 X 14 INCHES, INSIDE.

The Ink Rollers have our new invention, the Adjustable Trunnions, by which the rollers bear light or heavy on form, as desired. One of the greatest improvements ever put on a printing press. Saves use of bearers.

Press is powerful and rapid, yet readily understood and run by even a lad of ten. Every press we send out is fully warranted in every respect.

Circa 1899

Union Rotary Job Press

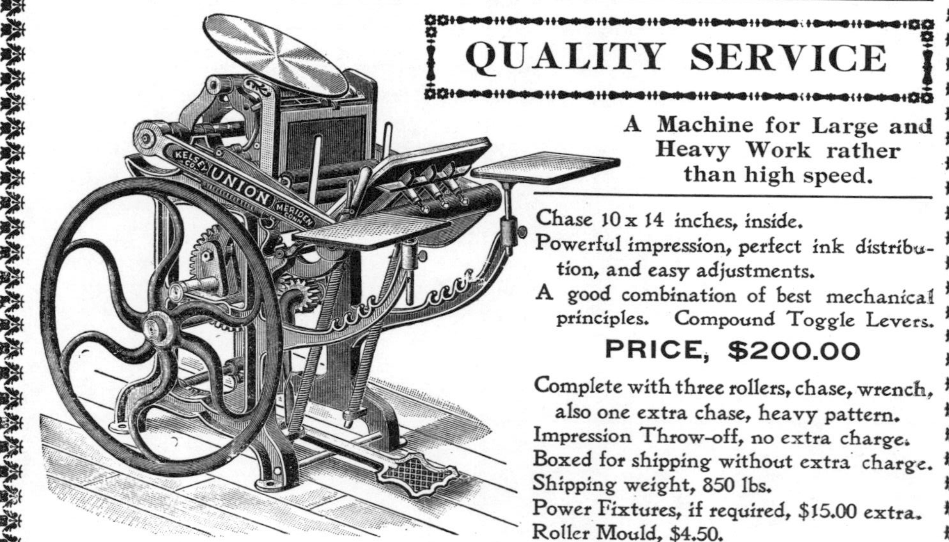

QUALITY SERVICE

A Machine for Large and Heavy Work rather than high speed.

Chase 10 x 14 inches, inside.
Powerful impression, perfect ink distribution, and easy adjustments.
A good combination of best mechanical principles. Compound Toggle Levers.

PRICE, $200.00

Complete with three rollers, chase, wrench, also one extra chase, heavy pattern.
Impression Throw-off, no extra charge.
Boxed for shipping without extra charge.
Shipping weight, 850 lbs.
Power Fixtures, if required, $15.00 extra.
Roller Mould, $4.50.

Complete Outfit — A FULL AND EXCELLENT SELECTION FOR GENERAL PRINTING. — **$300**

Union Job Press,	$200.00	Leads, Bodkin, etc.,	$2.90
Furniture and Quoins,	3.00	Composing Stick,	1.50
Fifteen Fonts Type,	57.10	Rule and Lead Cutter,	7.50
Type Cases,	22.50	Dashes, Rules, etc.,	3.00
Black and Colored Inks,	2.50	Total,	$300.00

Extra Rollers, $1.80 each. Chases, $2.00 each. Ink Fountain, complete, readily attached, $15.00
(Fountain only required by those having long runs. May be ordered with press, or can be bought afterward.)

INCREASING busin ss demands better facilities or you don't keep up with the times. Buy a Union Press, with speed of 1,000 per hour. It has many valuable improvements; depressible grippers, spring chase lock, handy boxes over chase for gauges, pins, paste, etc., adjustable feed boards, roller racks under press, ink plate for hand roller and a tool box.

The peerless movement, compound toggle leverage, the most powerful direct action. Three rollers over full form. Quick regulation of impression and roller adjustment. There is a positive dwell on impression and a long rest for feeding. Chase 10 x 14 inches inside.

Press is powerful and rapid, yet readily understood and easily run. Every press we send out is fully warranted in every respect.

A large variety of printing can be executed on this machine with much saving of money if you do your own printing, or substantial profits printing for others.

Note the same press with different prices.

KIDDER'S

SELF-FEEDING & DELIVERING

JOB PRINTING PRESSES.

Printing, and Ruling or Bronzing from the Web or continuous sheet, an established revolution in the Job Printing Business.

Nearly 100 of these Machines already in Use.

MANUFACTURED IN THREE SIZES: HALF, QUARTO AND EIGHTH MEDIUMS. OTHER SIZES IN PROPORTION.

This engraving represents the Eighth Medium size. Its ordinary practical working speed for first-class mercantile printing, is SIX THOUSAND to SEVEN THOUSAND impressions per hour.

Size of Chase, inside, 8x12 inches.

For full particulars, references, prices, etc., address,

THE KIDDER PRESS MANUFACTURING CO.,

140 High Street, Boston, Mass.

BRANCH OFFICES AND AGENCIES:

New York, N. Y., 13 Spruce Street .... H. H. HARADON, Agent
Chicago, Ill., 81 Jackson Street .... F. HINCKLEY, Agent
St. Louis, Mo. .... BUXTON & SKINNER, Agents
Philadelphia, Pa., 124 Exchange Place .... J. R. SMITH, Agent
Cincinnati, O., 168 Vine St. .... ALLISON, SMITH & JOHNSON, Agents
Syracuse, N. Y. .... W. A. VANDERCOOK, Agent

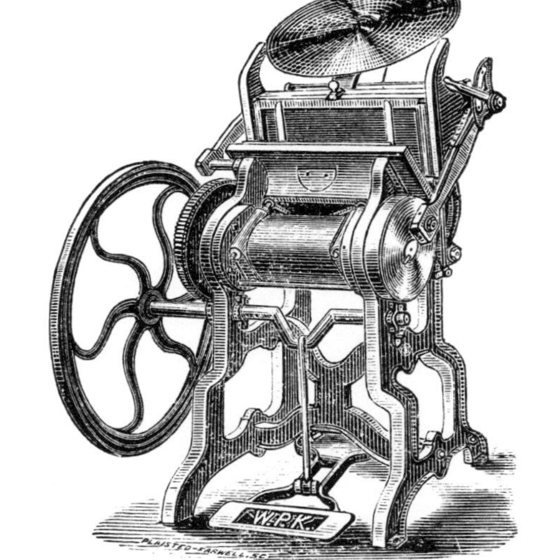

Kidder Press manufactured by Standard Machinery Co., Dover, N.H.
Circa 1875

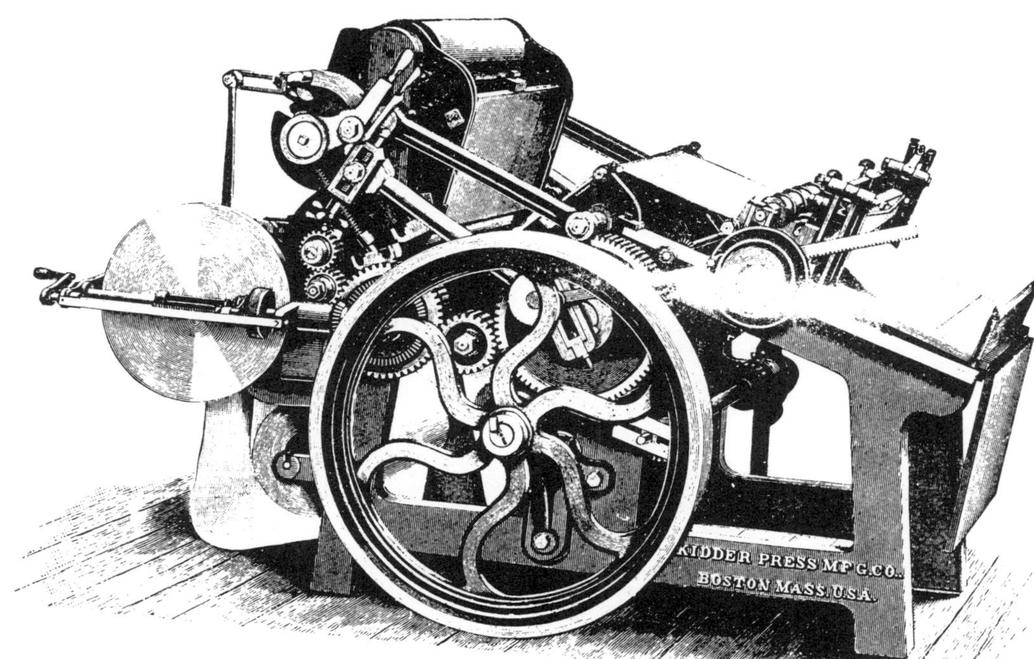

Kidder Roll-fed Platen Press. Circa 1895

. . . The New Style Noiseless

LIBERTY JOB PRESS

Its Special Features are entirely Unique, and not to be had on any other Job Printing Press. * * * *

HIGHEST PREMIUM AWARDED WHEREVER ON EXHIBITION.

LATEST AWARD:—First Prize, the Gold Medal, at the International Exhibition in Brussels, 1888.

More than 10,000 in Use all over the World.

IN USE IN THE GOVERNMENT PRINTING OFFICES OF THE UNITED STATES, GERMANY, AUSTRIA, RUSSIA, FRANCE, SPAIN, TURKEY, PORTUGAL, MEXICO, BRAZIL, CUBA, ETC.

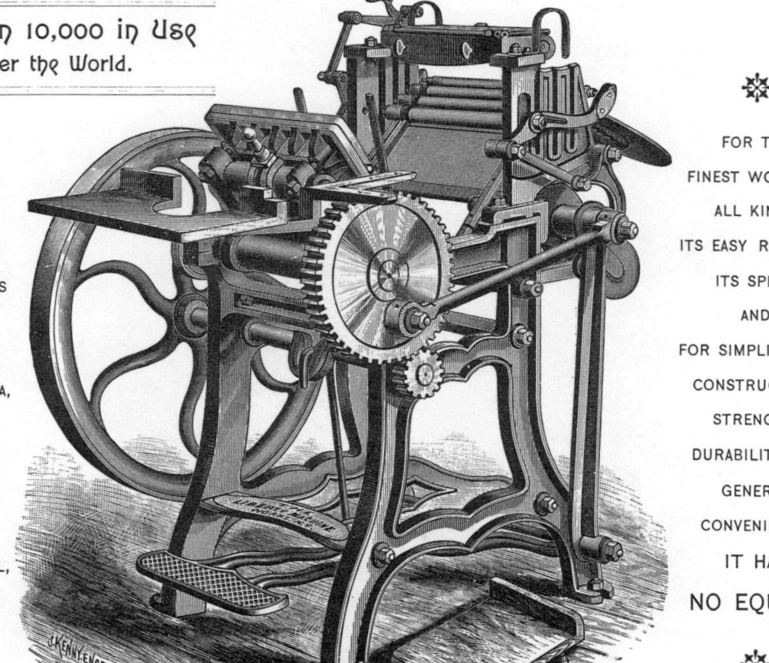

FOR THE FINEST WORK OF ALL KINDS, ITS EASY RUNNING ITS SPEED, AND FOR SIMPLICITY OF CONSTRUCTION, STRENGTH, DURABILITY AND GENERAL CONVENIENCE, IT HAS NO EQUAL!

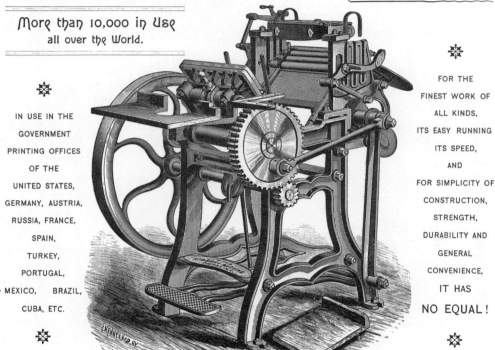

THE lightest running job press made. The most perfect distribution ever obtained on a job press. The only job press whose form rollers can carry full-sized riders. Patent noiseless gripper motion, worked by cam movement and without springs. Patent combined brake and belt shifter. New and original knifeless fountain, which can be regulated by feeder while press is in motion. Positive throw-off, so constructed as to add strength and durability to the press.

SIZES AND PRICES:

No.	Inside regular chase	Inside skeleton chase	Price	Fountain, if ordered with press	Skeleton Chase, each	Boxing
No. 2	7 x 11 in.	7½ x 11¾ in.	$200	$25.00	$3.50	$6.00
No. 2a	9 x 13	9½ x 13¾	250	25.00	4.00	6.00
No. 3	10 x 15	11 x 16	300	25.00	4.50	7.50
No. 3a	11 x 17	12 x 18	350	25.00	5.00	9.00
No. 4	13 x 19	14 x 20	400	25.00	5.50	10.00
No. 3x	11 x 17	12 x 18	375	25.00	5.00	9.00
No. 4x	13 x 19	14 x 20	425	25.00	5.50	10.00
No. 5	14½ x 22	15½ x 23	500	25.00	6.00	15.00

3x and 4x are extra heavy, for box makers, etc. Steam fixtures and brake, $15.00 extra. SEND FOR FULL DESCRIPTIVE CATALOGUE.

THE LIBERTY MACHINE WORKS, 54 Frankfort St., NEW YORK,

SOLE MANUFACTURERS.

Circa 1895

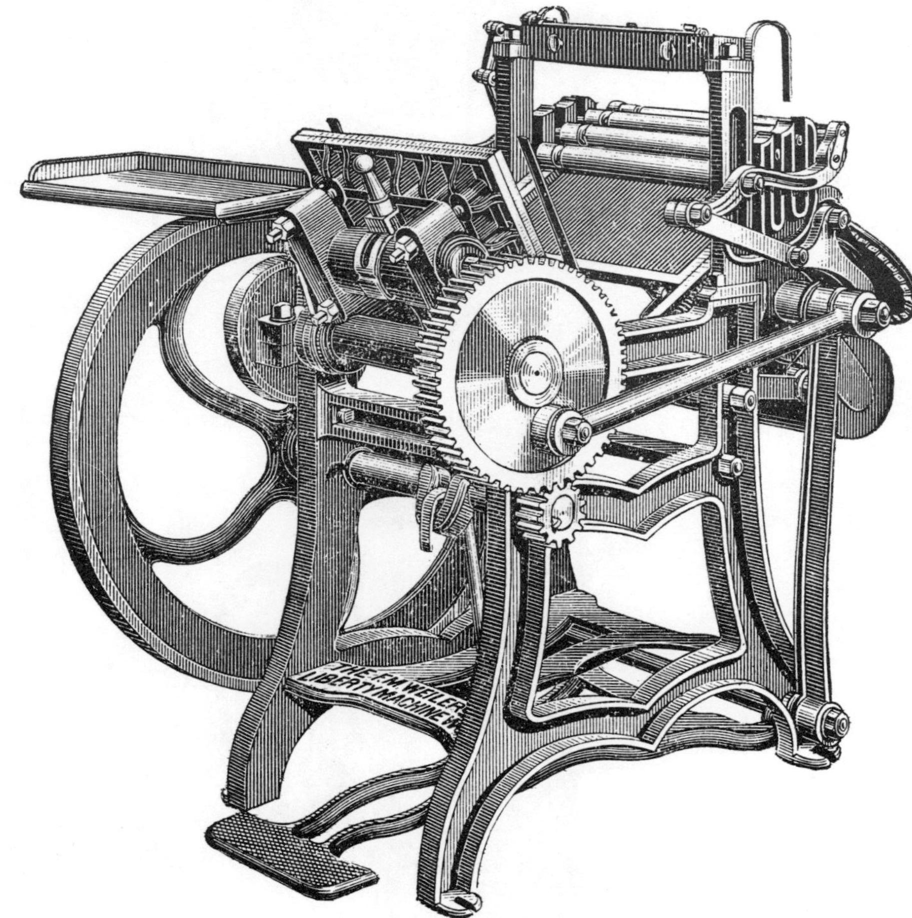

Liberty Job Press with throw-off.

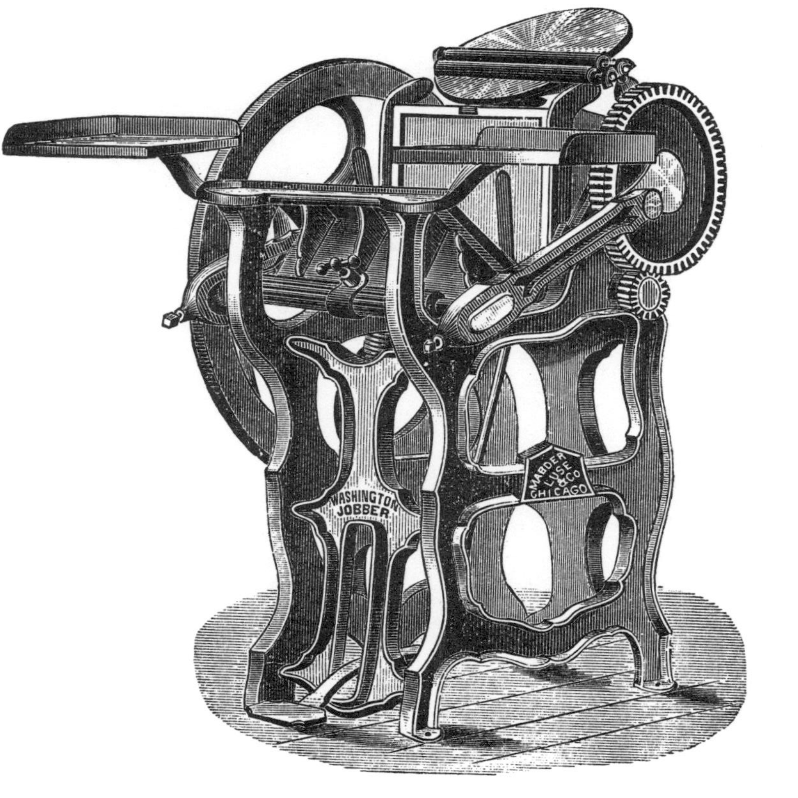

Washington Jobber manufactured for Marder & Luse Co. in Chicago.

Monitor Press manufactured by Monitor Press Co. of New York.
Circa 1875

Universal, style one, with double latched throw-off.
Manufactured by National and sold by American Type Founders.

National Jobber by National Printers Warehouse in New York City.
Circa 1892

A. & B. NEWBURY,

PRINTING PRESS AND MACHINERY MANUFACTORY,

COXSACKIE, N. Y.

Our Country Jobber.

Our Lead Cutter.

Our Proof Presses.

Circa 1867

THE NEW EUREKA JOBBER.

This Press has been in use but a few months, and is proving one of the most satisfactory in market. It occupies but little room, is simple, durable, cheap, and is operated with the greatest ease.

The distribution is by disc, the fountain is between the disc and bed, and is so arranged that the first roller takes the ink and the rest distribute it. It has three rollers, with adjustable bearers to regulate the pressure of the rollers on the form, and may be thrown off instantly for extra distribution. The impression may also be thrown off at once, so that neither rollers nor platen touch the form. The frame of the Press is made in one casting, and all the parts are made with a view of firmness and strength. The shafts are cast steel and the driving pinion wrought iron, and the Press may be run at any speed that the operator can feed with safety.

PRICES:

Half-Medium,	**13 1-2 x 19**	**inches inside of Chase,**		**$450**
Quarto-Medium,	**10 x 16**	**"**	**"**	**350**
Eighth-Medium,	**8 x 12**	**"**	**"**	**250**

Fountain, $25. Steam Fixtures, $15.

These prices include two sets of roller stocks, roller mold, three chases, wrenches, and boxing.

All presses delivered at the manufactory.

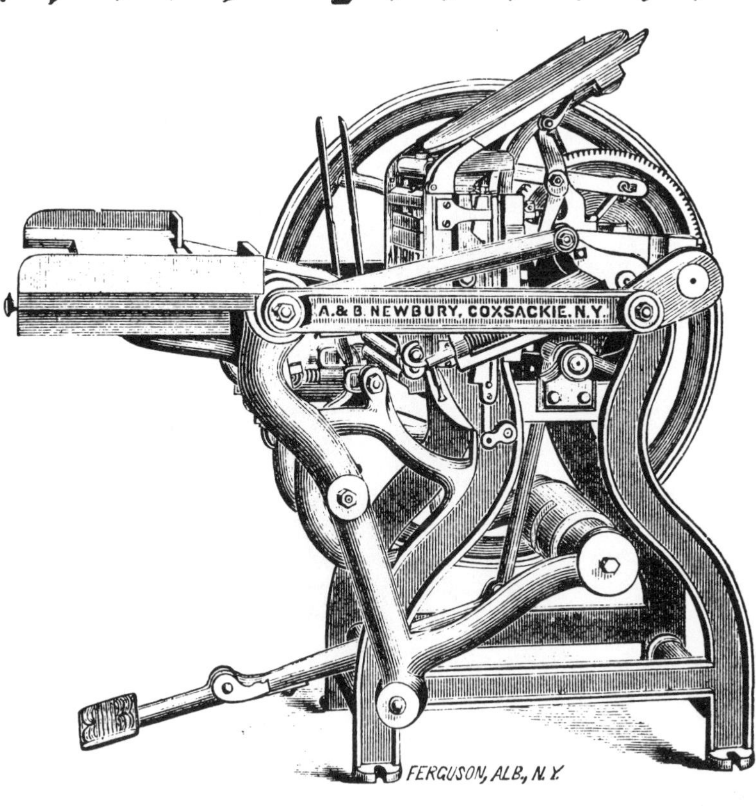

Circa 1874

NEW · CHAMPION · PRESS

Chase 6x10 in.; weight, 300 lbs.,	$ 60	Chase 10x15 in.,	Plain, Throw-off,	$150
" 8x12 " " 600 "	85	" 8x12 "	Finished, "	120
" 9x13 " " 725 "	100	" 9x13 "	" "	140
" 10x15 " " 1000 "	135	" 10x15 "	" "	190
" 8x12 " Plain, Throw-off,	100	" 11x17 "	" "	240
" 9x13 " " "	115			

Steam Fixtures, $12. Ink Fountain, $10. Boxed and delivered free in N.Y. City.

Easiest running; simple in construction; the equal of any other job press; every one warranted; for fine as well as for heavy work; two weeks' trial allowed. Send for circular.

NEW CHAMPION PRESS CO.

A. OLMESDAHL, MANAGER,

Machinists and Manufacturers and Dealers in Job Printing Presses,

No. 41 Centre Street, New York.

Circa 1887

NEW CHAMPION PRESS

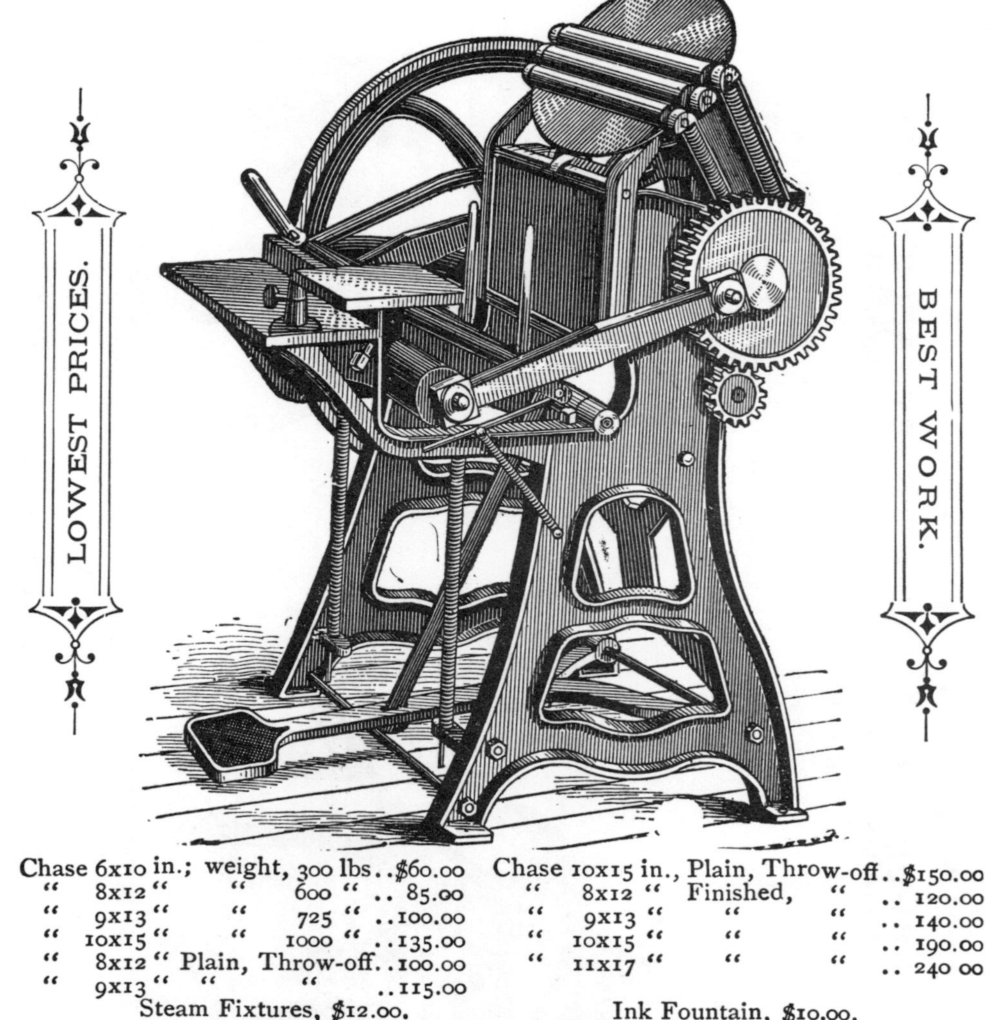

Chase 6x10 in.; weight, 300 lbs.	..$60.00	Chase 10x15 in., Plain, Throw-off	..$150.00
" 8x12 " " 600 "	.. 85.00	" 8x12 " Finished, "	.. 120.00
" 9x13 " " 725 "	..100.00	" 9x13 " " "	.. 140.00
" 10x15 " " 1000 "	..135.00	" 10x15 " " "	.. 190.00
" 8x12 " Plain, Throw-off	..100.00	" 11x17 " " "	.. 240 00
" 9x13 " " "	..115.00		

Steam Fixtures, $12.00. Ink Fountain, $10.00.

BOXED AND DELIVERED FREE IN NEW YORK CITY.

Easiest running; simple in construction; the equal of any other job press; every one warranted; for fine as well as for heavy work; two weeks' trial allowed. Send for circular.

A. OLMESDAHL,

Manufacturer and Dealer in PRESSES,

41 CENTRE STREET, NEW YORK.

Circa 1888

The "CALIFORNIA RELIABLE" JOB PRESS

COMPLETE WITH

New Patent Throw-off, Ink Fountain and Depressible Grippers,

WITHOUT EXTRA CHARGE.

Manufactured by Palmer & Rey of San Francisco. Circa 1888.

Golden Gate Jobber

Price, - - $110.00 Boxing, $3.00

Size inside chase 7 × 11 inches.

PRICE OF EXTRAS. — Chases, $1.00 each. Roller Cores, 60 cts. each. Roller Moulds, $2.75. Side Steam Fixtures, $10.00

The entire frame of the Press, including the bed, being cast in one solid piece, it cannot spring or get out of line, even if it does not set on a level floor. It can be run with ease, the speed being limited only by the capacity of the person feeding. It has a simple impression adjustment, and is complete with two chases, two rollers, brayer and ink table, wrench and gauges; also extended shaft for adding side steam fixtures.

LIBERAL DISCOUNT FOR CASH.

Manufactured by Palmer & Rey of San Francisco. Circa 1892.

Medals were awarded this press at the San Francisco Mechanics Exhibitions of 1886 and 1887.
Cut of 8x12 size.
PRICES
For each press complete, with PATENT THROWOFF, PATENT FOUNTAIN, and BOXED with FREIGHT PAID.
14x20 - $390
10x15 - 250
8x12 - 160
Side Steam Fixtures and Shifter - $10
Overhead Steam Fixtures - - $20
Either size same price.
SIMMONS-CUNNINGHAM SF

Reliable Jobber manufactured by Palmer & Rey, San Francisco. Circa 1886.

Peerless-Gordon manufactured by Peerless Printing Press Co. Circa 1891.

POTTER'S JOB PRESSES,

Babcock's Patent.

Sizes and Prices:

	INSIDE CHASE.	WEIGHT.	PRICE.
BILL-HEAD,	6x10 inches,	550lbs.,	$165.
QUARTO,	10x14 inches,	1,200lbs.,	300.
HALF MEDIUM,	12½x20 inches,	2,300lbs.,	425.

☞ Ten per cent. must be added to the above rates, on account of the enhanced prices of iron and labor.

Circa 1864

POPULAR PRINTING MACHINERY.

POTTER'S PRESSES AND STEAM ENGINES

No. 8 SPRUCE STREET, NEW YORK.

FACTORY:

WESTERLY, RHODE ISLAND.

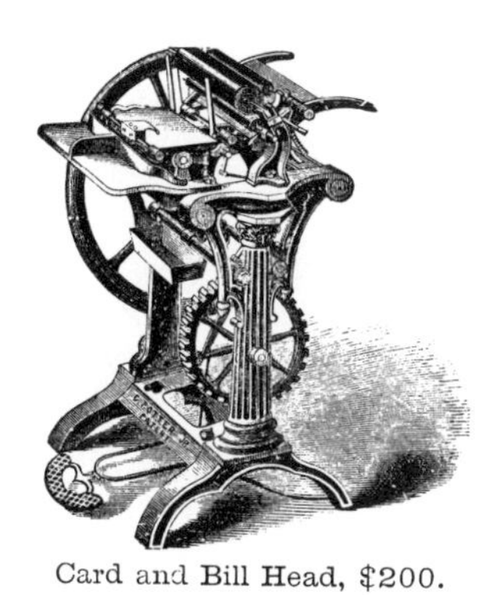

Card and Bill Head, $200.

Price $1,200.

Boxing $50.

Country Newspaper and Job Press.

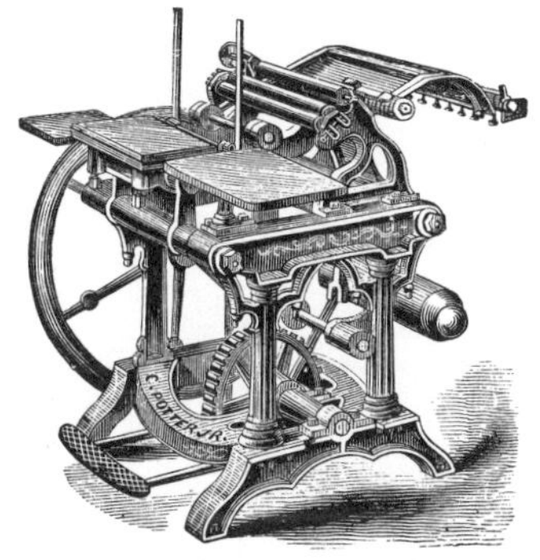

Quarto-Medium Jobber, $375.

PRINTERS AND THE TRADE GENERALLY

ARE RESPECTFULLY INFORMED THAT

C. POTTER, J'R & CO'S PRESSES are the only ones that have the COMBINED CYLINDRICAL and TABLE DISTRIBUTIONS;

WHICH is the BEST and MOST PERFECT distribution (in the opinion of leading Printers) to be found on any of the modern Drum Cylinder Printing Machines. The importance of efficient distribution can not be too highly estimated.

Circa 1866

THE PROUTY JOB PRESS.

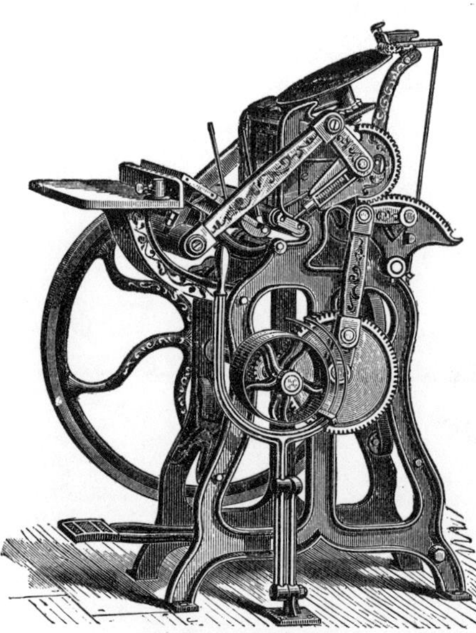

EIGHTH MEDIUM.

SIZES.

Eighth, chase inside	....	6½ x 10
Large Eighth	".	8½ x 12½
Quarto	".............	10 x 15

Prices.

Eighth, including boxing,......	$125.00
Large Eighth,.....................	200.00
Quarto.	275.00

Boxing Large Eighth, $4; Quarto, $8.

"OFFICE OF RAND, AVERY & CO.

"BOSTON, Sept. 24, 1880.

"GENTLEMEN:—It gives us pleasure to be able to heartily commend the working of the PROUTY PRESS furnished by you some three or four months since. It has accomplished all you claimed for it, and bids fair to become a popular member of our busy hive. Your obdt. servants,

RAND, AVERY & CO.

Printers who have not received our latest (24 page) Pamphlet, PRINTED ON our EIGHTH PRESS, will receive the same, with other samples of work, by sending postal to our address.

QUARTO MEDIUM.

The attention of printers is directed to our new Large Eighth (chase, inside, 8½ x 12½), of which cut and full description will be printed shortly on this page.

MANUFACTURED BY

THE PROUTY PRESS CO. 52 Federal St. Boston, Mass.

Circa 1881

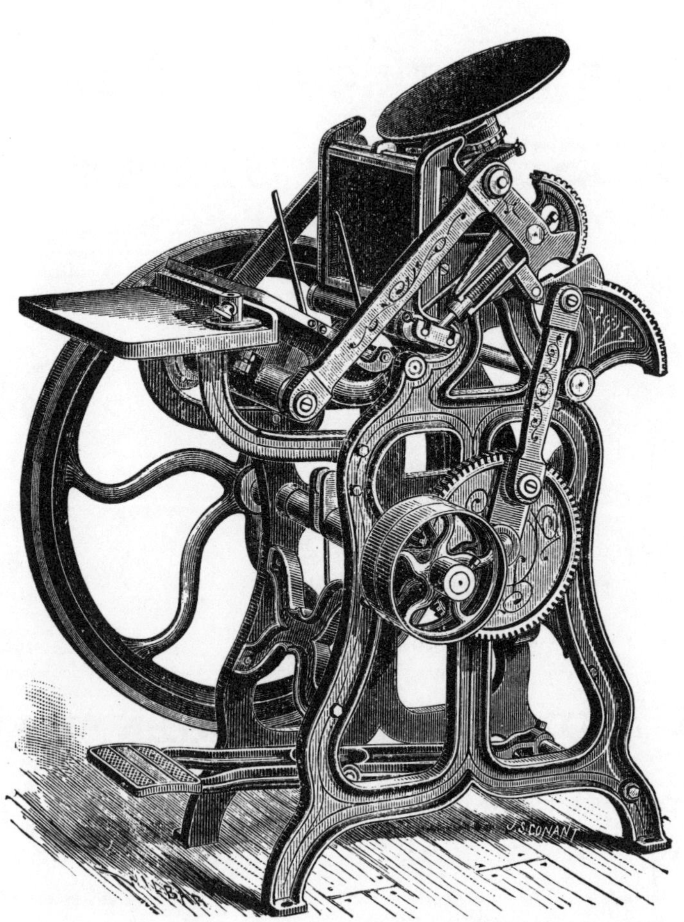

Prouty Jobber, Improved Model, manufactured by George W. Prouty & Co. Circa 1890.

The·Perfected·Prouty·Job·Press

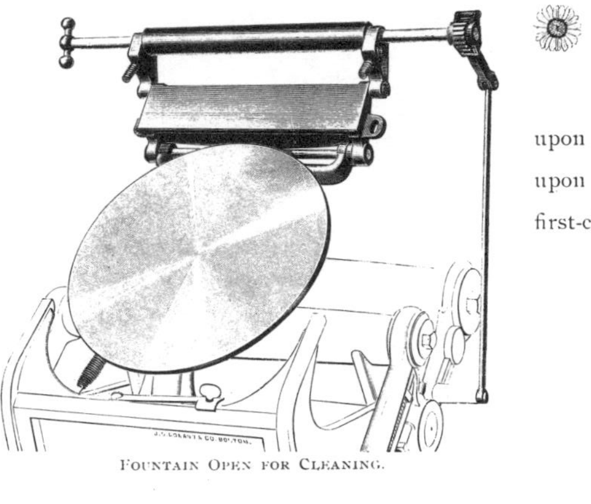

Fountain Open for Cleaning.

Constructed from an entirely new plant, upon the interchangeable system, and placed upon the market strictly on its merits as a first-class machine.

Speed and durability coupled with smoothness of operation, and absence of noise and grind, are points worthy of your consideration.

PARTICULARS ON APPLICATION.

GEO. W. PROUTY & CO.

No. 49 FEDERAL STREET, BOSTON, MASS., U. S. A.

Circa 1888

GEO. W. HUNT'S SUPERIOR

JOB PRINTING PRESS.

WITH AUTOMATIC BRAYER AND INK DISTRIBUTOR.

Built at REMINGTON ARMORY, Ilion, N. Y.

New York, Jan. 19th, 1889.

Messrs. E. Remington & Sons, Gentlemen—

I take pleasure in testifying to the merits of your excellent machine, known as Hunt's "Superior" Job Printing Press, which we have had in use in our office for the past five months with the most satisfactory results. For beauty of finish, strength, accuracy of register, and distribution of ink, it is indeed "superior" any to job press we have ever had. The Automatic Brayer and the ink throw off are in themselves a sufficient recommendation to insure its popularity among intelligent printers.

Wm. J. Hearfield.
Manager for J. H. Warner,

Endorsed by J. H. WARNER,
Bank Stationer, Lithographic Printer, and Blank Book Manufacturer,
119 Fulton Street, New York.

We are prepared to deliver the SUPFRIOR—size 11x16 inches, inside of chase. Price, including Fountain, Automatic Brayer and Ink Distributor, 4 Chases (including 1 extra large-size, 1 patent chase for small forms, and 2 regular size), two sets of Roller Stocks and Truck Rollers, 1 Roller Mold, Adjusting Wrench and Oil Can, $325.00. Size of smaller Press now under way, 9x13 inches inside of chase. Extras: Steam Fixtures, $15; Extra Fountain, $10; Ink Dropper $10; Boxing, $6.

E. REMINGTON & SONS, Salesroom 281 & 283 Broadway, N. Y.

Circa 1890

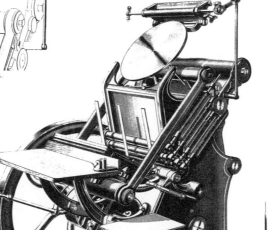

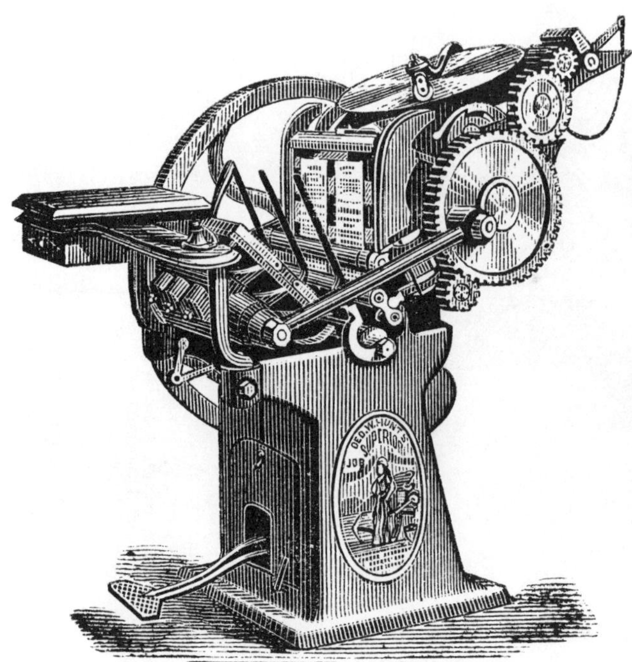

GEO. W. HUNT'S "SUPERIOR" Job Printing Press.

SIMPLE, COMPACT, and POWERFUL.

Automatic Ink Distribution.

INKING and Impression suspended at one operation at will.

Grippers adjustable to the form or tympan.

Solid carrier heads for the Ink Rollers.

Paper Table Cabinet finish.

E. Remington & Sons.

281 & 283 Broadway, N. Y.

Circa 1880

SUPERIOR

ROTARY JOB PRESS

WITHOUT THROW-OFF.

No. 1,	Chase, 6 x 10	inches,	Two Rollers..	$65 00
No. 2,	" 8 x 12	"	Three " ..	85 00
No. 3,	" 9 x 13	"	" " ..	95 00
No. 4,	" 10 x 15	"	" " ..	125 00

WITH THROW-OFF.

No. 2,	Chase, 8 x 12	inches,	Three Rollers,	$100 00
No. 3,	" 9 x 13	"	" "	110 00
No. 4,	" 10 x 15	"	" "	140 00

EXTRA FINISH, WITH THROW-OFF.

No. 2,	Chase, 8 x 12	inches,	Three Rollers,	$120 00
No. 3,	" 9 x 13	"	" "	140 00
No. 4,	" 10 x 15	"	" "	190 00

No. 1 has two rollers, two chases and wrench. Nos 2, 3 and 4 have three cast rollers, three extra stocks, three chases, roller mold and wrench.

Prices include boxing and cartage for all.

The Superior Press is strongly built, light running, and is guaranteed to print a full form without springing.

Circa 1892

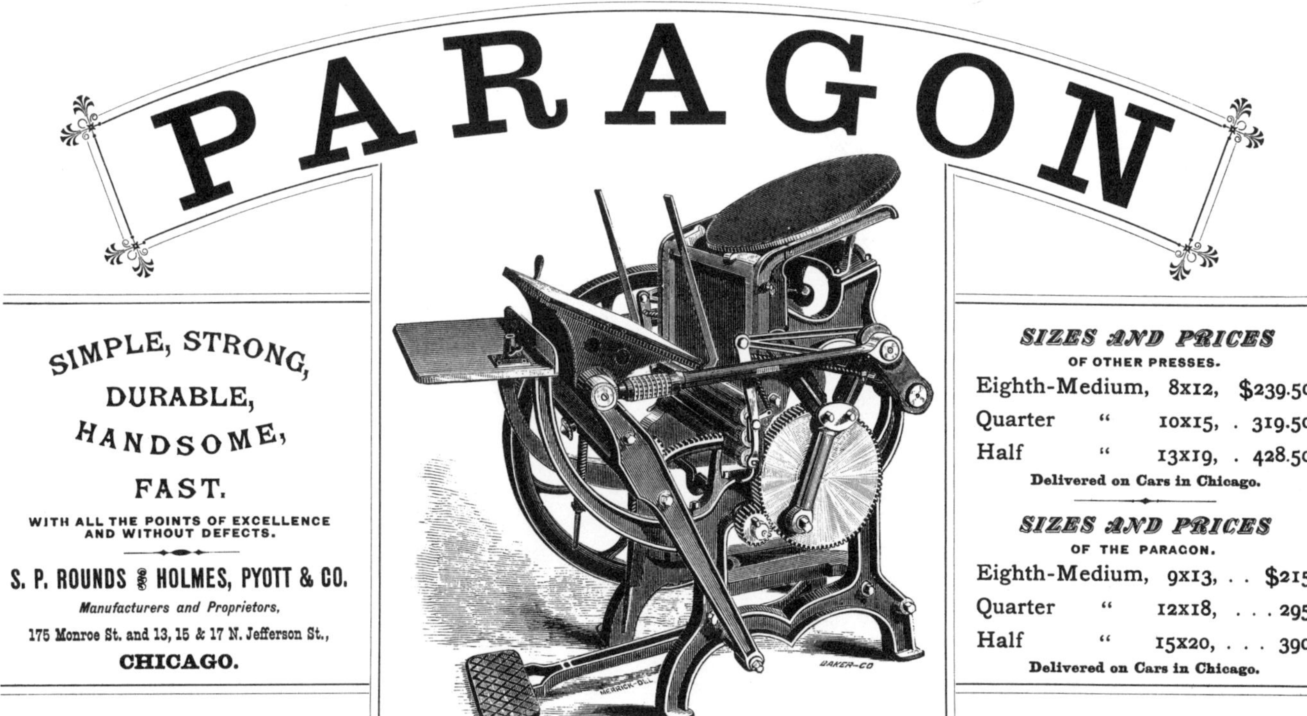

A New and Elegant Job Printing Press.
AS ITS NAME INDICATES, THE
PARAGON
SIMPLE, STRONG,
DURABLE,
HANDSOME,
FAST.
WITH ALL THE POINTS OF EXCELLENCE AND WITHOUT DEFECTS.
S. P. ROUNDS & HOLMES, PYOTT & CO.
Manufacturers and Proprietors,
175 Monroe St. and 13, 15 & 17 N. Jefferson St.,
CHICAGO.
SIZES AND PRICES
OF OTHER PRESSES.
Eighth-Medium, 8x12, $239.50
Quarter " 10x15, . 319.50
Half " 13x19, . 428.50
Delivered on Cars in Chicago.
SIZES AND PRICES
OF THE PARAGON.
Eighth-Medium, 9x13, . . $215
Quarter " 12x18, . . . 295
Half " 15x20, . . . 390
Delivered on Cars in Chicago.
AMONG ALL THE MODERN JOB PRESSES NOW BEFORE THE TRADE.

Circa 1878

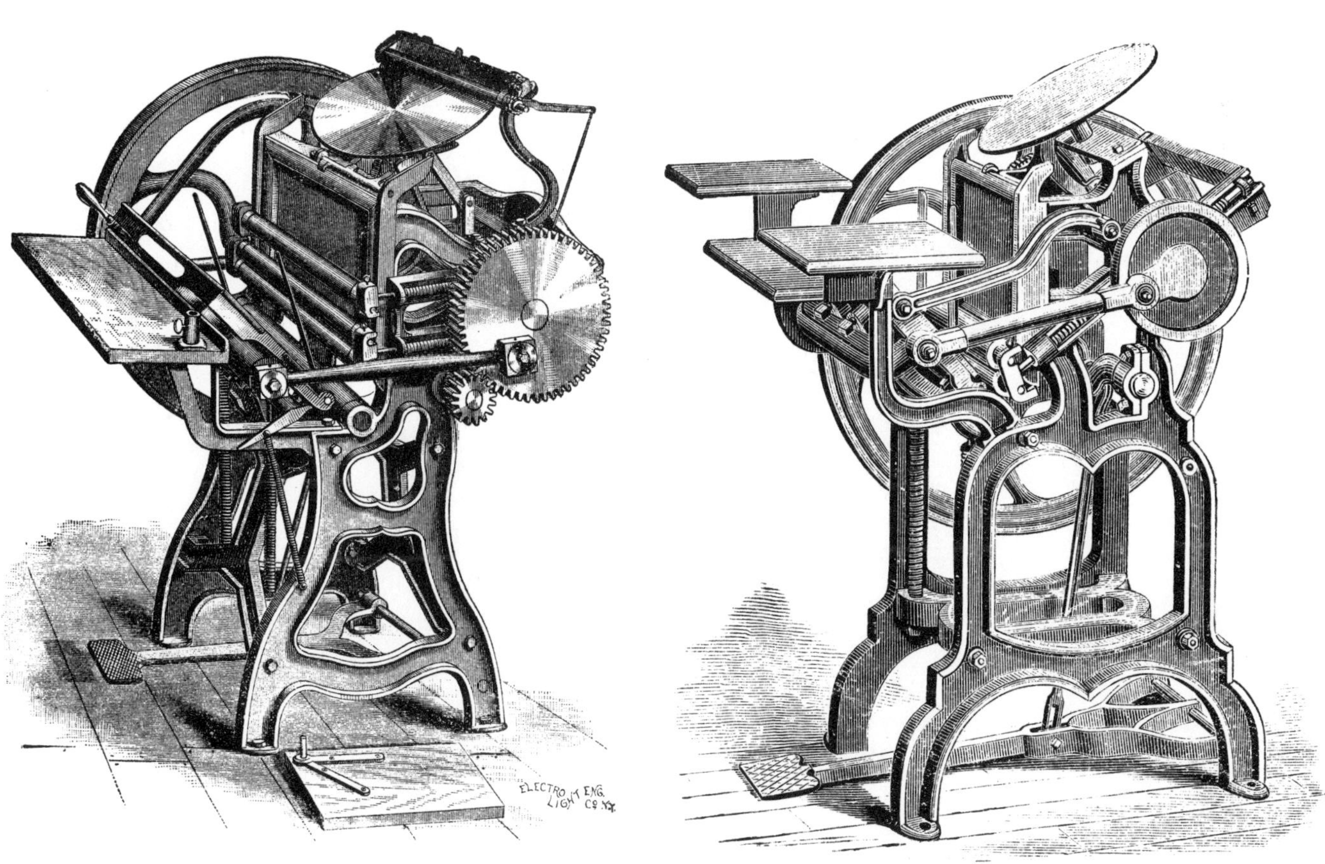

Champion Jobbers made by unknown manufacturer.

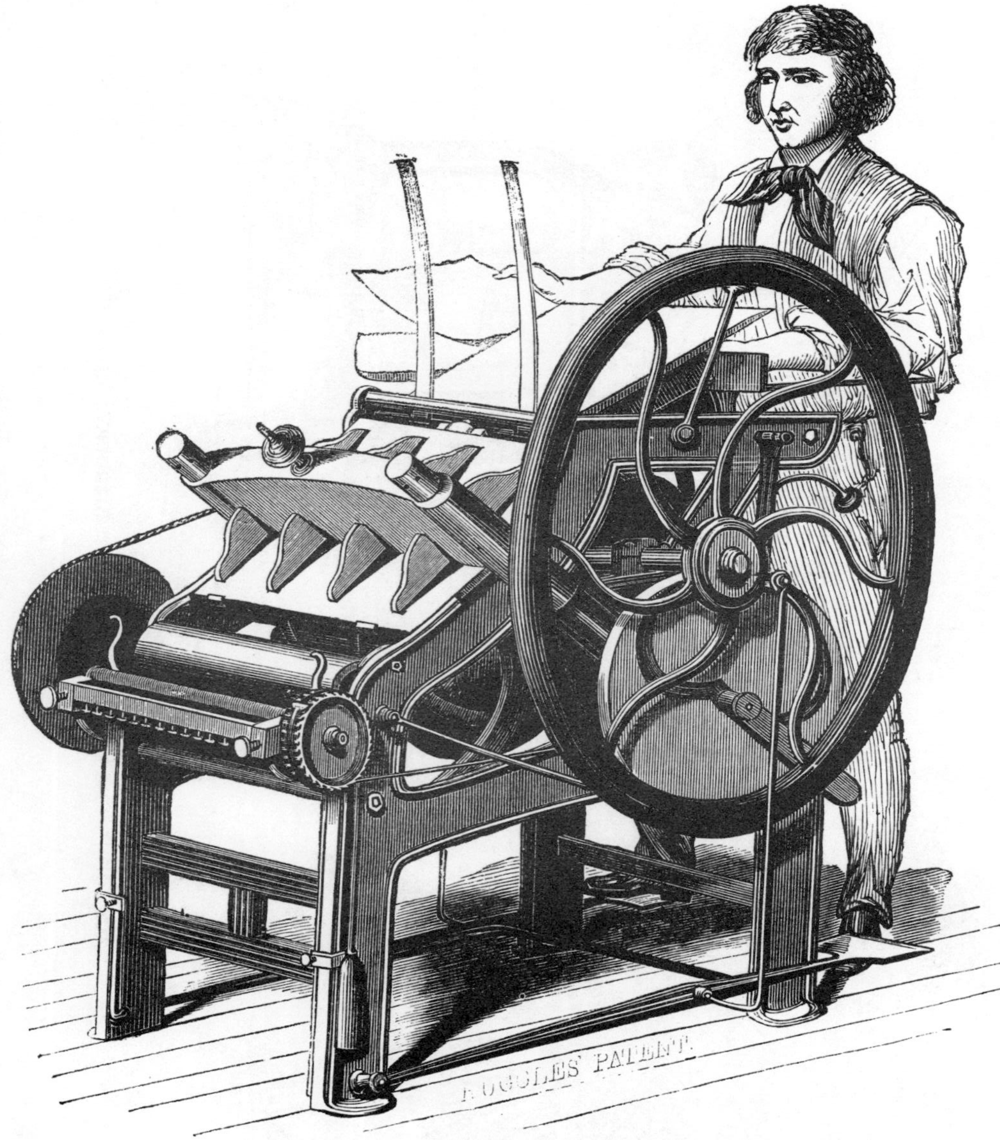

COMBINATION JOB ENGINE PRESS

THREE SIZES—HALF & QUARTER MEDIUM & LETTER, $550, $400 & $300

A Medal and Diploma awarded by the Am. Institute of N. Y., Fair of 1855.

Manufactured by S.P. Ruggles Power Press Manufacturing Co., Boston.
Circa 1858

BEST IN THE WORLD.

CHALLENGE JOB PRESS

MANUFACTURED BY

SHNIEDEWEND & LEE CO., CHICAGO.

EIGHT SIZES MADE.

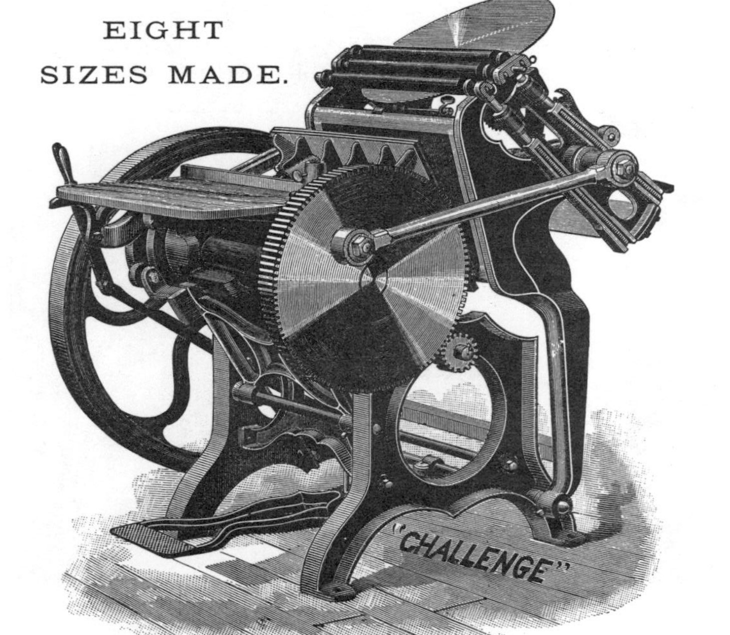

It will yield a quicker return for the money invested. It will give better satisfaction on all classes of job work than any other press in the world.

THE OPINIONS BELOW ARE ENTITLED TO CONFIDENCE. READ THEM.

SHNIEDEWEND & LEE CO. CHICAGO, September 8, 1888.
The four 10 x 15 Challenge Presses, with fountains, you put into our office two years ago, have fully equaled your recommendations. They are in perfect order, and have given entire satisfaction.
KNIGHT & LEONARD CO.

SHNIEDEWEND & LEE CO. CHICAGO, September 11, 1888.
We find the half medium, 13 x 19, Challenge Press made by you to be first-class in every particular. The same has given us good satisfaction.
RAND, MCNALLY & CO.

SHNIEDEWEND & LEE CO. LOUISVILLE, KY., September 19, 1888.
We are using the Challenge Press bought of you daily, and the more we use it the better satisfied we are with it. The working qualities cannot be beaten.
H. C. FORSMAN.

SHNIEDEWEND & LEE CO. APPLETON, WIS., September 29, 1888.
Our 9 x 13 Challenge Press is the only decent one we have in our office, and we wonder how we ever got along without it. It works beautifully, and has saved us many dollars since it has been running.
RYAN BROS.

FOR CIRCULARS, PRICE LIST AND TERMS ADDRESS

SHNIEDEWEND & LEE CO., MFRS., 303-305 DEARBORN STREET, CHICAGO.

These presses were manufactured from 1884 to 1893.

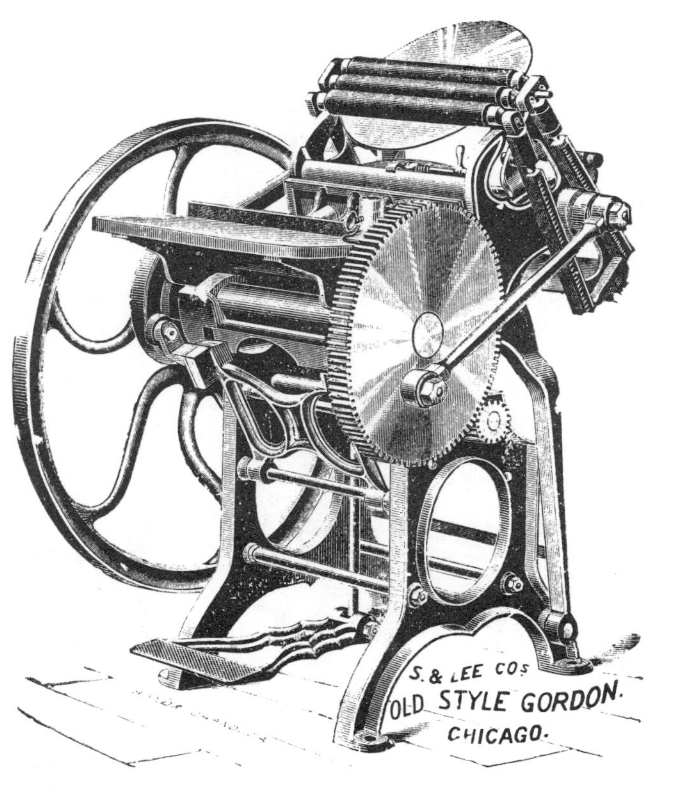

Gordon, old style, manufactured by Shniedewend & Lee Co. Circa 1885

Same press as on the left with an ink fountain attachment. Circa 1890

SMITHIAN
JOB
Printing Presses.

Will do the best quality of work!

Are the easiest to run!

Handiest! Fastest! and Cheapest Press in the World!

Two Sizes.

EIGHTH MEDIUM,
Chase 7x11,
Price, $235,00.

QUARTO,
Chase 10x14½,
Price, $365,00.

Terms Cash.
Delivered in New York City.
Satisfaction Guaranteed!

EARLE H. SMITH,
SOLE AGENT,
No. 34. PARK ROW,
NEW YORK.

☞ Send for Circular.

Circa 1872

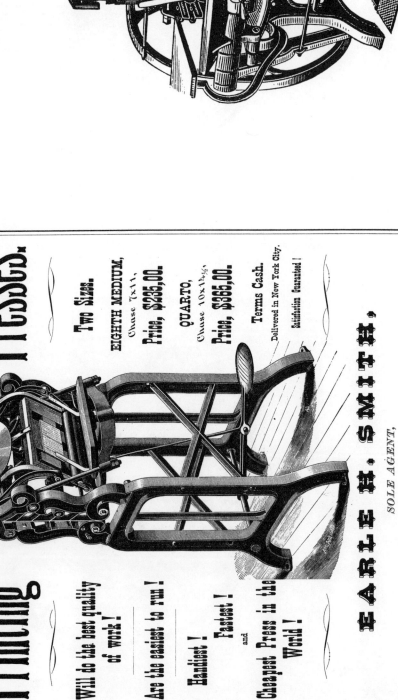

Chromatic Printing Press designed to print three colors in one impression.
Invented and manufactured by Suitterlin, Claussen & Co. of Chicago.
Circa 1871

IMPROVED CHROMATIC PRINTING PRESSES.

DESCRIPTION.

The basis of the Inking Apparatus is a triangle with the three sides planed. To these sides are attached three Chases which can be easily and quickly detached for the purpose of changing the arrangement of the colors. Segments, or Color Sectors are provided of various widths, corresponding with the various sizes of type. The curved part of these Sectors corresponds with the curve of the Cylinder, and the base of the Sectors is twenty ems pica in length. The compositor having a color form to arrange, places the three Sector Chases on the stone by the side of the form, and after selecting the Sectors for each color proceeds to "make up" in the Chases, taking care where a Sector is placed in one Chase, to "blank out" the same space in the other Chases with ordinary Furniture, Slugs or Leads as may be required. A dry proof of the form will aid the compositor in determining whether the Sectors have been "made up" in unison with the lines of type they are to color. The Sectors are locked up by means of the screws in bottom of Chase.

The forms are then given to the pressman who attaches the Sector forms to the sides of the triangle, thus forming an Inking Cylinder in three sections. Three sets of distributing Rollers, one for each color, supply ink to the three sections of the Cylinder. These sections in turn transfer the ink to the form Rollers, in correspondence with the lines of type to be colored.

The pressman then proceeds to "ink up" and make ready as with one color. It will be seen that by this arrangement the colors are made up in the composing room, thus permitting the use of the press for other work until the colors are arranged, besides taking much less time in arranging the Sectors than in the old manner.

For working black or any one color the Press is provided with two Shells or half Cylinders which can be secured in a moment, thus making a plain Cylinder for one color, with more inking surface and three times the distribution of ANY other jobber.

The Inking Cylinder is very large; giving ample supply of ink to the various colors.

Each Color has its Vibrating Distributing Rollers, with lateral motion, giving as much Distribution to each color as is given to the ordinary one color Job Presses.

No Sectional Rollers being used, any line of type or cut may be printed in two or three colors without blending, leaving the line of demarcation perfectly clear and distinct.

The type and Distributing Rollers are similar to those of any Job Press, and can be detained from passing over the form at pleasure.

The impression can be thrown on or off almost instantaneously, and is easily and accurately adjusted. No springing of the platen with the strongest impression.

The form may be placed in any part of the bed, and work equally as well as in the center.

A verv simple device securely fastens and easily unfastens the Chase. They run smoothly and noislessly either by steam or Treadle. SPEED—1,000 to 2,000 per hour, depending upon the ability of the feeder.

Circa 1873

The A. B. TAYLOR JOBBER

Is now a fixed fact, and can be seen at our Factory at

No. 3 HAGUE STREET, New York.

It has many points of excellence over any other built. The Press is easily worked, being the most simple in construction, the most compact in size and the best distribution, it being cylindrical, with four rollers passing over the full form, the same rollers passing over the cylindrical portion of the cylinder not occupied by the flat surface on which the form is placed; another most convenient advantage *is* that the form can always be corrected on the Press without removal.

The desire of the INVENTOR is that those wishing to purchase the best JOB PRESS built, can easily satisfy themselves by a personal examination, when all the merits of this NEW JOBBER will be better appreciated than can be explained in this brief description.

Sizes and Prices of the A. B. TAYLOR JOBBER.

No. 2 Card and Circular Press, 7 by 11 inside chase, $250.00, boxing $6.00. Fountain, $20.00 extra.

No. 3 Quarto Medium, 10 by 15 inches inside chase, $425.00, boxing $7.00. Fountain, $20.00 extra.

No. 4. Half Medium, 13 by 19 inches inside chase, $550.00, boxing $10.00. Fountain, &c., $20.00 extra.

Steam Fixtures for either size $10.00 extra.

Three Chases, two sets Roller Stocks, one Roller Mould, one Hand Roller, and two Wrenches go with each Press.

The A. B. TAYLOR PRINTING PRESS AND MACHINE COMPANY,

NEW YORK CITY.

Circa 1871

COLT'S ✶ ARMORY ✶ PRINTING ✶ MACHINE.

New, Perfect, Practical.

THE INSPECTION OF PRINTERS IS CONFIDENTLY INVITED.

The Colt's Armory Press was Designed, Patented and is for Sale Exclusively by

JOHN THOMSON,

143 Nassau St.,

NEW YORK,

TO WHOM ADDRESS FOR PARTICULARS.

Circa 1888

Circa 1885

THE JUSTLY CELEBRATED OLD STYLE GORDON PRESS

— WITH —

THORP'S PATENTED IMPROVEMENTS

KNOWN AS THE

"THORP-GORDON."

Absolutely the Best

— IN —

MATERIAL USED,
GENERAL WORKMANSHIP,
EASE OF RUNNING,
CONVENIENCE AND SPEED OF OPERATING
AND
QUANTITY AND QUALITY OF WORK PRODUCED.

Fully Guaranteed

TO BE

SUPERIOR

. . TO ANY AND ALL . .

OLD STYLE GORDON PRESSES

NOW IN THE MARKET.

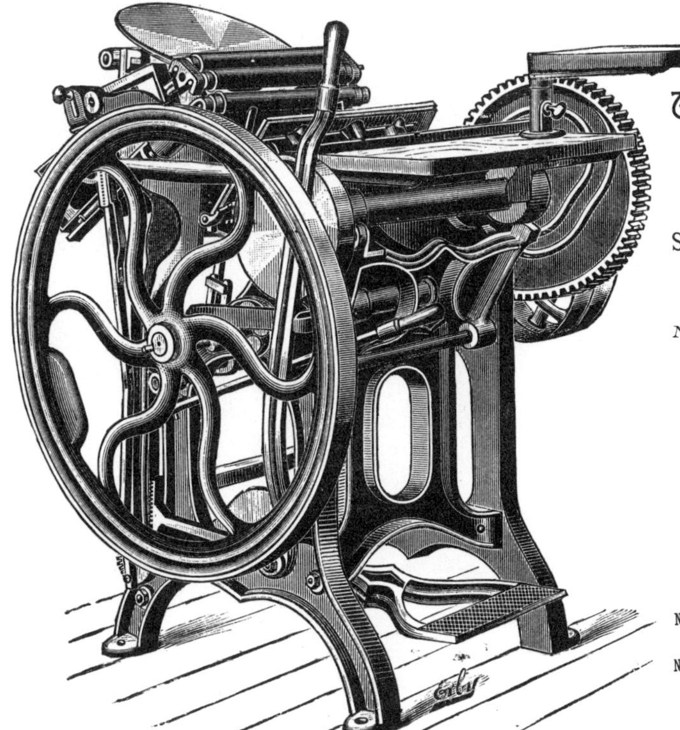

The Twin Roller Fountain.

(PATENTED)

Strong, Durable, Efficient
— AND —
EASILY MANAGED.

NO DRY INK.
NO DIRT.
NO WASTE.
NO DELAY.

Complete Distribution.
Quickly Changed.
Easily Cleaned.
Always Ready.

SIZES AND PRICES.

No. 1, for 7x11 and 8x12 Improved Thorp-Gordon Presses, - - - - - - $15.00

No. 2, for 10x15 and 11x17 Improved Thorp-Gordon Presses, - - - - - - $20.00

IT LEADS THEM ALL

Among the many features of this Press, which place it in advance of the Old Style Gordon Presses of today, are the following:

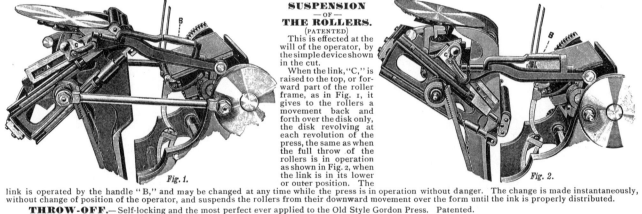

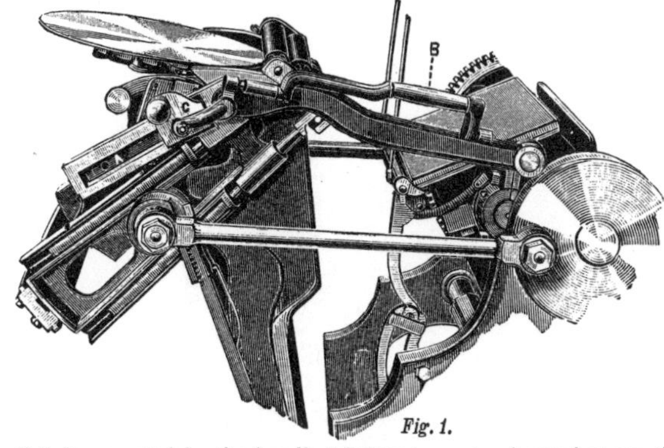

Fig. 1.

SUSPENSION — OF — THE ROLLERS. (PATENTED) This is effected at the will of the operator, by the simple device shown in the cut. When the link, "C," is raised to the top, or forward part of the roller frame, as in Fig. 1, it gives to the rollers a movement back and forth over the disk only, the disk revolving at each revolution of the press, the same as when the full throw of the rollers is in operation as shown in Fig. 2, when the link is in its lower or outer position. The link is operated by the handle "B," and may be changed at any time while the press is in operation without danger. The change is made instantaneously, without change of position of the operator, and suspends the rollers from their downward movement over the form until the ink is properly distributed.

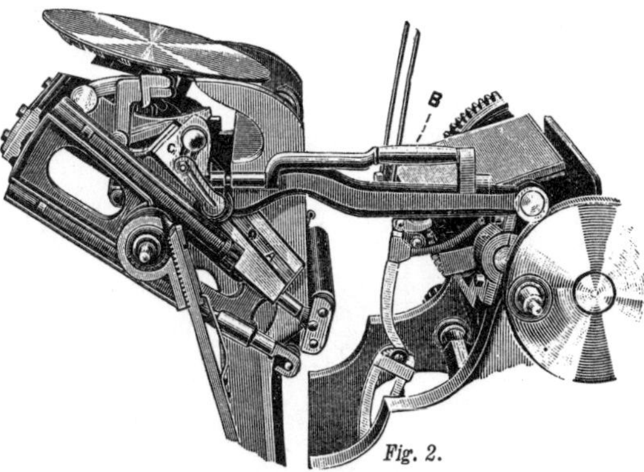

Fig. 2.

THROW-OFF.—Self-locking and the most perfect ever applied to the Old Style Gordon Press. Patented.

ANTI-FRICTION BOX.—This extends out from the side frame to a point where the entire weight of the fly-wheel, crank shaft and treadle are sustained, reducing the friction to a minimum and making this absolutely the easiest running press in the market. Used on all except the two smaller sizes, which run sufficiently easy with the LONG BEARING box used on these sizes. Patented.

SOLID BRACE GIRT.—We have introduced a Solid Brace Girt in the frame of these presses, which takes the place of the brace rods heretofore used, and imparts a degree of solidity to the machine not attainable by the old method of construction, and which greatly increases the durability and efficiency of the press. See cut.

DEPRESSION OF THE GRIPPERS.—Very simple and effective. The grippers may be brought to the platen at any time without danger of accident.

Interchangeable parts, Improved Distribution (patented), **Improved Spring Chase Lock, Hardened Steel Cam Rollers, Steel Side Arms (forged from the solid bar), Steel Shafts, Gear (cut from the solid), Solid Disk-Bracket, Solid Locking Frame, Tongue and Groove Joints.**

Strong, substantial and thoroughly well built. Favor us with your orders and secure the best.

PRICE LIST.

7x11 Inside Chase, with Throw-off, $150.00, Fountain, $15.00		10x15 Inside Chase, with Throw-off, $250.00, Fountain, $20.00	
8x12 " " " " 165.00, " 15.00		11x17 " " " " 300.00, " 20.00	

Steam Fixtures...$15.00

Securely boxed and delivered free on board cars or boat at Cleveland. Three chases, two sets roller stocks, roller mold, brayer and wrenches are furnished with each press. When the mold is not required, rollers will be cast or two extra chases substituted therefor. Write for cash discounts.

THE THORP-GORDON PRESS CO., Manufacturers, 71-73 Ontario St., CLEVELAND, OHIO.

The Thorp-Gordon was manufactured from 1886 to 1890.

LATE IMPROVEMENTS INTRODUCED

IN THE CONSTRUCTION OF THE

STANDARD JOB PRESSES

RENDERS THEM NOW

THE STRONGEST PRESS IN THE MARKET.

All Strain Bearing Parts are Made of Steel.

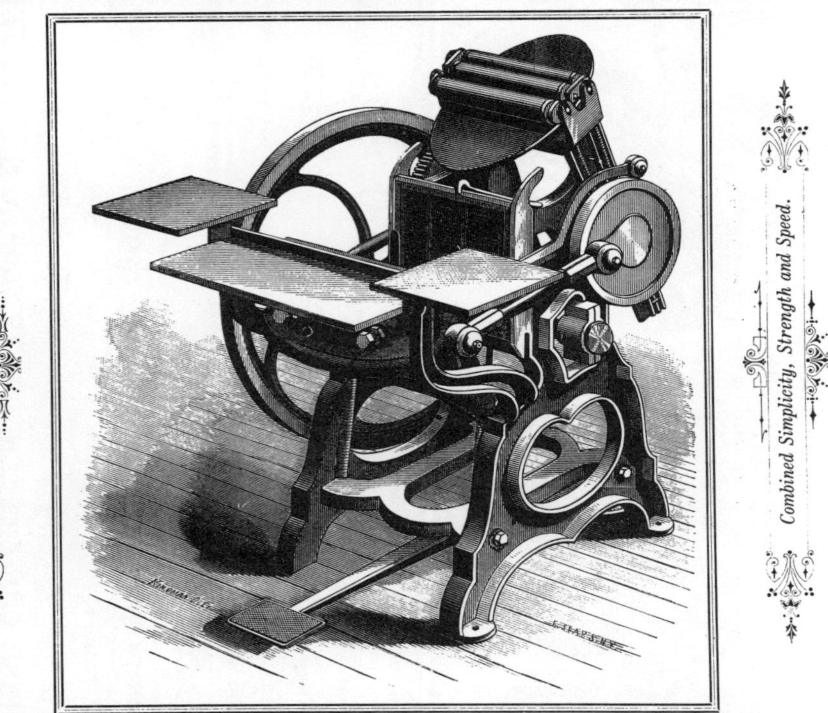

Combined Simplicity, Strength and Speed.

DURABILITY SPEED AND CHEAPNESS

THE STANDARD has all the essential features of a first class JOB PRESS. All the moving parts are perfectly balanced—making it the easiest and smoothest running Press in the market. Among the many admirable features of this Job Press, we mention the following: Ease in running! Every moving part is so very accurately balanced that all dead weight, loss of power and unnecessary friction and wear is obviated! Convenience in working! The Impression is easily adjusted. The Grippers can be brought to the Platen, for adjustment, at any point instantly, and resume their position automatically! The Chase is locked in position by a simple and effective device—the most convenient and complete ever used for the purpose! The Disk is instantly removed from the Press to wash up or warm the ink!

The Press can be run at a very high rate of speed, without injury, owing to its simplicity and the very accurate balance of its parts. The convenient arrangement of the Feed Tables, and the steady, noiseless motion of the Press, admit of the greatest rapidity in feeding. It is neat in appearance, strong and durable. The Chase and Rollers are inter-changeable with Gordon's New Style. One Roller Mold, two sets of Stocks, three Chases, are furnished with each press. Below we give numbers, sizes and prices. These Presses are furnished with or without Throw-off and Fountain, (not-shown in cut) and every press is fitted for the steam fixtures, which can be attached in a moment.

We also furnish with No. 4, a chase 10½x15½ inside, which will often "help you out" on a larger form.

The TYPOGRAPHIC GAZETTE—12,500 copies—is printed, two pages at time, on one of our No. 4 Standard jobbers.

STANDARD PRESSES—SIZES AND PRICES:

			With Throw-Off.	With Throw-Off and Fountain.	Boxing.
No. 3, Eighth Medium,	8x12 inside chase,	$200	$225	$250	$6.00
No. 4, Quarto,	" 10x15 " "	275	300	325	7.00

Steam Fixtures, $15.00.

Thorp-Gordon Press Co.manufactured the Standard Job Press. from 1876 to 1881.

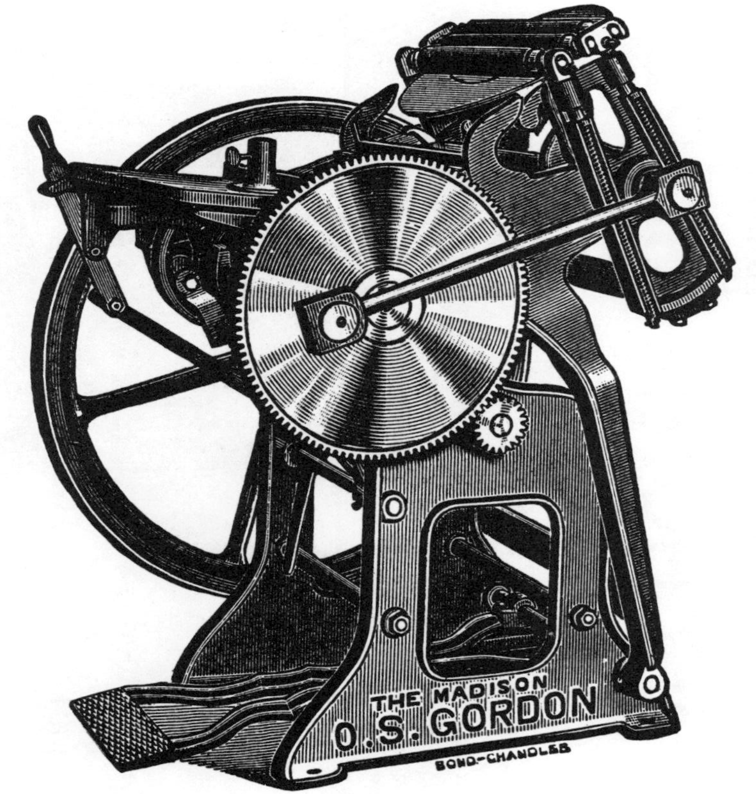

The Madison Gordon, old style, manufactured by W.G. Walker & Co., Madison, Wisconsin. Circa 1890.

Price-List of Printing Material for sale by JOSEPH WATSON, New York City.

The Improved Samson Press.

THE SAMSON PRESS, on account of its simplicity, durability, and efficiency, commends itself alike to the amateur and the practical printer. It is now (1895) ten years or more since we first began its sale, and the general expression by the purchasers has been that of complete satisfaction in these respects. We now make two grades of the No. 2, 3, and 4 Samson Presses, the difference, with the exception of the impression throw-off, being almost entirely in the finish or appearance of the press. In the first or best grade, in addition to the impression throw-off, the fly-wheel has a turned or faced surface, the gears are cut, the side-arms or draw-bars are of steel, the blank wheels and gear have polished surfaces, and the crank shaft extends far enough on the right hand side to admit of the attachment of steam fixtures. The second grade has a plain fly-wheel, cast instead of cut gears, and with iron instead of steel draw-bars, but which are sufficiently strong to sustain the strain necessary to print a full form. The impression throw-off can be added to this grade, if ordered with the press, at an additional expense of $15.00. The only difference between the two grades, other than those mentioned, is that the best grade, having cut instead of cast gear, may run a little easier, when first purchased, than the other—a difference, however, which disappears with use. In all other respects the one grade is just as good the other. Both grades have steel shafts through platen carrier and large gear wheel.

This cut shows the Samson Press with our sectional feed-boards, the ordinary ones, however, being sent unless otherwise ordered.

The No. 1 Samson is made of the second grade only, except where an impression throw-off is ordered with the press, in which case the gears are cut and the fly-wheel faced. With the No. 1 are sent two cast rollers, two extra roller stocks, two chases, roller mould, and wrench, while with all the larger sizes are sent three cast rollers, three extra roller stocks, three chases, roller mould, and a wrench. The No. 5, 6, and 7 presses are made in the best grade only. Although furnished with treadles, the No. 5, 6, and presses are rather too heavy to be run by foot, steam or other motive power being generally used.

The rate of speed at which these presses can be run varies from five hundred to fifteen hundred or more per hour, depending upon the skill of the operator, the size of the press, and the kind of printing done.

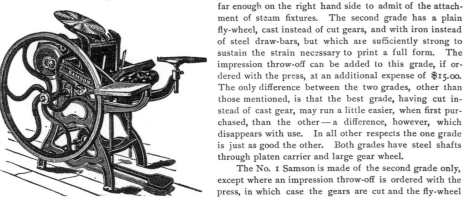

	Chase	Weight	Best Grade.	Second Grade.
Samson No. 1,	chase 6 × 10 inches;	weight, 300 pounds,	....	**$ 65.00**
Samson No. 2,	" 8 × 12 "	" 600 "	..............**$115.00**....	**85.00**
Samson No. 3,	" 9 × 13 "	" 725 "	.... **125.00**....	**95.00**
Samson No. 4,	" 10 × 15 "	" 1050 "	.... **160.00**....	**130.00**
Samson No. 5,	" 11 × 17 "	" 1400 "	.... **200.00**	
Samson No. 6,	" 13 × 19 "	" 1600 "	.... **285.00**	
Samson No. 7,	" 14½ × 22 "	" 2300 "	.... **350.00**	

PRICE-LIST OF EXTRAS.

	No. 1	No. 2	No. 3	No. 4	No. 5	No. 6	No. 7
Cast rollers, each,	.70	.80	1.00	1.25	1.65	1.95	2.50
Recasting, each,	.35	.40	.50	.65	1.00	1.25	1.50
Roller stocks, each,	.35	.40	.50	.65	1.00	1.20	1.50
Roller trucks, each,	.20	.25	.25	.30	.30	.30	.30
Chases, each,	1.00	1.25	1.50	1.75	1.80	2.00	3.00

Impression Throw-off, for second grade, $15.00 extra. Steam Fixtures, $12.00. Ink Fountain, $12.00.

Joseph Watson of New York manufactured the Samson Press from 1885 to 1895.

Price-List of Printing Material for sale by JOSEPH WATSON, New York City.

THE United States Press.
TUTTLE N.Y.
THE UNITED STATES PRESS.

THE UNITED STATES PRESS is similar in construction and appearance to the Young America Presses, with the addition of an iron frame upon which it is mounted, a fly-wheel and a treadle, with the necessary connections to transform it into a rotary press. We manufacture three sizes of this press. They are not so stoutly built as the SAMSON, and therefore not so well adapted to the use of the practical printer, but for the ordinary office work of the amateur they will generally prove satisfactory. The smaller size—the Fifty Dollar Rotary—we can commend to all as a remarkably cheap and efficient press, and one which will satisfy in every respect. They can be run at a speed of from 1500 to 2500 an hour. Two cast rollers, two chases, roller mould, and wrench accompany each press.

NEW YORK, Sept. 26, 1887.
The No. 1 United States Press has been in use in our office for several years. It is first-class in every respect, and any person using it will be amply rewarded for their outlay.
R. W. LAPPER & CO.,
54 W. B'way. Mercantile Printers.

United States No. 0, (chase 5½ × 8¼ inches; weight, 250 pounds,)........................ **$50.00**
Boxing, $2.00. Ink Fountain, $7.50 extra.

United States No. 1, (chase 6 × 9¾ inches; weight, 267 pounds,)........................ **60.00**
Boxing, $2.50. Ink Fountain, $7.50 extra.

United States No. 2, (chase 8 × 12 inches; weight, 345 pounds,)........................ **75.00**
Boxing, $3.00. Ink Fountain, $7.50 extra.

PRICE-LIST OF EXTRA ROLLERS, &c.

	No. 0.		No. 1.		No. 2.	
Rollers, complete, each......	$ .65.	Postage, $ .18	$ .75.	Postage, $ .20	$1.10.	Postage, $ .30
Roller stocks, each.........	.35.	Postage, .09	.40.	Postage. .09	.65.	Postage, .14
Recasting, each............	.30.	Postage, .18	.35.	Postage, .20	.45.	Postage, .30
Roller trucks, each.........	.20.	Postage, .02	.20.	Postage, .04	.25.	Postage, .05
Chases, each...............	.70.	....	.75.	....	1.25.	

The United States press was manufactured from 1877 to 1895.

NEW YORK JOB PRESS.

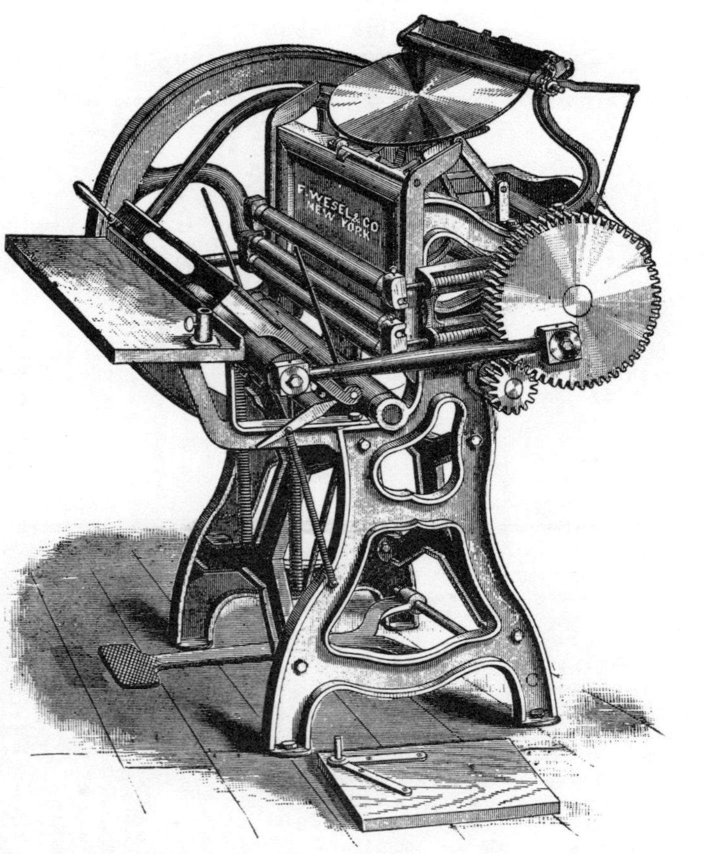

EVERY PRESS IS WARRANTED TO BE PERFECT IN ALL ITS PARTS, AND TO BE FULLY CAPABLE OF DOING FIRST-CLASS WORK.

	WITHOUT THROW-OFF.	WITH THROW-OFF AND CUT GEARS.	EXTRA FINISH WITH STEEL SIDE ARMS.
6×10	$60.00	—	—
8×12	85.00	$100.00	$120.00
9×13	95.00	115.00	140.00
10×15	125.00	150.00	175.00
11×17	—	—	225.00
14×21	—	—	325.00

F. Wesel of New York manufactured this press. Circa 1890.

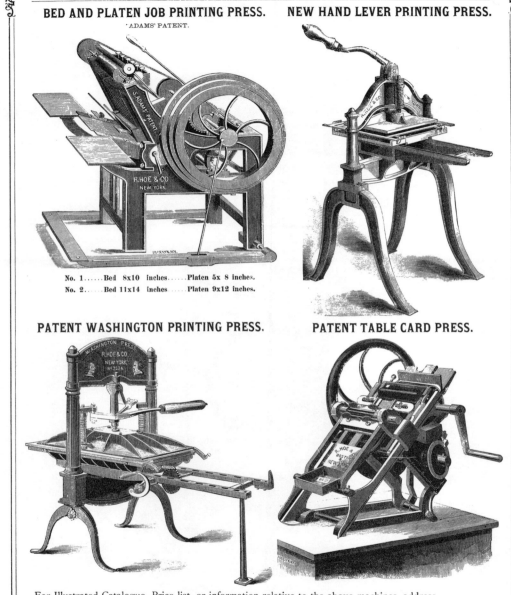

BED AND PLATEN JOB PRINTING PRESS.

"ADAMS' PATENT.

No. 1......Bed 8x10 inches......Platen 5x 8 inches.
No. 2......Bed 11x14 inches......Platen 9x12 inches.

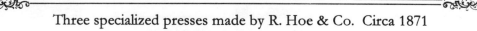

NEW HAND LEVER PRINTING PRESS.

PATENT WASHINGTON PRINTING PRESS.

PATENT TABLE CARD PRESS.

For Illustrated Catalogue, Price-list, or information relative to the above machines, address

R. HOE & COMPANY,
31 Gold Street, New York.

Three specialized presses made by R. Hoe & Co. Circa 1871

Lever presses

Lever presses are often included in the same category as platen presses, because they are a scaled-down version of the platen press. Some of the lever presses or tabletop presses were capable of doing the same quality work as regular floor model platen presses. They were usually heavy, had four adjusting screws for the platen, and were fastened to a sturdy workbench of the proper height. An 11 x 16" was advertised as suitable for a small town printer since the cost was reasonable and the press could put out a small-sized newspaper.

There were three types of levers, often referred to as handles, used on these presses. They were the side lever press, the single front lever press and the double front lever press. Some of the side levers could be changed from right to left as preferred by the printer. Others had a stirrup handle at the end of the lever. The Chicago, Caxton and Baltimore were presses that had single front levers, whereas the double front lever with a connecting bar was used on the Model and Kelsey.

Many of the small presses came in two styles: hand inked with a brayer, and self-inking with rollers. These presses needed at least two rollers of the largest diameter possible to produce the best inking. Some small hand inked rail presses sold for $3.00 in an outfit that included type. One is illustrated on page 209. Most of the rail presses were only toys and could not print well.

Some of the other presses made in the small sizes were also more like toys. The larger sizes, such as the 7 x 11", were still small enough to be mounted on a tabletop and they were operated by a hand lever rather than a foot treadle or a motor. One hand on the lever brought the platen and bed together while the other hand fed and removed the paper.

In England, as early as the 1830's, wealthy families bought miniature hand presses referred to as Parlour Presses, to print their own calling cards, poetry, etc. Samuel Orcutt, of Boston also made small hand presses but they were not very popular as the amateur printers in the United States preferred the lever press.

Commercial printers needed a high-speed press for printing cards and tickets. George P. Gordon produced the bench mounted Lightning, which was said to print 8,000 to 10,000 cards an hour from a continuous roll, with a built-in knife that cut the card after each impression. Franklin L. Bailey patented a card press in 1857 and gave it to the Hoe Co. to produce. A crank handle turned this press. It claimed to print 1,000 to 2,000 cards an hour, using an automatic feeder that fed individual cards into the press, then dropped them into a trough. Hoe adapted this press for ticket printing in 1865. It was known as the Hoe Patent Numbering Card Press in their 1867 catalog. Though not lever presses, these were tabletop presses. In 1860 B.O. Woods designed a lever press miniature of the Gordon press, called the Novelty press, marketed by Kelly, Howell and Ludwig of Philadelphia.

Even though professional printers used some of these presses, most were found in homes of amateurs. The excitement of printing attracted many hobbyists. While the professional printer used these small presses for printing business cards, envelopes, billheads, and similar small work, the amateur produced little booklets of poetry and journals for himself and his friends.

Commercial printers resented the lever press manufacturers because they encouraged the amateur printers to buy the same equipment they were using. Some of these hobby printers were doing commercial printing on the side.

Many of these neophyte printers were enticed by ads in the classified section of newspapers and magazines, such as the Harper's Bazaar and the Sears Roebuck Catalog. One ad offered a "Complete Printing Outfit for $30." Many of the miniature presses were called Boys' Presses and advertised with copy stating "No Boys Should be Without a Printing Press."` The kits, called outfits, had a small press, and often included 4 fonts of type, a composing stick, planer, furniture, leads, ink, and cases. Others added tweezers, gold and silver bronze and cards.

William Kelsey, of Meriden, Connecticut, was one of the entrepreneurs who wanted to take advantage of this new market. Kelsey made the small jobber a very popular item. Wanting to capture the young amateur printer, he advertised his first press in 1872, before it had been perfected. He came out with the Excelsior in 1875, which had a good toggle action and an inking system using the rotary disk. Kelsey didn't seem to mind that William Braidwood of New York called his card and job press an Excelsior, or that there already was a press in England by that name. Kelsey absorbed several of his competitors including B.O. Woods, J. Cook & Co., Joseph Watson and Curtis & Mitchell. It is interesting to note that J. Cook was Kelsey's landlord at one time. Kelsey's business looked so good that Cook went into competition with him. The William Kelsey Co., which became the best known of the dozens of manufacturers of lever presses in the 1800's was still selling lever presses and supplies to schools and amateur printers as late as the 1980's.

There were at least 25 firms making these small presses from 1880 to the early 1900's. Golding Company made the Official table press, 6 x 9" with elaborately painted decoration, and a miniature version called Junior, 2 1/2 x 3 1/2". Two other competitors were Chandler and Price, Cleveland, Ohio, with their Pilot press, and the Sigwalt Co. of Chicago. Both companies remained in business until well in the 1970's.

Manufacturers, and there were many, also sold supplies, type, cases, paper, ink, etc. Before 1900, there were so many different companies selling these small presses it was difficult to tell who manufactured the presses and who distributed or sold them.

Pilot Lever Press manufactured by Chandler & Price of Cleveland. Circa 1886

THE FAVORITE PRESS.

SELF-INKING.

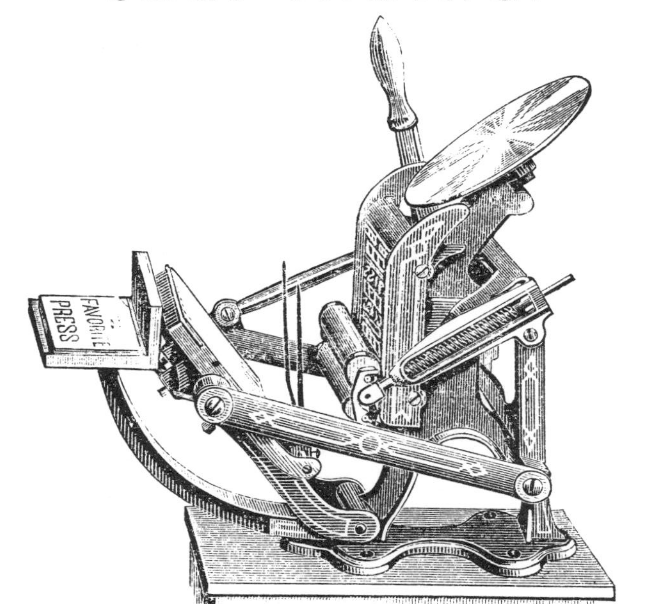

Size inside Chase, $4\frac{1}{2} \times 6\frac{1}{2}$. Price, $16.00.

This includes Chase, Two Rollers and Key Wrench.

Manufactured by Curtis & Mitchell of Boston. Circa 1888

THE

Caxton and Caxtonette Presses

SELF INKING.

Caxton Press, 4 x 6 inches, inside chase, $13.00
Caxtonette Press, 3 x 4½ in., inside chase, 8.00

Caxton weighs 38 lbs. Caxtonette weighs 24 lbs.

Two Rollers and One Chase with each Press.

These Presses are strong, compact, and thoroughly built. They have four impression screws on the back of the bed, for adjustment of the impression. Two rollers pass entirely over the form twice at each impression, and a revolving ink disc insures good distribution. They are quickly operated, and are capable of doing excellent work. A full form can be printed on them without straining the press.

For Printing Cards, Tags, Envelopes, &c., they have no equal.

Manufactured by Curtis & Mitchell of Boston. Circa 1880.

Manufactured by Curtis & Mitchell of Boston. Circa 1885.

THE MODEL PRINTING PRESS.

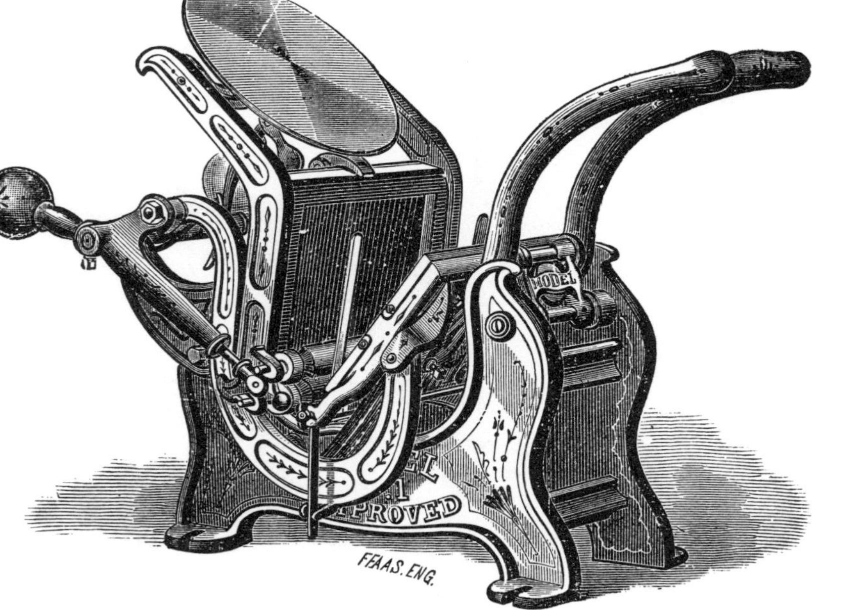

Improved No. 1 Self=Inking Model Press.

Inside size of Chase, 5 x 8 inches. Price, $18.00.

Boxing, $1.00.

Among printing presses the above MODEL No. 1 is the Acme of Perfection. It has received thousands of unsolicited testimonials as to its merits and adaptability for all kinds of plain and fancy printing.

SPECIAL $16.00 PRINTING OUTFIT, NO. 1, ONLY $12.00.

Four fonts of Type (to value of).....	$8.00	Four Type Cases, 12½x12½, 49 boxes..	1.20
Spaces and Quads for above type.....	1.00	Full set Iron Quoins and Steel Key....	.85
Three cans Printing Ink, assorted....	.75	Imposing Stone, 9x12 inches..........	1.00
Two lbs. Leads and one Brass Dash..	.40	Composing Stick, 8 inch..............	.80
Ten yds. Furniture and Reglets.....	.50	Four-inch Hand Roller...............	.50
Bottle Ink Reducer and one Planer...	.50	Shooting Stick and Tweezers..........	.50
		TOTAL	**$16.00**

THE ABOVE MODEL PRESS AND OUTFIT, NO. 1, COMPLETE, $30.00.

TYPE TWEEZERS

GOOD TWEEZERS	15c.	TWEEZER and BOBKIN Combined..	40c.
NICKEL-PLATED, Best	25c.	BOBKIN, With Handle	10c.

MITER BOXES AND SAWS.

Wooden, 13½ ems wide, each	.50	Fine-tooth, high-back SAW	.75
Wooden, 3 inches wide, each	.60	Back Saw, for wood or metal	1.25

Manufactured by J.W. Daughaday of Philadelphia. Circa 1883.

THE MODEL PRINTING PRESS.

Improved No. 2 Self=Inking Model Press.

Inside size of Chase, 6 x 9 Inches. Price, $25.00.

Boxing, $1.50.

This PRESS is one of the most popular sizes. The extrême simplicity of its construction, and the excellence of its work have met all the requirements for Business, Professional and Educational use. In the illustration we show it in the position when taking an impression.

SPECIAL $20.00 PRINTING OUTFIT, NO. 2, ONLY $15.00.

Four fonts of Type (to value of).....	$8.00	One doz. type Cases, and Cabinet....	6.00
Spaces and Quads for above type.....	1.00	Full set Iron Quoins and Steel Key....	.85
Three cans Printing Ink, assorted....	.75	Imposing Stone, 9x12 inches..........	1.00
Two lbs. Leads and one Brass Dash..	.40	SMALL MALLET, Hardwood	.25
Ten yds. Furniture and Reglets.....	.50	Four-inch Hand Roller...............	.50
Model Ink Reducer and Cleaner.......	.25	Shooting Stick and Tweezers..........	.50
		TOTAL	**$20.00**

THE ABOVE MODEL PRESS AND OUTFIT, NO. 2, COMPLETE, $40.00.

FOR CLEANING INK ROLLERS AND INK DISC USE THE MODEL'S INK REDUCER, Price, 25c. Rubber Blanket for platen bed, 25c. per sq. ft.

BALTIMOREAN No. 2.

HAND-INKING. SIZE OF CHASE 4 x 6.

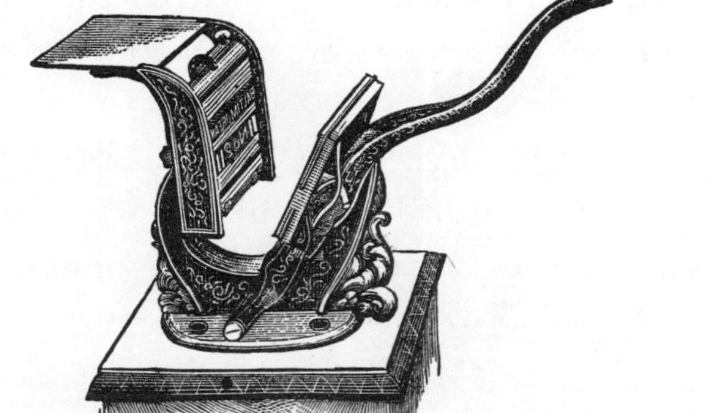

This is a very cheap press, considering the size and the superior manner in which the Press is made.

PRICE OF PRESS WITH ROLLER AND ONE CHASE, BOXED, . $10.00
With outfit of 4 Fonts Type, Nos. 51, 56, 57 and 71 with Composing Stick, Planer, Furniture, Leads, Ink, Cases, &c. $15.00

BALTIMOREAN No. 3.

HAND-INKING. SIZE OF CHASE 5½ x 8.

This is an excellent size for ordinary printing, requiring a cheap and perfect press. It is large enough for Letter Heads, Bill Heads, Cards and Small Circulars.

PRICE OF PRESS WITH ROLLER AND ONE CHASE, BOXED, . $14.00
With outfit of 5 Fonts Type, Nos. 51, 56, 57, 61 and 71 with Composing Stick, Planer, Furniture, Leads, Ink, Cases, &c. . . . $20.00

Manufactured by J.F.W. Dorman of Baltimore. Circa 1880.

BALTIMOREAN No. 2.

No. 2, Self-Inking, size of Chase 4¼ x 6¼, ... PRICE, $16 00
With outfit of 4 Fonts Type, Nos. 51, 56, 57 and 71 with Composing Stick
Planer, Furniture, Leads, Ink, Cases, &c. . . . . . " 21 00

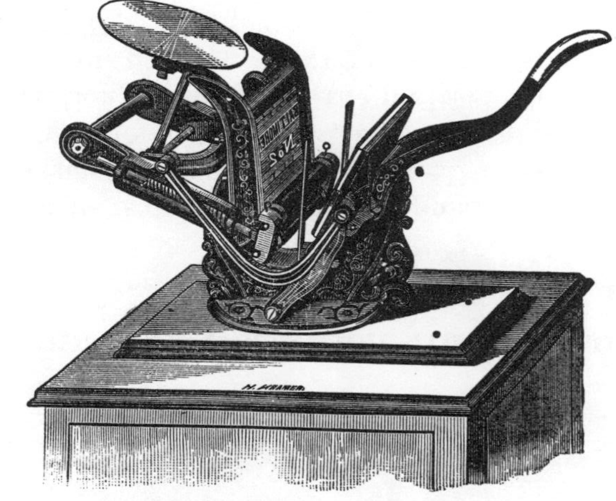

OUR PRESSES

HAVE MANY VERY ESSENTIAL IMPROVEMENTS.

1st. The Chase is fitted with screws, by which a larger form can be locked up than with quoins. This is much more convenient either for Printers or Amateurs.

2d. The Rollers are made of the very best composition, at a greater expense than the ordinary compounds generally used, and are warranted to last much longer. This supplies the most important adjunct to any Printing Press, for, without perfect rollers, it is impossible to do good printing.

3d. The Rollers are put up separate in strong wood boxes with slide lid, which preserves them when not in use or during shipment.

These improvements will be appreciated by all who use our presses.

When comparing our Prices with the same size Presses of other Manufacturers, please take this into consideration.

All Presses are delivered to the Depot, in this City, without charge for Boxing or Cartage.

BALTIMOREAN No. 3.

No. 3, Self-Inking, size of Chase 5½ x 8, ... PRICE $25 00
With outfit of 5 Fonts Type, Nos. 51, 56, 57, 61 and 71 with Composing
Stick, Planer, Furniture, Leads, Ink, Cases, &c. . . . " 31 00

THESE Presses are adapted for all small printing, and have no equal of the same size. We give with Nos. 2 and 3, two Chases, an Oil Can and Hand Roller, besides the usually accessories. One Chase has screws. The other is plain. Only one Chase goes with No. 1 Press or Nos. 2 and 3 Hand Inkers.

THE BALTIMOREAN SELF-INKERS have lately been very much improved by connecting the ink arms at the back with an iron rod; this prevents the arms from ever becoming loose or out of place. It enhances the value of these presses very considerably. The connecting rod that works the ink rollers is crooked, so that any length sheet can be printed. The handles are nickel plated, and the Press is screwed to a fancy walnut board, so that it can be used without fastening it down to the box or table. They are by far the finest finished Press made.

THE MARYLAND PRESS.

Will Print a Card 1½x2 inches.

THE MARYLAND PRESS is an improvement on the usually made hand inking presses of this size. It is made for practical use, and not simply to sell cheap. It is beautifully japanned. Every press is tried, and none sent out but what we can warrant as perfect.

Price of Press with Roller, - - - - - - $1.50.
With Outfit including 1 font of No. 52 Type, 50 Blank Cards, Ink and Furniture in a box, $2.50.

BALTIMOREAN No. 1.

Hand-Inking. Will print a Card 2½x4.

This is the most complete hand-inking press made, beautifully designed, elegantly constructed, and tastefully finished. This press is capable of doing a great variety of small Printing, such as, Cards, Envelopes, &c.

Price of Press and Roller, Boxed, - - $3.75.
With Office of one Font of No. 71 Type, 50 Blank Cards, Ink and Furniture in a Box, - - - - - - $5.00.

BALTIMOREAN No. 1.

Self-Inking. Will print a Card 2½x4.

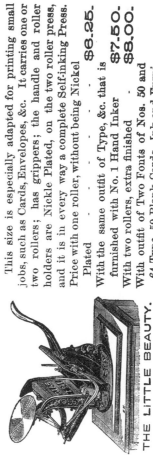

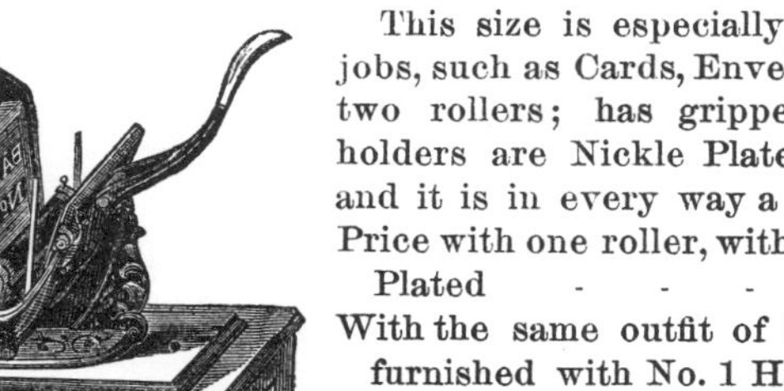
THE LITTLE BEAUTY.

This size is especially adapted for printing small jobs, such as Cards, Envelopes, &c. It carries one or two rollers; has grippers; the handle and roller holders are Nickle Plated, on the two roller press, and it is in every way a complete Self-inking Press.

Price with one roller, without being Nickel Plated - - - - - - - - $6.25.
With the same outfit of Type, &c. that is furnished with No. 1 Hand Inker $7.50.
With two rollers, extra finished - $8.00.
With outfit of Two Fonts of Nos. 50 and 64 Type, 50 Blank Cards, Ink and Furniture in a Box - - - - $10.00.

Manufactured by J.F.W. Dorman of Baltimore. Circa 1880.

MONUMENTAL No. 1 LEVER.

WITH IRON STAND. CHASE 6 x 9.

THIS gives a view of the Lever Press, showing it on an Iron Stand. This is a very powerful, well built and finely finished Press. It is a great improvement over all other Lever Presses. Requiring very little power to work it, so that a boy eight years old can manage it with ease.

We give with the Lever Presses, Two Chases, Two Ink Rollers, Wrench, Walnut Delivery Table, Hand Roller and Oil Can. One Chase has screws.

PRICE,—WOOD STAND, ... $40.00
" IRON " 45.00

MONUMENTAL LEVER No. 2

WITH IRON STAND. SIZE OF CHASE 8 x 12.

A PERFECT Press, strongly built and well finished, and will do as good work as the highest price Job Press. Each Press is supplied with all the modern appliances for convenience in operating: including two Chases, (one with improved lock-up screws,) two Rollers in a box, Wrench, Walnut Feed and Delivery Tables, Hand Roller, Ink Plate and Oil Can. Weight of Press with iron stand 450 pounds.

PRICE—ON WOOD STAND, ... $65.00.
" " IRON " . . . . 75.00.

Manufactured by J.F.W. Dorman of Baltimore.

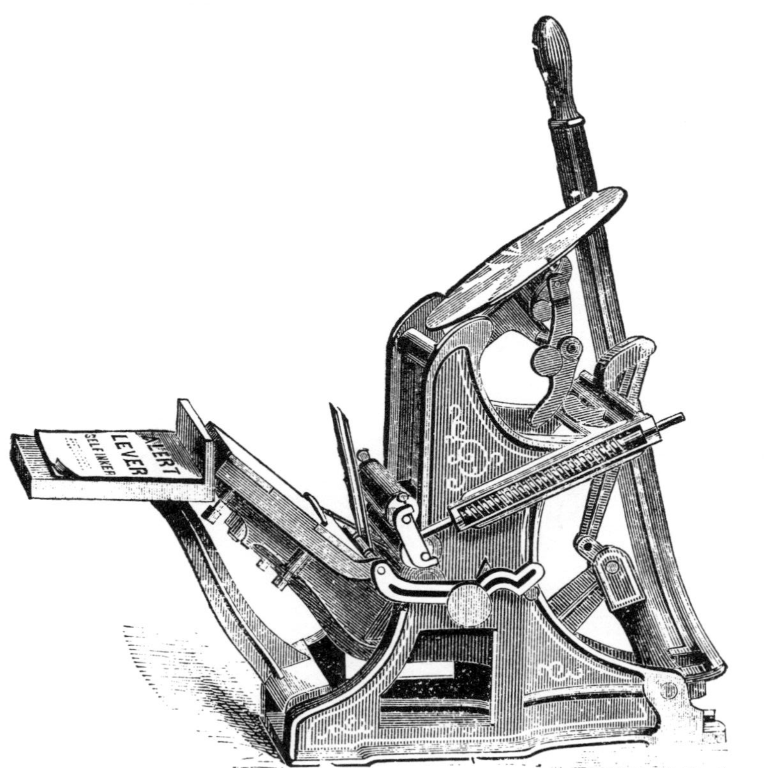

ALERT SELF-INKING

LEVER PRESS.

No. 1, Size inside Chase 5 x 8, $25.
" 2. " " " 7 x 10, $40.

The delivering table can be instantly disengaged from the press, if desired for convenience in getting at the under part of the press.

Manufactured by W.B. Gorham & Co. of Boston. Circa 1888

THE BOSTON PRINTING PRESS
GORHAM & Co
BOSTON
MASS.
DETATCHED VIEW OF LEVER

For the accommodation of those who would like the Boston presses without treadle or cabinet, we shall sell them so; the prices given being for the press alone, without anything else. A treadle, complete, and ready for application to either size, will be furnished for $1.50 extra. We believe the presses, cabinets and outfits, as shown on the preceeding page, are more economical than to buy the presses alone in this way. Circa 1878

BOSTON PRESS.

No. 1
3 ½ x 5 ½
$5.00
Roller, 50 Cents Extra

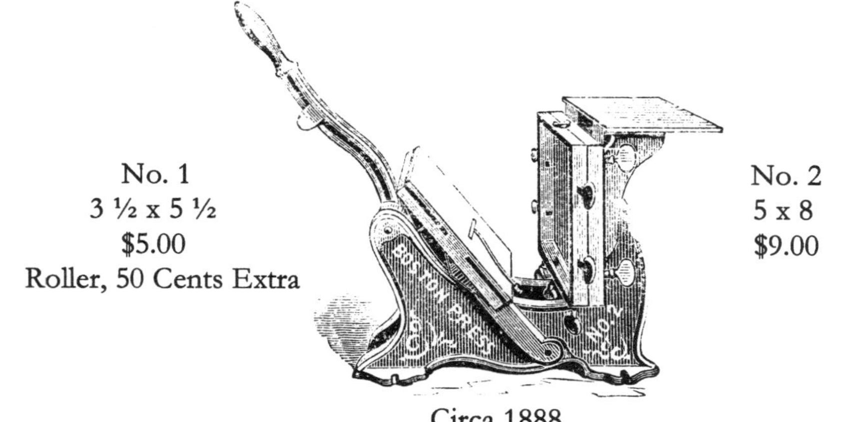

No. 2
5 x 8
$9.00

Circa 1888

BOSTON PRINTING PRESS. No. 2.

[Patent applied for.]

The above is a new engraving of the Boston No. 2 Press, and conveys a better idea of it than the one upon the cabinet. This cut shows our Nonpareil bottom gauge which will be found almost indispensable when once used. We send it for 50 cents extra.

Weight of Press, boxed, 96 lbs.

SIZE INSIDE CHASE, 5 X 8. - PRICE $13.00

Circa 1878

Gorham & Co., Boston, Mass.

THE BOYS' PRESS.

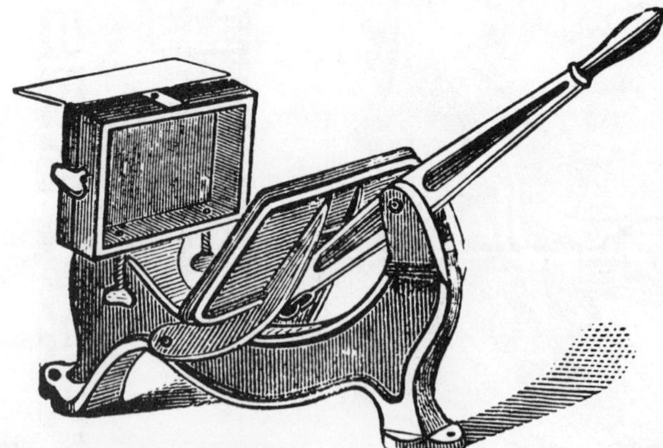

SIZE INSIDE CHASE, 3 x 4¾. - PRICE, $5.00

INCLUDING

Furniture, 1 Font Type, Spaces and Quads for do. Leads, Can of Ink, Type Case, Ink Roller, Ink Board,

Circa 1878

IMPROVED EMPIRE LEVER PRESS

Patent allowed December, 1874.

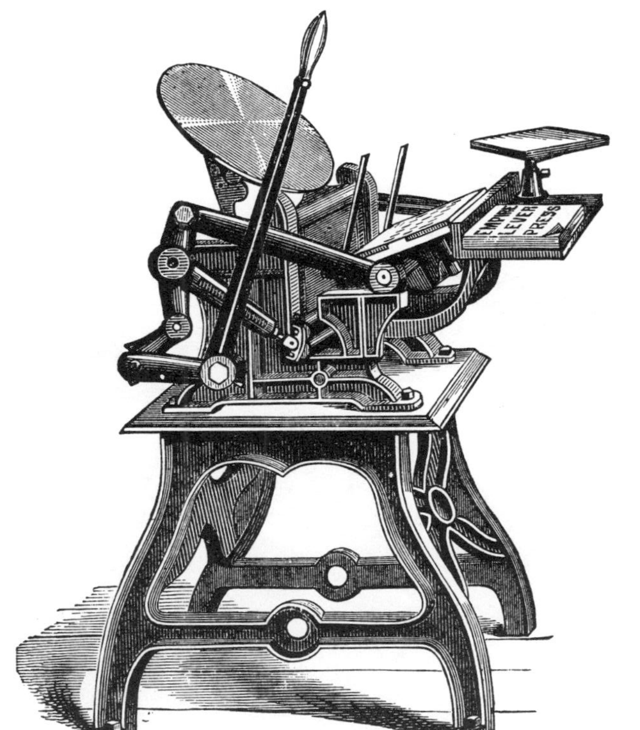

SIZE INSIDE CHASE, 8 X 12. - PRICE, $70.0(

This includes the following articles:

Two Chases, Two Ink Rollers, Rubber Blanket, Wrench, Hand some Walnut Feed Board and Delivery Table, Hand Roller, Ink Board and Oil Can.

The Empire Lever Press is made precisely the same as the Rotary except in a different arrangement of tl parts and the substitution of a lever for the balance wheel and treadle. Except in the rapidity of its operatic there is no difference between this press and the Rotary, the quality of workmanship being precisely the sam

Our Empire Presses have been entirely remodelled and many very important changes made. Everythi has been carefully figured out to attain the highest perfection. The press is now entirely noiseless and wor very easily. We have also had new side frames made, which adds greatly to its appearance as well as strengt

Please take particular notice that we have discontinued the manufacture of tl Hand-inking Empire Presses.

We invite special and critical attention to our presses of all grades. Please compare them with others a we are satisfied the result will not be to their disadvantage.

We sell this same press without stand for $60, including all the extras.

Manufactured by Gorham & Co. in Boston. Circa 1878

Small Card Press.

In this Press the form is placed on an inclined bed, and receives ink from two rollers. The impression is given by a cam and may be regulated by platen screws. It has adjustable feed-guides, a large distributing cylinder, card rack and receiver, and is well adapted for long service. The removal of a bar, easily effected, allows the platen and guides to be thrown back and thus exposes at one glance bed, platen, guides and rollers, greatly assisting correction, making ready or cleaning-up. The movements are simple and the motion easy, enabling the operator to print from 1,000 to 2,000 per hour. Platen 4 × 5 inches.

A Roller Mould, two sets of Roller Stocks and three Chases are furnished with the press.

Price, $125.

Boxing and Carting, $3.50.

Driving Pulley, Fast and Loose Pulleys, Counter-shaft, Hangers and two Cone Pulleys, for steam power, extra, $50.

Circa 1867

OFFICIAL PRINTING PRESSES.

Junior	prints 2x3 in.	***Hand-Inking,***	***$ 3***
		Self-Inking,	***5***
No. 1,	prints 3x4½ in.	***Hand-Inking,***	***6***
		Self-Inking,	***10***
No. 2,	prints 4x6 in.	***Hand-Inking,***	***11***
		Self-Inking,	***16***
No. 3,	prints 5x7½ in.	***Hand-Inking,***	***$17***
		Self-Inking,	***25***
No. 4,	prints 6x9 in.	***Hand-Inking,***	***25***
		Self-Inking,	***35***
No. 6,	prints 8x12 in.	***Self-Inking,***	***60***
		Rotary Power,	***100***

These prices include Inking Rollers, Chase, Wrench and Walnut Base Board. The Rollers are cast and the machine is all complete, ready to operate as soon as received.

The size of the sheets printed on this press is not limited by the size of the press, as it will print sheets with large margins without soiling them.

When there is much work to be done with the press, it is convenient to have one of each of the following extras:—An extra chase; a screw-chase, for holding a full form of type; an extra machine roller and a hand roller and ink-plate, to assist in holding and distributing the ink.

	Jr.	1	2	3	4	6
Chase,	$0.30	$0.40	$0.50	$0.60	$0.75	$1.10
Screw Chase,	.50	.75	.90	1.05	1.25	1.75
Rollers, each,	.30	.40	.55	.70	.85	1.20
Roller Cores, each,	$0.20	$0.25	$0.30	$0.40	$0.50	$0.70
Roller Mold,	1.50	1.75	2.00	2.25	2.50	3.00
Hand Roller & Plate,	.50	.75	1.00	1.00	1.25	1.50

THE OFFICIAL.

The Strength and Simplicity of Its Construction.—The entire Frame and Bed are one casting, from refined iron, and are so designed that the bed is *centrally supported* by the frame. The construction of the press is such that the power or strain is *compression*, and the bed and platen are so supported by cross braces, that it is impossible to spring them under the heaviest impression. The power, which is amply sufficient to print a full form of type, is obtained by a lever operating a toggle movement situated inside of the frame.

The Artistic Beauty of its Design and Finish is acknowledged by all who see it. The press stands on a round base or pedestal, combining beauty and strength. It is finished in enamel, which is almost as hard and durable as the iron itself, and is beautifully ornamented, making it very attractive and pleasing to the eye.

Its Conveniences for Making Ready.—A perfectly *square and even* impression is obtained by four adjusting screws under the platen. The platen has positive bearings, so that it is impossible for it to wear loose and slur. The impression is lessened or increased as desired, for printing either a small or large form of type, and for the varying thicknesses of paper and cardboard, by means of a *single screw* at the end of the Rocker. This regulates the impression quickly, equally and positively. By this invention most of the difficulty of making ready is overcome, and a great saving of time is made. Besides the above great advantages possessed by this press, the Inking Rollers and Distributor, and the form of Type and Platen, are in the most desirable position for making ready and operating. The Chase is reversible, and, on being put in its position on the press, is held firmly, as if by magic, without the aid of spring or screw.

The Ease and Rapidity of Operation.—The Platen swings on a Rocker, and is thereby perfectly balanced at every point in its movement, therefore requiring very little power, and is almost noiseless in its operation. The Hand-Inking Presses can readily be worked at the rate of 500 impressions an hour, and the Self-Inking Presses at the rate of 1000 and upwards an hour.

The Quality of Work that can be Produced from it.—It is adapted to meet the wants of the most exacting and discriminating, being capable of doing the finest work that can be done on any press, with either black or colored inks. It is so simple in its construction and so easily adjusted, that the most inexperienced can at once readily comprehend it.

Its Surety of Keeping in Perfect Working Order.—The parts of the press being few and very simple, render it very durable. There being no gearing or springs to be strained or broken, there will be no occasion for repairs. With proper usage it will last a life-time.

HAND-INKING OFFICIAL PRESS.

The Inking Attachment.—The distribution is complete, being obtained by a rotating disk and two rollers, which have a full movement on the disk. The rollers are carried twice completely over the type at every impression, inking the type thoroughly. The rollers are held by a new and simple device, so that they have an even pressure on the type, and the springs cannot be strained.

The Quality and Price Considered, no other Press can equal it for its design, which is so beautiful; for its construction, which is so simple; for its conveniences for making ready, which are so desirable; for its ease and rapidity of operation which are unequaled. All these desirable features are patented or have patents pending.

At the Centennial International Exhibition it received the highest and only award given to Self-Inking Hand Power Presses, and attracted visitors from all parts of the world. Many were sold to be taken abroad, as souvenirs of the exhibition and specimens of American taste and ingenuity. Among these sales were several to the representatives of European nations for their polytechnical schools.

Weight, packed, ready for shipment:

No.	0	1	2	3	4	6
Weight, lbs.	15	30	60	93	130	260

Circa 1877

Manufactured by J. Cook & Co., later by Kelsey both of Meriden, Conn.
Circa 1877

One Dollar

Printing Press.

For the boys who simply wish to print cards, or others who only desire to print a few lines, we make a simple lever press at one dollar which will print 1x2½ inches, on any size sheet. All iron and steel and does *good work*. Put up complete with Ink, Roller, Font of neat Card Type, price $2.50

(Can be sent by mail for 80 cents extra).

Sold by Kelsey & Co. of Meriden, Conn. Circa 1889.

THE

EXCELSIOR

PRESSES.

$3

$6

$15

$30

$50

Manufactured by Kelsey & Co. in Meriden, Conn. Circa 1889.

DESCRIPTION OF HAND INKING EXCELSIOR PRESSES.

PRICE LIST.

No. 1 Chase 2⅛x3½ inches, weight boxed about 16 lbs, $3.00
No. 2 3⅛x5⅛ inches, about 30 lbs,
No. 2½ 4½x7½ inches. about 60 lbs. 8.00
No. 3½ 5½x9½ inches about 100 lbs. 14.00
No. 4½ 7¼x13¼ in. about 175 lbs. 25.00
No. 5 10½x15½ in. about 290 lbs. 44.00

☞ Boxing for shipment, *free*. 1 Chase, 1 Ink Table, 1 Feed Table Bracket, with each press.

The press is well shown by the engraving. The body of press, A, is a solid casting with the bed. The chase, B, holds the type; it is made on our *patented* plan, having a bottom plate, which saves using an imposing stone, prevents a *pi*, or mixing of the form of type if by accident it is not well locked in chase. This chase is a *great* advantage to beginners as no discouraging mishaps can occur. With *other* style presses accidents will retard progress, which *cannot* occur with an EXCELSIOR. On swinging platen, D, rests sheet to be printed. A downward pressure on lever, E, gives the impression. The lever is *double*, has *two* connections with platen, which gives great power and prevents all twist or spring; it is as powerful as a side lever but far superior as it does away with side arms so that a sheet with *any* size margin may be printed. Ink is spread on ink table, C, (which is removable for cleaning,) and applied by a convenient hand roller. Our ink tables have an original arrangement to prevent handle of roller becoming inked. Impression is regulated by hand screws through the bed and adjusted to a *hair*, quickly and perfectly. Our chase fastening is *not equaled;* chase slides to place without *hand fastening*, self-locking, and *never* can work loose. NO EXCELSIOR PRESS is *cheaply* made but has *steel* bearings, *best* of screws, etc. Feed tables, F, are used to hold work being printed; one free with every press, except No. 1 size which is too small to need it. All presses print within ⅛ inch of full size of chase as screws are used to lock up the forms. Speed of press depends upon circumstances; from 300 to 1000 per hour are run according to size of sheet and dexterity of user.

EXCELSIOR SELF-INKING PRESSES.

The mechanical arrangements are almost precisely the same as in the hand-inkers, excepting that inking rollers are added which are operated by the action of the press. The arms which carry the inking rollers are moved by a connecting bar from the platen. The circular ink table revolves at each impression, giving perfect distribution, and the rollers pass twice over the form at each impression. Gripping fingers attached to the platen hold sheets in place for printing and remove them from the type. The advantage of the self-inker over the hand-inker is mainly in speed. Speed is increased because both hands are free, one to feed in paper, the other to work the lever. Any printer having a good run of work, or expecting it, *needs* a self-inker because from 600 to 2,000 impressions may be run, saving 50 per cent. in time. And anyone who will frequently have jobs of several thousand copies needs a fast press. But those whose work is limited to an occasional job, or small jobs of a few hundred, will be *entirely satisfied* with a hand-inker, and we advise it, unless they feel willing to pay slightly higher for the sake of a more complete machine and a little easier work.

	Price.
No. 1 Excelsior Self-Inking Press.—Chase 2½ by 3½ inches; weight, boxed, about 20 lbs.,	**$5.00**
No. 2 Excelsior Self-Inking Press.—Chase 3½ by 5½ inches; weight, boxed, about 35 lbs.,	**9.00**
No. 2½ Excelsior Self-Inking Press.—Chase 4½ by 7½ inches; weight, boxed, about 65 lbs.,	**16.00**
No. 3½ Excelsior Self-Inking Press.—Chase 5½ by 9½ inches; weight, boxed, about 110 lbs.,	**26.00**
No. 4½ Excelsior Self-Inking Press.—Chase 7¼ by 13¼ inches; weight, boxed, about 175 lbs.,	**50.00**
No. 5 Excelsior Self-Inking Press.—Chase 10½ by 15½ inches; weight, boxed, about 290 lbs.,	**85.00**

Each Press furnished with one Patent Chase, one pair Ink Rollers, one Ink Table, one Feed Table Bracket.

CABINET FORM.

When it can be afforded, order your press with a Cabinet, as shown in first engraving. It has places for 10 type cases, drawer for tools, etc., and brackets for holding a case when setting type. Price only $3.50. (With 10 cases, $9.50.)

TREADLES.

Foot Treadles furnished for any press above, with spring complete, for $2.00 extra. In some cases it is an advantage, though it is seldom necessary.

FEED TABLES.

At side of the self-inker is shown a little table on a bracket. It makes easier feeding. One bracket given with every press, on which any shaped board desired may be fastened. Extra brackets 30 cents each.

Nos. 1 and 2 Self-Inkers carry one Roller and no Grippers, being used mostly for cards.

Manufactured by Kelsey & Co. in Meriden, Conn. Circa 1880.

EXCELSIOR PRESS

9 X 13 INCHES.

Chase 9¼ x 13¼ Inches. Weight, boxed for shipment, about 350 lbs.

PRICE, $85.00

Heavy. Strong. Durable.

Made on the new improved lines that mark the superiority of the **Excelsior.** This size is capable of doing a large variety of jobs.

With the $135.00 outfit shown on opposite page a full line of commercial printing can be executed.

11 x 16 EXCELSIOR PRESS

PRICE, $160.00

Chase 11¼ x 16¼ Inches.

Weight, boxed for shipment, about 550 lbs.

This is a new and up-to-date machine, with all the patented features of the **Improved Excelsior,** and of a size particularly adapted for the use of printing offices in small towns, as the capital invested is not large, and the machine will execute all kinds of job work. It can also be used to get out a fair-sized newspaper.

This press and outfit, price $230 makes a comprehensive printing plant for a thriving town.

THE BEST PRESS FOR THE LEAST MONEY!

ENTERPRISE

PRINTING PRESSES.

The **Enterprise Presses** receive the highest commendations from those who have seen or used them, and are generally acknowledged to be the BEST small presses made. With the self-inking attachment perfect distribution of ink is obtained, but the chief advantage gained is the much greater rate of speed at which the press can be worked. The chases to all Enterprise Presses have screws to lock up the form, so that matter almost the size of the chase can be printed. The chases having a bottom, a composing stick can be dispensed with, especially on the smaller sizes where not too heavy to handle. Card printers will find these presses exactly suited to their wants We claim that **for Card and small work the Enterprise Self-Inkers are unequaled.** A fair trial will convince you of their excellence.

CHASES FOR ALL ENTERPRISE PRESSES ARE MADE WITH A BOTTOM.

PRICES OF ENTERPRISE SELF-INKERS.

No. 1, Chase inside, 2½ x 4 inches. .... $6 00 | No. 2, Chase inside, 3¼ x 5½ inches......... $10 00

☞Each press is provided with chase and two machine rollers, being in perfect working order when shipped. The No. 1, being designed more especially for card printing, has no grippers, as they are not needed when cards are worked. No. 2 complete with grippers.

PRICES OF ENTERPRISE HAND-INKERS.

No. 1, Chase inside, 2½ x 4 inches...........	$3 00	No. 3, Chase inside, 6 x 8½ inches..........	$15 00
No. 2, " " 3¼ x 5½ "	5 50	No. 4, " " 7 x 10½ "	20 00

Chase and Hand Roller with each press. The ink-table can be instantly detached for cleaning. It is made with a rest for the handle of the ink roller, attached to a stud beneath, which can be turned under the ink table when not in use; when turned up the handle of the roller is kept entirely clear of the ink Other devices do NOT accomplish this. ☞**All Enterprise Presses Boxed Free.**☜

PRICES FOR EXTRAS.

Extra Chase for No. 1 Press	$0 80
" " " " 2 "	1 00
" " " " 3 "	1 65
" " " " 4 "	2 50

EXTRA INK TABLES FOR HAND-INKERS.

No. 1 Press....................................	$0 25
No. 2 " with rest	40
No. 3 " " "	85
No. 4 " " "	1 25

EXTRA INK DISCS FOR SELF-INKERS.

No. 1 Press....................................	$0 80
No. 2 "	1 00

EXTRA INK ROLLERS FOR SELF-INKERS.

No. 1 Press, with stocks, each	$0 40
No. 2 " " " "	50

When new rollers are required, old stocks can be returned, and will be re-covered for 25 cts. each.

IMPORTANT NOTICE!

Type, Presses and Printing Materials, selected from any other Catalogue, furnished at manufacturers' prices, and at short notice. In ordering, mention from what book.

Manufactured by J. Cook & Co. of Meriden, Conn.
Kelsey purchased the company.

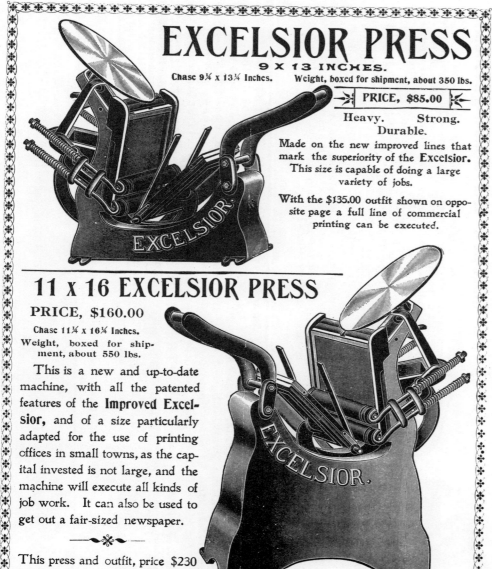

NONPAREIL PRINTING PRESS

Hand-Power Self-Inking

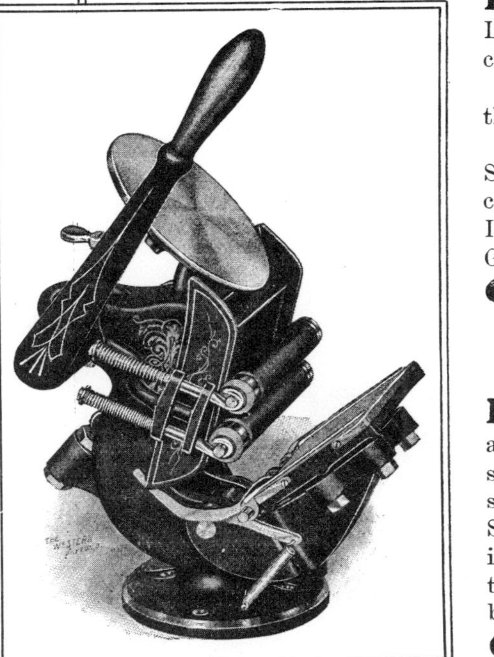

Press No. 21. This is a Side Lever Self-Inking Press. The Size of chase inside measure is $2\frac{1}{2}$ x 4 inches.

The ink-rollers will cover the form thoroughly and evenly.

This outfit complete with a font of Standard Metal Type, 5 A caps; Type case with 48 compartments; Tube of Ink; Wood Furniture; Tweezers; Gold and Silver Bronze; Cards, etc.

Complete, - $8.00

Press No. 22. This is also a Side-Lever Self-Inking Press, it is similar in character to the No. 21 as shown in cut, but has a larger chase. Size of chase inside measure, 3 x $4\frac{1}{2}$ inches. The outfit furnished with this press is similar to press No. 21 but has 6 A, 10 a font of metal type.

Complete, - $12.50

Press No. 23. This is a Side-Lever Self-Inking Press, it is the simplest and most durable press ever built. Every part is accurately fitted by expert mechanics. It works smooth and easy.

Size of chase inside measure, 4 x 6 inches. This outfit complete with a font of Standard Metal Type, 6 A caps and 10 a lowercase; one Type case with 72 compartments; Spaces and Quads; Wood Furniture; Leads and Slugs; Tube of Ink; Gold and Silver Bronze; Cards, etc.

Price Complete, - - $20.00

Made by Sigwalt Manufacturing Co. of Chicago.

NONPAREIL PRINTING PRESS

Hand-Power Self-Inking

Press No. 24 This Press is a Side Lever, Self-Inking, Hand-Power Printing Press, it is built with as much care and skill as any piece of machinery that goes into the best equipped printing office.

The size of chase inside measure, 5 x $7\frac{1}{2}$ inches.

All material used is carefully selected, manufactured in the best modern mechanical style, all parts are thoroughly inspected before assembled in the press.

This outfit is complete with a font of Standard Metal Type, 9 A caps and 15 a lower case, or small letters; Leads and Slugs; Wood Furniture; Spaces and Quads; one Type case with 72 compartments; one pair of Tweezers; tube of Ink; Cards, etc.

Complete, = $31.25

Press No. 25. This is a Side-Lever Self-Inking Hand-Power Printing Press. Size of chase inside measure, 6 x 9 inches.

This press will print a form the full size of the chase and is far superior to any other press on the market. This outfit complete with a font of Standard metal type, 9 A caps and 15 a lowercase; spaces and quads; leads and slugs; wood furniture; type case with 72 compartments, ink, etc.

Price Complete, = = $43.75

CHICAGO PRINTING PRESS

...SELF-INKING...

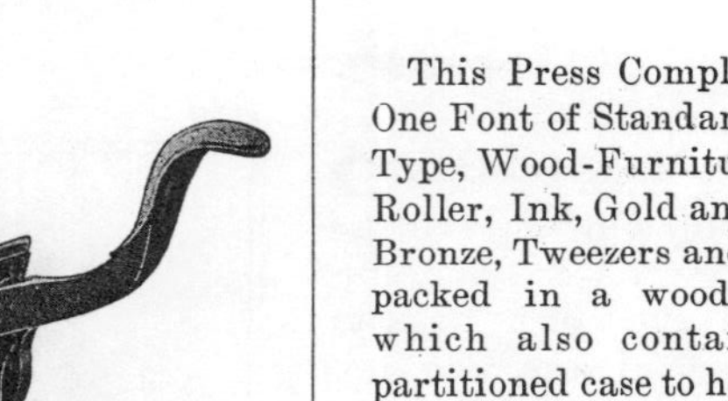

This Press Complete with One Font of Standard Metal Type, Wood-Furniture, Ink-Roller, Ink, Gold and Silver Bronze, Tweezers and Cards, packed in a wooden box, which also contains one partitioned case to hold type.

No. 9, Size of Chase, inside measure 2⅛x3¼ in. price complete **$3.50**

No. 10, Size of Chase, inside measure 2½ x 4 in. price complete **$5.00**

This Press same as No. 10, is made with two rollers, thus giving better distribution of ink and equality of color. The same equipment furnished as with No. 9 and 10.

No. 11, Size of Chase, inside 2½x4 in. price complete **$6.00**

Made by Sigwalt Manufacturing Co. of Chicago.

CHICAGO PRINTING PRESS

SELF-INKING

Press No. 15 is a side lever Self-Inking Press as shown in cut. Size of chase inside measure, 1½ x 2½ inches. Outfit complete with a font of Short Metal Type, Wood-Furniture, Ink-Roller, Ink, Gold and Silver Bronze, Cards, etc.

Price Complete . $2.00

PRESS NO. 16 is a side lever Self-Inking Press as shown in cut. Size of Chase inside measure 1⅞ x 2⅞ inches.

Outfit complete with a font of Standard Long Metal Type. Wood-Furniture, Ink, Gold and Silver Bronze, Cards, etc.

Price Complete - $3.00

The Lightning Press.

SINCE the introduction of cheap printing presses, card printing has become a business of great importance, and hardly a village in the country but has one or more persons engaged in its prosecution. This arises from the fact that most persons have a very natural desire to see their names in print, and can have that desire gratified at a trifling expense by having a few address cards printed. The field for the enterprise of the card printer is a large and profitable one, and the capital required small—two features of the trade which combine to make it an attractive one to persons of small means. Card printing has usually, been done on presses with a speed varying from three hundred to fifteen hundred impressions an hour.

The need of a press capable of being worked at a greater rate of speed than the presses in general use led us to turn our attention in that direction, and the result is the beautiful machine to which we have given the name of the LIGHTNING CARD PRESS, and which, owing to a new idea successfully carried out in this press, can be run at a speed of from twenty-five hundred to four thousand impressions an hour, varying with the skill of the operator. The side-guage on the platen, against which the end of the card is placed, on receding from the bed, is unlocked and forced suddenly to the left, — delivering the card at the side of the press, in view of the operator. The side-guage, after the delivery of the card, relocks itself, and is ready to receive another. The speed over the presses having an automatic card-drop is gained by the instant delivery in the Lightning Press, while in the former it is dependent on the simple dropping of the card by its weight beneath the press. Another advantage gained by this method of delivery is that it is applicable to envelopes, tags, and even thin paper circulars, while the other is limited to cards alone. The press is operated by a lever which can be used at either side, at the will of the operator.

THE LIGHTNING PRESS.

Price, (chase, 3 × 5¼ inches ; weight, 48 pounds,) **$30.00**

Extra rollers, each, complete, 65 cents. Postage, 8 cents. Stocks alone, each, . 35 cents. Postage, 4 cents.
Recasting rollers, each, ... 30 cents. Postage, 8 cents. Extra chase, ... 50 cents. Postage, 25 cents.

Young America Press Co., 35 Murray St., New York.

THE LIGHTNING PRESS.

Since the introduction of cheap printing presses, card printing has become a business of great importance, and hardly a village in the country but has one or more persons engaged in its prosecution. This arises from the fact that most persons have a very natural desire to see their names in print, and can have that desire gratified at a trifling expense by having a few address cards printed. The field for the enterprise of the printer is a large and profitable one, and the capital required small — two features of the trade which combine to make it an attractive one to persons of small means. Card printing has usually been done on presses with a speed varying from three hundred to fifteen hundred impressions an hour.

The need of a press capable of being worked at a greater rate of speed than the presses in general use led us to turn our attention in that direction, and the result was the beautiful machine to which we have given the name of the LIGHTNING CARD PRESS, and which, owing to a new idea successfully carried out in this machine, can be run at a speed of from twenty-five hundred to four thousand impressions an hour, varying with the skill of the operator. The side-gauge on the platen, against which the end of the card is placed, on receding from the bed, is unlocked, and forced suddenly to the left, delivering the card at the side of the press, in view of the operator. The side-gauge, after the delivery of the card, relocks itself, and is ready to receive another. The speed over the presses having an automatic card-drop is gained by the instant delivery in the Lightning Press, while in the former it is dependent on the simple dropping of the card by its weight beneath the press. Another advantage gained by this method of delivery is that it is applicable to envelopes, tags, and even thin paper circulars, while the other is limited to cards alone. In the Lightning Press we use our new device for fastening the chase in position on the bed, being dropped instantly into place, where it remains securely fastened. The press is operated by a lever which can be used at either side, at the will of the operator. The method of adjusting the impression is the same as that used on the Young America Presses, except that the impression screws are attached to the platen instead of the bed. The ink table is a disk, which receives a quarter turn at each impression. Two inking rollers pass completely over the form, giving perfect distribution of ink. A feed-board, not shown in the engraving, is attached to the front of the press. The press itself presents a neat and attractive appearance, and, as it is sold at a very reasonable price, one or more should be in the possession of every person who desires success in the art of card printing. No less than eight of these machines are in operation in the town of Nassau, New York, at the date of the issuance of this circular, and the number is being added to constantly. J. B. HUSTED, ESQ., postmaster of that town, and a well-known card printer, now possesses three of them.

But one size of the Lightning Press is made. With each press is sent a screw chase, two rollers, and a wrench. It will be boxed, and delivered, free of charge, to the express, or on board of the cars, in New York city, on receipt of the price.

Circa 1875

THE

YOUNG AMERICA PRESS.

The Young America Press was first manufactured and sold by us in 1871, and has had a very large sale. We have received and published hundreds of unsolicited testimonials to its extraordinary merits, and a large proportion of that testimony has been from persons who have owned or been familiar with other presses. At the time of its introduction, there were but three other cheap printing presses in general use, the Lowe, the Cottage, and the Novelty. The Lowe Press was the first press made for popular use, being introduced in 1856. The impression was made by a conical roller, hung, larger end outward, in a lever pivoted to a post at the rear of the bed. When the roller was swung around, it carried with it the tympan, which was hinged to the rear part of the press, between the post and the bed. The Cottage Press was brought out in 1860. The impression on this press was produced by a cylinder, the bed being propelled beneath it by a crank. Several years later the Novelty Press appeared, and was the first cheap press made on the bed and platen principle; but then, as now, it was without side-arms, and the impression regulated by moving the legs on the lower part of the platen in or out, as occasion might seem to demand — a contrivance entirely inadequate to effect the end aimed at.

THE YOUNG AMERICA PRESS.

To the novice in printing one press seems to be as good as another, and it is only by dear-bought experience that he arrives at a different conclusion. To the practical printer the size of the chase is by no means evidence that it will print a full form of that size, endorsed even by the assertions of the manufacturer that the bed will not spring under a full form. The only true test of the worth of a printing press is to fill the chase full of small type, and then take an impression. If that impression does not present a uniform appearance throughout, and cannot be readily made to do so by the means provided for that purpose, you may be sure that the press is a defective one, and cannot be relied on. If, on the contrary, the impression be an even one, the centre presenting the same appearance as the sides and end of the form, and that appearance be maintained for any length of time without further adjustment, you may feel certain that the press on trial, so far as printing well is concerned, will not disappoint you. A press which will print a full form well will also print a single line equally well; but it by no means follows that a press which will print a form half the size of the chase in a satisfactory manner will have the same power over three fourths or a full form. This applies especially to presses without side-arms, and without which it is almost a mechanical impossibility to produce a satisfactory press. It is, indeed, possible, by overlaying the bed or platen of such a press, to make it do its duty in a feeble way; but it is at a great expenditure of time and strength, as the overlays have to be added to at frequent intervals, and more power is required to operate a press which yields in ever so small a degree at the point of impression. An inspection of the presses in use in regular printing offices will show what immense strength of material is needed in any kind of press to secure durability and efficiency.

The inventor of the Young America Press was a practical press-builder. The points he aimed to secure in this press were simplicity, durability, efficiency, and ease of working. Under the supervision of a practical printer, no expense was spared to make it absolutely perfect; and to-day, notwithstanding scores of other presses have been introduced, it is a long way ahead of its rivals in the points

Circa 1875

Young America Press Co., 35 Murray St., New York.

essential to a good printing machine. It will be seen, on comparison, that in regard to strength of construction, ease of adjustment, as well as the power to print a chase full of type, the Young America is fully equal to any press made, of whatever cost. Its superiority over all others of that class is too notorious a fact to be disputed at this day. Of the thousands which have been sold in the last five years, there is not one (unless broken by accident) that is not as good as the day it was purchased.

The Young America is a bed and platen press, having its toggle-bar in the rear, behind the bed. The feet of this toggle-bar are hinged to the frame of the press, one at each side. The ends of the toggle-bar are connected by two side-arms with the platen, the lower part of which is hinged to the frame-work. On the smaller sizes the press is operated by a lever connected directly with the toggle-bar. Depressing the lever raises the toggle-bar to a horizontal position, and, by means of the side-arms, draws the platen up to the bed, and gives the impression. On the Quarto press a second toggle, with two joints, is introduced, one joint being the lever which projects towards the operator, and the other having its point just beneath the upper toggle-bar. When the end of the joint nearest the operator is depressed, the rear end of the other joint is raised, carrying with it the upper toggle-bar. This arrangement enables us to print from a full form with less power than is required to work a smaller one on other presses. The double-toggle presses are operated by hand or foot, or both together, as may be most desirable.

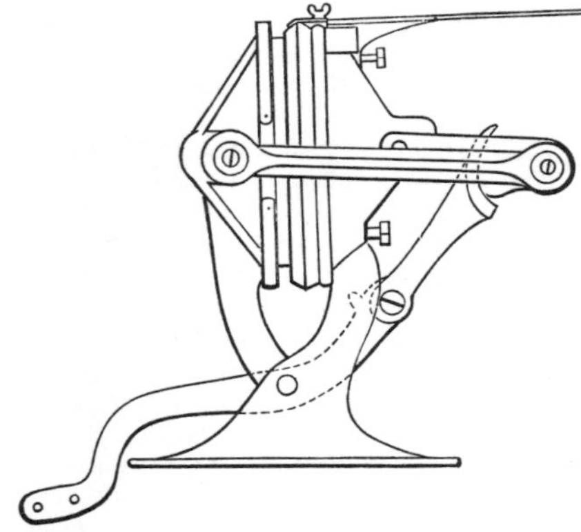

THE YOUNG AMERICA QUARTO PRESS.

In the appliances for adjusting the impression we have adopted the plan used on all good presses. The bed is attached to the framework by a single bolt in the centre, with an impression screw at each corner. This, in connection with the side-arms, allows the type to be placed upon any part of the bed, and contributes to the durability of the press. If, from constant use for many years, some parts of the press are worn more than others, yet the quality of the printing will not be affected, because every part of the surfaces of the bed and platen can be made, by the use of the four impression screws, to retain the exact distance from each other necessary to do good printing. Attached to each press is an adjustable card guage and an ink table, removable at pleasure, and the Note, Billhead, Letter, and Quarto presses have gripping fingers, for removing the printed sheet from the type.

The rate of speed to be attained on the Young America Press will depend entirely on the skill of the operator. While some of our patrons assert that they have printed at the rate of one thousand impressions per hour, we could only assure from three to five hundred as the probable result.

Owing to the great durability of these presses, we are enabled to guaranty that we will take in exchange, at any time, unless broken, a small press for a larger one, of the same kind, on payment of the difference in price.

One chase, one ink roller, and an ink table accompany each press without additional charge.

THE YOUNG AMERICA PRESS

OUR business experience in connection with printing presses for popular use dates back to 1857, when we engaged in the manufacture and sale of the Lowe Press, in Boston, Mass. This press was invented by one S. W. Lowe—hence its name. The impression was made by a conical roller, hung, larger end outward, in a lever pivoted to a post at the rear of the bed. When the roller was swung around, it forced down the tympan, which was hinged to the rear part of the press, between the post and the bed. Notwithstanding its defects, great numbers were sold; but its manufacture has long since ceased, and it is rarely that one of them is seen in use.

In 1860 we opened an office in New York city for the sale of printing presses and material, and in the same year we brought out the Cottage Press, which was somewhat of an improvement on its predecessor. This press also had an extensive sale, but in its turn superseded by other and better presses. In 1872 we began the manufacture of the Young America Press, first as a hand-inking press, and then, four years later, adding to it the necessary fixtures to make it a self-inker.—Many new presses have been put upon the market since its introduction, but in our opinion it has never been excelled, if equalled, by any other in simplicity, durability, and efficiency. It is a bed and platen press, having its toggle-bar in the rear, behind the bed, and its feet hinged to the frame of the press, one at each side. The ends of this toggle-bar are connected by two side-arms with the yoke, or platen carrier, the lower part of which is hinged to the frame-work. The machine is operated by a lever connected directly with the toggle-bar. Depressing the lever raises the toggle-bar to a horizontal position, and, by means of the side-arms, draws the platen up to the bed, gives the impression, and at the same time forces the two inking-rollers up over the type, on to the top of the press, which revolves at each impression. While the impression is being taken, the rollers are on the ink-table. The rollers pass completely over the type and well up on the disk, insuring a good distribution of ink. The lever can be used on either side of the press as may be desired.

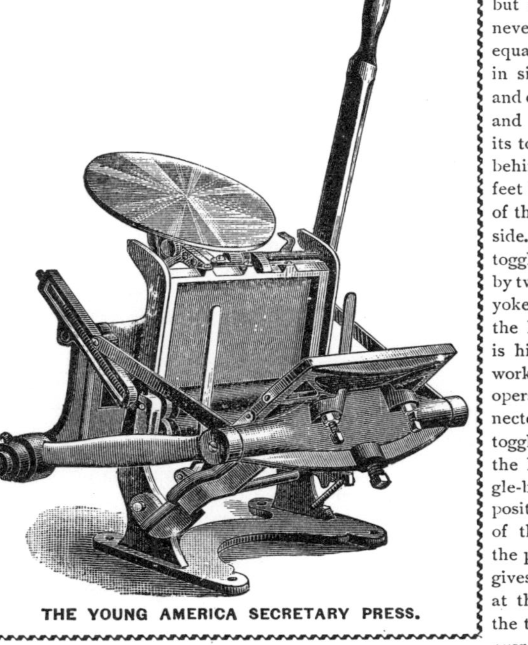
THE YOUNG AMERICA SECRETARY PRESS.

In the appliances for adjusting the impression we have adopted the plan used on all first-class presses. The platen is attached to the yoke by a single bolt in the centre, with an impression screw at each corner.

Circa 1875

Young America Press Co., 35 Murray St., New York.

THE AMERICAN PRESS.

In now presenting to the public our series of SELF-INKING PRESSES, we do so with the positive assurance that they will be found unequalled for SIMPLICITY, DURABILITY, EFFICIENCY, and CHEAPNESS. An examination of the cheap self-inkers will disclose the fact that to a poor press has been added a poorer inking apparatus, and the combination advertised as a great improvement. To have the type properly inked is as necessary to secure good printing as an even impression, and in our new presses the desired result is attained in a most satisfactory manner. Two inking rollers pass completely over the form, the ink being taken from a disk, which revolves at each impression, insuring a perfect distribution.

THE AMERICAN EAGLE PRESS. THE AMERICAN UNION PRESS.

The main features of the AMERICAN and YOUNG AMERICA PRESSES are nearly alike. They are both perfect in their way, and either will give satisfaction. As will be seen from the price-list, some of the presses have an automatic card-drop, whereby the cards, as fast as printed, are delivered in front of the press. This device increases the speed from fifteen to twenty-five per cent., and can be detached, if desired, in a moment. As with the YOUNG AMERICA Presses, the name does not indicate the class of work to which they are adapted. On either press an entire chase-full of type can be printed easily and distinctly. The smaller sizes are operated by a lever at the side of the press. The UNION is operated by our patented double-toggle, combination hand-and-foot lever, by which large forms can be

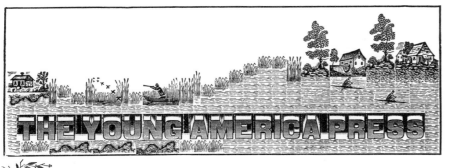

THE LAST AND BEST PRESS

DURING the last twenty-five years we have produced many printing machines, some of more and some of less merit. In this press, to which we have given the name of "THE LAST AND BEST," we have endeavored to combine the excellences which have characterized the others with such improvements as our long experience in the manufacture and sale of printing presses has shown to be desirable.

Without enumerating all the good features of our new press, simply claiming that it will be found equal in all respects to any press made, we desire to call attention to one improvement which renders it superior to all others. By an inspection of the cuts, it will be seen that the entire bed of the press, with its chase, can be swung up into a horizontal position, so that, if desired, the type can be transferred directly from the composing stick to the chase upon the bed of the press, and there locked up, without (as in most other presses) the type having to be first placed on an imposing stone or other smooth, flat surface, and then locked up before being placed upon the press. It is often a considerable trouble with the inexperienced amateur printer, owing to defective spacing or inequality in sizes of type, to raise the form after it is locked up. In the Last and Best this difficulty is obviated. In the making of corrections in the form of type, also, the new improvement is of great benefit. Every printer has time and again experienced the annoyance arising from being obliged to take the form from the press, in order to make alterations and to correct typographical errors. Some persons have the idea that the bed of this press swings up with every impression. Such is not the fact, the bed changing its position from the perpendicular to the horizontal only when desired. The grippers can be depressed to the platen at will, the chase is securely fastened, and yet easily detached, and the lever can be placed on either side of the press. For printing outfits, those recommended on another page for the Young America Secretary and Union Presses will answer for these,—outfit No. 7 for the smaller, and outfit No. 9 for the larger press.

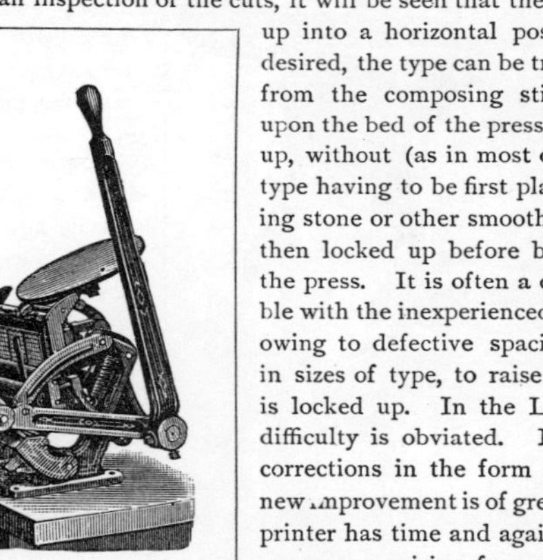

Last and Best No. 1, (chase 7 by 10 inches; weight, 155 pounds,)—boxing, $1.00 extra—... **$40.00**
Last and Best No. 2, (chase 10 by 15 inches; weight 400 pounds,)—boxing, $1.50 extra—... **85.00**

Two composition or cast rollers, one chase and a wrench accompany each press.

PRICE OF EXTRA ROLLERS, &c.

	Last and Best No. 1.	Last and Best No. 2.
Rollers, complete, each..........	80 cts. Postage, 25 cts.	$1.25. Postage, 60 cts.
Roller stocks, each..........	50 cts. Postage, 10 cts.	.80. Postage, 20 cts.
Recasting, each..........	40 cts. Postage, 25 cts.	.50. Postage, 60 cts.
Roller trucks, each..........	20 cts. Postage, 4 cts.	.25. Postage, 4 cts.
Chases, each..........	$1.00	1.25.

Manufactured by Joseph Watson of New York. Circa 1875

THE CENTENNIAL PRESS.

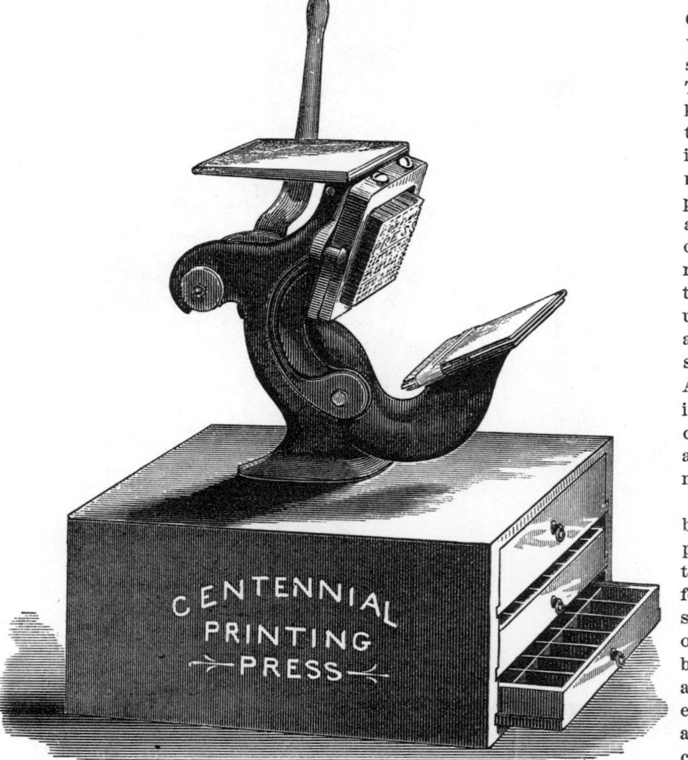

In the introduction of the Centennial Press we had in view the production of something cheap and good. That it is cheap every one knows, and the wonder is that we are enabled to sell it at so low a price. We make two sizes of this little press, the smaller exchangeable for the larger, with the difference in price. We have received many recommendations from those who have used the Centennial Presses, and which generally express surprise at their efficiency. An investment of five dollars in one of our Centennial offices has netted its owner over a hundred dollars in three months.

The Centennial, as shown by the cut, is a bed and platen press, worked by a lever at the side. The large press has four impression screws, the smaller none, the impression on the latter being regulated by paper. An ink table is attached to each press, and each press is furnished with an ink roller, screw chase, card gauges, and our patent automatic chase-fastener.

While this beautiful little machine meets the general demand for a low-priced printing press, and is capable of doing good work, and gives general satisfaction, we only claim for it that it is just as good as most of those for which from three to five times as much is asked. If a perfect press be desired, it can be had in the YOUNG AMERICA and AMERICAN PRESSES, and for which the Centennial is exchangeable.

Manufactured by Joseph Watson of New York. Circa 1875

The Folio Novelty Press

Price of Press, $150.00

Weight, 550 lbs.

Prints a form 14 by 19 in.

Size, 14¾ by 20 in.

Benj. O. Woods & Co., Manufacturers,

49 Federal Street, - - - - Boston, Mass.

AGENTS,

E. F. MAC KUSICK, 6 MURRAY STREET, NEW YORK.

KELLY, HOWELL & LUDWIG, 720 FILBERT ST. PHILADELPHIA, PA.

S. P. ROUNDS, 175 MONROE STREET, CHICAGO, ILL.

ORDERS MAY ALSO BE SENT TO

Rowley Brothers & Co., Utica, New York. Ludden & Bates, Savannah, Georgia.

Detroit Paper Company, Detroit, Mich. A. C. Bakewell & Co., Pittsburg, Penn.

The Folio Press is constructed entirely of iron, in a very superior style of workmanship and finish. It possesses great strength, and the platen being moved by two toggles instead of one, as in the other sizes of the Novelty Press, secures for it vastly increased power and consequent ease of operation. It possesses all the points of excellence that have made the other sizes of the Novelty so popular and which have secured for them a sale of over eight thousand presses.

A full form, 14 by 19 inches, or a newspaper, 22 by 32, of four pages, may be printed on it, one page at a time, with much greater ease and at three times the speed of any of the different hand presses made, such as the "Washington," "Tufts," "Adams" etc., and much more rapidly than any other press not run by artificial power, while for ordinary job work, whether large or small, the press is all that could be desired either for speed or superiority of work.

A simple glance at the construction of the press is sufficient to show that it is vastly superior for convenience of working, to any of the others, which, together with its light weight, (five hundred and fifty pounds,) and low price, as compared to the others, renders it very much more desirable.

With each press are furnished one each Folio, Quarto and Octavo Chases, one each 20, 10 and 5 inch roller stocks with extra spindles and a 20 inch Roller-mould. Price of extra chases, each, $2.00.

Each press is set up ready for instant use when dispatched to the purchaser.

In addition to the price of the press, purchasers will be required to pay freight from the manufactory in Athol, Mass., but no press will be dispatched until full payment therefor is made.

Circa 1875

QUARTO NOVELTY PRESS.

(PLAIN ONLY.)

Size of chase inside, 10 × 14 ½ in.

Prints a form of type 9 × 14 inches.

Weight of press, boxed, 200 pounds,

Price of press, boxed, 50 Dollars.

Manufactured by Benjamin O. Woods & Co. Circa 1875

The Standard Lever Press manufactured by H.H. Thorp of Cleveland. Circa 1876.

"UNCLE SAM" PRESS.

No. 1, Chase 3¼ x 5¼ inches.
Hand-inking, $6 00 | Self-inking, $10 00
Boxing, No. 1, 50 cents extra.
No. 2, 5 x 8 inches inside of chase,
Hand-inking, $10 00 | Self-inging, $20 00
Boxing, No. 2, $1.00 extra.
Every requisite for immediate use included.

Manufactured by W.C. Evans of Philadelphia. Circa 1880.

NEWBURY'S PATENT JOB AND CARD PRESS.

This press is fast winning favor among printers throughout the country. Its cheapness recommends it to their notice, and its utility brings it into favor It is built in a substantial manner, and is simple in all its arrangements. It is adapted to all kinds of work, from a coarse bill to the finest of fancy printing. Will give from 800 to 1,000 impressions per hour, according to the kind of work. It is well adapted to printing in colors, as the ink may be cleaned from the distributing disc almost instantly. In working cards they are fed into feed-slides and deliver themselves. Paper is fed on a spring frisket, and has to be placed on and taken off by hand. We furnish adjustable steel stops for feeding paper, so that a perfectly accurate register may be obtained. The inking and distributing is all done by the impression lever, so that all that is required is to work the lever with one hand and feed with the other. The distribution is a flat plate which revolves a little at every impression, giving a most perfect distribution. It is, in fact, all that is necessary for a Power Jobber, and the price is so low that no printer need be without one. We box and ship them ready for operation, with directions for adjusting and operating them.

Prices of Jobber.

Half Foolscap size, Platen 7 by 11¾ in.......................................$65 00
Extra Roll Stocks, per set.. 1 00
Extra chases.. 75

These prices include boxing and carting; also one set of Roller Stocks, Roller Mold, Chase, and Paper Registers.

TERMS OF PAYMENT.—Cash previous to shipment, or send money by Express, to e paid on delivery of press.

Proof Press.

We are also manufacturing a superior article of Proof Press, similar to those in general use, except that it has no flanges on the roll, the guides for it being on the bed, so that the roll can be used advantageously for taking proof of a full form on the stone. We make them to set on counter, without frame or with frame, ink box, roller frame, and stock.

PRICES—9x28 inches inside of bearers, $25; with frame, ink box, roll frame, and stock, $35.
16x28 inches inside of bearers, $35; with frame, ink box, roll frame and stock, $45

Newbury's Mitering Machine.

We have just introduced this little Machine in our manufactures. Its simplicity and the perfect accuracy of its work must recommend it to the Craft. It is adapted to both squaring and mitering rules, and may be adjusted to any angle by means of an index on its bed; the work is done by means of a steel cutter turned by a crank, and it cuts so rapid that it can be used advantageously for squaring rules to a length where there is from ⅛ to ¼ inch variation. Price $12 50.

Salesroom, 16 Murray-st., New York. Address, A. & B. NEWBURY, Windham Centre, Greene Co., N. Y.

Circa 1863

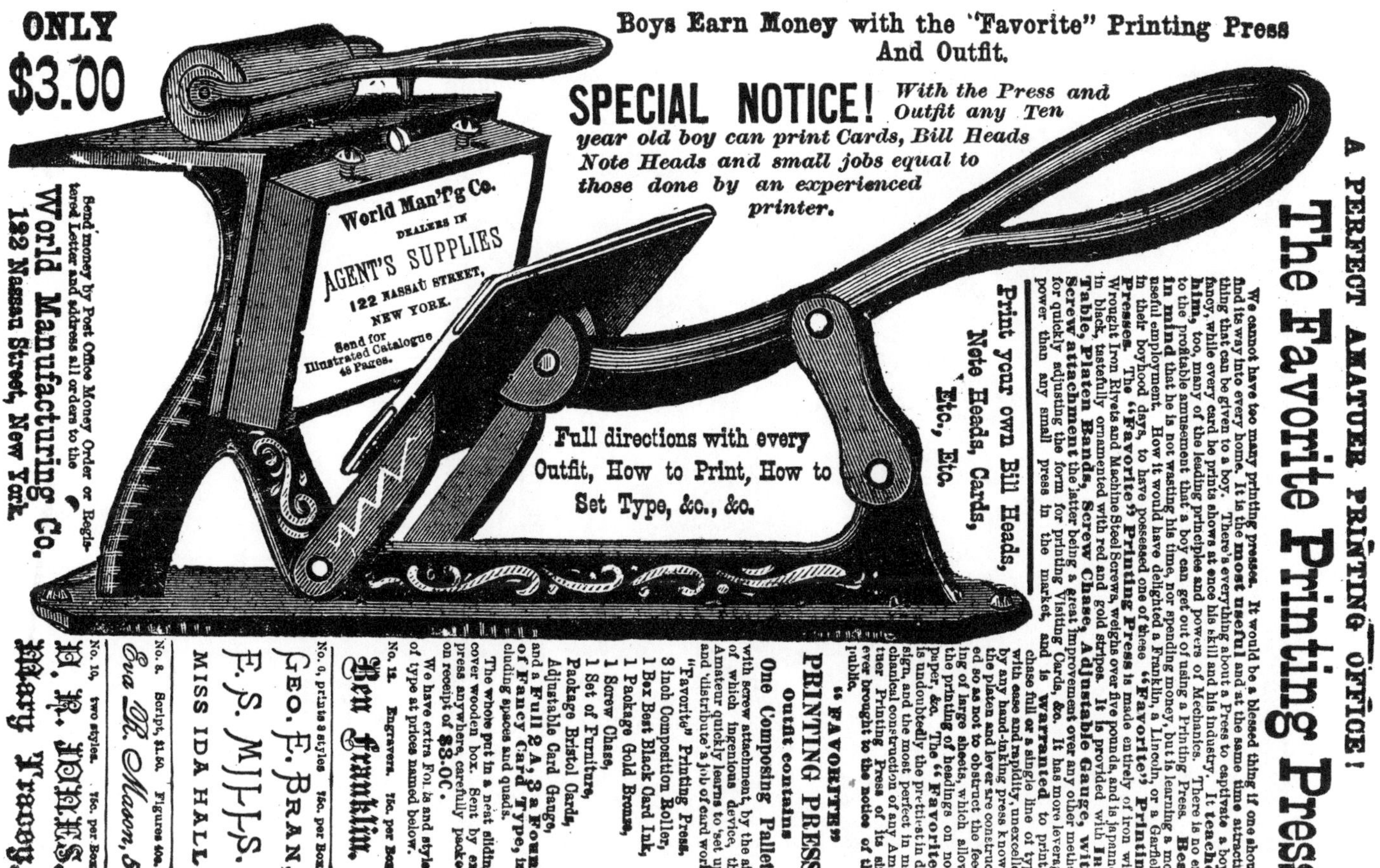

One of many Rail Presses made in the United States. Circa 1883

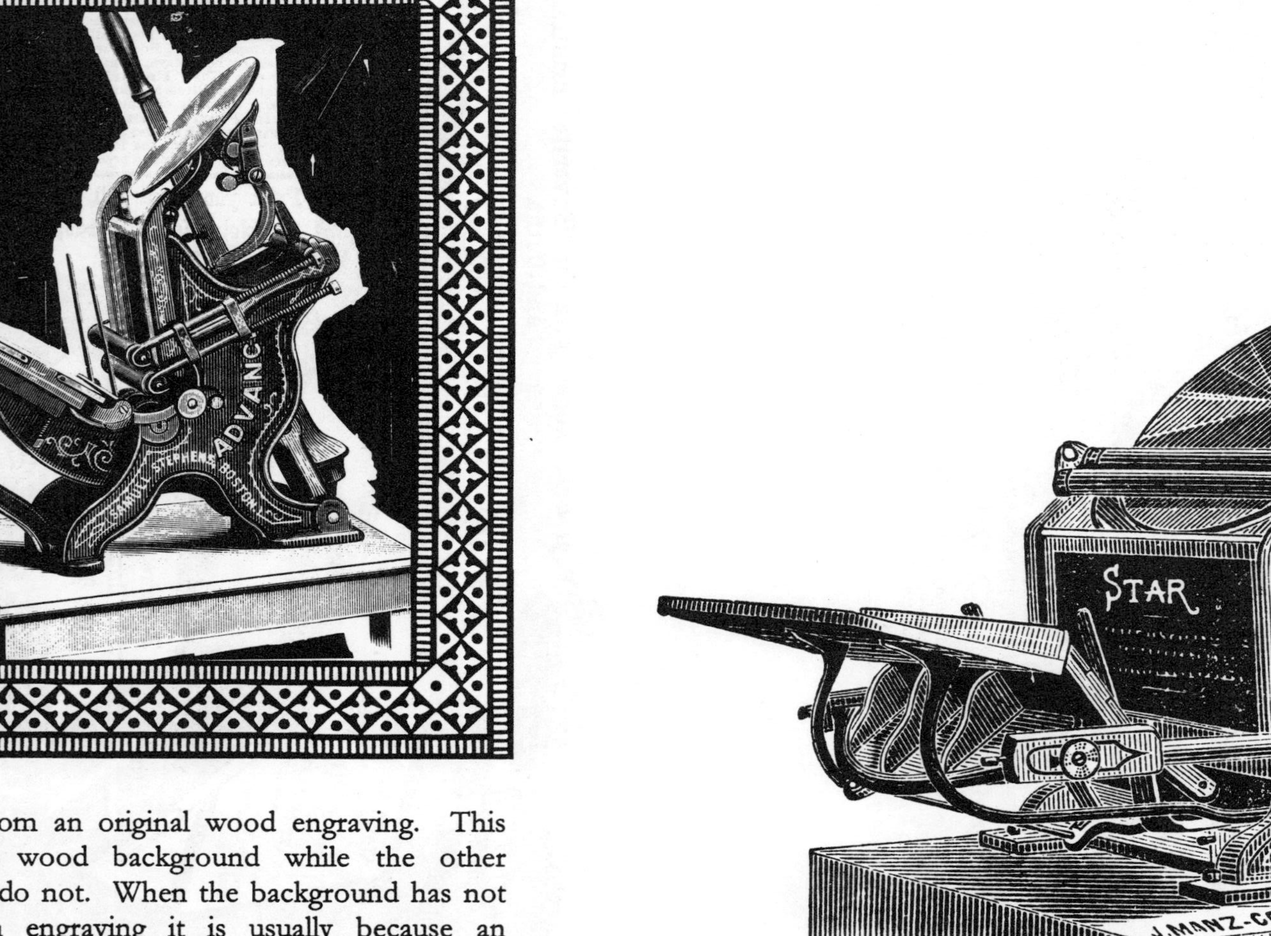

The above is a proof from an original wood engraving. This illustration has a solid wood background while the other illustrations in this book do not. When the background has not been removed from an engraving it is usually because an electrotype was made from the original and the unwanted background was routed away. Thus the original could be saved as a pictorial source and used over and over again.

Circa 1888

Star Lever Press manufactured by J.M. Jones Co., Palmyra, New York.
Circa 1882

Lithographic presses

In 1798, using a stone to write a laundry list, Alois Senefelder revolutionized the printing industry by discovering a method of chemical reproduction on stone. To make a lithograph, the artist drew an image in reverse, directly on a limestone, using a grease crayon. By applying certain chemicals to the stone's surface the picture was etched into the stone. Water kept the non-image area clean. The basic premise of lithography is that grease and water don't mix. Artists used this new medium enthusiastically as it provided them with a fast, accurate, and economical way to reproduce their work.

In the 1820's, the printing industry recognized the benefits of the lithographic method as an easy way to transfer small detailed designs to a stone, and economically print labels, certificates, bank notes, etc. Lithographic shops were set up first in Boston, then in Philadelphia and New York. They employed artists who specialized in maps, sheet music, illustrations, business stationery, advertisements, stock certificates, and insurance policies. The lithographic technique better rendered the fine detail and unusual calligraphy in these beautiful items.

Limestones from the banks of the Danube River in Bavaria, Germany were used. The thickness of the stone had to be in proportion to its other dimensions or the stone could crack. Some of these stones were as thick as 3 inches.

In 1850 there were only twenty-five lithographic establishments in the United States, although this process was less expensive than making illustrations using engravings or copper plates. The image could also be removed from the stone and the stone reused. Lithography finally came into its own in the last quarter of the century when the Hughes & Kimber Co. built a steam-powered litho press in London. It was imported to this country about 1865, and shortly thereafter the R. Hoe and Company started building steam-powered litho presses. While in France, Richard Hoe saw the lithographic press that Mr. H.A. Marinoni produced. He suggested that Marinoni apply for a U.S. patent and assign it to the Hoe Co. By 1869 Hoe was producing this press. There were approximately 450 hand-powered lithographic presses and thirty steam-powered presses in use by some fifty establishments in the United States in the 1870's.

The basic design of the lithographic press and the cylinder press was similar as they both delivered the sheets to the back and used a moveable bed. Their function was quite different though. The lithographic press had an ink distribution system plus a water system for dampening the stones. The lithographic press had an adjustable bed that could be raised or lowered to allow for the difference in thickness of the stones.

All the presses illustrated in this section printed from stones, with the exception of the Huber. The Huber press printed from zinc plates that were mounted around a cylinder. The zinc plate, like the stone, printed directly on paper. Offset lithography, which is printing from a rubber blanket, was not developed until early in the twentieth century.

When Alois Senefelder developed his first lithographic presses he also experimented with pressure in order to get a better transfer. On one press the stone was placed in the bed and covered with felt or leather, which added resiliency to prevent the stone from cracking when it passed under the cylinder. The cylinder mechanism could exert the right amount of pressure on the paper to get a good print from the stone. A second press had a traveling bed and used a wide scraper under which the stone, with a felt or leather pad, passed in order to make an impression.

> Senefelder states in his book, The Invention of Lithography:
> "The foregoing shows that a good lithographic press must have these two properties
> (1) It must not pull or shift the paper in the least.
> (2) It must produce a uniform impression without weak spots or streaks."
> "The other properties it needs in common with other presses, such as: -
> (3) It must be powerful enough to produce the necessary pressure.
> (4) It must combine the greatest possible speed with this power.
> (5) It must be easily operated, to save the workman.
> All these qualities combined are not to be found in any press hitherto applied to lithography".

Color lithography was introduced in 1835, and was in demand as a cheaper means of mass-producing color illustrations. Producing posters and other artwork could require up to ten or twelve special colors, each on a separate stone.

With the advent of the steam-powered press 5,000 impressions could be pulled in a day rather than 400. The much sought-after Currier and Ives prints, as well as theatrical and circus posters, exemplify the outstanding contributions made by the lithographic press in American printing during the nineteenth century.

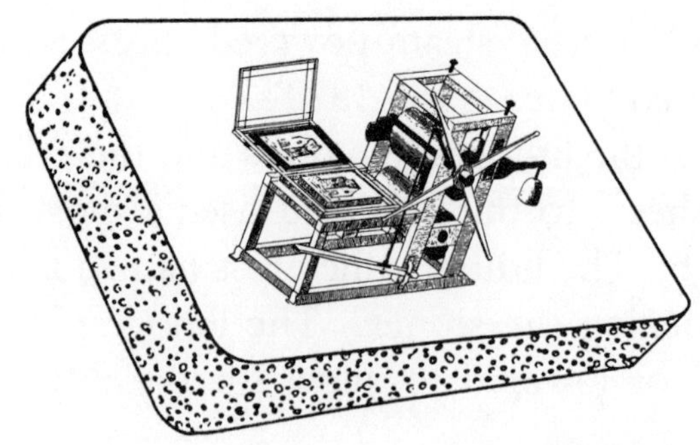

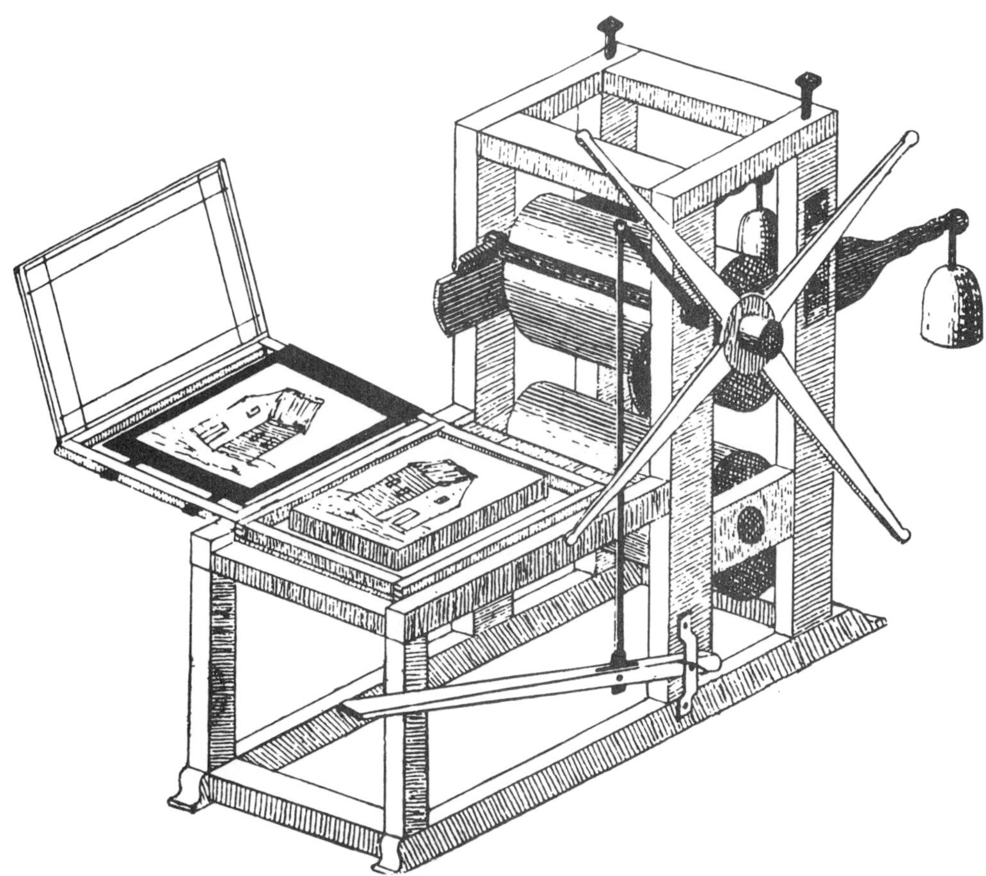

Senefelder's wood production litho press. Circa 1817.

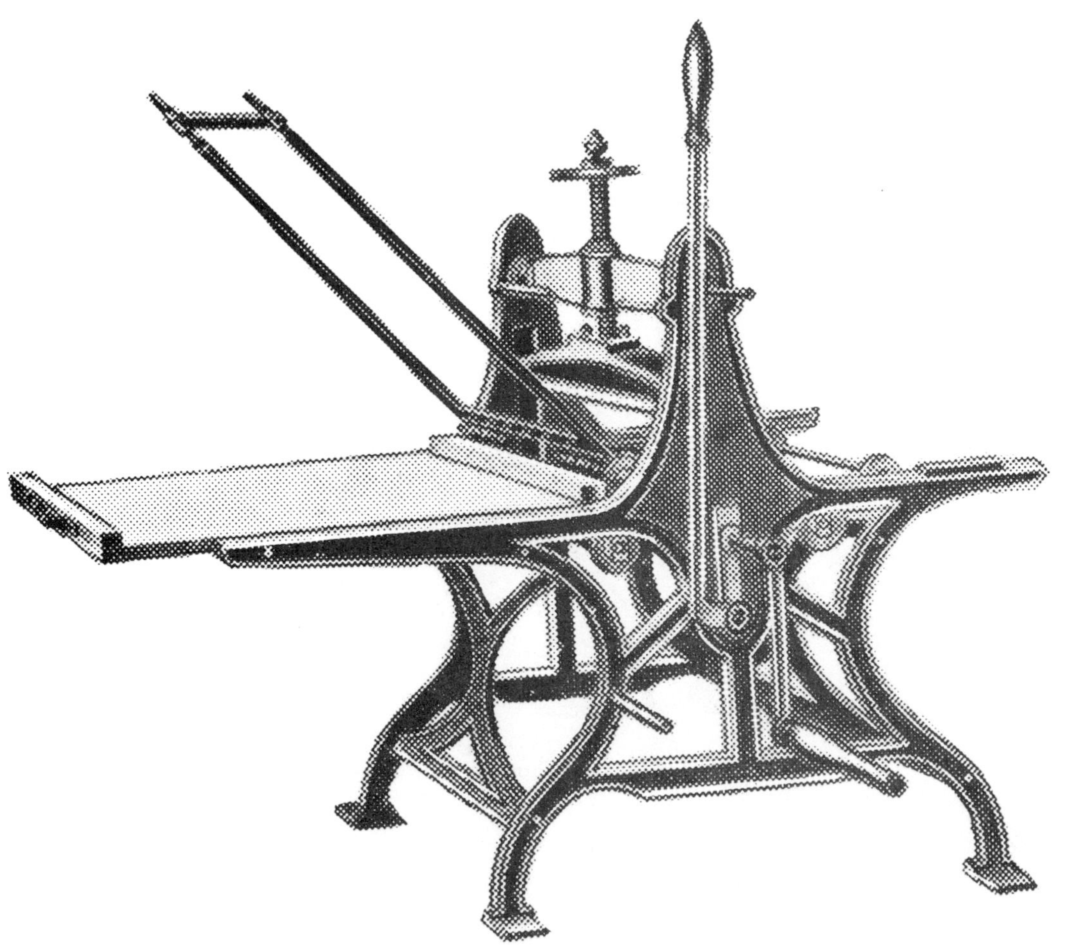

A typical hand lithography press from the mid 1800's.

JOSEPH BICKERTON'S PATENT IMPROVED LITHOGRAPHIC CYLINDER PRINTING MACHINE

FOR CHROMO, CHALK, AND EVERY OTHER DESCRIPTION OF WORK.

AT SPEEDS VARYING FROM 500 TO 1,000 PER HOUR.

PARTICULARS AND PRICES ON APPLICATION.

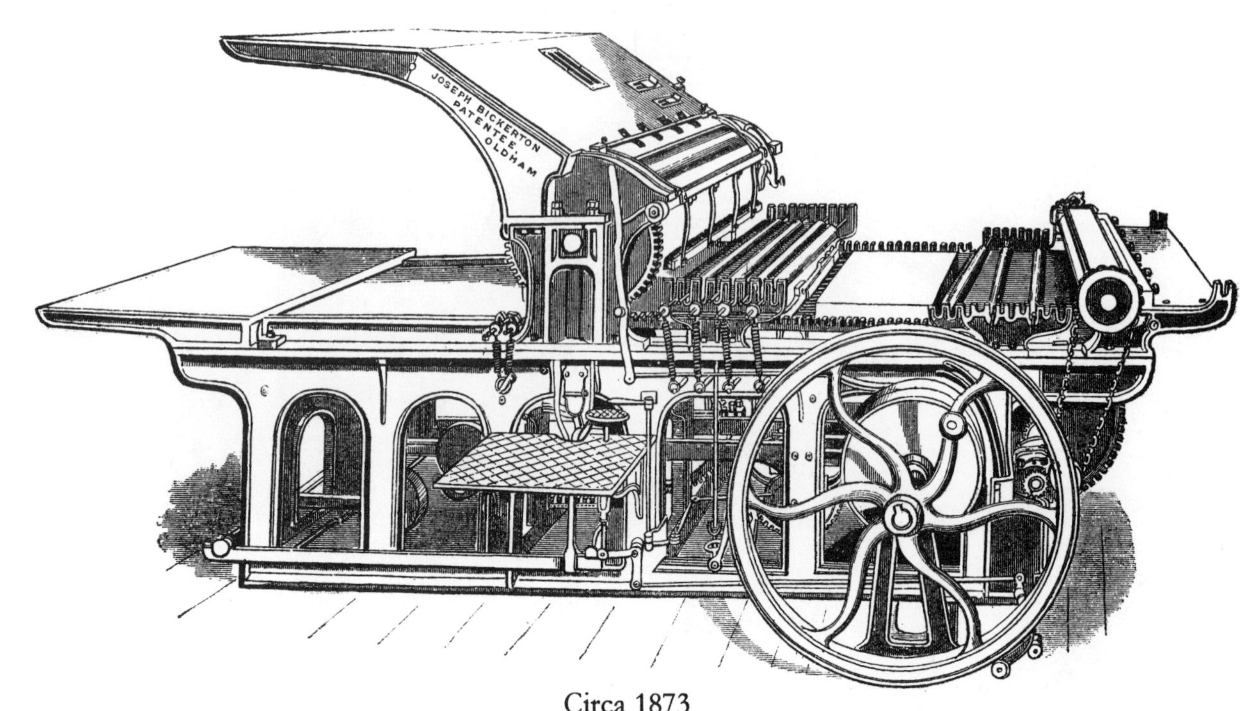

PARTICULARS AND PRICES ON APPLICATION.

Circa 1873

THE BRONSTRUP LITHOGRAPHIC HAND PRESS

THE above cut represents the BRONSTRUP LITHOGRAPHIC HAND PRESS, long and favorably known to Lithographic Printers, and by them preferred to any other make. These presses are neatly, yet strongly built, and will be kept up to the high standard of excellence that has made them *the* favorites with those who use Lithographic Hand Presses. The following testimonials, from two of the largest lithographic establishments in Philadelphia, will be sufficient to show the esteem in which they are held:

Circa 1886

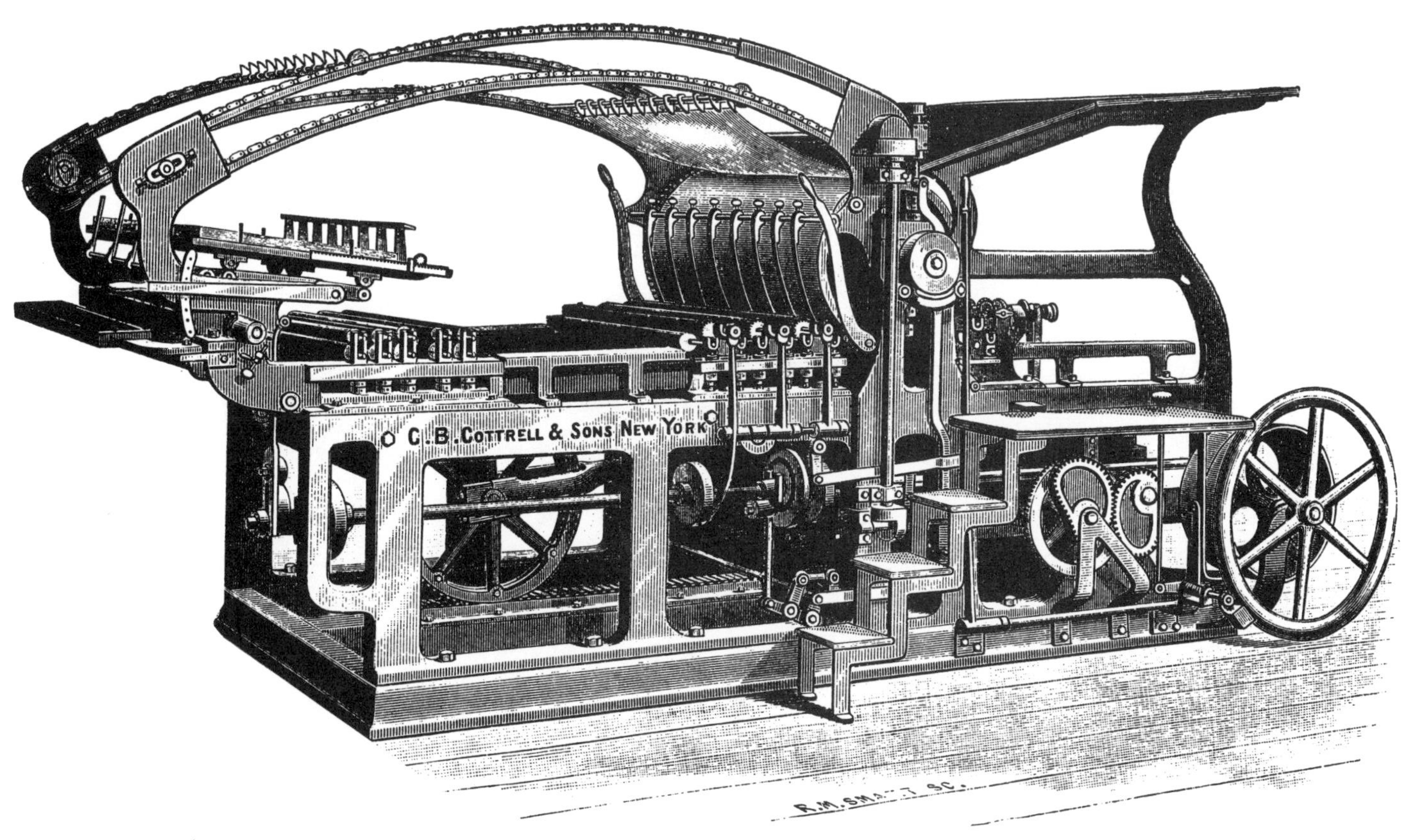

C.B. Cottrell & Sons Flatbed Lithographic Press with new front sheet delivery. Circa 1890.

DEMY LITHO MACHINE.

THIS MACHINE IS CAPABLE OF DOING FIRST-CLASS WORK, THE PARTICULAR ADVANTAGE BEING THE USE OF A SMALL DIAMETER OF CYLINDER, MAKING TWO TURNS FOR ONE LENGTH OF TRAVEL. THE BOARDS BEING FLAT, CAUSES PERFECT REGISTER WITHOUT POINTS.

Circa 1873

Fuchs & Lang Litho Hand Press, not geared.

Halligan Lithographic Stone Press. Circa 1895.

R. Hoe & Co. Flatbed Stone Press. Circa 1885.

THE HUBER

Rotary • Zincographic • Printing • Press

PATENTED.

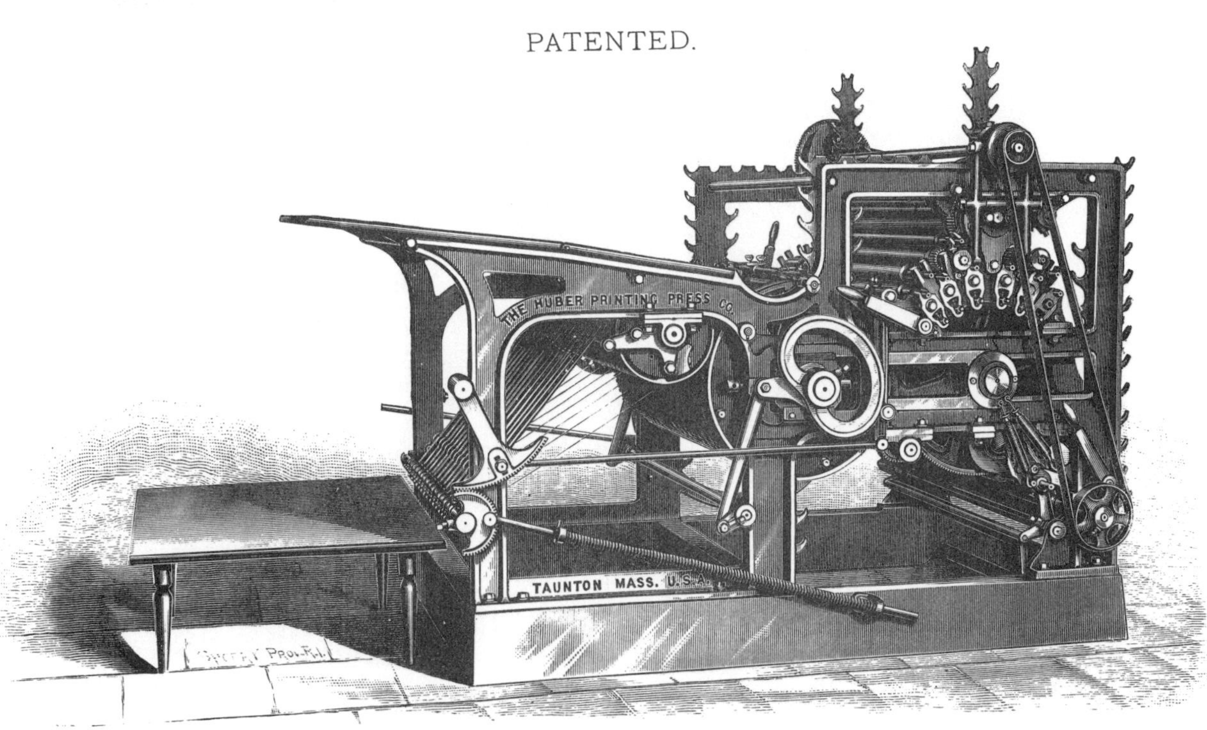

This press printed from zinc plates instead of stones, directly on the paper. Circa 1888.

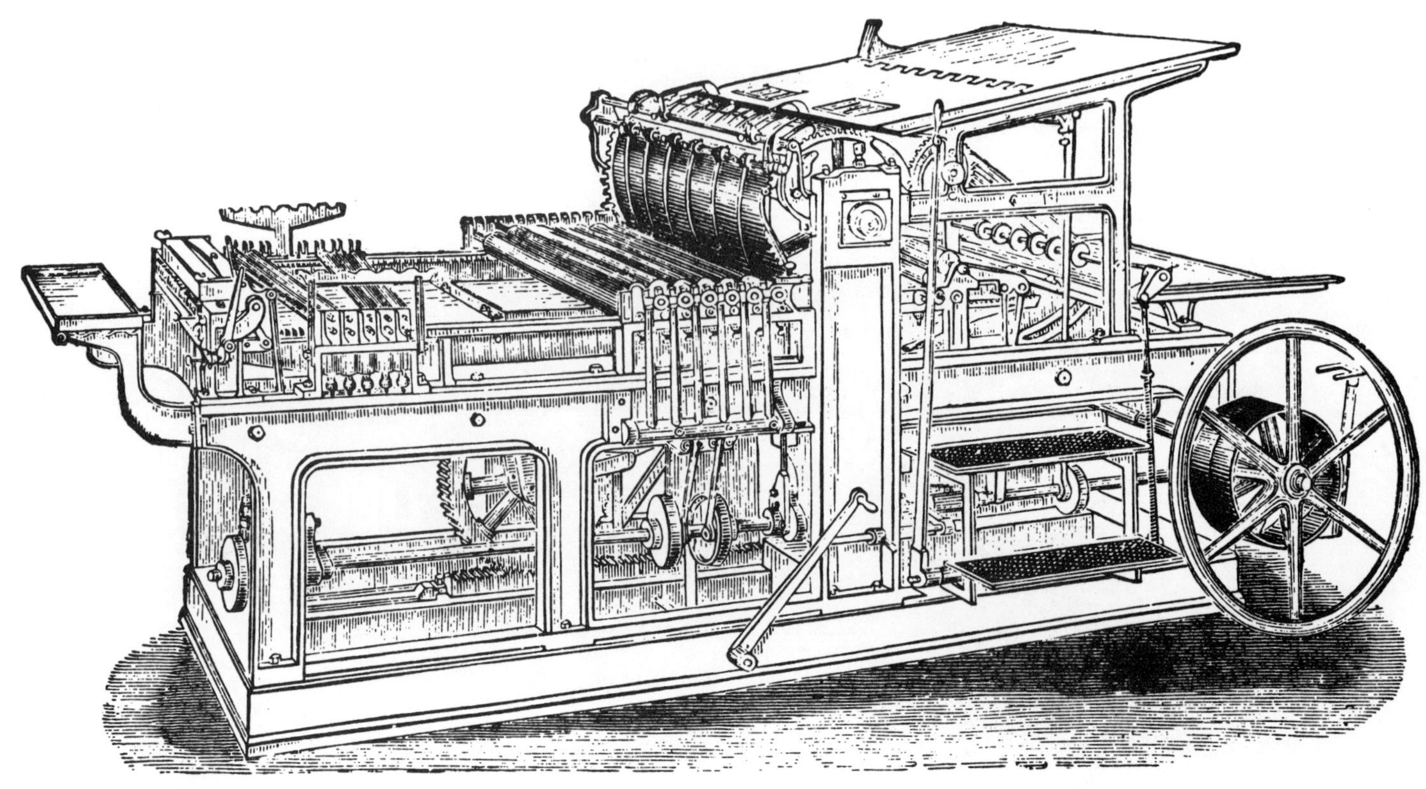

Hughes & Kimber Lithographic Steam Press manufactured in England. Circa 1866.

"Improved Lithographic Power Press."

Sole Agents, - George Meier & Co.,

IMPORTERS OF

BRONZE POWDERS, LITHOGRAPHIC STONES, INKS, COLORS AND MATERIALS,

P. O. Box 3462. NEW YORK. *135 and 137 William Street.*

Manufactured by Klein, Forst & Bohn in Germany. Circa 1884.

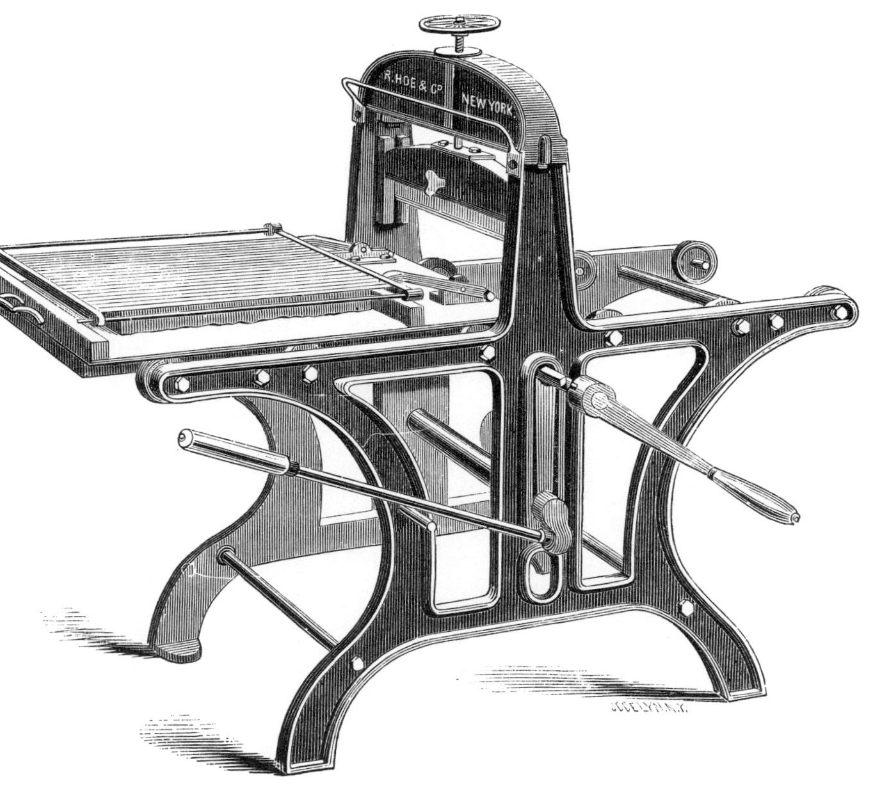

New Style Lithographic Press.

It is made of the best materials, is strong, simple, convenient, and works with great ease. The roller under the bed is geared in presses of the larger size, but is so arranged that it may be used with or without the gearing. The bed is made sufficiently long always to cover the roller, thus protecting it from dirt or grease from the scraper, and at the same time having a more even movement.

Sizes and Prices.

	Size of Bed.	Size of Stone.	Price.
No. 1	20 × 26	18 × 24	$200.00.
" 2	24 × 32	22 × 30	250.00.
" 3	28 × 40	26 × 37	300.00.
" 4	32 × 46	30 × 43	350.00.
" 5	36 × 52	34 × 48	425.00.
" 6	42 × 60	39 × 56	500.00.

Circa 1868

Karl Krause, Leipzig.

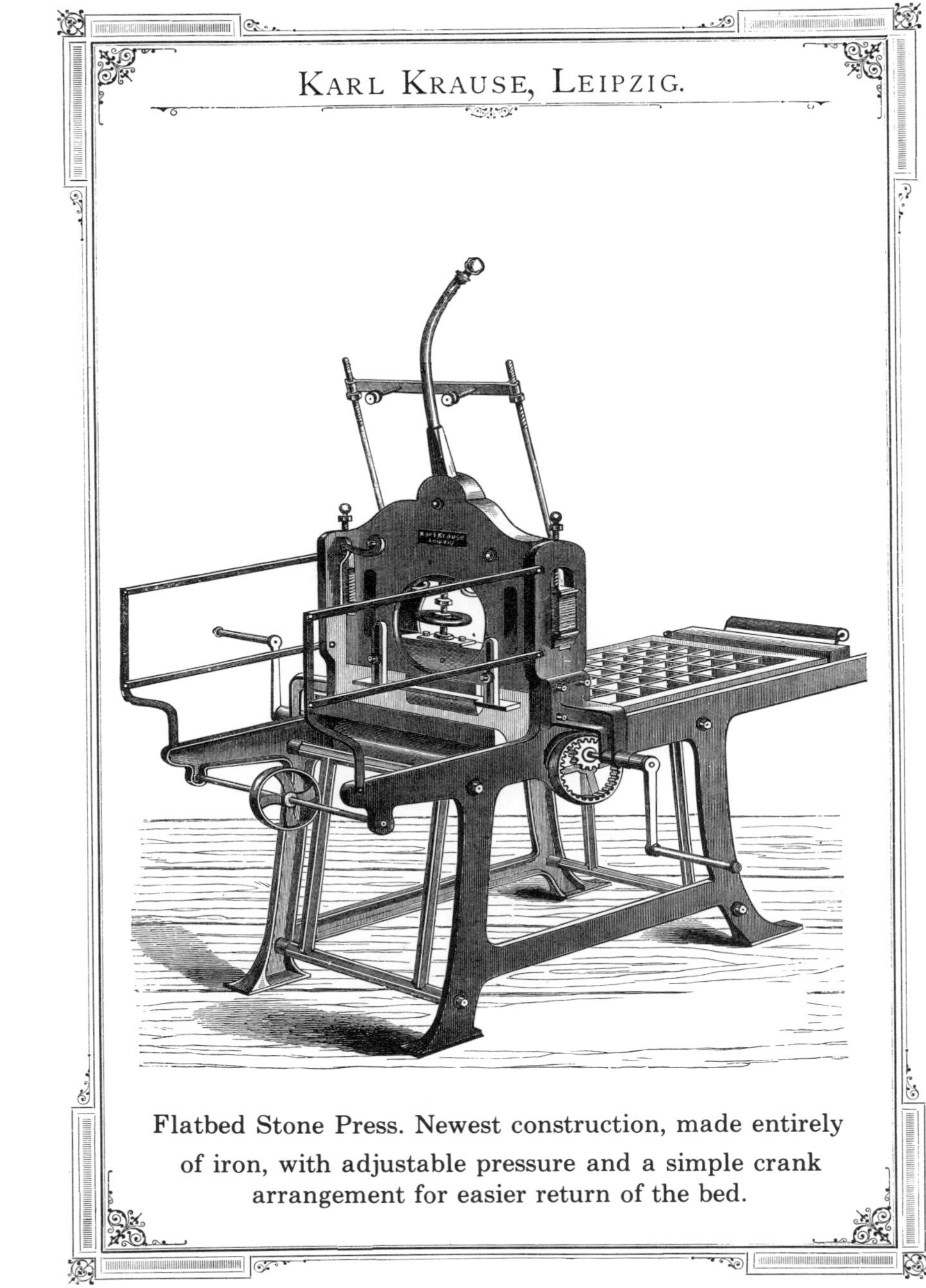

Flatbed Stone Press. Newest construction, made entirely of iron, with adjustable pressure and a simple crank arrangement for easier return of the bed.

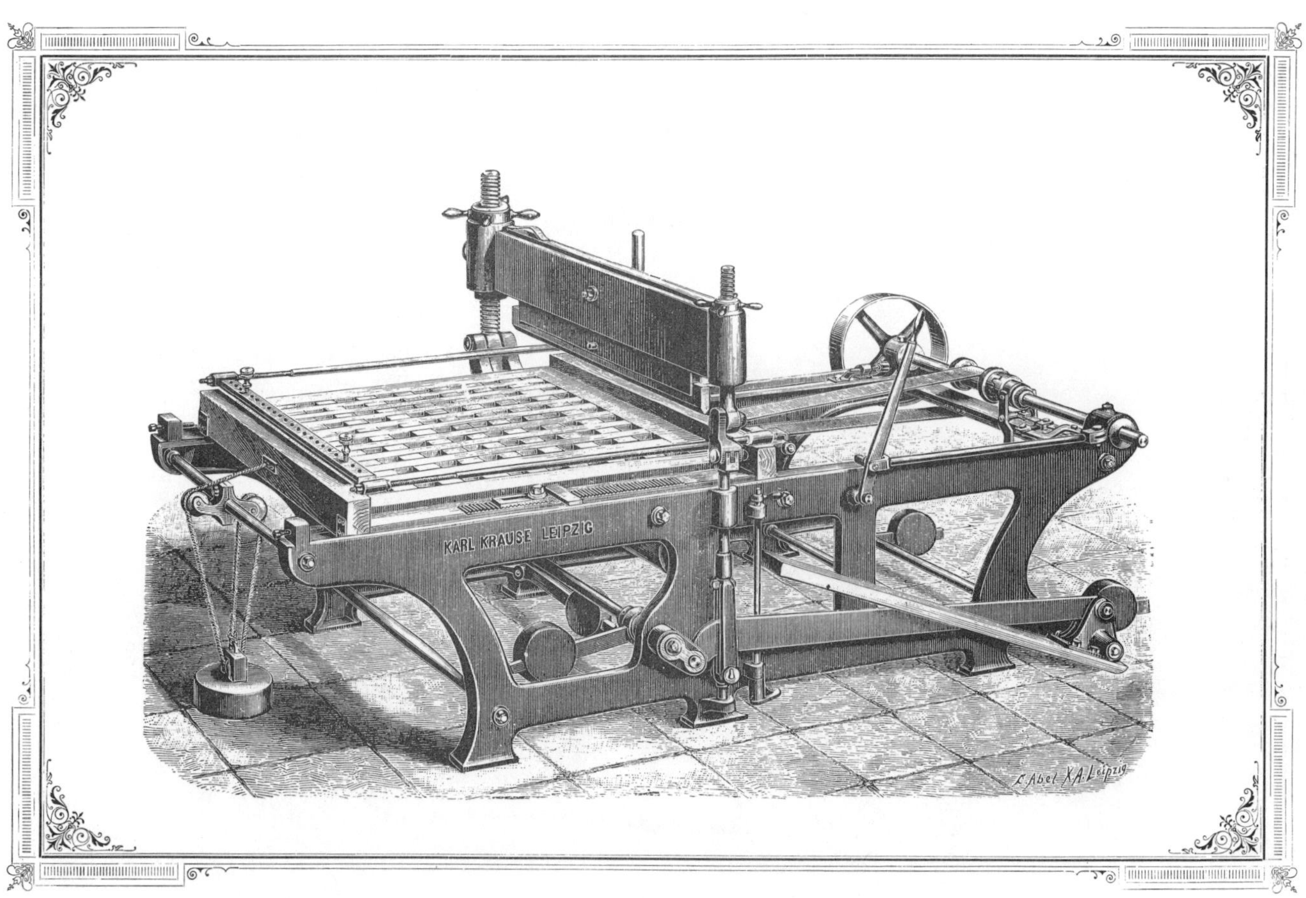

Karl Krause's Foot Treadle Stone Litho Press, especially suited for the transfer of large forms. The stone is positioned according to width.

KOENIG & BAUER'S

New and Improved Lithographic Steam Press.

FUCHS & LANG,

29 WARREN ST., NEW YORK, Sole Agents for the United States and Mexico.

CHICAGO, 79 DEARBORN STREET.

Circa 1885

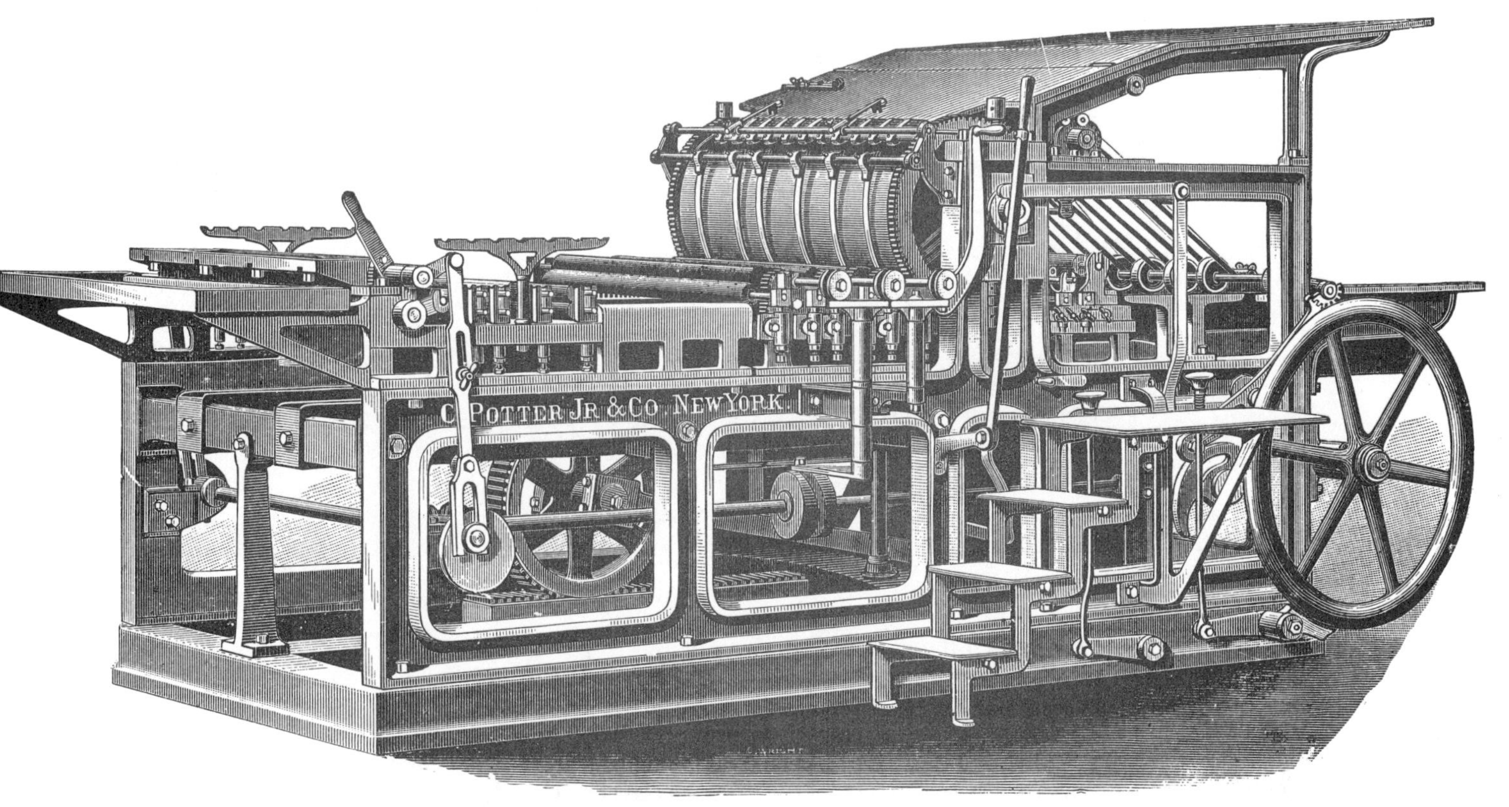

Potter Lithographic Press – 6 roller, rack, cam and table distribution, tapeless delivery, impression trip back-up and water fountain.

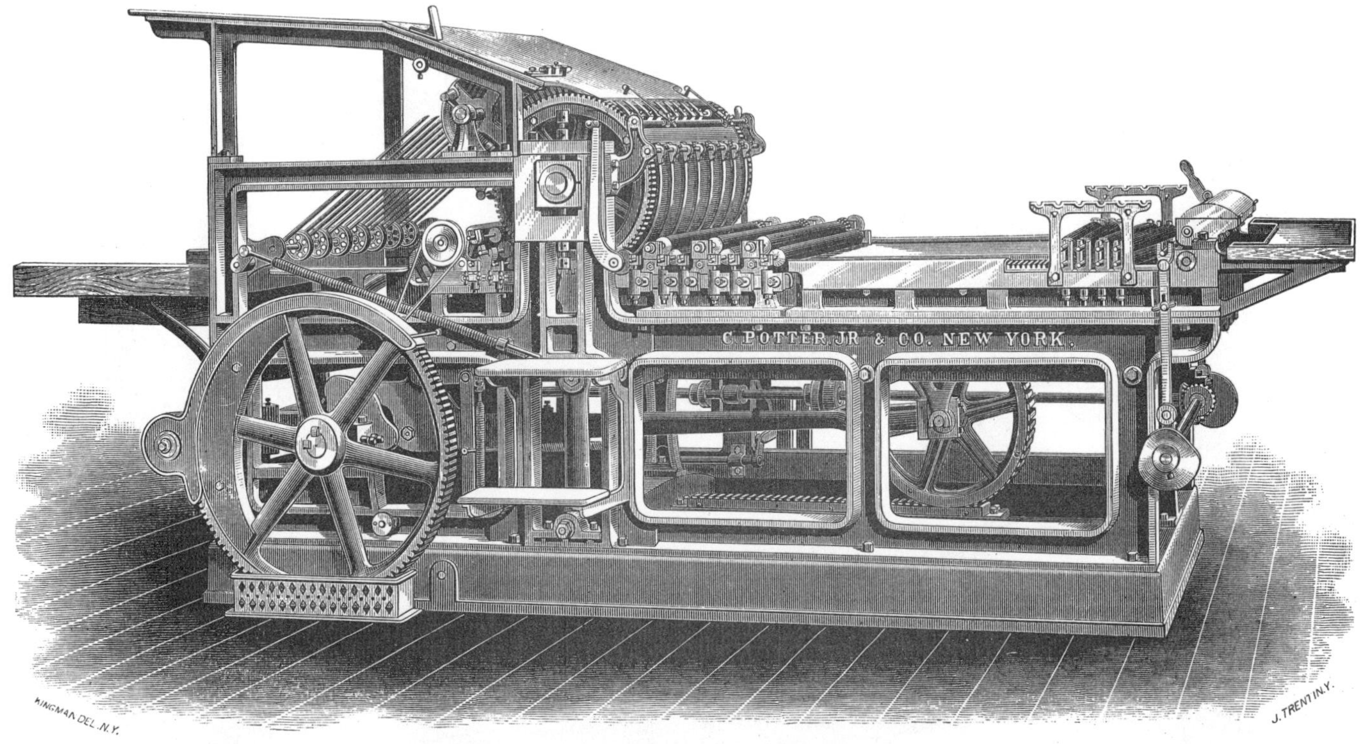

THE POTTER LITHOGRAPHIC PRESS.

THE BEST IN THE MARKET.

WESTERN AGENTS: H. HARTT & CO., 162 S. CLARK STREET, CHICAGO. **OFFICE: 12 AND 14 SPRUCE STREET, NEW YORK.**

Circa 1885

THE PARAGON.

The only Perfect Registering Colour-work Litho. Machine.

Circa 1873

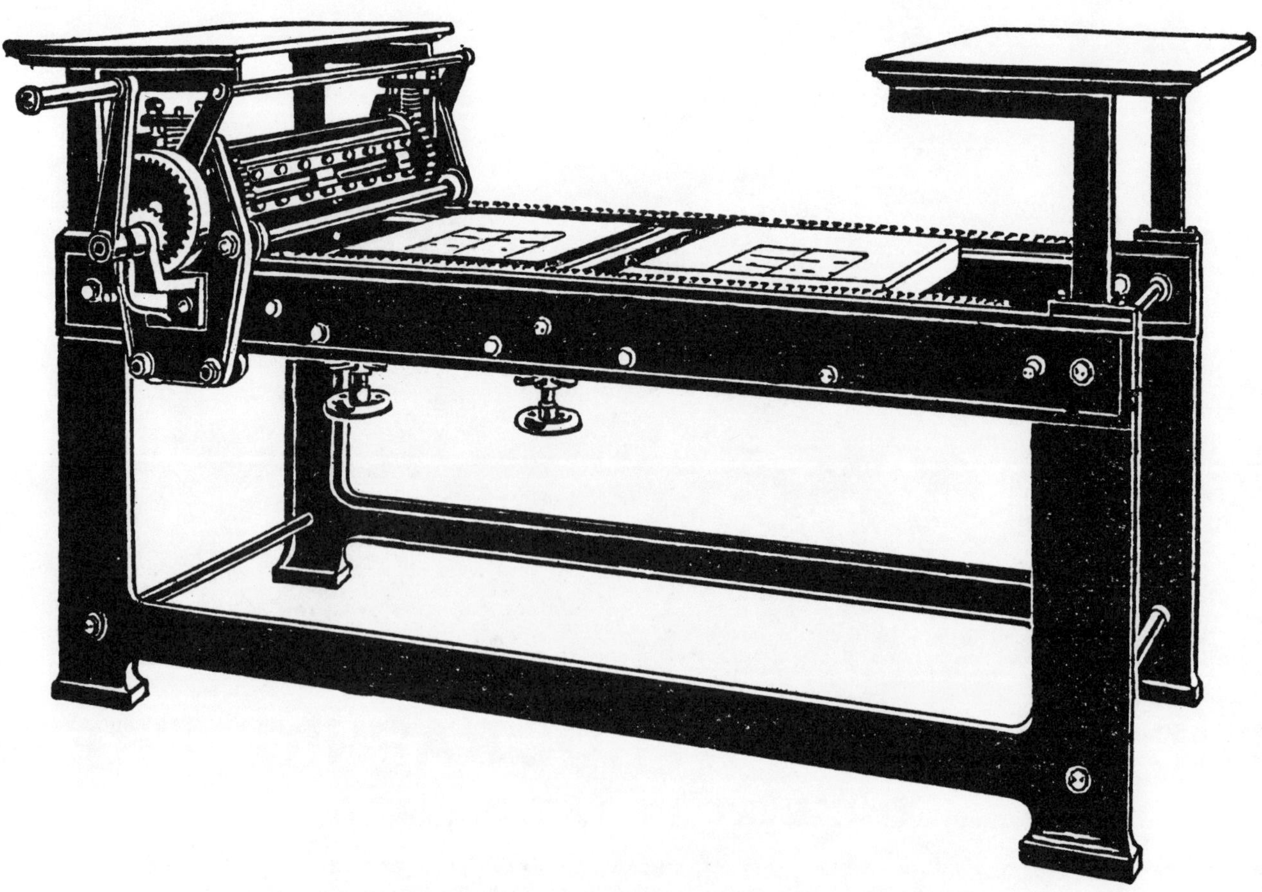

Lithographic tin-printing hand press for short runs of heavy gauge tin.

Rotary presses

The rotary press, with all its complicated, interacting parts, is by far the most fascinating and exciting of all the printing press developments of the nineteenth century. Although the hand press, the cylinder press, and the platen press were being manufactured and improved, some inventive, forward-thinking mechanical geniuses were working on ways to increase press speed to meet the tremendous demand for the printed word. Three types of presses are included in this chapter under the name of Rotary Presses:

1. Rotary printing cylinder or Type Revolving Press fed with sheets of paper.
2. Rotary printing cylinder fed with rolls of paper (web-fed)
3. Flat bed press fed with rolls of paper (web-fed)

The cylinder press had limited speed because of the reciprocal motion by which that press could deliver the printed sheets. The only way to increase the speed was to have a continuous printing cylinder. Flat stereotypes were used successfully in the 1830's but it was difficult to accurately bend them for mounting on a printing cylinder. This problem was solved by placing the set lines of type in a curved device called a turtle. The type was locked up in this turtle, which was then mounted on the printing cylinder. With this innovation the Type Revolving Press, patented in 1847, was well suited to print newspapers. Type revolving presses were made with anywhere from two to ten printing cylinders. There was one man as feeder for each cylinder, plus a take off-boy. These multiple cylinder presses could run at 2,000 revolutions per hour. A 10 cylinder press with 10 feeders could produce 20,000 sheets per hour.

In 1859 an improved type-revolving press was introduced capable of perfecting or printing on both sides of the sheet at the same time. Perfecting presses had an on-going problem of set-off, i.e. ink transferring onto the back of the next sheet. To overcome this problem some presses were fitted with slip-sheets. When better drying inks were developed this problem disappeared.

However, as press speeds increased, use of the turtles on a high-speed roll-fed press was dangerous. In the 1860's the process of casting curved stereotypes, made from a matrix that had been pressed into the type, was developed. The curved stereotype began to replace the turtles on type-revolving presses. Duplicate stereotype plates were also used, thus cutting press time in half. Hoe, Kidder, Babcock, Miehle and Harris and others manufactured type-revolving presses in the United States until about 1876. Hoe made 175 type-revolving presses in a 20-year period. It was ten years later that the more innovative Linotype was introduced which enabled type to be set much faster.

"Endless sheets", paper made in rolls, was invented in France in 1798 but was not made in the United States until 1817. Interestingly enough, one early roll-fed press was developed by papermaker James Trench, who patented the press in order to use the rolls of paper made by his mill in Ithaca, New York. DeFoe's Robinson Crusoe and a common spelling book were the first two books printed on both sides of the paper, by Trench.

The roll-fed rotary press solved the problem of feeding and taking off the printed work as the paper sizes and speed of the sheet-fed rotary presses increased. When William Bullock of Pittsburgh received his patent for the first roll-fed rotary newspaper press in 1863, he had an open field. His innovative press cut the roll of paper into sheets and then fed them into the printing cylinders. Bullock's success with the web fed press led other manufacturers to develop similar presses with added features such as in-line folders which increased the output of the newspapers.

By 1873 presses were made that could print 12,000 8-page newspaper sheets per hour. By 1876 the sheets could be folded in-line, allowing presses to produce 24,000 4-page folded newspapers per hour. Improvement of the single-reel newspaper press evolved into presses that used multiple rolls of paper that were printed from several cylinders at one time. By 1882 a 2-roll press could produce 24,000 4, 8, or 12 page folded newspapers per hour. In 1884 Hoe introduced a double width web press.

The R. Hoe & Co., one of the first to manufacture the rotary press, had been lured to the European market. Because European governments taxed paper by the sheet and did not allow printing on rolls of paper, Hoe could only offer sheet fed rotary presses abroad. After England repealed the sheet paper tax in 1861, France followed in 1871, and roll fed presses became available in Europe. By 1888 there were 15 newspapers in London using a total of 85 web-fed presses. Of these, 29 were made by Hoe, who had earlier opened a factory in London which employed 100 men to make these presses.

In general smaller newspaper shops also wanted higher press speeds but did not want to get involved with the complications of curved stereotypes. They were appeased with roll-fed flatbed presses that delivered folded newspapers. This came about in 1889 when Paul Cox of Battle Creek, Michigan invented the Duplex press, later followed by similar presses designed by Scott and Campbell.

The demand for higher quality printed work than newspaper presses could produce at that time led to the more sophisticated design of an "art" rotary sheet-fed press. The flat electrotype, developed in 1840, was a fine quality printing plate. The presses, printing from curved electrotypes, produced better quality illustrated work in magazines, books and catalogs.

By 1890, printers were eagerly utilizing the tremendous capabilities of the roll-fed rotary presses, with the curved electrotype plates. The appetite of the Americans for books, magazines, catalogs, advertisements, etc. was finally satisfied by the high speed, good quality, and cheaper printing made possible by the rotary presses.

It is hard to believe that at the beginning of the nineteenth century newspapers were printed one page at a time on a hand press at a rate of 250 sheets per hour by two men. Yet by the end of the nineteenth century the web-fed rotary press printed 90,000 4-page folded newspapers in an hour.

William Bullock's first newspaper rotary press. Circa 1865

THE BULLOCK PRINTING PRESS

Circa 1872

Campbell Web Perfecting Newspaper Press capable of speeds up to 12,000 per hour.
Circa 1876.

Campbell Perfecting Newspaper Press with a folder.

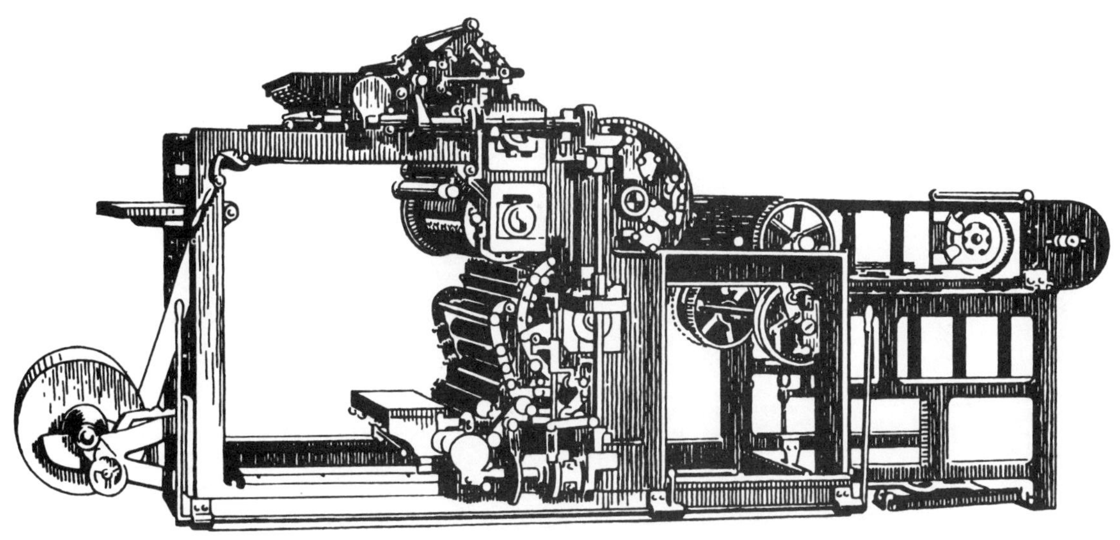

C.B. Cottrell & Sons Rotary Web Perfecting Press. Circa 1890.

Cox "Duplex" Perfecting Press with two flatbeds.

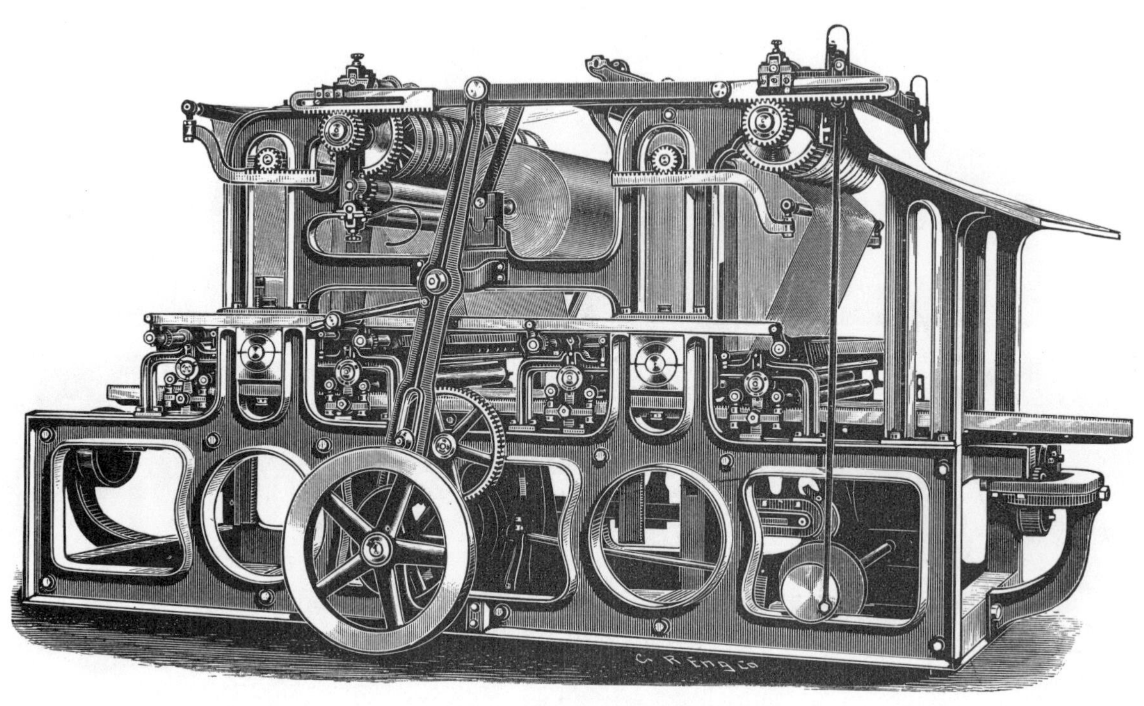

Cox "Duplex" Sheet-Perfecting Press.

Cox Stereotype Web Perfecting Press with folder.

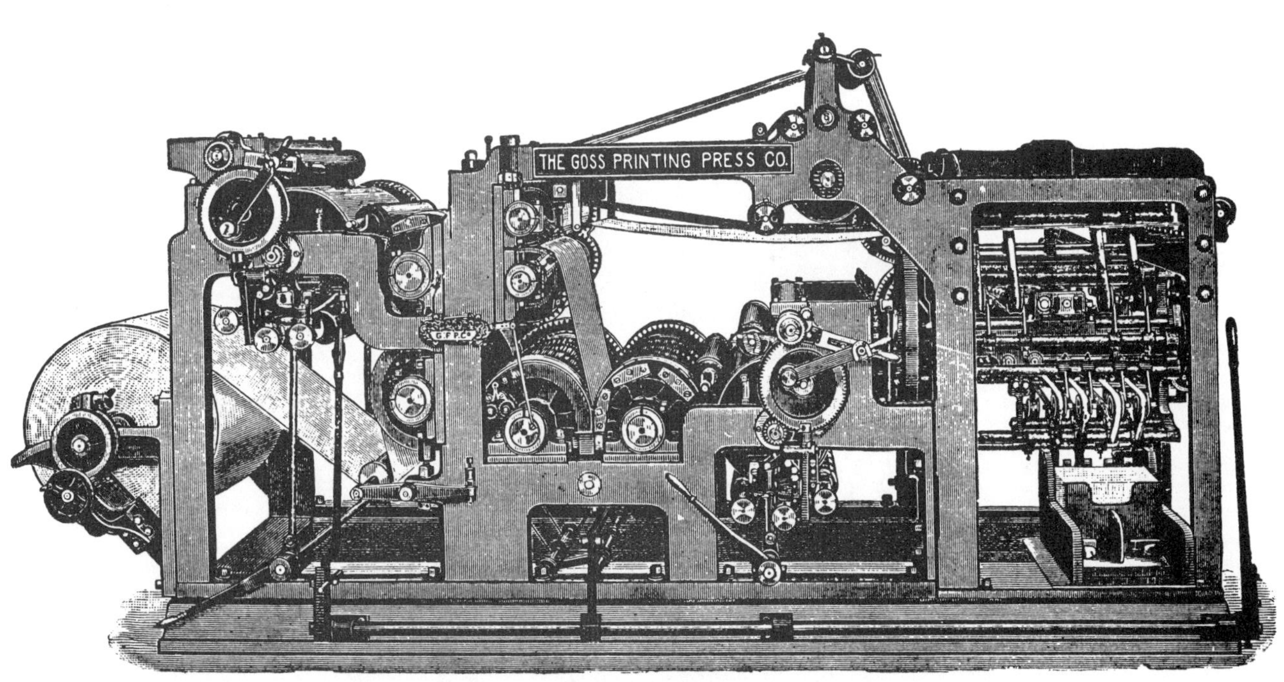

Goss "Clipper No. 1" newspaper press with capability of 8000 4 or 8 page newspapers per hour. Circa 1885.

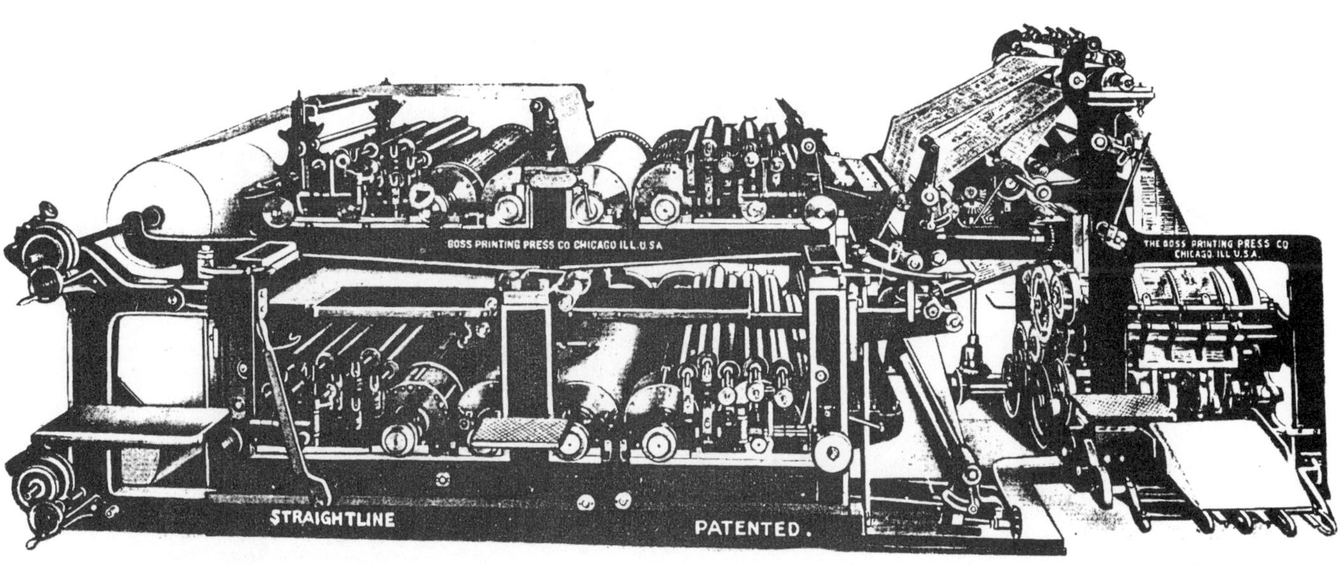

Goss "Straightline" Press. A two deck press with a capacity of 12, 16 or 20 pages at a speed of 12,500 newspapers per hour or half the pages at twice the speed. Circa 1891.

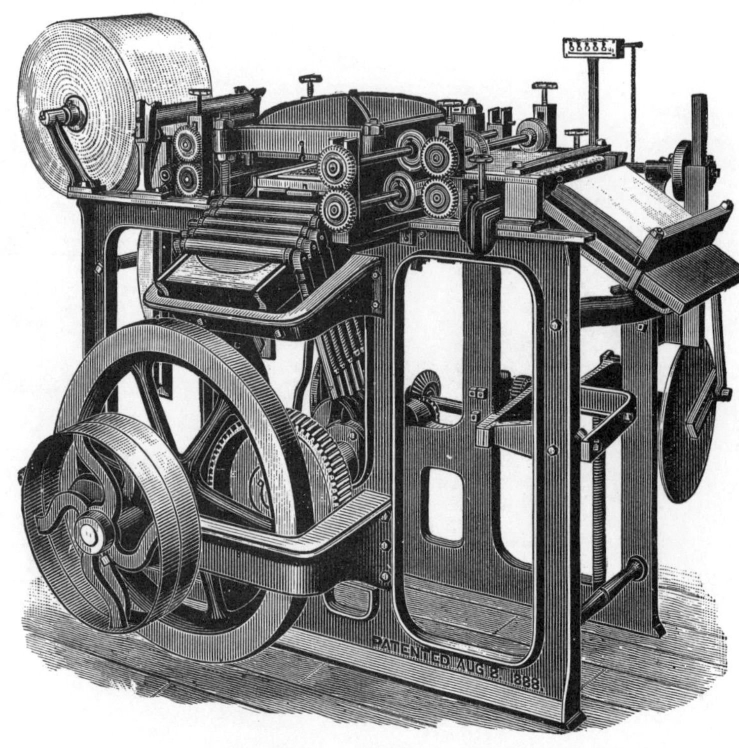

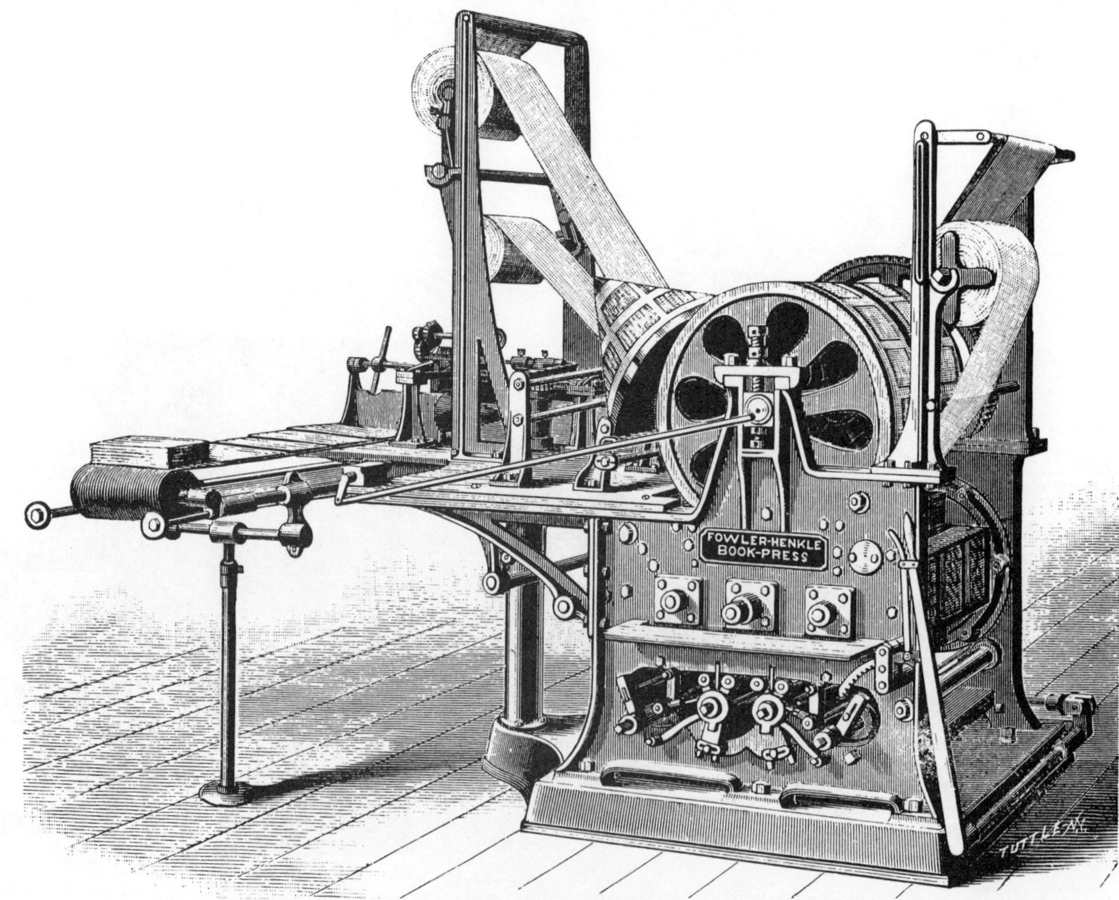

Fowler-Henkle Book Press. A perfecting press delivering collated sheets in 32 page signatures. Manufactured by American Printing Press Co. Circa 1891.

Two Cylinder Type-Revolving Printing Machine.

Four Cylinder Type-Revolving Printing Machine.

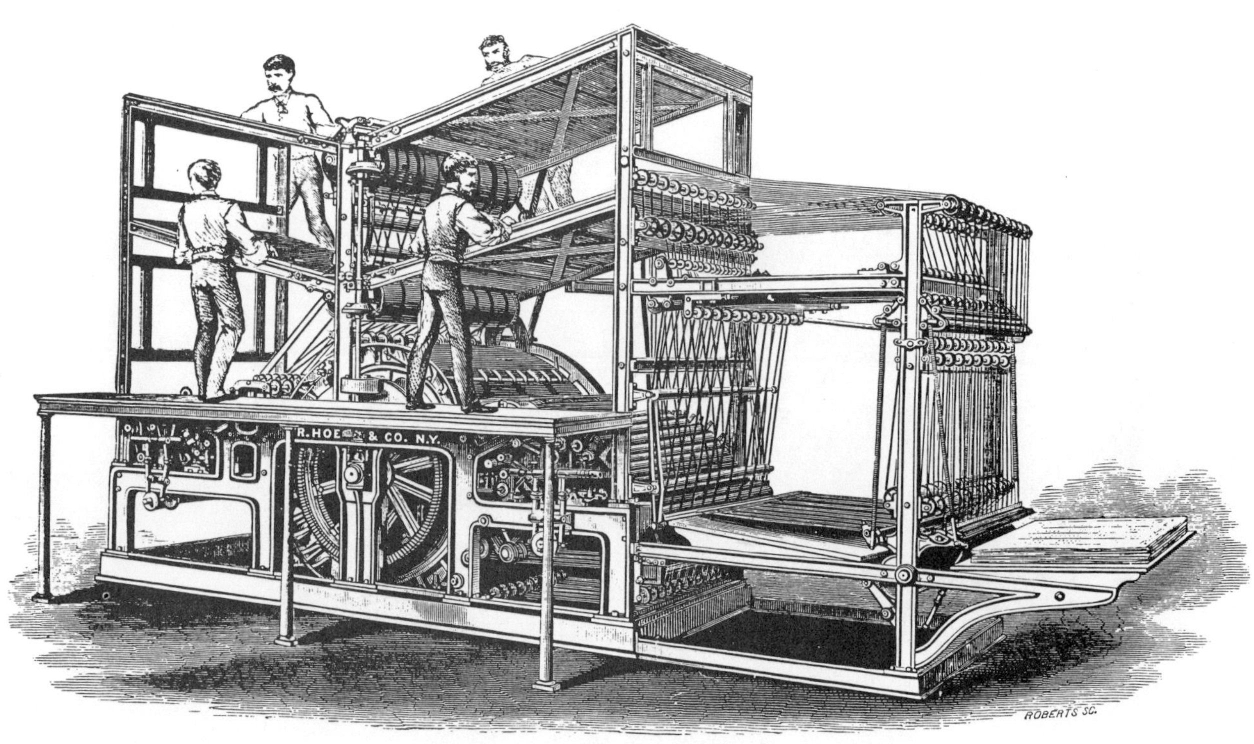

Hoe Rotary Stereotype Newspaper Perfecting Press printing cut sheets with four feeders doing 8000 sheets per hour. Circa 1852.

Six Cylinder Type-Revolving Printing Machine.

Hoe Ten Cylinder Revolving Newspaper Press producing 20,000 sheets per hour.
Circa 1855

Hoe Rotary Art Press. For printing magazines with halftone illustrations from curved electrotype plates. Four sheets are fed separately printing on one side of the paper at a time. Circa 1890.

R. Hoe & Co.'s first stereotype perfecting press with a folder. Circa 1875

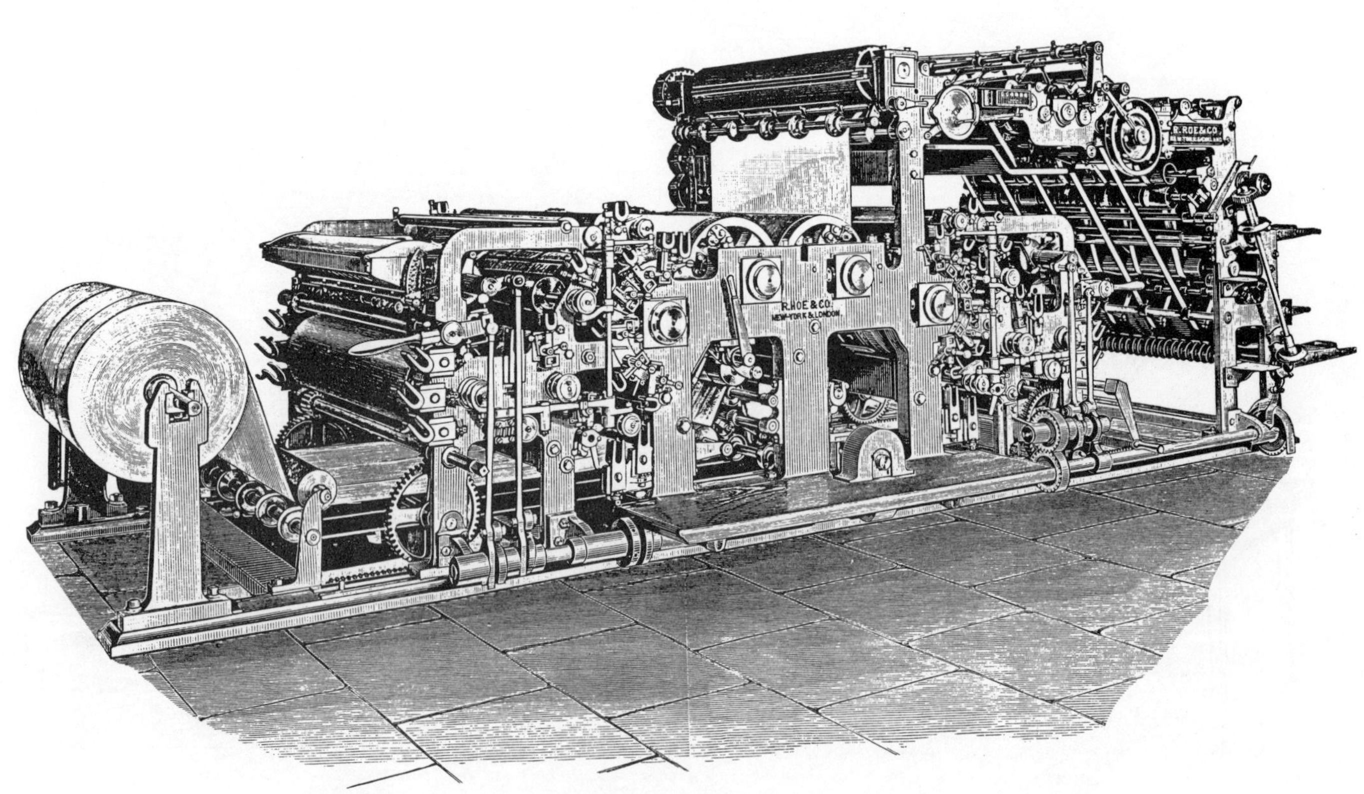

Hoe "Century" magazine and book electrotype perfecting press. Designed for fine magazines and book work. The sheets are delivered cut and folded in signatures at a running speed of 6000 per hour. Circa 1886.

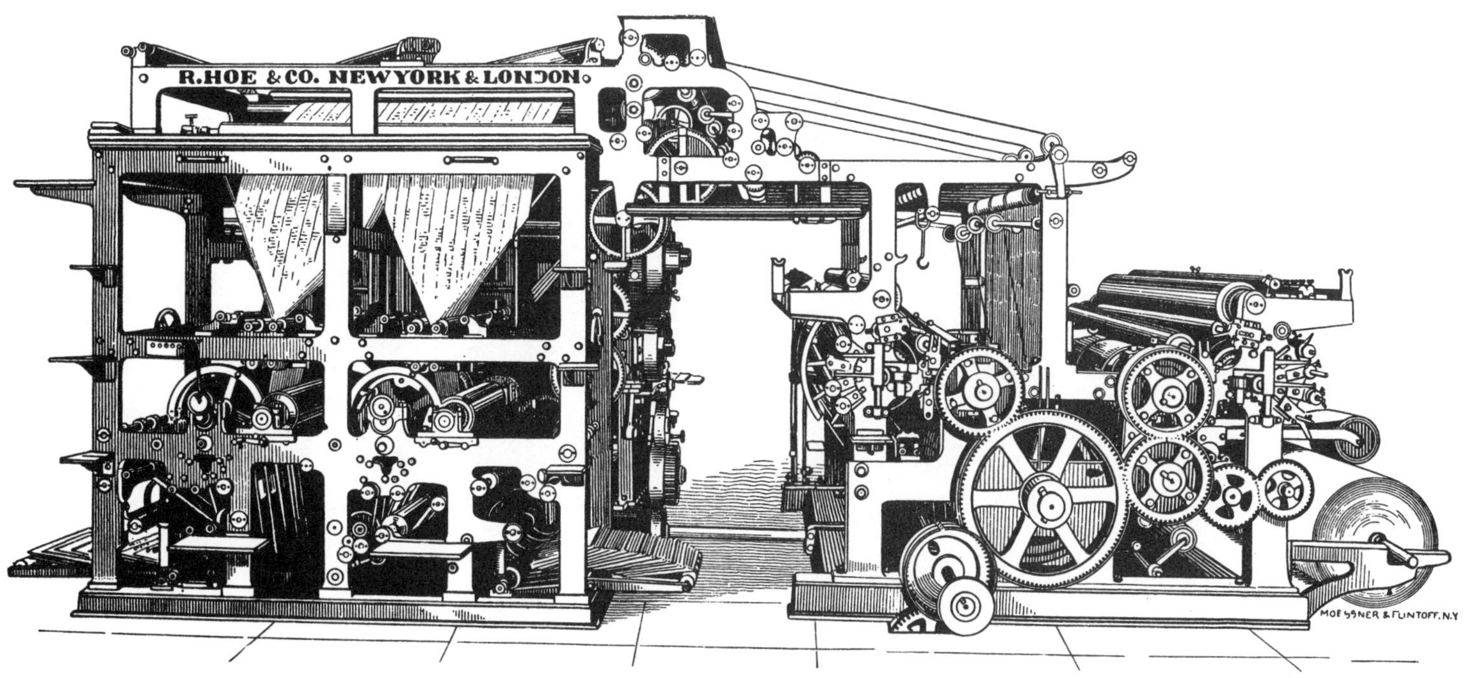

Hoe "Quadruple" Stereotype Perfecting Press with folder. An hourly capacity of 48,000-4, 6, 8 page newspapers or 24,000-10, 12, 14,16 page newspapers or 12,000-20, 24 page newspapers. Circa 1887.

Hoe "Sextuple" Newspaper Perfecting Press. Three deliveries capable of printing 72,000-4, 6, 8 page newspapers to 24,000-24 page newspapers per hour folded, counted and pasted (optional). Circa 1889.

Type Revolving Book Perfecting Press.

As the name indicates, it is on the rotary principle, the forms being secured on the surface of two large horizontal cylinders. This system, as it does away with the reciprocating motion, admits of a greater speed in printing than any other. The distribution of the ink also is more perfect, there being room for six or more ink rollers to each form. It is equally well adapted to letter-press, stereotype and wood cut work, and will print from 1,500 to 2,000 perfected sheets per hour, the only limit to its speed being the capability of the feeder to supply the sheets.

As it dispenses with the registering apparatus, and is furnished with our patent self-acting sheet flyer, only one attendant is required for the largest sized press.

Circa 1852

Two-Color Rotary Press

FOR PAPER AND COTTON BAG PRINTING

F. X. HOOPER'S TWO-COLOR ROTARY PRESS

SPEED AS FAST AS CAN BE FED

ABSOLUTELY PERFECT REGISTER

Size Bag, ... 33 x 44
Size Form, ... 19 x 24

LARGER SIZES MADE TO ORDER. WRITE FOR FURTHER PARTICULARS

PRINTS FROM CURVED STEREOTYPE PLATES

F. X. HOOPER, 600 to 608 Water St. Baltimore, Md.

Circa 1893

Kidder Web Perfector with traveling tympan. Circa 1896.

Koenig & Bauer Twin Rotary Newspaper Press manufactured in Germany. Circa 1890.

Potter Two Deck Web Rotary Newspaper Press. Circa 1896

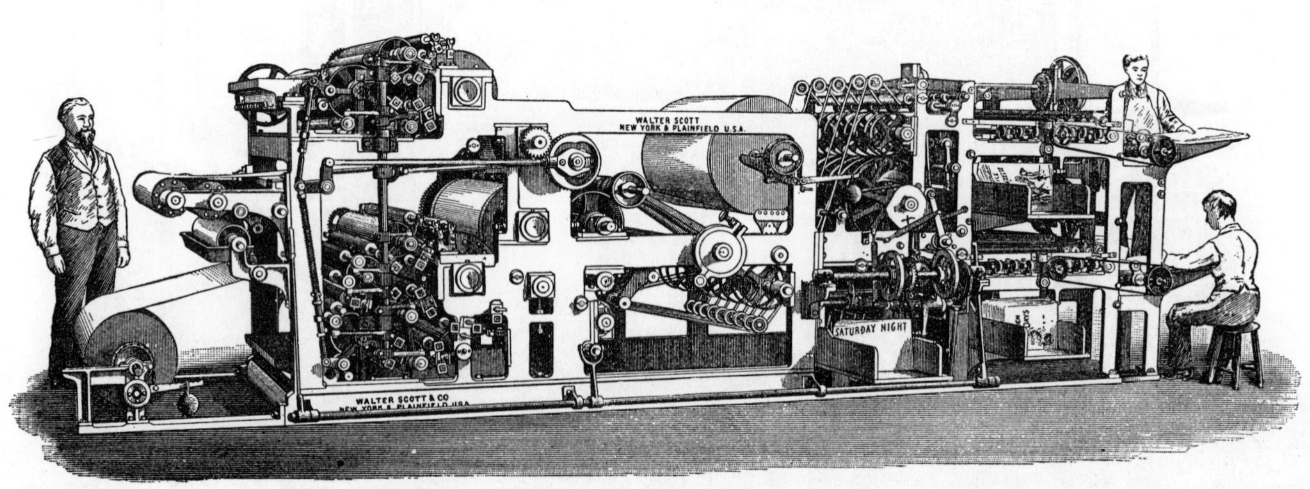

THE SCOTT WEB PERFECTING MACHINE.

Especially designed for Illustrated Periodicals and Fine Book Work. Guaranteed to produce work equal in quality to four roller two-revolution or stop-cylinder presses. Speed, 6,000 per hour.

Circa 1888

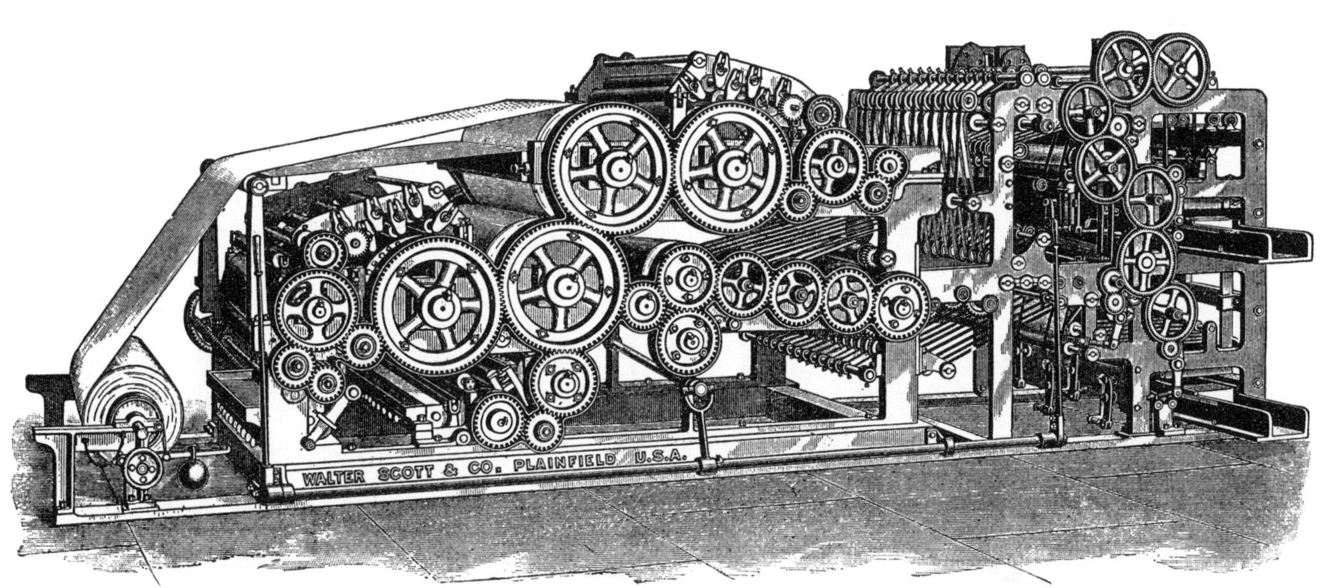

THE SCOTT WEB PERFECTING AND FOLDING MACHINE.

Adapted for Almanac and ordinary Book Work. Speed, 12,000 per hour.

Circa 1888

Scott Flatbed Web Perfecting Press. Capable of printing and folding 4, 6 or 8 page newspapers at speeds of 3000 to 4000 per hour. Circa 1891

Scott Two-Color Roll-fed Rotary Press with a sheeter and double folder. Circa 1891.

Scott Newspaper Press with a folder. Circa 1895.

miscellaneous equipment

There are so much miscellanea in the printing process that a whole book could be written about it. The tasks facing the nineteenth century printer were achieving better quality and faster output, while still making a profit. The auxiliary equipment shown in this chapter helped the printer achieve these goals.

The need for power was very important. Choosing the right steam engine was paramount. The steam engine had to drive all the equipment in a plant. The presses were driven by the pulleys from the overhead shaft that was engaged by a clutch. This arrangement required a large monetary investment that could have been equivalent or greater than the cost of a press. In 1884 electric motors were developed, giving the printer another way of driving his equipment.

Printing with the hand press required ink balls, then brayers and finally, an inking apparatus. The lithographic process was enhanced through the use of bronzing machines. The platen press depended on only a few miscellaneous items – furniture, a mallet, a planer and quoins.

Cylinder presses required an array of auxiliary equipment from plate shavers and saws to shooting sticks. The rotary press needed another set apparatus. They required a wetting machine to condition the newsprint and other papers. Rotary printing cylinders first required a curved turtle, and then later stereotyping equipment for curved plates. The stereotyping process required a half dozen separate pieces of equipment. The electrotyping process required another completely different set. This procedure needed a Blackleading machine, a hydraulic or toggle press to make molds, and other machines for coating and plating.

Some printers who wanted to diversify their business installed a Plate Printing Press for engraving stationery.

Type and engravings had to be proofed before printing. Of the many proof presses that were made, only a couple are illustrated in this section. Several of the same style proof presses had a large drum, some covered with felt. Many printing plants continued using a hand press to make proofs, although the hand press had to be adjusted to allow for the thickness of the brass or wood galleys. Smaller shops just used a felt covered planer or a proof roller to make proofs.

One kind of proof press came to newspapers in an unusual manner. Dr. Miles, of Elkhart, Indiana gave a proof press to small newspapers in exchange for advertising space for his patent medicines. He had the proof press made with "Miles Nervine" cast on one end and "Miles Heart Cure" on the other end.

Tools of the trade are always interesting and those illustrated here are certainly no exception.

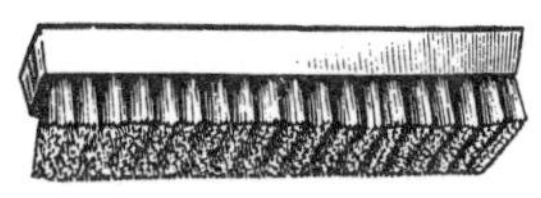

R. Hoe & Co's Ready Proof Press.

THIS machine consists of a cast-iron table, or bed and railway, supported by a cast-iron frame. The solid cast-iron cylinder is of weight sufficient to give the requisite impression, and has a flange at each end to prevent it from running off the track ; the surface of the cylinder is turned parallel to the bed, and is covered with a blanket. The railway stands above the level of the bed as much as the height of the type and the thickness of the galley bottom.

The frame is furnished with a closet to hold the ink-roller and damp paper, The closet door, when let down (as shown in the cut), can be used as a distributing table.

The machine should stand level, so that the cylinder will rest at either end. When a proof is wanted, place the galley with the matter in it on the bed, ink it, lay on the slip of paper and roll the cylinder to the other end of the railway.

PRICE, including proof roller, $65.00
Boxing and Carting, ... 2.50

Circa 1860

YOU WANT IT.

KENNEDY'S HAND PASTER.

PATENTED, NOV. 7, 1882

THIS Invention consists of a tight box, moulded out of pressed brass into graceful shape, with a handle and a revolving wheel, so constructed that the flow of paste can be regulated to a nicety, or the line made coarse or fine as the nature of the work or the quality of the paper may demand.

The paster is carried in the hand, while the sheets are being folded, between the thumb and forefinger, without the least inconvenience, and the pasting is done with the consumption of scarcely any appreciable extra time.

This invention did not grow out of a happy accident but of a long-felt necessity.

It enables the country publisher to cut and paste his paper; to do away with "inside pages;" to keep the size of his paper down to the level of every day business, and to add, making it a regular part of his paper—a two, six, or eight paged supplement—"to expand"—to the extent of business on demand.

It is of great value to the Paper-Box Manufacturer, the Map Maker, the Book-binders, the Job Printer, and all others who want an even and straight line of paste. PRICE—Including Two Wheels, Four Gates, etc., **$3.50.** FOR SALE BY

Marder, Luse & Co.,
CHICAGO.

Or by the Inventor
W. M. KENNEDY, Dixon, Ills.

LABOR SAVING

CHERRY FURNITURE

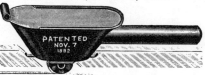

ABOVE CUT REPRESENTS A SINGLE FONT WITH CASE.

Height, 32 inches; width, 14 inches; depth, 12 inches.
Size Stamped on end of each Piece.

Convenient and Durable. Finished in Oil.

This Furniture is planed perfectly smooth, finished in oil, and made 2, 3, 4, 5, 6, 8 and 10 ems Pica wide, and accurately cut to 10, 15, 20, 25, 30, 40, 50 and 60 ems long, with size stamped on end of each piece.

PRICE.

Single Font, with stained Case, 560 pieces $8 00
Double " " " " 15 00

MARDER, LUSE & CO.,
CHICAGO, SAN FRANCISCO AND MINNEAPOLIS.

Circa 1883

C. KRATZ, SOUTHERN MACHINE WORKS,

EVANSVILLE, IND.

S. P. ROUNDS, General Agent, 175 Monroe St., Chicago.

3 Horse Power	*Cash,*	*$275*
5 " "	*"*	*350*
8 " "	*"*	*600*

Free on board here. Boxing and Chimney extra.

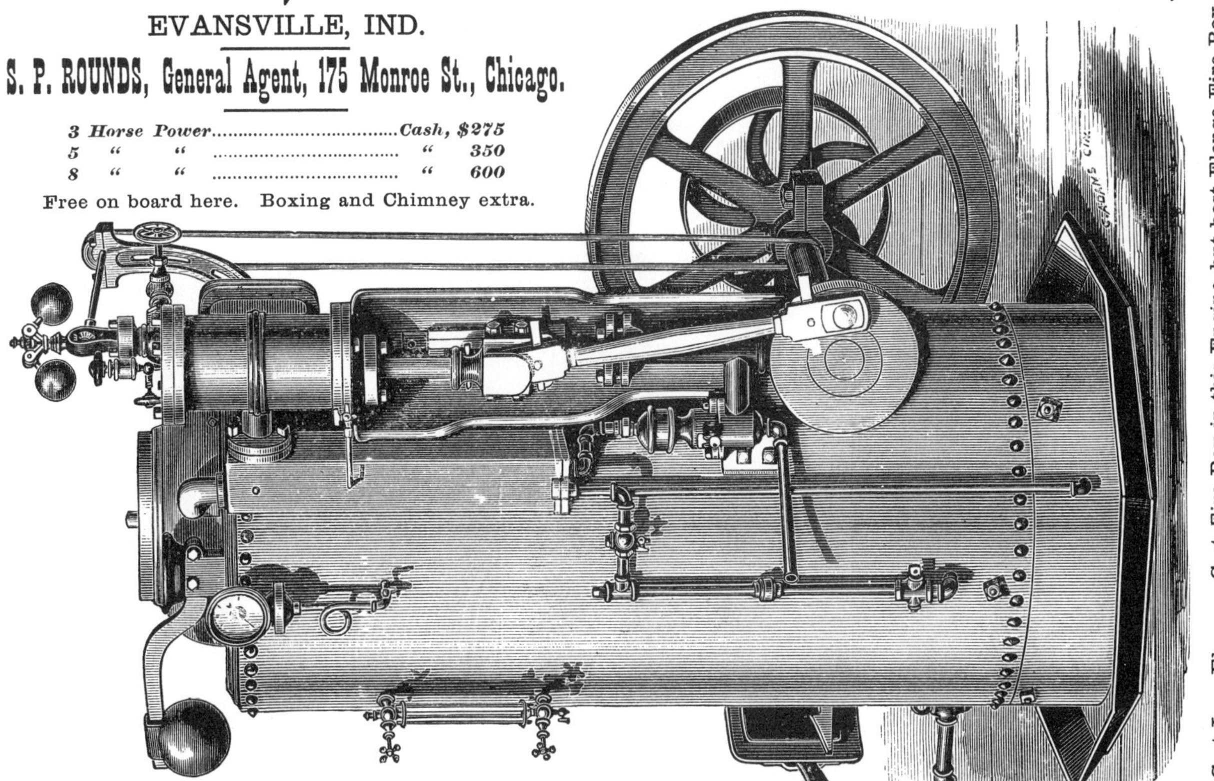

No Cast Iron Flues or Cast Fire Box in this Engine, but best Flange Fire Box and Lap Welded Flues. No burning off tops of Flues. No Malleable Iron used on this Engine. The only Engine that uses its Exhaust Steam twice to heat water before entering the Boiler. All Bearings and Connections are Adjustable.

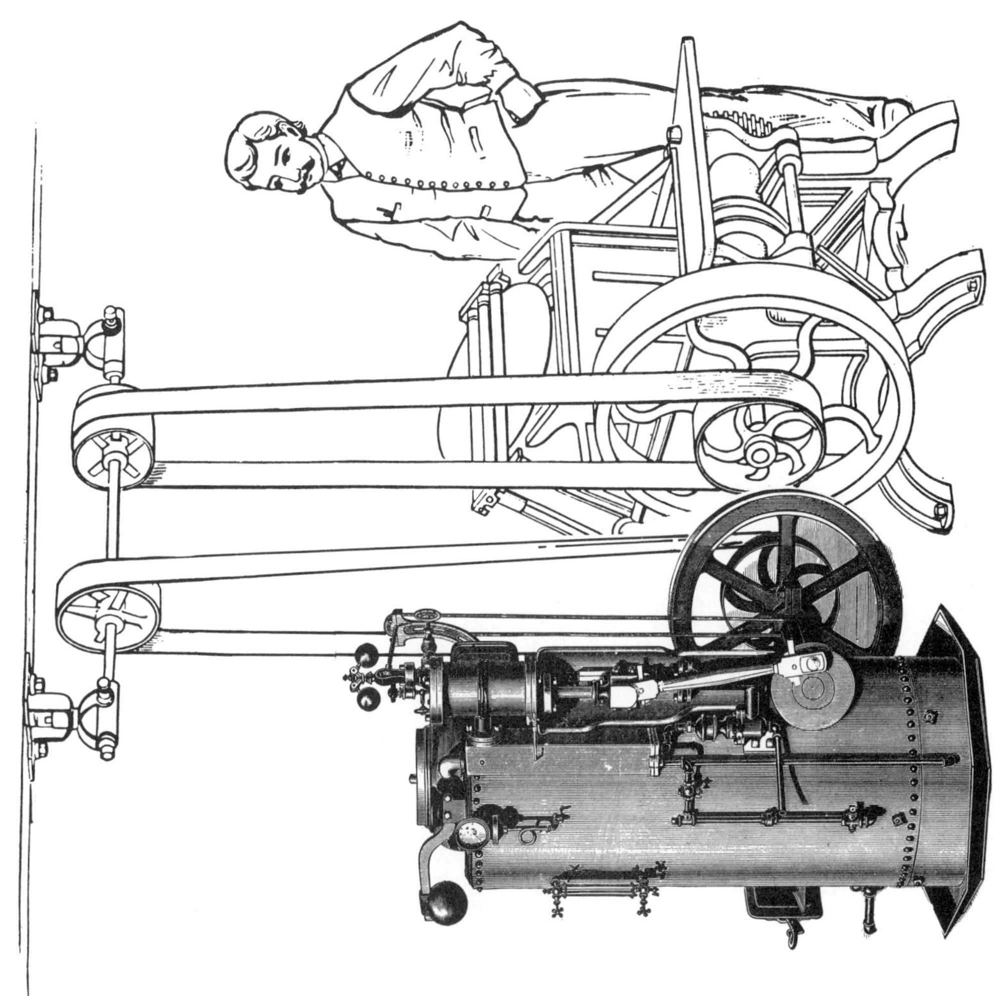

PETER WALRATH,

CHITTENANGO, N. Y.

MANUFACTURER OF

Light Portable Steam Engines

EMBODYING

Safety, Simplicity, Durability, Economy in the use of Fuel, &c.,

At Least Possible Expense.

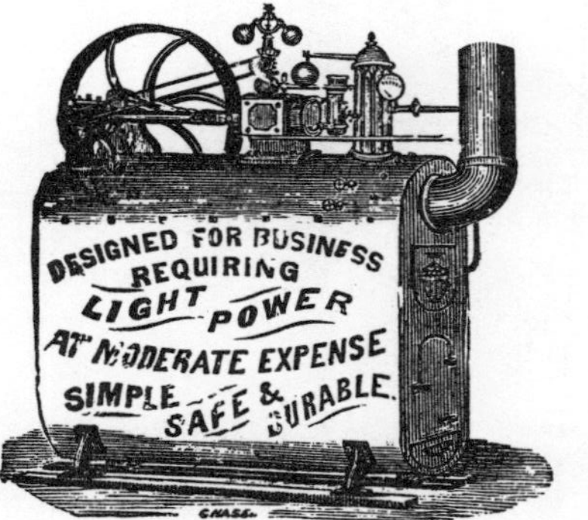

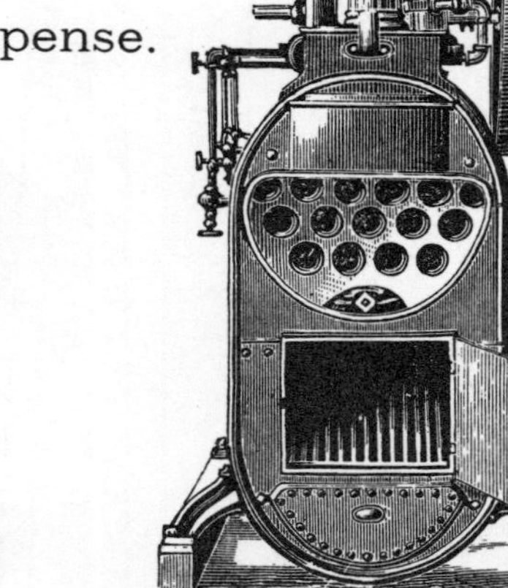

ESPECIALLY DESIGNED FOR THE USE OF

PRINTERS.

Their simplicity insures ***Perfect Ease of Management and Safety to anyone,*** however uninstructed in the use of any Engine—which end has been attained by the Builder through very special and protracted effort. Every provision for ***Safety from Fire*** is made, and the Engine rendered safe as a common stove. For ***Capacity in proportion to space occupied,*** it has no rival. It requires but very little room, and is easily set up, requiring only a firm base for its two timbers, and needs no brick work. It is supplied with a most reliable ***Self-Acting Pump, Governor, Steam Gauge, &c.,*** and is lacking in none of the requisites of a first-class, light Engine.

Persons having labor to perform requiring a light power, will find it to their advantage to ***SEND FOR A CIRCULAR,*** and examine the above mentioned Engine, therein fully described, with Price List, Testimonials, etc., etc.

Address,

PETER WALRATH,
CHITTENANGO, MADISON CO., N. Y.

S. P. ROUNDS, Gen'l Western Ag't,
175 Monroe Street, CHICAGO, ILL.

P. S. The Boiler employed is much more durable than the common upright Boiler, and is superior in every respect.

THE NILES ENGINE.

All Engines warranted to develope the rated horse power with a pressure of sixty pounds of steam. Prices given on application.

Is specially adapted for any purpose requiring an engine of from four to twelve horse power.

The engine and boiler are mounted together on a substantial cast iron base, forming a complete power outfit, simple and durable, and economical in performances. The engine is not attached to the boiler, but is erected on the same base with it, thus preventing all injurious effects of expansion and contraction.

Each engine is provided with a heater into which exhaust steam escapes, heating the feed water, thereby saving fuel and preventing the injection of cold water into the boiler.

The engine is horizontal, with long steam chest and short steam passages, and the cylinder is provided with a hot air jacket. The connecting rod is a wrought-iron forging with gun-metal brasses, adjustable for wear. The main shaft is of steel, and the bearings are unusually large, with simple devices for taking up wear.

The engine is completely equipped with governor, fly-wheel, oil cups, stop valves, and drip pipes.

The boiler is made entirely of wrought iron of the very best quality, and is of ample size to furnish the engine with steam when exerting its maximum power, having fifteen square feet of heating surface per horse power.

The tubes are arranged for complete circulation, and are entirely below the water line, preventing the possibility of leakage.

The trimmings are the best, comprising gauge cocks, glass water gauge, steam gauge, safety valve, check valve, blow-off cock, and feed pump. Purchasers will do well to consider the superiority of the Niles Engine as a power outfit before looking elsewhere.

PULLEYS, SHAFTING AND HANGERS.

Pulleys, Shafting and Hangers, of the best material, furnished to order on short notice. Estimates made on receipt of description of room to be occupied, and number and sizes of presses to be used.

CINCINNATI TYPE FOUNDRY,

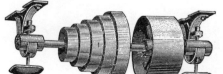

Brass Shooting Stick.

Ready Roller Proof Press.

Jones' Rocking Proof Planer.

Double Cylinder Inking Apparatus, with Roller Frame.

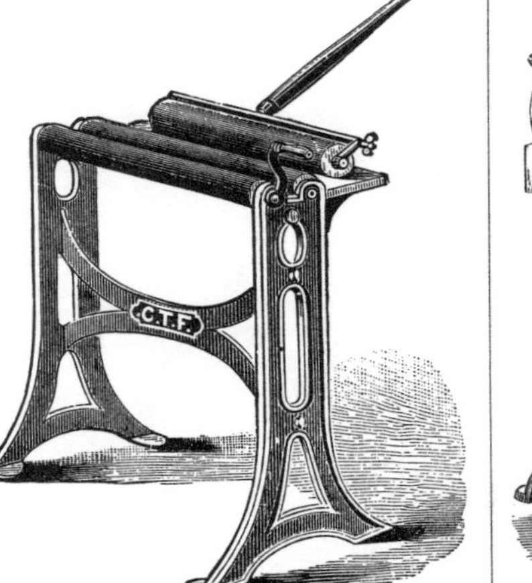

Steel Shooting Stick.

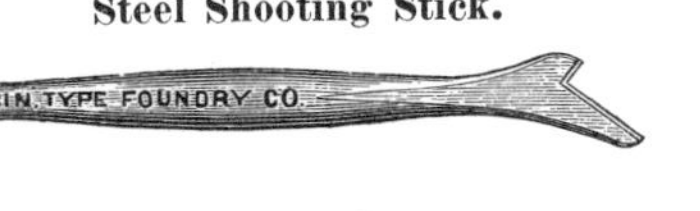

Novelty Proof Press.

Roller Frame for Single Cylinder Inking Apparatus.

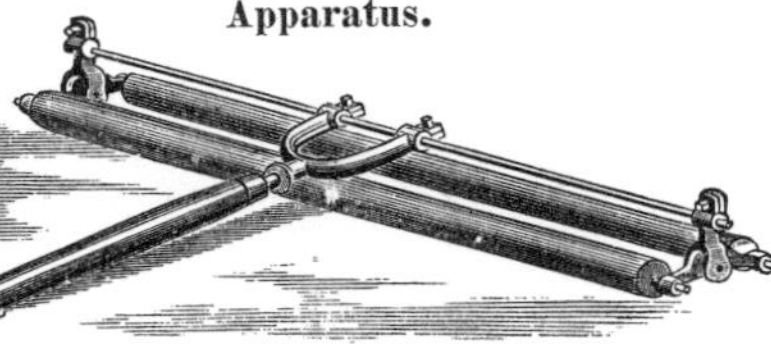

Single Cylinder Inking Apparatus.

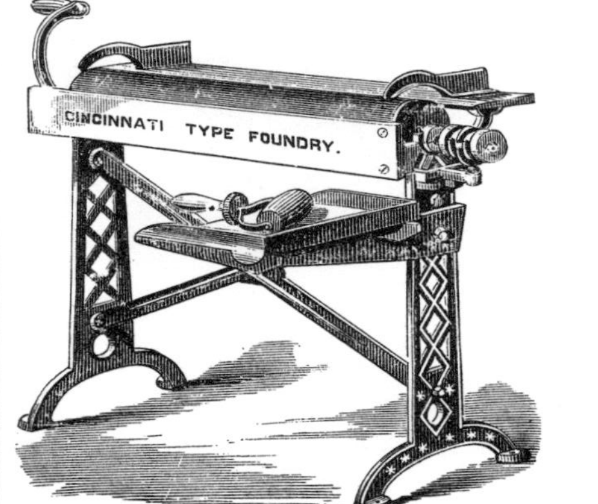

Manufacturing Stationers' and Plate Printers' Machinery

Envelope Cutting Presses.
Envelope Folding Machines.
Embossing Presses for Monogram and Relief Color Printing.
Bookbinders' Embossing Presses.
Hat-Tip Presses.

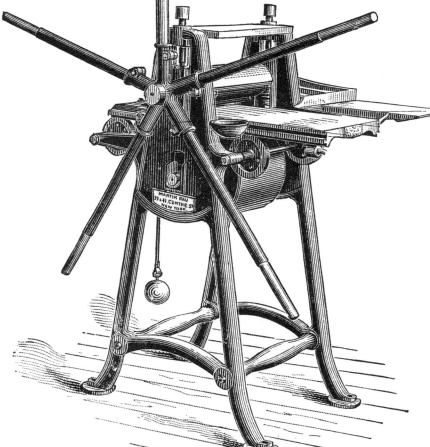

NEW STEEL PLATE PRESS - Guaranteed Best in the Market.

MARTIN RAU, *MANUFACTURER.*

39 AND 41 CENTRE STREET, *NEW YORK.*

Circa 1893

CASTING BOX AND MELTING FURNACE.

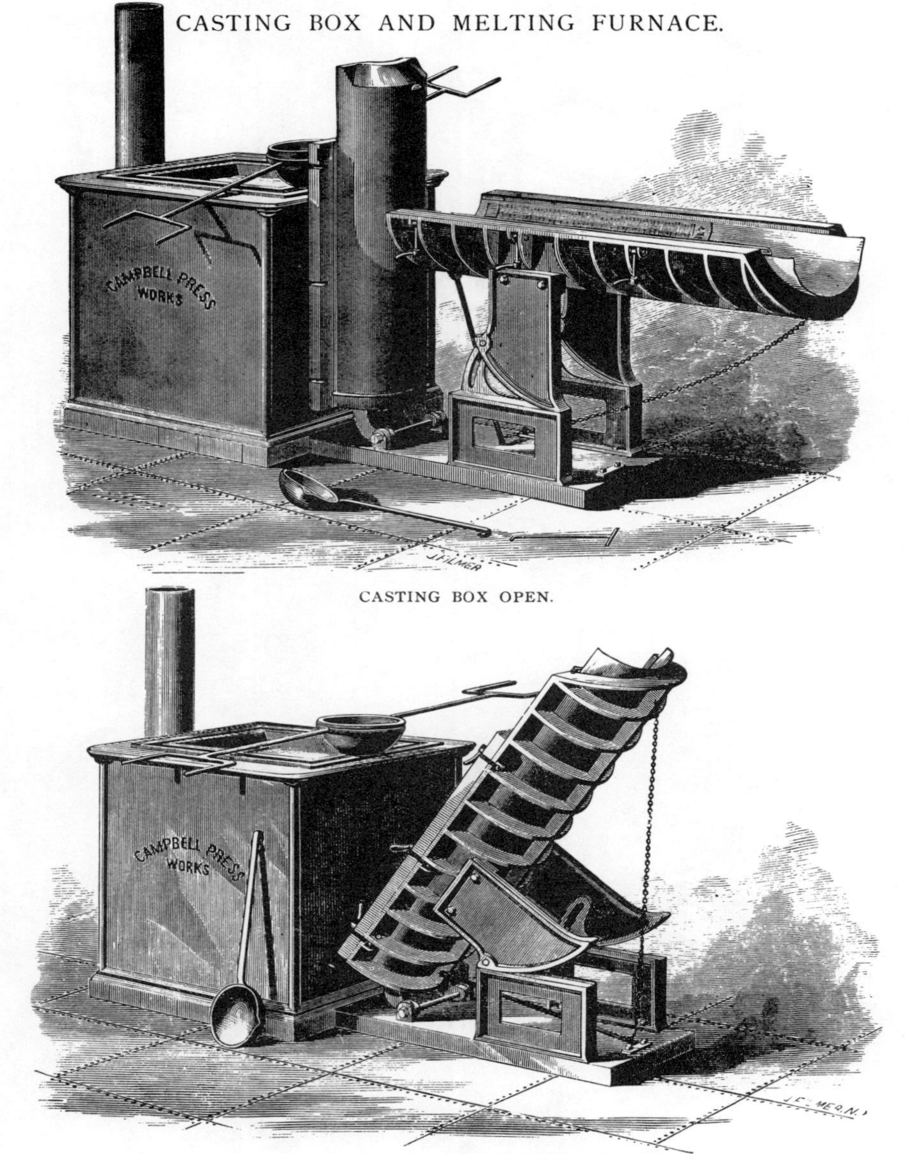

CASTING BOX OPEN.

CASTING BOX CLOSED.

THE CAMPBELL PRINTING PRESS AND MANUFACTURING COMPANY.

CASTING BOX AND MELTING FURNACE.

The Casting Box and Melting Furnace, as represented on preceding page, requires no explanation — its use being at once apparent. The holding, or guide-bars, for the matrices, on the casting-boxes, are FIXTURES, and cannot be removed, which makes them very convenient for instant use and easy handling.

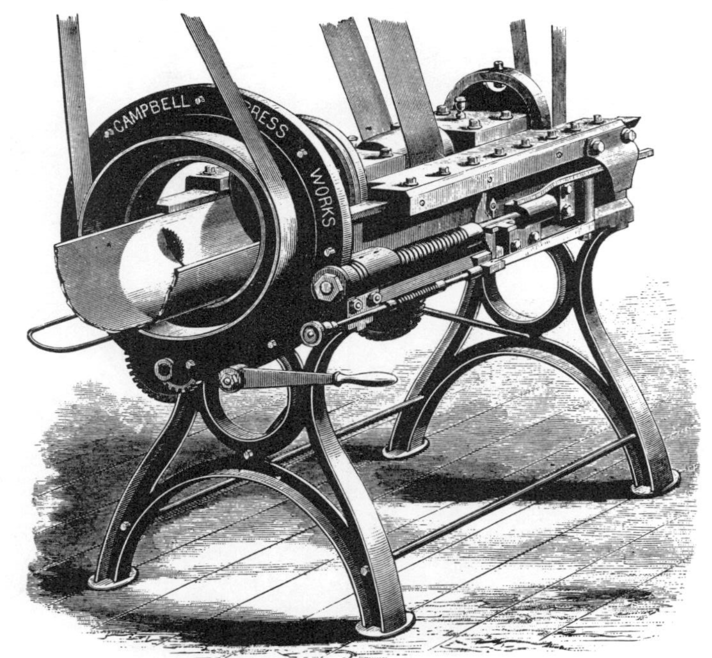

PLATE-FINISHING MACHINE.

The above engraving gives a fair representation of one of our new Finishing Machines, a detailed description of which is unnecessary. IT IS BY FAR SUPERIOR TO ANYTHING OF THE KIND EVER BEFORE PRODUCED. Into this machine the plate is placed on its removal from the Casting Box, and is finished for immediate use at one operation in less than TWO MINUTES.

With our three machines previously described — the Matrix, Casting Box, and Finisher — A PERFECT PLATE SHOULD BE MADE IN FROM TEN TO FIFTEEN MINUTES; and the face of the letter should be as clean and sharp as the type itself.

39 BEEKMAN ST., NEW YORK. WYTHE AVE., HEWES AND PENN STS., BROOKLYN, E. D.

Stereotype Apparatus.

OUR moulds, or matrices, are made by a process which insures a PERFECT FACE TO EVERY LETTER, without the slightest damage to its hair-lines; and our plates are cast and finished, from first to last, by MATHEMATICALLY ACCURATE AND ARBITRARY MACHINERY, which preclude any variation or imperfection.

The DRYING MACHINE is also improved and simplified for rushing the mould, and insuring a perfect cast of the pages.

Our methods and machinery dispense with one-half of the ordinary work of the stereotyper, and the time consumed from locking up the forms until ready for the press is not more than fifteen minutes.

So absolute is the action of all the machinery in the casting and finishing room, that any attempt by the workmen to make an imperfect or an unequal plate, from any reason or motive whatsoever, would inevitably result in its destruction — thus preventing the greater and more irretrievable disaster of an accident or break upon the press at the most critical moment.

MATRIX MACHINE.

This is constructed with a hot-bed; the form being removed from the traveling imposing table by a rounce, similar to that used on the hand-press, to run the form under the platen. The impression is given by means of a lever, and the beating is by hydraulic force, applied by repeated blows on the head of a ram in the platen. In effect, this is like the brush; the only difference being in the use of a *felt*, instead of the ordinary bristle. The brush, roller and hydraulic power, as ordinarily applied, are hard on the type, and destroy the hair-lines in the forms on which they are used. By our new method the letters have a PERFECT FACE, and that without the slightest damage whatever to any of the hair-lines. The mechanism is so arranged, that when the blow is applied on the head of the ram, it produces a perfectly even pressure over the whole form; and the mátrix is held so firmly in position on the form, that DOUBLE IMPRESSIONS ARE IMPOSSIBLE.

New Rotary Wetting Machine.

ONE of the most difficult operations connected with printing from the roll, or web, is that of WETTING THE PAPER UNIFORMLY AND EVENLY THROUGHOUT ITS LENGTH AND BREADTH. No web press can run with speed and safety unless the paper on which it prints has been first carefully rewound, tested and dampened. To insure the perfect performance of these three initiatory steps, we have invented and constructed a very simple machine, of which the above is a representation. This performs all these important operations in a reliable manner, and thus prevents the usual ***breaking*** of the sheet, as is frequently the case by the machines and methods now in vogue. By the above machine the water is so regularly and evenly distributed throughout THE ENTIRE roll that it is in condition for immediate use.

The sprinkling arrangement is another application of centrifugal force, by which the water is mechanically disintegrated DROP BY DROP as it falls upon the metal discs which revolve beneath the reservoir, as shown. By this method a single drop of water can be distributed over a superficial yard of paper. This being the case, it is a very simple and easy matter to give the paper the exact quantity of water required.

The paper rolls, as rewound, strained and dampened, are very compact, and will retain their moisture for twenty or thirty days. The capacity of this machine is six thousand sheets per hour.

Vertical Steam Engine.

This engraving represents a high pressure steam-engine, which, as it occupies but little space, is admirably adapted to the impelling of machinery for printing and other manufacturing purposes where room is valuable. It is remarkable for symmetrical proportions, compactness and great strength.

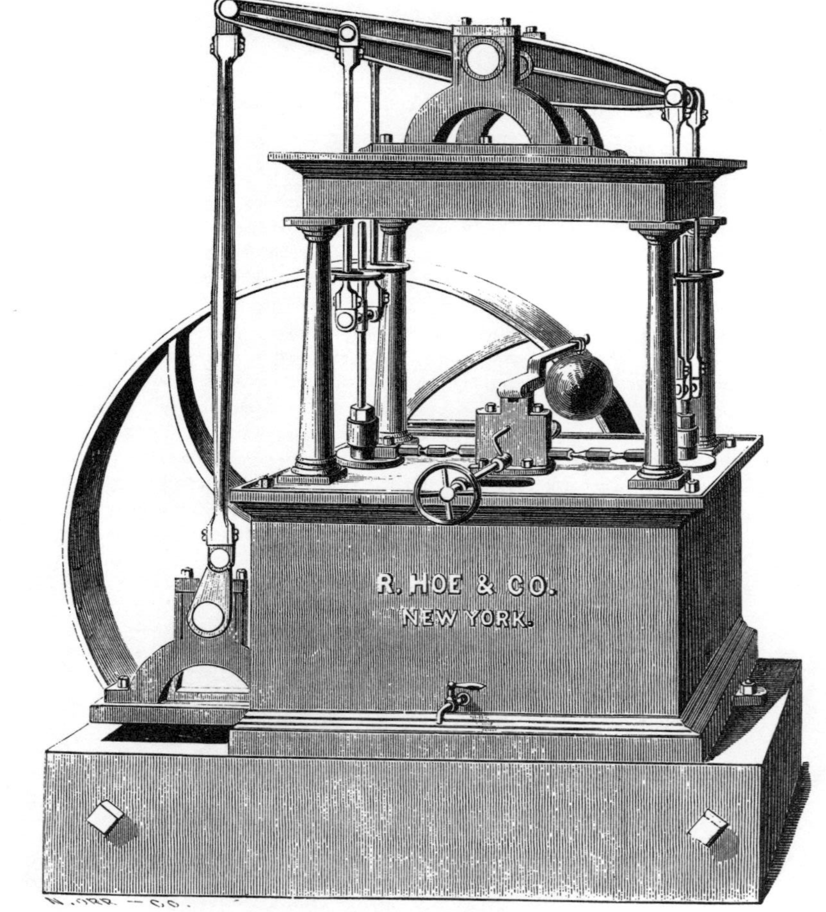

Double Vertical Steam Pump.

This handsome and durable Pump is sufficiently explained by the cut. It is finished in the most thorough manner. The joints are made without packings. Any number of presses may be operated by it by means of the proper connections. Running at its usual speed of fifty revolutions per minute, it will raise the platen of a twelve-inch hydraulic press at the rate of one inch and a half per minute. The cistern should be frequently cleansed and supplied with pure water.

Space occupied on floor, 4 feet × 6 feet 8 inches. Capacity of Cistern, 55 gallons. Height, 6 feet. Weight, 2,400 pounds.

Price $1,000.

Terms of Payment—Cash at manufactory in New-York.

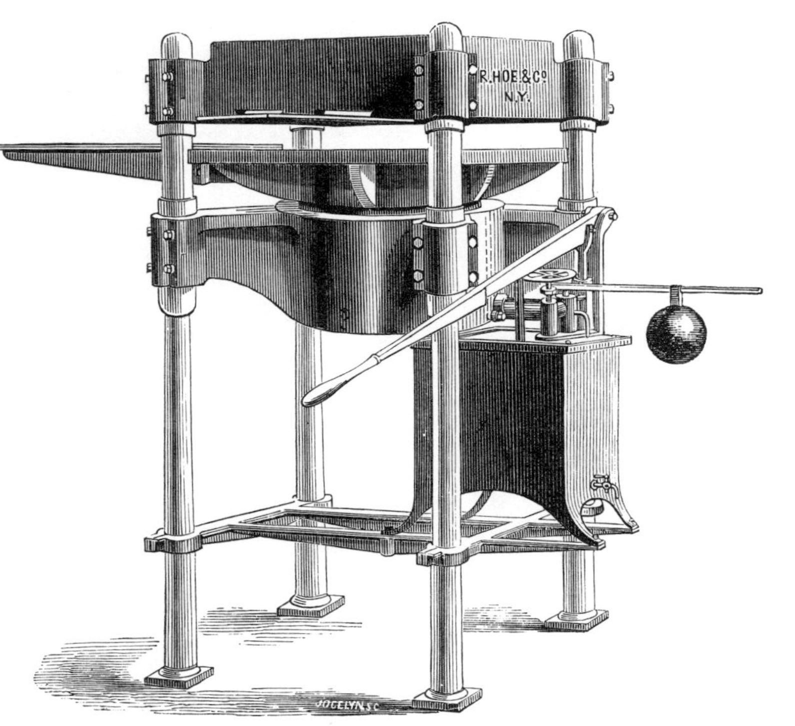

Hydraulic Press for Electrotype Moulds.

This Press, especially designed for the above purpose, is very convenient, compact and powerful. The platen is provided with a projecting table, upon which the form and mould are prepared before being placed in the press. The pump is supported by a frame-work on the cistern below the cylinder, and has a safety valve so graduated as to give any required pressure.

Price, $1,000.

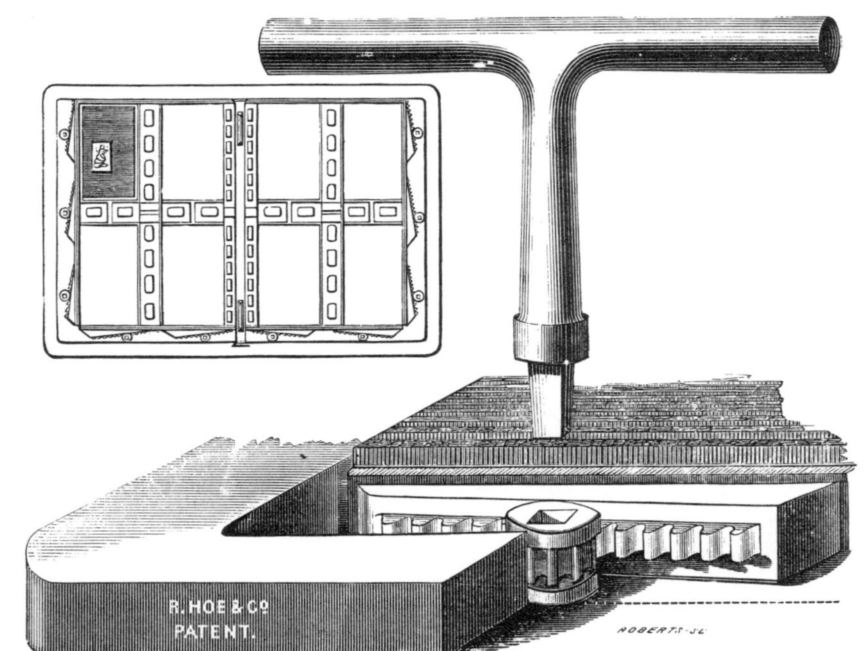

Patent Mechanical Quoins.

This invention is intended to dispense entirely with the usual method of locking up type forms.

The Quoins or pinions are operated by a key, which in turn operate on the geared side and foot stick. The power thus gained is sufficient to enable the operator to lock up a form complete: in which condition it is secure, and will remain any length of time.

The operation is so clearly described in the above engraving that any further description is hardly necessary.

Price List of Quoins for the Foot of the Page.

The Quoin complete,	4	inches long	$0.25.
" "	$4\frac{3}{4}$	"	0.28.
" "	$5\frac{1}{2}$	"	0.30.

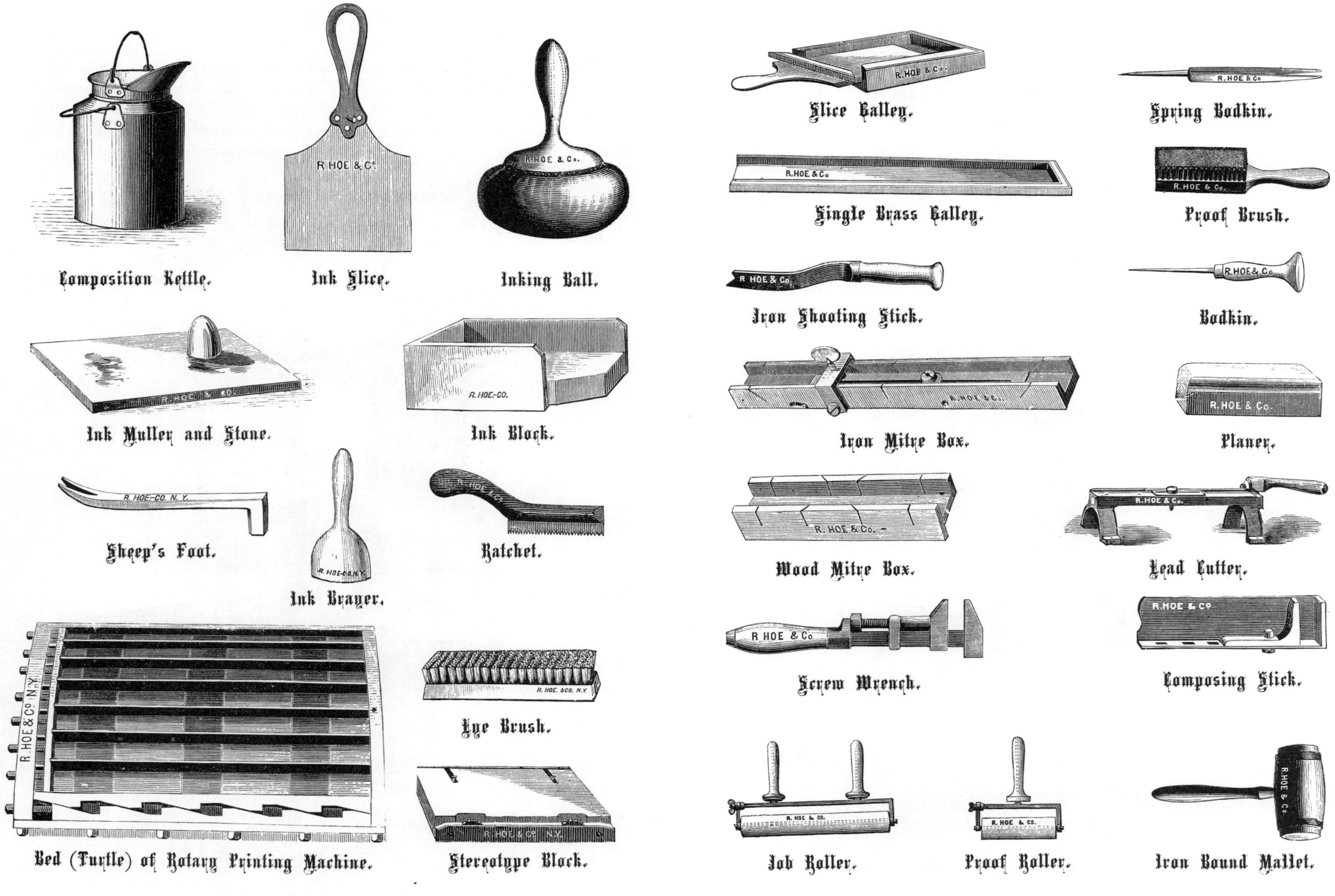
Composition Kettle.
Ink Slice.
Inking Ball.
Ink Muller and Stone.
Ink Block.
Sheep's Foot.
Ink Brayer.
Ratchet.
Bed (Turtle) of Rotary Printing Machine.
Lye Brush.
Stereotype Block.
Slice Galley.
Spring Bodkin.
Single Brass Galley.
Proof Brush.
Iron Shooting Stick.
Bodkin.
Iron Mitre Box.
Planer.
Wood Mitre Box.
Lead Cutter.
Screw Wrench.
Composing Stick.
Job Roller.
Proof Roller.
Iron Bound Mallet.

Curtis Stereotype Outfit.

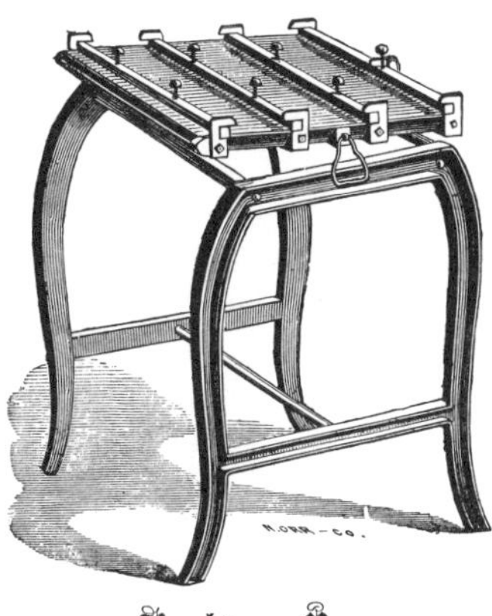

Backing Pan.

(FILMER'S PATENT.)

Stereotype Melting Furnace, Clay Process.

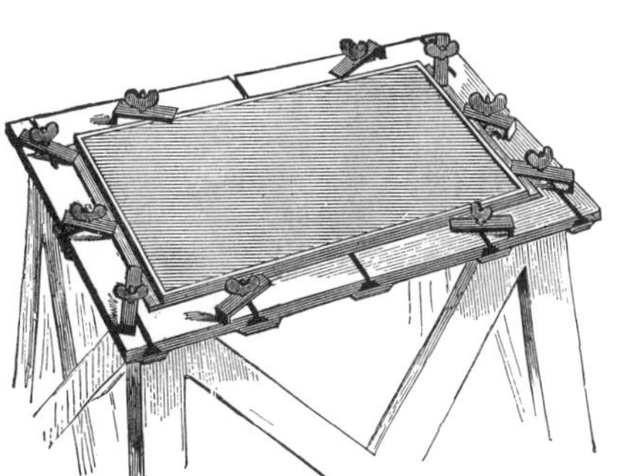

Moulding Pan.

(FILMER'S PATENT.)

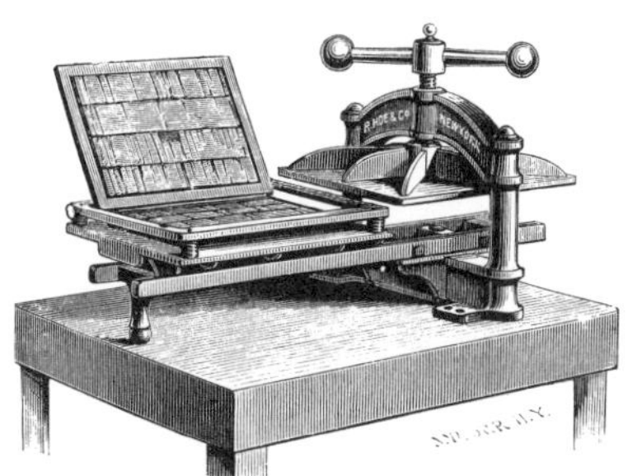

Press for Stereotype Moulding, Clay Process.

Stereotype Planing Machine.

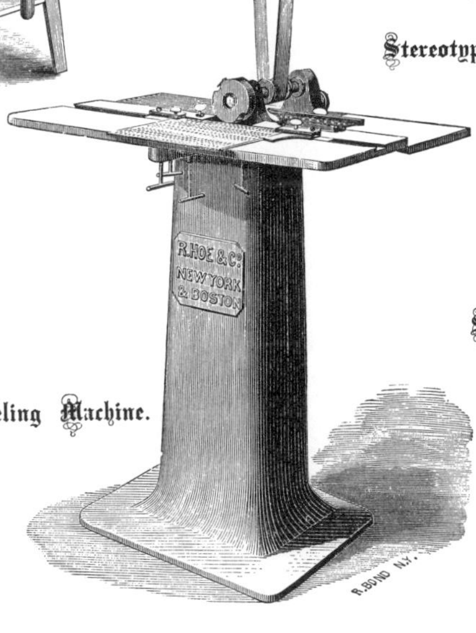

Stereotype Shaving Machine.

Stereotypers' Saw Table.

Patent Stereotype-plate Beveling Machine.

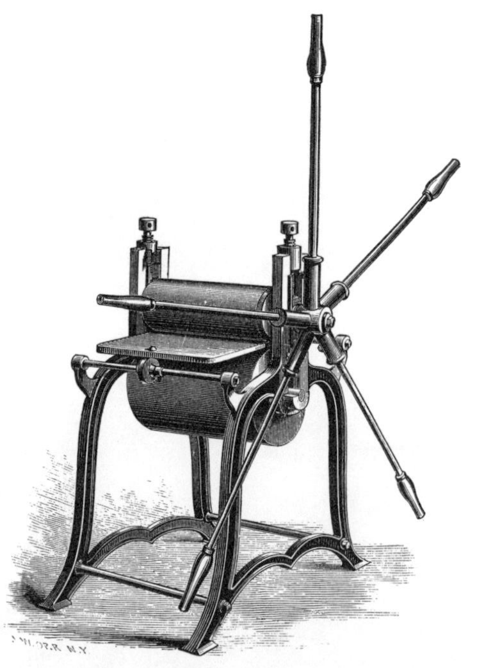

Iron Copper-plate Press.

THE side frames, cylinders and bed are made of cast iron; the cylinders are turned, and the bed planed perfectly true. The shafts through the cylinders, the braces, arms and screws are of wrought iron; the bearings of composition.

Every material connected with Copper-plate Printing supplied.

Sizes and Prices.

Bed 10 inches wide	$150.00.	Bed 24 inches wide	$325.00.
" 12 " "	175.00.	" 26 " "	370.00.
" 15 " "	200.00.	" 28 " "	415.00.

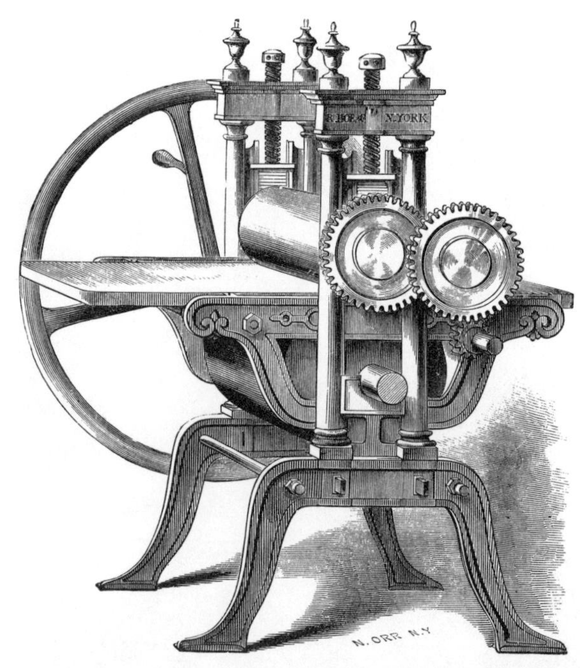

Geared Copper-plate Press.

THIS is a heavy and powerful Press, of a new style, capable of printing the largest sized plates. The frame is strengthened by internal wrought iron tension rods. The Press is double-geared, and the bed is guided by side anti-friction rollers. It has a fly-wheel and crank for working by hand, or it may be run by steam power.

Sizes and Prices.

Bed 34×60	$1,250.00
" 34×66	1,350.00

TERMS OF PAYMENT—Cash at manufactory in New-York.

Blackleading Machine.

(ADAMS' PATENT.)

THIS machine performs quickly and neatly the disagreeable operation of blackleading the wax moulds for electrotyping. The mould is placed on the turn-table of the traveling carriage, in front of the operating brush, under which it is passed slowly backwards and forwards by the motion of the crank. If the moulds are small, several may be placed in the machine at once: one 12×18 inches can be blackened in two minutes. An apron under the machine catches the powder and prevents waste.

Price, $440.

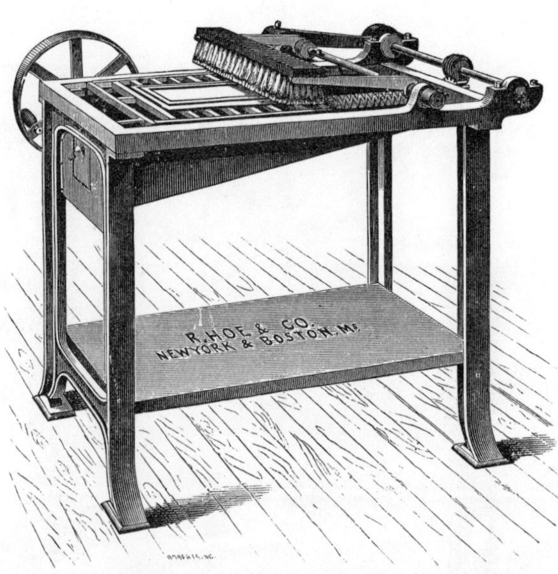

Blackleading Machine.

THIS Machine performs quickly, thoroughly and silently the disagreeable operation of blackleading the wax moulds for Electrotyping. The mould is placed on the travelling carriage in front of the brush, under which it passes slowly backward and forward. A mould 12 × 18 inches can be leaded in from two to three minutes, and the smallest boy can work the machine with ease. If the moulds are small, several may be put in at once. A cover prevents the dust from flying, and an apron catches the powder and prevents waste.

Sizes and Prices.

Size.	Dimen. of Mould.	Price.	Boxing and Shipping.
No. 1, will blacken,	12 × 18 inches,	$300	$10.00
" 2 " "	18 × 24 "	375	12.50
" 3 " "	24 × 30 "	450	15.00

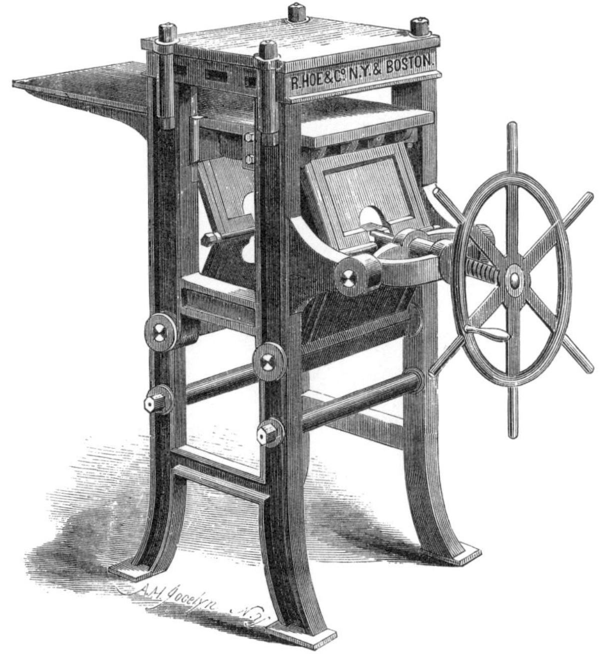

Toggle Press for Electrotype Moulds, with Solid Head.

In this machine the pressure is given by two toggle joints which are operated by a screw and crank wheel. The platen is provided with a projecting table where the form and mould may be arranged.

Size of platen, 16 × 19½ inches. Weight boxed, 1,040 lbs.
Price, $400.
Boxing and Carting, $5.

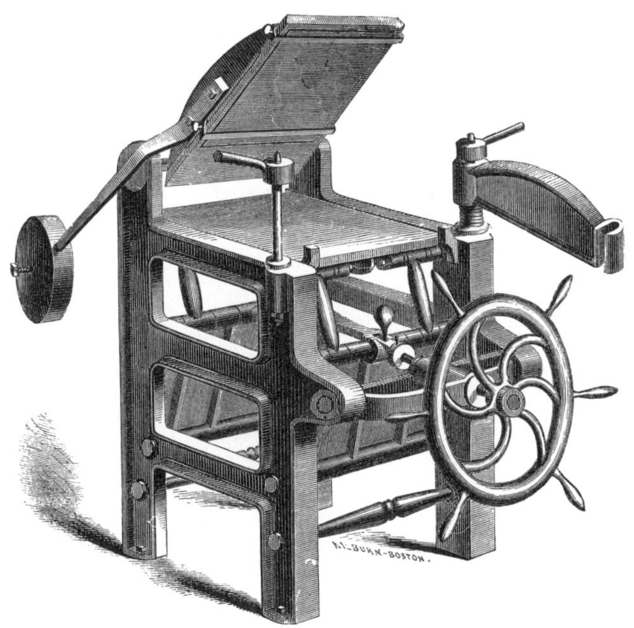

Toggle Press for Electrotype Moulds, with Swinging Head.

This Press is similar in principle to that on preceding page, but the head is hung on pivots and so counterbalanced that it can be readily thrown up, leaving the whole bed exposed.

Size of bed, 17 × 21 inches.
Price, $600.

Terms of Payment—Cash at manufactory in New-York.

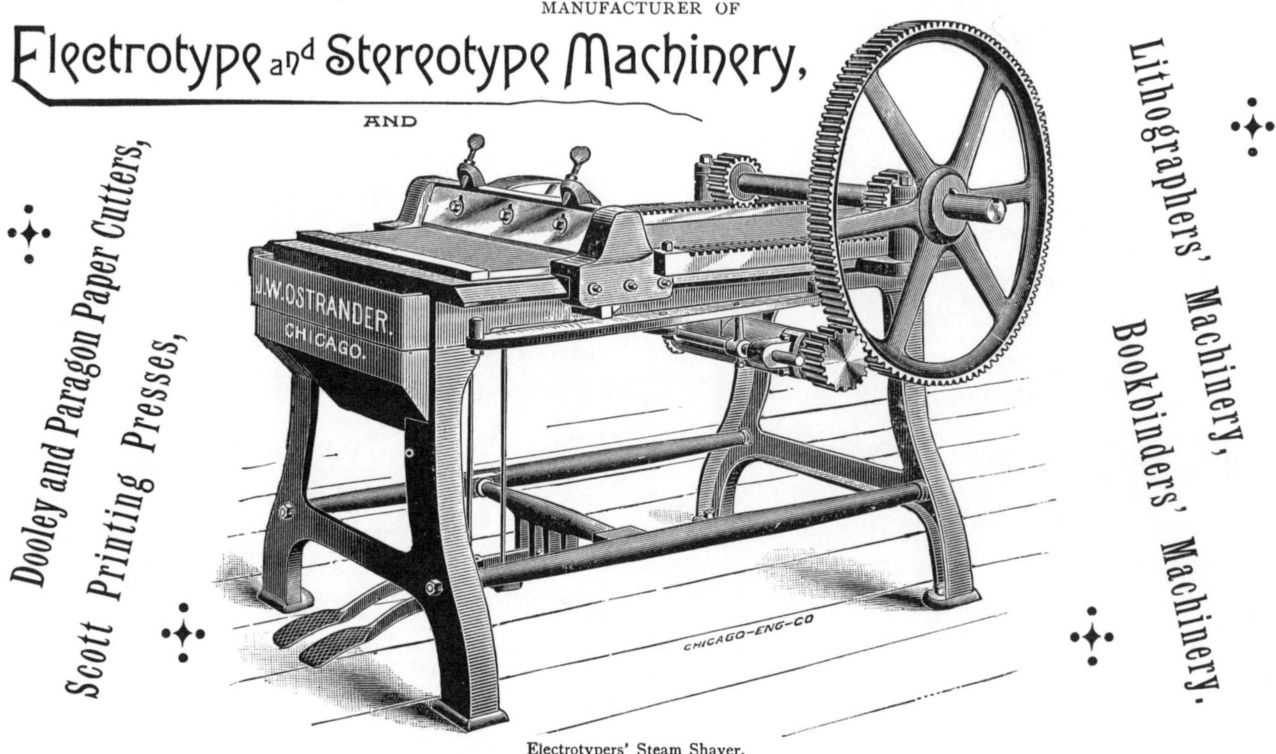

Scott Dampening Machine used to moisten newsprint before printing. Circa 1895.

addendum

Chandler & Price Press Serial Numbers

Year	7 x 11	8 x 12	10 x 15	12 x 18	14 x 20	14 1/2 x 22
1884	301		302			
1885	501		502			
1886	653		556			
1887	797	25001	858			
1888	1053	25053	1138		25002	25100
1889	1181	25379	1456		25034	25104
1890	1265	25811	1834		25088	25144
1891	1365	26365	2336		25248	25156
1892	1461	26981	2902	22001	25402	25308
1893	1533	27521	3568	22022	25438	25340
1894	1587	27989	4048	22068	25498	25366
1895	1697	28711	4822	22176	25682	25440
1896	1801	29701	5842	22303	26002	25742
1897	1935	30555	6702	22458	26202	25928
1898	2041	31627	7602	22670	26456	26162
1899	2165	32901	8656	22901	26682	26372
1900	2355	34207	9908	23136	27050	26738

Bibliography

Allen, Lewis M., *Printing with the Handpress.* Van Nostrand Reinhold Company. 1971
Burke, Jackson, *Prelude to Albion, a History of the Development of the Hand Press.* 1940
Caldwell, David A., *Chandler & Price Serial Number List.* Caldwell Press. 1995
Comparato, Frank E., *Chronicles of Genius & Folly.* Labyrinthos. 1979
Comparato, Frank E., *Old Thunder's American Lightning.* Journal of the Printing Historical Society. 1978
Cottrell, Donald C., *The Cottrell Company (1855-1955) Color Press Pioneers.* The Newcomen Society in North America. 1955
Electrotype and Stereotype Handbook, International Association of Electrotypers & Stereotypers, Inc.
Goss – Supporting the Power of the Press since 1885. Rockwell International. 1984
Green, Ralph, *Works of Ralph Green,* Ye Olde Printery. 1981
Halbmeier, Carl, *Senefelder The History of Lithography.* Senefelder Publishing Co. 1926
Harris, Elizabeth & Sisson, Clinton, *The Common Press.* David R. Godine. 1978
Hoe, R. & Co.'s Catalogue of Printing Presses and Printers' Materials. 1881
Hoe, Robert, *A Short History of the Printing Press.* 1902
Jubilee Publication on the 150th Anniversary, 1817-1967. Schnellpressenfabrick Koenig & Bauer. 1967
Kainen, Jacob, *George Clymer and the Columbian Press.* Book Club of California. 1950
Logan, Herschel C., *The American Hand Press.* The Curt Zoller Press. 1980
Moran, James, *Printing Presses.* University of California Press. 1973
Paper and Press, 1891
Peat, David W., *Peat's Apercu of Small Presses.* David W. Peat. 1998
Problems of Pressmanship. C.B. Cottrell & Sons Co. 1903
Saxe, Stephen O. & Depol, John, *American Iron Hand Presses.* Yellow Barn Press. 1991
Senefelder, Alois, *The Invention of Lithography.* The Fuchs & Lang Mfg. Co. 1911
Silver, Rollo G., *The American Printer, 1787-1825,* University of Virginia Press. 1967
Sterne, Harold E., *Catalogue of Nineteenth Century Printing Presses.* Ye Olde Printery. 1978
Superior Printer. 1887
Sutton, Walter, *Western Book Trade.* Ohio State University Press. 1961
Thomson, John, *Colt's Armory Platen Press.* John Thomson Press Company. 1909
Tucker, Stephen D., *History of the R. Hoe & Co., 1834-1885.* American Antiquarian Society. 1973
Wilkes, Walter, *Die Entwicklung der Eisernen Buch Druckerpresse,* Verlag Renate Raecke. 1983
Wings to the World, The Rapid Electrotype Company. 1933

index

Acme 19
Acorn 6
Adams 13, 20, 77
Advance 210
Albion 3
Alden 121
Aldine 138
Alert 147, 193
Alexandra 3
Allen 19
American Power Press 83
American Type (ATF) 67, 166
Army Press 48
Asteroid 125

Babcock 21-27
Bagley & Sewell 28-29
Baltimore 137
Baltimorean 190-191
Barnhart Bros. 88
Ben Franklin 153-154
Benton, Waldo & Co. 121
Bickerton, Joseph 214
Boston 193-194
Boston & Fairhaven 69-70, 138
Boys' 194
Braidwood, William 133
Bronstrup 4, 214
Bullock, 225

California 169
Campbell 30-43, 226, 246-247
Caxton 188
Centenial 206
Challenge 44-45, 122, 176
Champion 168, 175
Chandler & Price 123-124, 187
Chicago 202
Chromatic 178-179
Cincinnati Type Foundry 4, 13, 45-50, 125-130, 244-245
Clipper 140
Clymer, George 5
Colt's Armory 180
Columbian 5, 132, 133, 188
Complete 131
Cook, J. & Co. 197, 200
Cope, R.W. 3
Cope & Sherwin 10
Cottrell & Babcock 51-52
Cottrell, C.B. 53-62, 215, 227
Cox. 63, 227-228
Cranston, J.H. 64-67
Curtis & Mitchell 132-133, 187-188

Damon & Peets 134
Daughaday, J.W. 135, 189
Dauntless 152
Degener & Weiler 136
Demy 215
Diamond 118
Dokum & Sons 138
Dorman, J.F.W. 137, 190-192
Duplex 227-228

Eckerson 230
Emmerich 253
Empire 148, 195
Enterprise 200
Eurika 167
Evans, W.C. 208
Excelsior 133, 160, 198-200

Fairhaven 69-70
Favorite 134, 187, 209
Foster 5
Fowler-Henkle 230
Franklin 68, 144-145
Fuchs & Lang 216, 220

Gally, Merritt 139
Globe 154
Globe Mfg. Co. 140-141
Golden Gate 169
Golding 70, 141-143, 196
Gordon 68, 124, 134, 144-146, 153, 156, 177
Gorham, W.B. 147-148, 193-195
Goss 229
Gump. M.L. 150
Halligan 216
Hamilton & McNeal 149
Harrild & Sons 68
Henry 83
Hird 92
Hoe, R. & Co. 5-13, 20, 71-82, 151, 184, 195, 217, 219, 231-236, 242, 248-253
Hooper, F.X. 236
Huber 83-85, 217
Hughes & Kimber 218
Humphrey, Hassler & Co. 92
Hunt, George W. 173-174

Ideal 44
Imperial 10
Island City Mfg. Co. 197
IXL 197

Jennings, P.J. 152
Johnson Peerless 154
Jones, J.M. 140, 154-158, 210
Julien, H. 86

Kellogg, A.N. 159
Kelsey 86, 159-162, 197-200
Kennedy, W.M. 242
Kidder 87, 163, 237
Klein, Forst & Bohn 218
Koenig & Bauer 87, 220, 237
Kratz, C. 243
Krause, Karl 10, 219-220

Last and Best 206
Leader 158
Liberty 136, 164
Lightning 156, 203

Madison 114, 182
Marder, Luse & Co. 154, 242
Maryland 191
Medhurst, George 13
Miehle 88-90

Model 135, 189
Monitor 165
Monona 113
Montague 93
Monumental 192

National 122, 166
New Era 158
New York 150, 184
Newbury 91, 159, 167, 209
Niles 244
Nonpareil 126-130, 201
Novelty 207

O.K. 159
Official 143, 196
Olmesdahl, A. 168
One Dollar 198
Optimus 26-27
Ostrander, J.W. 254

Palmer & Rey 94, 169-170
Paragon 175, 222
Pearl 141-142
Peerless 140-141, 170
Pilot 187
Pioneer 94
Pony 89
Potter 94-102, 171, 221, 238
Progress 121
Prouty 111-115, 172-173

Ramage 4
Rau, Martin 245
Reliable 126, 170
Reliance 14
Remington, E. & Sons 173-174
Rounds, S.P. 175
Ruggles, S.P. 176
Ruthven. John 11

Samson 183
Scott 103-106, 238-240, 254
Senefelder 213
Shniedewend & Lee 14, 176-177
Shniedewend, Paul 14
Sigwalt 201,
Smith 7, 11-12, 178
Smithean 178
Standard 182, 208
Stanhope 12
Stansbury 13
Star 155, 157, 161, 210
Stephens, Samuel 210
Suitterlin, Claussen & Co. 178
Superior 173-174

Taylor, A.B. 107-110, 179
Thompson, John 180
Thorp-Gordon 181-182
Thorp, H.H. 208

Uncle Sam 208
Union Rotary 162
United States 183
Universal 139, 149, 166, 180

Vaughn 44
Victor 197
Victory 118

Walker, W.G. 111-115, 182
Walrath, Peter 244
Washington 6-8, 14
Washington Jobber 155, 165
Watson Joseph 183, 206
Wells, John 15
Wesel, F. 184
White, S.K. 89
Whitlock 69, 116-117
Woods, Benj. O. & Co. 207
World Mfg. Co. 209

Yorkston 150
Young America 203-205

Zincographic 217